Postmodern Apocaly

University of Pennsylvania Press
New Cultural Studies
Joan DeJean, Carroll Smith-Rosenberg,
and Peter Stallybrass, Editors

Postmodern Apocalypse

Theory and Cultural Practice at the End

EDITED BY
Richard Dellamora

University of Pennsylvania Press

Philadelphia

Permission is gratefully acknowledged to reproduce material from published works. A complete listing
can be found following the index in this volume.

Copyright © 1995 by the University of Pennsylvania Press
Printed in the United States of America

Library of Congress Cataloging-in-Publication Data

Postmodern apocalypse : theory and cultural practice at the end / edited by Richard
Dellamora.
    p.   cm. — (New cultural studies)
    Includes bibliographical references and index.
ISBN 0-8122-3320-4 (cloth : alk. paper). — ISBN 0-8122-1558-3 (pbk. : alk. paper)
    1. Apocalyptic art. 2. Postmodernism. 3. Arts, Modern — 20th century. I. Dellamora,
Richard. II. Series.
NX650.A6P67   1995
700 — dc20   95-19128
                                                                                     CIP

How can one be late to the end of history? A question for today. . . . It obliges one to wonder if the end of history is but the end of a *certain* concept of history.

Jacques Derrida, *Specters of Marx*, 1994

Contents

Illustrations

Preface

Postmodern Apocalypse. The phrase sounds apt, but do these two terms belong together? Consider, for instance, the word "modern" within the context of aesthetic discourse. If "modern" refers to avant-garde aesthetics, which insists on "making it new," then to be post- or *beyond* the modern is to be beyond those qualitative breaks in the temporal and spatial order that characterize apocalypse as a genre. If, in contrast, "modern" refers, as is usually the case today within anglophone literary studies, to the aesthetic closure within which the literary experimentation of James Joyce, D. H. Lawrence, and Virginia Woolf is judged to be contained, then to be post- means to be *beyond* closure in the field of newly opened textual possibilities. As a number of theorists have argued, the negative prospect of this infinite horizon is that it can imply mere repetition, a ceaseless doing again of deeds that issue in frustration and failure.

This last possibility helps explain a pervasive sense of unease in contemporary existence. The attendant lack of confidence in the possibility of shaping history in accord with human desire(s) provides the bass line of culture — political, economic, and aesthetic — in the fin de millennium. It is imaged, for instance, in a postmodern text like Philip K. Dick's "Survey Team," published as long ago as 1954. In Dick's technofable, planet Earth has been rendered uninhabitable as the result of an endless war. A group of inhabitants flees to Mars, the last planetary body within reach that might be capable of supporting human life. When they get there, they discover that Mars, like Earth, is a heap of "ruins. Nothing but ruins."[1] At the end of the story, they learn that six hundred thousand years earlier, the inhabitants of Mars had left their devastated planet to begin life afresh on Earth. "We've destroyed two worlds," says one of the surveyors: "Not one. Mars first. We finished up here, then we moved to Terra. And we destroyed Terra as systematically as we did Mars." "A closed circle," as another character says,[2] Dick's story provides a vivid example of narrative structure as repetition, which negates the apocalyptic dream of an escape into a new order of existence. And yet, as Frank Kermode, the leading modernist theorist of apocalypse, argues, while predictions of the end are continually being made, they are counterbalanced by what he describes as "clerkly scepticism," reminding the faithful that "arithmetical predictions of the End are bound to be discon-firmed."[3] The genre of apocalypse includes a concept of repetition that permits the writing of new stories about the end. Moreover, as I have said, Dick's story depends on the prior existence of apocalyptic narrative in order to make its own negation of apocalypse possible.

The authors of the essays included in this book are at one in believ-ing that, among today's educated classes, belief in apocalypse is liable to continual critique. Nonetheless, whether these writers respond to Jacques Derrida's posing of a humanist counternarrative to the rhetoric of nuclear deterrence or to Donna Haraway's cyborg manifesto as a criti-cal response to feminist apocalypticism during the 1970s and early 1980s, they are likewise at one in thinking that the uncircumscribed field of narrative at the fin de millennium continues to be structured, if only negatively, in relation to apocalypse. This unsettling realization requires cultural critics to subject to ever renewed analysis the framing of popular and political beliefs in apocalyptic narratives—whether it be in North American Christian fundamentalism or in the rhetoric of the National Security Agency during the early 1980s. But we also need to be aware of the seductive attraction of what some writers refer to as "apocalyptic desire." Similarly, the writing of history and cultural possibility beyond predicted but disconfirmed ends of history requires continual assess-ment of the implications, both positive and negative, of the current sense that temporality permanently resists human desire(s) for purpose, prog-ress, and finality.

On this point, there is considerable anxiety among these writers. Kevin Pask, for example, contends that "postmodern theorists" who celebrate the end of myths of the end of history believe that today it is impossible, undesirable, or both to imagine a world order other than that of transna-tional capitalism. Linda Howell, another writer, worries that Haraway's rejection of feminist triumphalism might be turned into a triumphalism of the cyborg whose effect would be to erase awareness precisely of those distinctions of class, race, and gender that Haraway is at pains to call to mind. It should be remembered, however, that each writer attempts to supplement critique with the figuration of possibility on the postmodern horizon. In this respect and within whatever limits, the collection shares in the aspirations of those, both in and outside the educated classes, in the West and in what until recently was referred to as the "Third World," who have imagined a better set of human possibilities.

The sense that these essays form part of an ongoing conversation de-rives from the circumstances in which they were conceived, written, and assembled. In May 1993, I organized two special sessions on Postmodern Apocalypse for the annual meeting of the Association of Canadian Col-lege and University Teachers of English, held at Carleton University in

Ottawa, Ontario. In addition to taking part in the panels, contributors met for a three-hour seminar in which they discussed what had occurred at the panels as well as additional papers. The seminar, which was open, benefited from the contributions of others, such as Jonathan Dollimore and Patricia Merivale, to whom I am grateful. It has been a great pleasure to see this collaborative work develop. I hope that other readers will find it useful in thinking through the difficulties of the fin de millennium.

Notes

1. Philip K. Dick, "Survey Team," in *We Can Remember It for You Wholesale: Collected Stories,* vol. 2, introd. Norman Spinrad (New York: Carol Publishing Group, 1992), 371.

2. Dick, "Survey Team," 376.

3. Frank Kermode, *The Sense of an Ending: Studies in the Theory of Fiction* (New York: Oxford University Press, 1967), 10.

Introduction

Richard Dellamora

Alone and teary-faced, Madonna sings "In This Life," an elegy for friends who have died of AIDS. Then, from offstage, over reverent sustained chords from the band, she recites from the Book of Revelations (including condemnations of "fornicators" and "idolators") while the troupe alternately mimes couplings and brawls. It's an ambiguous sequence, mourning the sexual freedom of the pre-AIDS 1970's, then hinting at biblical retribution.

(press account, "The Girlie Show," Madonna's 1993 tour)

In cultural history, there are a number of moments that provide an allegorical figure of a particular movement or style. The suicide of Virginia Woolf in March 1941 is one such moment. Woolf died expecting the invasion of Britain by the German army and knowing the violent ends which in that case awaited her and Leonard Woolf, her Jewish socialist husband.[1] Woolf's death seems to sound the knell for the refined aesthetic modernism of novels such as *To the Lighthouse* and, more generally, for the form of middle-class dissidence summed in the word "Bloomsbury." Raymond Williams says that the ethos of Bloomsbury emphasized "the supreme value of the civilized *individual,* whose pluralization, as more and more civilized individuals, was itself the only acceptable social direction."[2] Woolf's death demonstrated the vulnerability of Bloomsbury's attempts to reform politics by appeals to "social conscience" while asserting individual autonomy through aesthetic and personal balance in face of the human capabilities for individual and group destruction.[3]

If Woolf's death seems to signal the end of literary modernism, the suicide several months earlier of the Jewish, Marxist intellectual Walter Benjamin has become a touchstone of postmodernity.[4] Benjamin killed himself in the Spanish border village of Port Bou in order to avoid being returned to the hands of the Gestapo in Nazi-occupied France. His act testifies to the end of the capability of Euro-American world historical movements — communism, fascism, and liberal or socialist democracy — to dominate human meaning. In the "Theses on the Philosophy of History" that he wrote in the last year of his life, Benjamin pronounced the self-immolating end of Western history. But his refusal to be swallowed by Moloch continues to offer an oracular sign to the world on the far side of the end that we inhabit.

At Port Bou, the German federal states are providing funds to build a monument to commemorate Benjamin's death. The structure consists of a set of steps cut through a cliff face, ending in a glass wall that permits a view of the sea without affording access.[5] The Benjamin memorial signals in an especially moving way the implication of apocalypse and its negation in the history of the twentieth century. The stairway suggests the movement, temporal and spatial, upward from one order of experience to another. This trajectory characterizes a number of the shaping narratives of twentieth-century cultural politics: the utopian aspirations of modernist experimentation in the work of Le Corbusier and others; the dream of social transformation that motivated Russian Communists in the 1920s; and the existence beyond the end of the Third Reich to which millions of human beings were to be sacrificed. The negation occurs in the transparent glass barrier that separates those who climb the stairway from the vista that provides a natural metaphor of the infinity of the postwar order.

Both at the time and subsequently, World War II has been understood to signify a moment of rupture that permanently devalues the principles and aspirations associated with Euro-American tradition. The war signifies the end of the grand narratives that have shaped Western civilization for the past two hundred years. The political challenge that arises from this recognition is that which Jean-François Lyotard has described as the need to think of the future not in terms of a discredited universal telos but as "the beginning of" an "*infinity of heterogeneous finalities.*"[6] In this context, the sublime association of the marine horizon with an illimitable human future can be recuperated in relation to particular struggles engaging specific differences at particular times and places. This new situation demands a presentation of apocalypse that emphasizes those aspects of the genre that make it possible, in the words of Jacques Derrida, a leading contemporary theorist of apocalypse, "for the other tone, or the tone of another, to come at no matter what moment to interrupt a familiar music."[7] A number of the essays that follow take up this wager in considering apocalyptic tone in postmodern practice. Other writers emphasize the fact that a singular tone dominates much contemporary apocalyptic utterance.

At a time when the idea of an autonomous aesthetic sphere has collapsed, culture is characterized by a charged atmosphere of political contestation. Again, the Benjamin monument is a case in point. Criticism of the project in the right-wing tabloid press forced German Chancellor Helmut Kohl's Christian Democratic government to quietly let the project lapse. At the same time, Richard von Weizsäcker, the German president, who has characterized Benjamin as "a great German thinker and critic, with poetic power," remained a strong proponent. A council representing the leaders of the country's federal states agreed to a compromise whereby they will underwrite the cost of constructing the monument, designed by the Israeli artist, Dani Karavan. The marshaling of antagonistic forces and the complex maneuvering required to achieve worthy objectives is characteristic of cultural politics at the fin de millennium.

Benjamin's suicide can be read as a sign that he despaired about the possibility of such an outcome. It can also be read as a courageous protest against an order, triumphant at the time, that promised to extinguish both his liberty and his life. Admired today as the prophetic voice of contemporary cultural studies, Benjamin bequeaths to postmodern culture its most apocalyptic representation of human civilization. In the "Theses," Benjamin imagines "the angel of history":

His face is turned toward the past. Where we perceive a chain of events, he sees one single catastrophe which keeps piling wreckage upon wreckage and hurls it in front of his feet. The angel would like to stay, awaken the dead, and make whole what has been smashed. But a storm is blowing from Paradise; it has got caught in his wings with such violence that the angel can no longer close them. This storm irresistibly propels him into the future to which his back is turned, while the pile of debris before him grows skyward. This storm is what we call progress.[8]

Benjamin's inversion of progress as a single, ongoing catastrophe has powerfully affected cultural practitioners of the postwar period. Yet even this text can provide resource for presenting apocalypse otherwise. For example, Jonathan Boyarin, at the beginning of his study of the politics of Jewish memory, remarks: "Most commentators focus on the image of history as a continuing catastrophe. But . . . I want to emphasize the storm still blowing. . . . Part of the import of Benjamin's image is the lesson that we are always once again being driven out; in some sense we have always just lost paradise, hence we are always close to it. The ongoing state of emergency Benjamin also speaks of doesn't just meant that we are always in imminent danger, but also that something precious is eternally being lost."[9]

Boyarin argues that the continual loss of an apocalyptic point of origin invites a double response: the recognition of loss but likewise a continuing effort to recuperate a shared sense of alterity. With regard to Jewish identity, he calls for "the alternative (and in this sense traditional) resource of identifying with Jews as a collective through continuity (coextension in time) at least as much as through contiguity (coextension in space). Jews have always, it seems, used narrative to recreate their shared identities across time."[10] Boyarin's proposal has immediate political implications: for instance, in relation to the words of Saleh, a displaced Palestinian, who greeted the 1993 Israeli-Palestinian accord by saying:

> I don't feel good. . . . I was born in 1965 and all my life I have dreamed of seeing my village. Inside each of us is this village, this small paradise. For every family there is a tragedy.
> When I heard what we will get in this agreement, this was the conflict within me. But the Israelis, they are stronger, they are more advanced, so they will stay there.
> If peace will succeed in the coming future, maybe we will be one in the end. We must give up part to get part, to get peace. It is like King Solomon with the baby and we are the mother who must give up. So let me make my paradise in Ramallah [inside the Israeli-occupied West Bank]. But deep inside me is my village, inside me is this dream.[11]

Saleh's words suggest one way in which the "storm . . . blowing from Paradise" can enable continued existence and coexistence among otherwise antagonistic groups.

But apocalyptic narratives of group history can also be proclaimed in ways that create the conditions of new catastrophes. In the weeks following the accord, disturbances by both Palestinians and Jewish settlers in the West Bank threatened to disrupt it. After the random murder of Talal al-Bakri, a Palestinian vegetable seller, by Israelis at Qiryat Arba in the West Bank, a resident defended the action by appealing to the history of the Jews: "When you are attacked, you defend yourself. We are not going back to the ghetto. There's not going to be any Holocaust here."[12] The speaker invokes the memory of catastrophe within the history of his group as a way of negating the injustice currently done by Israelis to members of another group. He creates a memorial far different from Benjamin's.

In light of reports like these, it makes sense to reconsider the use and abuse of apocalyptic narrative and tone within postmodern culture. The present collection often focuses on apocalypse in relation to sexual difference. But, as Andrew Hewitt makes clear in the opening essay, critical theory provides examples of gendered narratives that are consonant with the peculiar engendering of history in fascist ideology. In *thinking apocalypse,* then, it is necessary at the outset to turn to World War II in order to rethink how history can be emplotted differently. Other essays interrogate other differences: in Jewish existence; in postfeminist resistance to the maxims generated by second-wave feminist critique in the United States; in the rap of Ice-T. Finally, in a cautionary example, Christopher Keep describes the desire for speed that propelled toward disaster both David Koresh and the officers of the law aligned against him at Waco, Texas.

Max Horkheimer and Theodor Adorno argue that fascism is not

merely something that happened in history but something that happened to it. Hewitt agrees—but puts in question the way in which theorists in the wake of Hegel, including Marxists, encode the future in a heterosexual narrative of coitus, conception, and birth. Fascist history cannot properly be recuperated within a dialectical narrative that fantasizes a cultural rebirth beyond the apocalyptic end of European fascism. The extent to which poststructuralist theorists such as Lyotard understand "Auschwitz" to be continually resistant to human desires to make sense of it is particularly important at the present moment when it is invoked by those who defend Israeli hegemony in the West Bank and by humanists who attack poststructuralist theory as an apology for the Holocaust.[13] To convert the destruction of Eastern European Jewry into an ultimate moral truth encourages the sublation of that truth into territorial claims that cannot be accommodated if Israelis and Palestinians are to live as neighbors. The installation of a moral end point in time implicitly projects an apocalyptic spatial grid across the West Bank. In the second essay in this book, Jonathan Boyarin considers the significance for postmodern apocalypse of the meaning of the term within Jewish tradition. Following Derrida's presentation of an "apocalypse without apocalypse"—that is, an apocalypse that includes apocalypse neither in its meaning of the revelation of an ultimate truth nor in its secondary meaning of a Final Judgment—Boyarin describes postmodern apocalypse as "endtime-without-judgment." The hope for peace in the Middle East depends upon the possibility that such an endtime can come into existence.

David Robson's essay, "Frye, Derrida, Pynchon, and the Apocalyptic Space of Postmodern Fiction," is the first of several that demonstrate the extent to which postmodern culture has been framed in apocalyptic metadiscourse since the late 1950s. Taking as a point of reference Thomas Pynchon's novel *Gravity's Rainbow* (1973), Robson argues that apocalypse is important not only in fiction but also in critical theory as exemplified by Northrop Frye's structuralism and Derrida's poststructuralist analysis of the rhetoric of nuclear deterrence in the first Reagan administration. Robson emphasizes the continual reworking of historical typologies both in his analysis and in what he refers to as the apocalyptic space of Pynchon's novel. As with Hewitt and Boyarin, he theorizes the cultural construction of postmodern time from a ground zero in the Europe of World War II. This effort propels both Robson and Pynchon backward into history to consider the prevalence of apocalyptic thinking in the writing of America's Pilgrim Fathers. At the end of the war, "Puritan eschatological hopes" appear in reconstituted form in the affirmation of the paramount role of the United States in defining a new world order. In *Gravity's Rainbow,* this order is usually envisaged in terms of a gnostic, paranoid narrative, whose end is signified in the phrase, "the Bomb." But Pynchon also imagines attempts to escape this absolute ending through perverse fantasy or the lyric celebration of romantic possibilities. Similarly, in considering Frye as the leading proponent of literary apocalypse in the 1960s, Robson balances Frye's validation of the apocalyptic emancipation or transfiguration of nature in human imagination against Derrida's subsequent deconstruction of such totalizing gestures.

In his essay, Ken Cooper notes the racist undertones of Western anxieties about nuclear proliferation that served to cover over the messianism of President Bush's rhetoric at the time of the Gulf War in 1991. In the final section of *Gravity's Rainbow*, Pynchon signals the advent of the Bomb with "a scrap of newspaper headline, with a wirephoto of a giant white cock, dangling in the sky straight downward out of a white pubic bush."[14] Pynchon's description metaphorically identifies the capability of nuclear annihilation with a specifically "white" hegemony. It is a mistake, however, to accept the metaphorical identification of "America" with a particular form of racism. Rather, "America" is a term whose meaning is continually contested by individuals and groups both within and outside the United States. Cooper shows that African-American writers resisted the (racial) logic of nuclear deterrence from the very outset. Beginning with W. E. B. Du Bois and Langston Hughes in the 1940s, a long series of writers, white and African-American, novelists and community leaders, called into question the phenomenon of what Cooper terms "arms-racism." Cooper reminds his reader of the price that men like Du Bois paid for expressing dissent. Du Bois, for example, who organized "Ban the Bomb" petitions, was indicted in 1951 as an unregistered foreign agent.

Mary Carpenter emphasizes the paranoid apocalyptic narratives that have shaped, at times disastrously, the existence of a variety of groups since World War II. She begins with an account of how the fiery end of the Branch Davidians echoes uncannily the prophecies of the Book of Revelation and notes the immense and continuing popularity of Christian fundamentalist texts such as Hal Lindsey's *The Late Great Planet Earth* (1970). Like Robson, Carpenter returns to moments in the history of literary criticism when the genre of apocalypse has been a significant focus and mode of cultural debate among figures such as Northrop Frye, Harold Bloom, and M. H. Abrams. Carpenter agrees with Steven Goldsmith that even when the discussion of apocalypse occurs within literary studies, it remains implicated in violence, if only because of the ease with which scholars negate the political implications of millenarianism by displacing it from politics to the supposedly autonomous realm of art.[15] Carpenter responds to this situation in three ways. First of all, she analyzes the sexual politics of these writers' rhetoric, commencing with a statement in *Fearful Symmetry* (1947), a study of the poetry of William Blake that Frye wrote during World War II. In the book, Frye identifies with Blake in projecting "The Great Whore of Babylon" as Woman, "the Medusa who turns men to stone, the *femme fatale* of the romantic poets whose kiss is death, whose love is annihilation, whose continual posing of the unanswerable riddle of life in this world is reflected in the mysterious female smiles of the Sphinx and Mona Lisa; and whose capacity for self-absorption has haunted art from ancient Crete to modern fashion magazines."[16] In the literary apocalyptics of the 1960s to 1980s, however, Carpenter also finds evidence of "an antipatriarchal and countercultural apocalyptic allied with feminism that I shall call a 'gay apocalyptic.'" During the same years, feminists "often appropriated the language of apocalypse, but in a rhetoric that explicitly underwrote a program of change and reform in *gender* politics." In the most troubling challenge that she poses to apocalyptic thinking, Carpenter asks whether feminists can effectively appropriate the genre. The feminist theologian, Elisabeth Schüssler Fiorenza, for instance, observes that Revelation "engages the imagination of the contemporary reader to perceive women in terms of good or evil, pure or impure, heavenly or destructive, helpless or powerful, bride or temptress, wife or whore. Rather than instill 'hunger and thirst for justice,' the symbolic action of Revelation therefore can perpetuate prejudice and injustice if it is not 'translated' into a contemporary 'rhetorical situation' to which it can be a 'fitting' rhetorical response."[17] Doubting whether such a translation can possibly be complete, Carpenter asks, how is it possible to recuperate apocalypse within feminist or gay critique?

Recently, James Creech has argued that "deconstruction is nothing if not a general economy of 'queering.'"[18] For that very reason, deconstruction can efface the restricted economy of queer identities. I consider the shifting borders of these two economies. Turning to the advent of poststructuralist theory in the United States in the 1960s, I observe that the struggle carried on between the proponents of literary modernism and emergent postmodernism implicated homophobic assault in the resistance to theory. Theory was targeted as signifying sexual perversity. Focusing on the (ab)use of the name of William Burroughs as a signifier in debates among Frank Kermode, Abrams, and Paul de Man, I argue that works like *Naked Lunch* and Burroughs's autobiographical fiction *Queer* represent modes of a specifically queer apocalypse, grounded in the social and psychological effects of homophobia in the United States at midcentury. In the second half of the essay, I argue that these struggles continue to be played out in current postmodern production. Ironically, David Cronenberg's film adaptation of *Naked Lunch* (1991) converts Burroughs's fiction and biography into a *modernist* apocalyptic narrative in which a metaphorical femininity (literally, Joan Vollmer, Burroughs's wife) needs to be sacrificed in order to enable the vocation of the artist.

The next section of essays deals with apocalypse in the contemporary media and the arts including the novel, film, music, and cyberpunk fiction. In "Can the Apocalypse Be Post?" Teresa Heffernan draws on Don DeLillo's novel *White Noise* to question Jean Baudrillard's contention that the implosion of the category of the "real" renders contemporary existence already apocalyptic. Baudrillard claims that the millennium will not occur: "We are already more or less disconnected from our history and thus also from its destination. That means, then, that time can slow as it nears its end and that the year 2000, in a certain way, will not take place."[19] In *America,* Baudrillard travels to "America" to find there the end put to Western civilization. But in a United States that is marked by the "ruins" of many cultures, both indigenous and imported, the end is signified for Jack Gladney, the protagonist of DeLillo's novel, not in the New World but in an obsession with Germany's Nazi past. Gladney's concurrent anxiety about dying resists the notion that the end can be either reduced to a sign or made authentic. Death marks a limit to the human will to master it by either means.

The first Reagan administration dealt in an apocalyptic rhetoric that derived from biblical sources familiar to the Christian fundamentalist fraction of his constituency. Kevin Pask displaces this rhetoric to the genre of science fiction and its (traditionally) utopian view of human possibilities. Pask argues that in popular culture at the fin de millennium the mapping of outer space as subject to military technology in the name of an intergalactic Pax Americana is reminiscent of a Reaganite fantasy of life in the 1950s. The film *Star Trek VI: The Undiscovered Country* (1991) offers yet another nostalgic image of returning "back to the future" of the days when, as Reaganites liked to think, the United States would be "secure" in its dominance of global politics. Pask further links Reaganite politics and contemporary liberalism as he finds it in Lyotard's *Economie Libidinale* (1974) and Francis Fukuyama's *The End of History and the Last Man* (1992). According to Pask, both these writers contend that, in the aftermath of the grand historical narratives, the only future that is at once conceivable and desirable is that of liberal capitalism. Tracking the analysis of the *Terminator* films in feminist and gay critique by Constance Penley and Jonathan Goldberg, respectively, Pask underscores the need to reframe discussions of the film within an awareness of postmodern capitalism. He argues that both *The Terminator* (1984) and *Terminator 2: Judgment Day* (1991) "deal with the consequences of the international division of labor — the replacement of relatively high-paying unionized jobs in North America by low-wage manufacturing work throughout the

Third World—as a gender crisis: the disappearance of the father (Kyle Reese), the 'cyborgization' of the mother (Sarah Connor), and even the 'recuperation' of the nuclear family in the return of the Terminator as a mechanically programmed father figure in *Terminator 2*." The nostalgia of the *Terminator* films unwittingly confirms what it appears to deny: namely, awareness of "the growing insecurity of the patriarchal nuclear family in an economy increasingly defined by female-headed households and a female or 'feminized' workplace."

Pask suggests that Donna Haraway's "A Manifesto for Cyborgs" has been a crucial theoretical intervention in the thinking of postmodern gender politics. Haraway takes as her point of departure the recognition by feminists in the United States during the mid-1980s that it is no longer possible to speak as though there were a unified subject of feminism — an acknowledgment that marks the end of second-wave feminist apocalypticism. As Haraway remarks:

Painful fragmentation among feminists (not to mention among women) along every possible fault line has made the concept of *woman* elusive, an excuse for the matrix of women's dominations of each other. For me — and for many who share a similar historical location in white, professional, middle-class, female, radical, North American, mid-adult bodies — the sources of a crisis in political identity are legion. The recent history for much of the U.S. Left and U.S. feminism has been a response to this kind of crisis by endless splitting and searches for a new essential unity. But there has also been a growing recognition of another response through coalition — affinity, not identity.[20]

Haraway reaches this conclusion mindful that if woman as a dialectical universal has come to an end, apocalypse in the form of "Star Wars," or what she refers to as "technological apocalypse," certainly has not. She proposes to pose against this prospect and its attendant desires "an effort to build an ironic political myth faithful to feminism, socialism, and materialism."[21] Writing in the spirit of this project, Linda Howell argues that the emergence of "technocultural feminism" has been necessary to resist the tendency for feminism to become the preserve of white middle-class feminists, whose agenda excludes the needs of others — including other women and, in particular, female industrial workers in the Third World. At stake in the manifesto, for Howell, is a cultural politics of difference articulated in local, historical terms — at the level of situated, embodied practices. This politics of difference motivates her critique of Derrida's limitation, in the essay on nuclear deterrence, of the concept of "literature" to the masterpieces of European (male) literary modernism.[22] In contrast, she analyzes the cultural work of three technocultural feminists — Constance Penley, Rosalind Petchesky, and Rey Chow — who assess the implications of the figuration of the female body as a biomechanical component of a global integrated circuit.

Peter Dickinson and Darren Wershler-Henry deconstruct the use and abuse of apocalyptic rhetoric in the representation of minority subjects. Situating himself as a seronegative gay man, Dickinson attempts "to listen, . . . actively, attentively, and sensitively," to "hear" the needs of his "Buddy," the interlocutor in the volunteer work that Dickinson does with AIDS Vancouver. Starting from Derrida's observation that "an apocalyptic superimprinting of texts" often implies the absence of a "paradigmatic text. Only relationships of cryptic haunting from mark to mark. No palimpsest (definitive unfinishedness). No piece, no metonymy, no integral corpus," Dickinson questions alternatively both the fetishizing and the disappearance of "a subject, a body, a corpus, a corpse," in the apocalyptic discourses that have proliferated around AIDS.[23] In Dickinson's citations, however, the subject-of-AIDS, naming him or herself, opens a future beyond the ends that impend. Alexander García Düttmann quotes a PLWA, who says: "Ever since I decided to speak in the language of truth [. . .], to speak of my AIDS and in its name — legitimated by this avowal — I rush headlong [*je me précipite*] after the virus, I allow myself to be led by it, to follow it, to love and to hate it, as if I were one of the survivors of some imminent apocalypse."[24]

Music/noise/composition (to use the terms of Jacques Attali): Gangster rap can signify any and all of them. "By its very tone, the mixing of voices, genres, and codes, and the breakdown of destinations, apocalyptic discourse can also, in dislocating destinations, dismantle the dominant contract or concordat."[25] Darren Wershler-Henry tests this wager in his essay, "O.G. Style: Ice-T/Jacques Derrida." The politics of positionality in Ice-T — the rap, the commodity, and the media event — are unusually complex. Wershler-Henry positions himself as the white male college student, pictured on the cover of Ice-T's album *Home Invasion*, who represents in turn the whites who comprise 75 to 80 percent of the purchasers of Ice-T's rap albums. This racial crossover suggests the reversibility of meaning possible in listening to Ice-T: "The rapper in-forms the rapt listener (the white college boy), the rapt (listener) wraps the rapper." But Ice-T is also "wrapped" in attacks made both on behalf of traditional order *and* political correctness. Common to both assaults is the view, as described by bell hooks, that finds "black militancy" to be "always too extreme in the white supremacist context, too out-of-order, too dangerous."[26] Moreover, Ice-T's music is subject to censorship — as Derrida suggests apocalyptic discourse often is. How does censorship affect the apocalyptic tone of Ice-T? Does it render it inaudible? Does it purify him and his listeners as a result of his departure from a major recording company for the independent Priority record label? Or is this "move" but one more ruse in the endless process of deferral known as commodification?

In a swift, incisive essay, Christopher Keep argues that the emphasis on speed that Derrida observes in both the rhetoric of nuclear deterrence and the Book of Revelation informs the responses of David Koresh and government agents at Waco. Keep rejects the humanist axioms of media coverage that attach responsibility to particular names such as that of Attorney General Janet Reno, while ignoring questions about institutional responsibilities and effects—including those produced by the media. He rejects too the marketing-based "sender-message-receiver" model of communication that attributes the disaster at Waco to an unfortunate "communications breakdown." Keep instances, instead, an "eschatology of speed," in which both defenders and besiegers were absorbed, that characterizes contemporary existence in its preoccupation with technological instantaneity. Ironically, it was Koresh's daily writing on the Book of Revelation that—like St. John's—continually deferred the end whose coming its author desired. This apocalyptic play was fatally interrupted on April 19, 1993, when Combat Engineering Vehicles, under the direction of members of the misnamed Hostage Rescue Team, "pushed the noses of their specially mounted battering rams through the pink plasterboard walls of Ranch Apocalypse, fired off their tear gas canisters, and withdrew." Keep's argument carries the implicit warning that the end of the Cold War leaves desire for "the big one" unabated. Even in its absence, nuclear apocalypse will continue to be played out, in a host of settings and transformations, some as yet unimagined, including the continuing possibility of actual use of nuclear weapons. In face of this desire, Keep asks what responsibilities exist and for whom?

The coda to *Postmodern Apocalypse* is Peter Schwenger's essay on William Gibson's cyberpunk fiction, *Agrippa (A Book of the Dead)*, which suggests the new terms within which avant-garde cultural practice occurs today. *Agrippa* combines engravings by Dennis Ashbaugh, crypted letter text, and hypertext. The text on disk mimes the ultimate apocalyptic book since it disappears—destroyed by a computer virus immediately after it unscrolls. Likewise, some of the illustrations fade when exposed to light while others require exposure to become visible. Schwenger explains Gibson's fascination with a self-destructing text in part by associating it with the memory of nuclear threat: Gibson's father worked on the Manhattan Project. But Schwenger contextualizes *Agrippa* primarily in aesthetic terms. Technogeneric innovation in this composite work occurs within the context of the tradition of the avant-garde. He cites Stéphane Mallarmé, a founder of modernism, who says of writing: "whatever truth emerged in the process only did so with the loss of an impression which, after flaring up for a brief instant, burned itself out."[27] Paradoxically, then, *Postmodern Apocalypse* ends with Schwenger's reminder that an aesthetic desire for the new continues to motivate the most current technotexts.

Do these new forms repeat the old norms or do they exceed repetition to become what Attali envisages as "composition"? "Composition, then, beyond the realm of music, calls into question the distinction between worker and consumer, between doing and destroying, a fundamental division of roles in all societies in which usage is defined by a code; to compose is to take pleasure in the instruments, the tools of communication, in use-time and exchange-time as lived and no longer as stockpiled."[28] Attali's formulation recalls the humanism of young Marx, who might have had a Beethoven quartet in mind when he remarked:

> Let us suppose that we had produced as human beings. In that event each of us would have *doubly affirmed* himself and his neighbour in his production. (1) In my *production* I would have objectified the *specific character* of my *individuality* and for that reason I would both have enjoyed the *expression* of my own individual *life* during my activity and also, in contemplating the object, I would experience an individual pleasure, I would experience my personality as an *objective sensuously perceptible* power *beyond all shadow of doubt.* (2) In your use or enjoyment of my product I would have the *immediate* satisfaction and knowledge that in my labour I had gratified a *human* need, i.e., that I had objectified *human nature* and hence had procured an object corresponding to the needs of another *human being.* (3) I would have acted for you as the *mediator* between you and the species, thus I would be acknowledged by you as the complement of your own being, as an essential part of yourself. I would thus know myself to be confirmed both in your thoughts and your love. (4) In the individual expression of my own life I would have brought about the immediate expression of your life, and so in my individual activity I would have directly *confirmed* and *realized* my authentic nature, my *human, communal* nature.
>
> Our productions would be as many mirrors from which our natures would shine forth.[29]

It is worth remembering that this text became generally available in English only in the 1970s. Since then, it has exerted considerable influence within the ambit of postmodernism. Despite the skepticism that makes latter-day radicals such as queer theorist Michael Warner shy away from phrases such as "*human, communal* nature," the search for a mode of sociality continues.[30] Analytic and affirmative deconstruction are equally pertinent to that desire at the present moment.

Notes

1. Mary Ann Caws, *Women of Bloomsbury: Virginia, Vanessa, and Carrington* (New York: Routledge, 1991), 31.

2. Raymond Williams, "The Bloomsbury Fraction," in *Problems in Materialism and Culture* (London: Verso, 1982), 165.

3. Williams, "The Bloomsbury Fraction," 167.

4. Although these allegories are historical fictions, they do throw constellations of factors into relief. I am aware too that one could make a case for Woolf's suicide

as an act that occurs *after* the modern just as one could argue that, if *To the Lighthouse* is a characteristically modernist text, Woolf's *Between the Acts*, published posthumously in 1941, is one of the first classics of postmodernism. The conjunction of Woolf and Benjamin interests me in the similarity of their ends. In this respect, I agree with Jean-François Lyotard, who argues that the discriminations to be drawn between the modernist and the postmodernist sublime are both fine and, at times, reversible. See Richard Dellamora, *Apocalyptic Overtures: Sexual Politics and the Sense of an Ending* (New Brunswick, N.J.: Rutgers University Press, 1994), 214 n. 5.

5. Information on the monument in this and the following paragraphs is cited from Christopher Phillips, "Germany to Build Benjamin Memorial in Spain," *Art in America* 80 (December 1992): 25.

6. Jean-François Lyotard, "The Sign of History," in *Post-structuralism and the Question of History*, ed. Derek Attridge, Geoff Bennington, and Robert Young (Cambridge: Cambridge University Press, 1987), 179 (emphasis Lyotard's).

7. Jacques Derrida, "Of an Apocalyptic Tone Recently Adopted in Philosophy," trans. John P. Leavey Jr., *Oxford Literary Review* 6, no. 2 (1984): 24.

8. Walter Benjamin, "Theses on the Philosophy of History," in *Illuminations*, ed. Hannah Arendt and trans. Harry Zohn (New York: Schocken Books, 1976), 257–258.

9. Jonathan Boyarin, *Storm from Paradise: The Politics of Jewish Memory* (Minneapolis: University of Minnesota Press, 1992), xvi.

10. Boyarin, *Storm from Paradise*, xvii.

11. John Kifner, "A Palestinian Version of the Judgment of Solomon," *New York Times*, Saturday, October 16, 1993, 2.

12. Clyde Haberman, "Violence by Settlers on West Bank Provoking Showdown with Rabin," *New York Times*, Monday, December 6, 1993, A4.

13. Richard Wolin, correspondence, *The New York Review of Books*, March 23, 1993, 66.

14. Thomas Pynchon, *Gravity's Rainbow* (New York: Viking Press, 1973), 693.

15. Steven Goldsmith, *Unbuilding Jerusalem: Apocalypse and Romantic Representation* (Ithaca, N.Y.: Cornell University Press, 1993), 2.

16. Northrop Frye, *Fearful Symmetry: A Study of William Blake* (Princeton, N.J.: Princeton University Press, 1947), 140. In context, the passage is yet more offensive since Frye conflates this gendered figure with a wide range of political, religious, and psychological evils. Likewise, since Medusa figures in Freud as the castrating feminine presence, the sight of whom turns men into homosexuals, the passage is as rife with homophobia as it is with misogyny.

17. Elisabeth Schüssler Fiorenza, *The Book of Revelation: Justice and Judgment* (Philadelphia: Fortress Press, 1985), 199.

18. James Creech, *Closet Writing/Gay Reading: The Case of Melville's* Pierre (Chicago: University of Chicago Press, 1993), 192.

19. Jean Baudrillard, "The Anorexic Ruins," in *Looking Back on the End of the World*, ed. Dietmar Kamper and Christoph Wulf and trans. David Antal (New York: Semiotext[e], 1989), 39.

20. Donna Haraway, "A Manifesto for Cyborgs: Science, Technology, and Socialist Feminism in the 1980s," in *Coming to Terms: Feminism, Theory, and Politics*, ed. Elizabeth Weed (New York: Routledge, 1989), 179–180.

21. Haraway, "Manifesto," 179, 173.

22. Jacques Derrida, "No Apocalypse, Not Now (Full Speed Ahead, Seven Missiles, Seven Missives)," *Diacritics* 14 (Summer 1984): 27–28.

23. Jacques Derrida, "Living On: *Border Lines,*" trans. James Hulbert, in *Deconstruction and Criticism* (New York: Continuum, 1979), 136–137. Given the alarming shift in the ethnic, racial, and gender demographics of AIDS in the U.S., one has to think as well of the color of bodies, literal and phantasmatic. See "Blacks Far More Likely Than Whites to Have AIDS, Agency Says," *New York Times,* September 8, 1994, A8.

24. Alexander García Düttmann, "What Will Have Been Said about AIDS: Some Remarks in Disorder," *Public* 7 (1993): 97.

25. Derrida, "Of an Apocalyptic Tone," 29–30.

26. bell hooks, "A Call for Militant Resistance," in *Yearning: Race, Gender, and Cultural Politics* (Toronto: Between the Lines, 1990), 186.

27. Letter from Stéphane Mallarmé to Eugène Lefébvre, May 17, 1867, in *Stéphane Mallarmé: Correspondance, 1862–1871,* ed. Henri Mondor (Paris, 1959), 245–246.

28. Jacques Attali, *Noise: The Political Economy of Music,* trans. Brian Massumi, foreword by Fredric Jameson, afterword by Susan McClary (Minneapolis: University of Minnesota Press, 1985), 135.

29. Karl Marx, *Early Writings,* introd. Lucio Colletti and trans. Rodney Livingstone and Gregor Benton (New York: Vintage, 1975), 277–278 (emphasis Marx's).

30. "Feminist and racial movements, along with the lesbian and gay movement, are frequently animated by displaced frustrations with atomizing conditions of market mediated life, frustrations that find expression in the otherwise misleading and damaging idea of 'community.'" (Michael Warner, "Something Queer about the Nation-State," *Alphabet City,* 3 [October 1993], 16.)

Part I
Jews, Gentiles,
and Fascists

Coitus Interruptus: Fascism and the Deaths of History

Andrew Hewitt

> Europe has two histories: a well-known, written history and an underground history. The latter consists in the fate of the human instincts and passions which are displaced and distorted by civilization. The Fascist present in which the hidden side of things comes to light also shows the relationship between written history and the dark side which is overlooked in the official legend of the nationalist states, as well as in the critique of the latter.
> —Max Horkheimer and Theodor W. Adorno, *Dialectic of Enlightenment*

If Adorno and Horkheimer are to be believed — and this essay seeks to rattle at that belief — then fascism is not merely something that happens *in* history, but something that happens *to* it. In fascism, a shift takes place from a "written history" to a history of the body: history bodies itself forth in the wake of fascism. Of course, the question raises itself whether this can, indeed, be taken as a definitive mutation in — or, rather, out of — historical consciousness; for as Jean-Joseph Goux has pointed out, "*Idealism is first of all a conception of conception.*"[1] The history of idealism, written history — "the official history of the nationalist state" — has to some degree always been modeled on a certain conception of the body. The shift to which Horkheimer and Adorno do attest, however, is a shift in our very conception of that body. If, as Goux argues, Hegel already glimpsed "the end of the end of a certain History and the beginning of another" in "copulation . . . , a practical coitus, no more and no less, of masculine and feminine," (*Symbolic Economies* 234), it is this belief in the reproductive powers of the human body that has now been lost. If, as Horkheimer and Adorno argue, "[t]he body cannot be remade into a noble object: it remains the corpse however vigorously it is trained and kept fit" (*Dialectic of Enlightenment* 234), I hope to show here how this corpse of history has been interred in those theoretical and narrative accounts of death that take fascism as their point of reference.[2] Specifically, I seek to show how the problematic of a nonreproductive history

of the body—polemically articulated in writings by Adorno and Jean-
François Lyotard—is narratologically displaced onto the question of
nonreproductive homosexuality in Alberto Moravia's *The Conformist*.[3]
The homosexual will be scapegoated as the instigator of that historical
rupture—both literally and figuratively, a coitus interruptus—that is
fascism.

What would it mean to model (post-)historical notions of apocalypse
on the political and historical phenomenon of fascism? For, indeed, fascism seems to have become the privileged modality of the apocalypse,
functioning both spatially as a totalitarian model of society's destructive
self-completion, and temporally through a rhetoric of "final" solutions,
of ends and of thousand-year regimes without end. An unfolding of history into the presence of totalitarian social space, fascism seems to body
forth the apocalypse in the form of the dialectic — as the self-sublation of
a philosophical and political tradition, an end thought both as completion or telos and as (self-)destruction. It is this dialectical understanding
of apocalypse that will be at issue here: if fascism is the end or death of
something, does it enact the notion of ending already encoded in the
thing it ends, or does it end what precedes it by imposing a new sense of
ending? What is the status of the end: is it integral or external to the thing
that ends? What does it mean to think apocalyptic ending through a
concept of totalitarianism that seems to displace questions of historical,
temporal continuity into the spatial realm of social structure? In short, if
we bespeak—through fascism—a "death" of history, is this a death by
natural causes? Can we posit an apocalyptic rupture when it is, in fact, the
concept of historical rupture itself that has been ruptured?

What I will be proposing here — beginning with a reading of Lyotard's
treatment of "Auschwitz" in *The Differend*—is an anti-apocalyptic reading
of fascism, or, at least, a reading that does not seek to reinstate the historical dialectic that fascism supposedly "ends" by subjecting fascism to an
interpretive hermeneutic.[4] Fascism is not to be made sense of—even as
the embodiment of the irrational. Before considering Lyotard's writings,
however, I should indicate a divergence between the concerns of his work
and the more limited, textual stakes of this study. By placing the emphasis
on Italian fascism—or, rather, on Alberto Moravia's presentation of it
through the life of *The Conformist*—I will necessarily shift the consideration of fascism somewhat from the essentially ethical concerns that
have accompanied Lyotard's somewhat synecdochic reading of fascism as
"Auschwitz."[5] The images that tie fascism to our representations of apocalypse have thus far been images of genocide, whether that genocide be
taken as the definitive historical repudiation of an intellectual tradition,
or as its horrible realization.[6] For this reason, though questions of anti-
Semitism and genocide are not central to the textual materials under

consideration here, I would like, nevertheless, to begin with a brief consideration of Lyotard's presentation of "Auschwitz" in *The Differend* as
a way of outlining what (historical) death has come to mean in and
through our understanding of fascism. Subsequently—using *The Conformist* as the point of articulation for such a consideration—I will seek
not only to acknowledge the ideological status of fascism as a definitive
rupture in the historical self-understanding of the twentieth century, but
further to demonstrate the investment of a "fascisticized" apocalypse in a
discourse of (hetero-)sexual—or what I shall call come to call "orgasmic"—normalcy. At issue, then, is the following: to what extent does the
historical phenomenon of fascism usher in a change in our historical
sensibility, and to what extent is any such change attributable to a reconfiguration of the categories of sexuality?

Lyotard's *Differend* can be read as a confrontation with the problematics involved in offering any modal (or apocalyptic) reading of fascism.
Taking issue with Adorno, one of the first philosophers to reflect (in his
Negative Dialectics) upon the ethical significance of genocide for speculative discourse, Lyotard seeks to resist a modal reading of "Auschwitz" —
its reduction, that is, to the level of a philosophical model. Reading
"Auschwitz" modally, Adorno reacts to his fear that any thought seeking
to represent "Auschwitz" to itself will necessarily trivialize genocide, reducing it, in turn, to the level of mere representation. Clearly, Lyotard is
sensitive to such fears, which also animate his own insistence upon the
nonlitigational nature of the differend, but he explains his critique of
Adorno in the following terms:

> For [Adorno], "Auschwitz" is a model, not an example. From Plato through
> Hegelian dialectics, the example has the function in philosophy of illustrating an
> idea; it does not enter into a necessary relation with what it illustrates, but re-
> mains "indifferent" to it. The model, on the other hand, "brings negative dialec-
> tics into the real." As a model, "Auschwitz" does not illustrate dialectics, be it
> negative. Negative dialectics blurs the figures of the concept, which proceed from
> the rule of the *Resultat*, and liberates the names that supposedly illustrate the
> stages of the concept in its movement. The idea of the model corresponds to this
> reversal in the destiny of dialectics: the model is the name for a kind of para-
> experience, where dialectics would encounter a non-negatable negative [*un néga-
> tif non niable*], and would abide in the impossibility of redoubling that negative
> into a "result." . . .
> The "Auschwitz" model would designate an "experience" of language that
> brings speculative discourse to a halt. (*The Differend* 88)

A modal (rather than exemplary) reading of "Auschwitz" is a reading
that will inevitably reinstate—albeit in negative form—the dialectical
mode of analysis that "Auschwitz" has supposedly discredited. Understanding "Auschwitz" as the sublation of a historical dialectic involves

making sense of something that must resist sense: the historical phenomenon that belies the historical validity of the dialectic is itself nevertheless accounted for in terms of that dialectic. Such a reading is, one might say, properly apocalyptic, in that it understands fascism as an end — as both a completion (telos) and as a destruction. Such apocalyptic thinking is intrinsically dialectic in its resolution of absolute negation and historical realization.

Lyotard objects that Adorno's presentation of "Auschwitz," while refusing mere reparation, nevertheless makes sense of senselessness, retaining the essentials of a historical dialectical (albeit in negated form) and thereby projecting beyond its own death the historical consciousness that has supposedly come to an end. This projection of the dialectical method beyond its own death ignores — from Lyotard's perspective — the ethical disfiguration enacted by fascism, and relies on a model of sublation and "beautiful death" that "Auschwitz" has rendered anachronistic. As a model, "Auschwitz" brings about its end from within the terms of the thing it supposedly ends — in this case, the dialectic. By asserting that "Auschwitz" "brings negative dialectics into the real," Adorno rejoins the idealist historical dialectic. Consequently, Lyotard argues that the end Adorno envisages is an end in both senses of the word: a rupture, but also a teleological completion. If "Auschwitz" cannot be made sense of, it would seem that it itself nevertheless makes sense — in Adorno's presentation — of the historical determinants that bring it about: it is not indifferent, as the example would be, and therefore it assumes a historical essence that is modally (though negatively) articulated.

I read *The Differend* as a countertext to Adorno, then, as precisely *non-apocalyptic* in tone; for if "Auschwitz" marks the end of our faith in a historical dialectic understood in either a teleological or an ontological sense, the apocalyptic, modal interpretation of fascism becomes merely restitutive. What I wish to examine, through my reading of Moravia, is how and why an apocalyptic reading of fascism — not only of "Auschwitz" — has asserted itself as a response to fascism. What are we seeking to restore in this "apocalyptic tone," in this movement beyond restoration or reparation?[7] What is the meaning of this "beautiful death" that philosophical thought has died? We should begin any such examination by asking exactly what it is that meets its end in "Auschwitz." What philosophical death occurs neither beyond nor beneath — but alongside — the death of millions of members of a race? Lyotard pursues this question in its essentially ethical dimension, arguing — correctly, I believe — that it is a certain conception of death itself that meets its death in fascism. It is my contention that this problematic of historical death (or the death of history) cannot be confined to the genocidal project of Nazism, and that the fascist imaginary in general reformulates the possibility of a historical death. Where Lyotard concentrates on the ethical dimension of "Ausch-witz," I wish to concentrate on the implication of a certain conception of death in dialectical thinking (and vice versa). Moravia's *Conformist*, I will contend, aims to construct a novelistic narrative of that death.

The form of death that meets its own end in "Auschwitz" is what Lyo-tard calls "beautiful death": for " 'Auschwitz' is the forbiddance of the beautiful death" (*The Differend* 100). This beautiful death is an ethical construct in which the death that confronts us is transcended through our compliance to a collective imperative legitimating that death. Lyo-tard argues that in any death that can acquire an ethical dimension and itself ground ethical actions "[t]he 'reason to die' always forms the bond of a we . . . " and that

by identifying oneself with the legislator who orders one's death, one nevertheless escapes the miserable fate of being the referent for every forthcoming phrase that may bear one's name: the scourge of the dead in Greek thought. One can only succeed in this by obeying the order, since by doing it, one decrees it anew as a norm. One thereby makes one's name enter into the collective name of the legislating authority, which is a constant addressor because it is a rigid designa-tor. . . . Such is the Athenian "beautiful death," the exchange of the finite for the infinite, of the *eschaton* for the *télos:* the *Die in order not to die.* (*The Differend* 100)

The "beautiful death" is at once an individual gesture and a collective project, assimilating the individual to the ethical collective at the moment of death. As a transcendent moment, then, the collective is predicated upon such deaths. Auschwitz is the forbiddance of any such beautiful death because of its characteristic anti-ethical, nonreciprocal configura-tion in which "that which orders death is excepted from the obligation, and that which undergoes the obligation is excepted from the legitima-tion" (*The Differend* 101). Lyotard insists that "the authority of the SS comes out of a we from which the deportee is excepted once and for all: the race. . . . But one cannot give a life that one doesn't have the right to have. Sacrifice is not available to the deportee, nor for that reason acces-sion to an immortal, collective name. . . . This death must therefore be killed, and that is what is worse than death. For if death can be extermi-nated, it is because there is nothing to kill. Not even the name Jew" (*The Differend* 101). The Jew is in no position to transcend his death by ac-quiescing to it in the name of the authority that demands it, since he does not inhabit a language game that allows him (or her) to occupy the ethical position of the command that demands death. The ethical divi-sion of interlocutors has been radicalized as a racial division, for in Nazi ideology the Jew *is* a Jew by virtue of this impotence. The Jew does not simply occupy a nonreciprocal position in language; "Jew" is the very *name* of that position (which is why not all Jews need to be jews). The Jews are constituted as a race within genocidal logic because they are defined as the recipients of the command, as those incapable of inhabiting the command as an ethical imperative. To make sense of "Auschwitz" (as Adorno does in rendering it the moment of a historical imperative, the moment of an absolute death) is to traduce its senselessness, to coerce meaningless slaughter into an essentially ethical and apocalyptic construct (the Holocaust).[8] Indeed, if such an endeavor seeks to make of "Auschwitz" a "beautiful death" we might see in it a recurrence — rather than a refusal — of fascist aestheticization.

This is one sense, then, in which we might speak of the death of history — as the death of "beautiful death," as the failure of death to inscribe the name of the dead not only into ethical discourse, but also into historical narrative. And indeed, this lost function of narrative acquires a further importance through Lyotard's contention that "[t]he people phrases itself by acting (by dying) and dies well by phrasing itself. Whoever is not of this people cannot hear, cannot tell, and cannot die well. This people alone is made up of 'true men,' that's the name one ethnic group calls itself by (D'Ans, 1978). . . . Nazism restores this genre of discourse, which modernity has brought to ruin" (*The Differend* 105). What Lyotard achieves with this exposition is the linkage of a genocidal project to a linguistic regimen from which the possibility of reciprocity has been eliminated. Fascism both urges upon us and witholds from us the importance of narrative phrasing. At the same time as it biologizes nation as race, fascism sunders the ethical and legitimational force of nationality. By radicalizing the positionality of interlocutors — by defining *as a race* those who may not speak — fascism withdraws itself from ethical discourse; and the modality of ethical discourse is, indeed, the dialectic. So, to answer again our question "What meets its end in Auschwitz?" we might answer: the dialectic as the discourse within which beautiful death is meaningful and communicable. To this extent, then, we might tentatively think phrasing as an alternative to the reciprocity of the dialectic; and yet the dialectic — as a historical necessity that has passed beyond any actual dialect or speech act — has itself also fallen prey to the closure of this phrasing. Lyotard seeks both to redeem a notion of dialectical interaction (a fact often overlooked) and to demonstrate its irredeemable phraseological closure.

I wish to draw now upon Lyotard's foregrounding of the dialectic as a mode of historical understanding, in order to argue that while the dialectic has supposedly been threatened (or negated) by fascism, it has nevertheless been reinstated in apocalyptic readings of fascism. For Lyotard, the dialectic that comes under attack in the historical phenomenon of fascism is a "phrase regimen" rather than a philosophical structure in the more limited sense. Lacking both the dialogical openness of a dialectic in the strict sense and the dependence on a linguistic referent (since fascism serves precisely to deprive its racial referent of language), this phrase regimen seeks to substitute meaning with coherence. Whereas the philosophical project seeks to negotiate the *differends* that arise between discourses that intersect but do not contradict, the phrase regimen seeks merely to produce meanings and results that the metadiscourse of philosophy must subsequently voice. But what are the stakes of the deceased dialectic? Lyotard differentiates from within the dominant "phrase regimens" of modernity (for example, "those of cognition and those of the Idea," *The Differend* 28) to assess what it is that the notion of the dialectic grounds for modernity. Without entering into the technicalities of his argument, we can observe that while Greece "placed the dialectical and rhetorical genres in the governorship of phrases," in the first French Republic (that is, in the paradigmatic nation-state) this ideological centrality is accorded to "the Idea, that is, dialectics in the Kantian sense, in particular the one whose stakes are in free causality (ethics)" (*The Differend* 141). What seems to be at stake politically in the collapse of a dialogical, dialectical notion of history is the nation-state as the ethical macro-subject of history.[9]

Worthy of note, though—both in the dictum just quoted and in the broader argument—is the characteristic dissociation of narrative from dialectic in modernity. Whereas in the Greek state it is "the dialectical and rhetorical genre or genres" that co-create legitimation, Lyotard claims that in the wake of Nazism "[t]he only way you can make a 'beautiful death' out of 'Auschwitz' death (nos. 156, 160) is by means of a rhetoric" (*The Differend* 109). The debate over "Auschwitz" brings to a head a division of dialectic and rhetoric implicit in enlightened modernity.[10] In what follows, I will contend that it is the rhetoric of apocalypse that has sought to make a beautiful death not only out of "Auschwitz" but out of all that fascism brought to a historical end. Clearly, it is just such a rhetorical reappropriation of fascism that Lyotard is concerned with when he asks: "If the name hidden by 'Auschwitz' is the death of the magical, 'beautiful death,' how could the latter, which sustains the speculative movement, rise up from its death in the camps? And, on the other hand, supposing that 'after Auschwitz' speculative discourse had died, does it follow that it leaves place only to subjective chatter and the wickedness of modesty? It is within speculative logic that this alternative is formulated. To accept it would be to perpetuate that logic" (*The Differend* 89). By reducing—or inflating—"Auschwitz" to the level of a model, by negating the modality it institutes in the assertion that no discourse can be *adequate* to it, we reassert the notion of adequacy that has itself become outmoded. Thus, Adorno's assertions play back into the mimetological structures that they reject.

Paraphrasing Adorno, Lyotard goes on to ask a question with which I would like to frame the question of literary treatments of fascism: "Is 'Auschwitz' and 'after Auschwitz,' that is to say, Western thought and life today, something that disputed speculative discourse? If so, is it frivolous? If not, what happens to and what becomes of the speculative which would not be speculative?" (*The Differend* 88). In moving toward a consideration of novelistic treatments of fascism, I would like to speculate on just what this "frivolous" might be. Is it frivolous only from the perspective of the speculative discourse that has supposedly been discredited? Or might it respond to the need to develop a discourse that does not reinstate the myth of the beautiful death, that does not aestheticize by reducing the displaced dialectical politics to a rhetorical aesthetic? I would like to play on this distinction of dialectic and rhetoric as a way of examining the possibility of a postfascist discourse by proposing that it is in the realm of the literary that the incommensurability of Lyotard's deliberative and narrative modes has been acted out — in rhetorical, apocalyptic mode.[11] Perhaps the paradox to be considered can be phrased as follows: the narrative of the end of dialectical politics potentially reasserts the notion of end (as telos) that it seeks to chronicle. A novel that makes sense of the end of the possibility of sense potentially undoes its own work, becoming "rhetorical" in the denial of its own phraseological closure. If this is the case, can we insist upon a notion of the literary as Lyotard's "frivolous" rather than as a rhetoric of "beautiful death"?

If narrative as a phrase regimen restores an aestheticized rhetorical death, we might examine the function of closure — the literary enactment of a "beautiful death" — as a way of understanding this rhetorical impulse in narrative. Furthermore, since this rhetorical function also leads to a mythic reconstitution of the nation as phraseological (inter-)subject, we might also hypothesize that it is specifically in the realm of dialectically legitimated national narratives — the traditional realm of the historical novel — that any crisis of representation will most immediately manifest itself. In turning to Moravia, we should recall that Lyotard by no means totalizes the dialectic as the equivalent of a modern episteme. The dialectic (in the Kantian sense) was tied specifically to the problematics of state and nationhood, and fascism seems to threaten the viability of any such national narrative. It is clear that the writing of *The Conformist* reflects (and, of course, by *reflecting*, in some sense negates) such a crisis of representability.

That the novelistic structure of *The Conformist* makes certain assumptions about historical representability is a fact by no means lost on Moravia. In response to a question on just this topic, for example, he has the following to say:

Do you believe in the possibility of an historical and national novel? One, that is, which in some way represents the recent or not so recent achievements of Italy? In other words, do you consider it possible to reconstruct happenings and destinies that go beyond the individual, and are outside their historical time? I would like to answer this question by asking others. Is it still possible to believe in History? Can national histories still exist in Europe? And what *is* the history of Italy, teeming as it is with defeats that are victories, and victories that are defeats, with the Risorgimento turning into Fascism . . . ?[12]

Moravia's response is thematically rich. First, it is quite explicit in its acknowledgment of the political and national implications of novelistic discourse: he questions both the possibility of a history and, more specifically, the possibility of a *national* history. But his comments reinstate the possibility of the representation of nation at the same time as they seek to question it. He *identifies* Italy with that sense of a crisis of representation: Italy is the place where victories become defeats and defeats victories, a land of dialectical reversals that find their sublation in the name of the nation. In other words, by the very same gesture with which he seems to question the integrity of history and the nation-state, Moravia reinstates a concept of Italy as a mutation in historical consciousness — apparently linked to fascism.[13]

With respect to Lyotard's foregrounding of the dialectic, what is interesting in Moravia's formulation is this repeated structure of "reversal," of victories that are defeats and defeats that are victories. It would seem that the possibility of a dialectical emergence from these simple reversals has been historically foreclosed — and that that foreclosure is paradoxically commensurate with Italy's nationhood. On the one hand, of course, this simple reversal is only a primitively dialectical gesture, insofar as it marks a purely determinate negation. Nevertheless, it might be that a simple reversal *is* that which lies beyond the dialectic, a historical consciousness *beyond* sublation, into which the historical dialectic will have sublated itself. It is in this latter vein, for example, that Goux has argued that "[w]hat follows absolute idealism can be conceived, perhaps, only through the figure of a reversal — but not a simple turnaround or hierarchical switch that would obliterate the process of evolution and breakthrough" (*Symbolic Economies* 235). If the notion of a reversal seems somewhat simplistic as a "beyond" of the dialectic, we might argue — against Goux — that his stigmatization of simple reversal is itself a classically dialectical gesture, and that his thinking of a beyond of dialectics is eminently dialectical. Is the death of the historical dialectic being transmogrified into a "beautiful death," Moravia's impossible national narrative itself grounding Italy as nation?

In fact, Goux's analysis will open up an entirely new terminology for the understanding of the dialectic and its moment of crisis as a political and philosophical structure in fascism. If we are to attempt to graft the terms of *The Differend* onto an analysis of the structure of death in *The Conformist*, it will be by way of Goux, who analyzes material and social reproduction in terms of a structure of homology that grafts an anthropological discourse derived from Engels onto the ontogenetic, Oedipal structure observed by Freud. Goux's thesis is that "[t]here is a spectacular congruence — too close-fitting to be accidental — between the logic of the sexual itinerary *from a mother to a woman* and the course of social history according to Engels: from nature as mother to a different, transformed nature" (*Symbolic Economies* 239).[14] The observation allows us, I think, to develop Lyotard's notion of the crisis of dialectical validation in a new direction. For Goux's analysis will eventually lead him to conclude that "[i]f the phylogenetic odyssey of libidinal positions of knowledge, through which social access to reality is gained, comprises a multiphased shift from inclusion in nature as mother, through a separation, and finally to an inclusive reciprocity with the *other* nature, human history through the present has been limited to the history of *man*: history is masculine" (241). The dialectical notion of history seems rooted in patriarchal structures, and in order for Goux's homologies to hold, it is necessary to read history as the history of a man, as a movement from mother to other: "the shift from primitive materialism to dialectical materialism (with idealism in between) entails a passage from a position of knowledge in which the subject reproduces his relation to his mother to a position of knowledge which, at the end of the typical libidinal trajectory (following paternal mediation), is congruent to the relation of the male subject to (a) woman" (237). Clearly, though, Goux is attempting to recontain the crisis of the dialectic, to position that crisis merely as a move from idealism to materialism, from Hegel to Marx. This recontainment, moreover, seems to involve a retention of rather strict — if reinterpreted — categories of gender that remain largely unencumbered by the more complex problematics of sexuality. What I will argue is that Goux partakes of precisely the rhetorical strategies Lyotard seems to indicate as necessary to the reconstitution of a beautiful death. Moreover, I will argue that Goux's inability to recognize the intrinsically idealist nature of the dialectic as structure results from a refusal to think beyond the strict limits of heterosexuality.

For Goux, apocalyptic thought reveals itself to be the thinking not only of "a certain [paternal] mode of historicity" (*Symbolic Economies* 217) — but as the mode of heterosexual thought. The crisis of the (gendered) subject reveals itself as a crisis of sexual relations. Thus, when Goux seeks to theorize the "reversal" he can only conjecture that "another mode of historicity, linked to another position of knowledge, works upon the preceding one: this working shapes the question of 'materialism' and of female sexuality" (217). This, I will contend is no reversal at all, or rather, merely a reversal in the limited predialectical sense of the word, a determinate negation of masculine heterosexuality from the position of a feminine that provides little by way of a real alternative.[15] Reversal is thought here strictly in terms of existing gender binarisms rather than through the prism of *sexuality*. Goux seems to identify the problem in terms of idealism as opposed to matter, when in fact the problem lies in the very structure of the dialectic, which is idealist in its very heterosexuality. (His own account of the movement from primitive materialism to a new materialism by way of idealism, for example, is itself an entirely idealist presentation.)

Given this fruitful conjuncture of gender, dialectic, and apocalypse in Goux's work, might we hypothesize that postdialectical, anti-apocalyptic thought would articulate itself through a language of sexuality rather than of gender? The reversal that apocalyptic thought cannot think is, in fact, an inversion — sexual inversion — a deconstruction of the dialectic, a "re-*vers*-al" and "re-*in*-scription." In fact, Goux does at certain points foreground the question of sexuality as the liminal imagination of a (post-)dialectical reversal, observing merely that "[i]f sexuality exceeds all procreative ends, investing itself in the erratic drift of signifiers, it is perhaps more because *human reproduction is not simply sexual* than because sexuality is not procreative. Reproduction, a subject's juncture with the matter of history, is no longer located in mindless copulation occasioned by sexual dimorphism, but is *social* production and reproduction" (*Symbolic Economies* 226; emphasis Goux's). Even here the strictly heterosexual organization of sexuality forecloses all but the most simplistic understandings of the reversal. Thus, while it is the socially reproductive function of sexuality that is stressed, this stress never serves to displace the biologically reproductive core of Goux's ultimately vulgar materialist heterosexism, or to suggest, in short, that "sexuality is not reproductive."

Could it be that the dialectical telos of Goux's model — the reversal in the deeper sense — needs to be thought *sexually* — as homosexuality — rather than in terms of gender? Certainly Goux resists any such interpretation with the most resolute and redoubtable heterosexuality. At the points where he does attempt to think the reversal in terms of sexuality, he returns to the idealist core of his own historical model — to Hegel — to suggest the configuration of a posthistorical libido, in which "Hegel glimpse[s] the 'end' of History — or, rather, the end of the end of a certain History and the beginning of another — as a copulation . . . , a practical coitus, no more and no less, of masculine and feminine" (*Symbolic Economies* 234). A practical coitus, no more and no less, of masculine and feminine — such are the sexual stakes of the historical reversal of the dialectic. But where would fascism fit into this schema? Or homosexuality? What I contend is that an apocalyptic (one might say, indeed, orgasmic) logic of heterosexuality, in which completion is projected as obliteration in *jouissance,* figures both fascism and homosexuality through the same trope — as a coitus interruptus.

Which brings us — by way of a rather long contextualization — to Moravia's *The Conformist,* and to the questions with which he, in turn, answered the question of the historical novel. The questions with which Moravia responded were all tied to his doubts about the validity of the nation-state as a public sphere, about the possibility of representation itself. Elsewhere, though, he obligingly answers questions with apparently straightforward answers; as for example, when he is quizzed about the motivation behind *The Conformist:*

What are the historical facts behind The Conformist?
The Rosselli murders. Furthermore, I wanted to add to this what I myself had known of fascism. Everything depends upon the equation: the protagonist is a fascist because he is homosexual.
This equation still seems true to me today: a fact that takes on a negative value on the individual level transforms itself (or thinks it does) into a positive value on the collective level. For example, d'Annunzio's decadentism is transformed into patriotism.[16]

The legitimational problems surrounding the nation-state as a vehicle of and for representation — the problem of the dialectic, to use Lyotard's terminology — are overdetermined at the level of the individual fascist psyche by a specifically *sexual* question: the sexual preference of the novel's hero, Marcello Clerici. The private vice of homosexuality becomes public as fascism — the political expression of an essentially decadent culture. But it is also important to examine the context of the question and the structure of the response, which link — at least for Moravia — the question of homosexuality and the question of the possibility of "phrasing." The question has, in fact, been sparked by Moravia's prior assertion that "once again I learned that it was impossible to write a novel on the basis of reality and historical fact" (*Alberto Moravia* 71–72; my translation). Fascism endangers the mimetic project. More than this, however, the passage suggests that fascism must be understood not simply as unrepresentable, but as the very *condition* of unrepresentability, as that which has rendered unrepresentable, for example, a mythology of nation closely tied to the project of self-narration.

But there is something in Moravia's passage from the aberrant *valore positivo* of fascism to the private vice, the *valore negativo* of homosexuality, that once again makes it possible to write a novel, and, more specifically, a novel about fascism. If fascism disfigures history and acquires an antirepresentational negativity, homosexuality—as the *valore negativo* on which it is supposedly based—serves as the negation of that negation; as the dialectical and determinate possibility of novelistic rerepresentation. *The Conformist*—as a mimetic treatment of fascism—reassures on two levels, then; first, it reassures by homosexualizing fascism in the figure of its protagonist, Marcello, thereby opening up the possibility of a postfascist return to a political and (hetero-)sexual normalcy. It is as if the collapse of the progressive public sphere (that is, of the bourgeois public sphere thought in terms of its own political sublation) were being identified with the emergence of homosexuality as a historically determinant character structure. Second, however—and more fundamentally—Moravia's project reassures by asserting the very possibility of a post-fascist representation.

But we begin to note also a recurrent structure, a structure of inversion familiar from the passage cited earlier: the Risorgimento becomes Fascism, just as the private vice becomes a public virtue. To this extent, we might say that Moravia partakes of an apocalyptic logic of reversal familiar—in different forms—from both Goux and Adorno. In the passage from the political structure of fascism to the libidinal structure of homosexuality, Moravia has retained the structure of the antirepresentational negative dialectic in order to revitalize the project of novelistic representation.[17] Thus we can conclude that in terms of the problematics of homosexuality and fascism, the relationship between the two will not have been one of historical causality, but rather of aesthetic recuperation: the novel forgets the very crisis of representation to which it supposedly attests. Fascist aestheticization is countered by what we might call—using Lyotard's terminology—a novelistic rhetoricization.

While it is not my intention, at this juncture, to elaborate on the vulgar psychoanalytic reading of homosexual desire encoded in Moravia's comments and pursued rather clumsily in the novel, it is necessary for other reasons to reconstruct Moravia's understanding of the Oedipal structure. For it is in and through the thematic of the Oedipal relation that he seeks to thematize not only questions of homosexual desire, but also of homosexuality as a model for the representation of the unrepresentable phenomenon of fascism. For this reason, let me provide a brief plot synopsis by way of case history. The novel's hero, Marcello Clerici, is first presented as a sadomasochistic child from a disrupted family. He is isolated from his friends both by an excess of masculine cruelty (significantly, when Marcello seeks to involve his friend Roberto in a game of killing lizards "Roberto, in refusing his proposal, had invoked maternal authority in support of his own disgust" [*The Conformist* 14]), and by an excess of physical femininity (he is teased and taunted as "Marcellina" by his schoolmates). From the very outset, then, Marcello's pathology is presented in terms of a confusion of gender, a confusion in which the extremity of one gender trait seems to have been exacerbated by the presence of traits of the opposite gender. This confusion is elaborated — by a conflation of effeminacy and homosexuality that is all too familiar — into a specifically *sexual* dilemma.

As a child, Marcello is seduced by Lino, the chauffeur from a local villa — though both at the time and in later life he suspects that he was more active than passive in this seduction. Lino lures the child to his room, where he makes sexual advances, only to recoil in shame at his own lust. When he urges the none-too-reluctant child to "Shoot, Marcello . . . kill me . . . yes, kill me like a dog" (64), Marcello complies, then steals away undetected. This murderous encounter acquires all the importance of a primal scene in Marcello's subsequent development, as he seeks both to live up to the guilt he has brought upon himself and to make good the ostracization from bourgeois society that such guilt involves. Understandably, Marcello is attracted by fascism, which responds to this double bind by rendering cruelty itself the norm: as a fascist he can both acknowledge and repudiate his guilt as a political and existential condition.[18] The body of the novel subsequently concerns itself with Marcello's betrayal of a former professor — Quadri, an anti-fascist exile in Paris — and with his compulsive linkage of the sexual and the political. Combining his honeymoon with a secret assignment that will lead to Professor Quadri's death, Marcello develops a passion for Lina, the professor's younger wife, who in turn develops a passion for Marcello's own wife, Giulia. The novel ends several years after the completion of this mission that led to the death of both Quadri and his wife. At the time of the fall of the Duce, Giulia and Marcello venture out onto the streets of Rome to witness the fall of the dictatorship that will guarantee their own fall from social favor. While making love in the park they are interrupted by a parkkeeper, Lino, who never died in the original incident that had formed the basis for Marcello's entire politico-sexual fascination with normality. At the novel's conclusion, Marcello and his family are killed by an enemy bomber while escaping from the city.

In his presentation of the etiology of Marcello's homo-fascism, Moravia seems obsessively concerned that we should Oedipalize both structures, that we understand the emergence of both homosexuality and fascism within the structural and historical parameters of the Oedipal construct. In presenting now the forms taken by Moravia's Oedipalization of political and sexual structures, the question I seek to keep in mind is that of the importance of such structures to Moravia's own project as a novelist of fascism. Indeed, Goux will already have averted us to the essentially *historical* role of the paternal: "Insofar as he guarantees the permanence of sameness in reproduction, it is the father and not the mother who is responsible for life and for the essential tendency of the living. He is the representative of reproduction, the signifier of vital perpetuation, and even, therefore, taking it one step further, the guarantor of eternity" (*Symbolic Economies* 22). Writing of "a 'paternal' hegemony that, rather than being added on to sexual difference as history, determines *a certain mode of historicity*" (217), Goux makes clear that what is at stake in Moravia's Oedipal construction of homo-fascism is the recuperation of a structure of historical representation (coded in limited, dimorphic terms of gender) that fascism supposedly sunders. In other words, while I do not contend that fascism should be accorded the position of "the unrepresentable" as such (which would constitute a re-aestheticization of politics under the sign of the sublime), we should nevertheless note how (through the restoration of the Oedipal structure) representation does, indeed, seek to make good that which fascism has provisionally destroyed.

Marcello's relation to his father can best be presented retrospectively, from the position of its disruption and the father's fall from sanity. What the eventual institutionalization of Marcello's father seeks to suggest, of course, is the displacement of the patriarch from the position of authority, from the position of phallic and representational privilege (to invoke Goux's system of homology). However, it is by this very displacement that the representational force of the father reasserts itself (and, subsequently, that historical mimesis becomes possible for Moravia, the novelist). The father retains his position of authority by forging and centering the system of decentering and displacement through which he is himself represented. In other words, the thematic attempt to present both homosexuality and fascism as *disruptions* of the Oedipal structure is met by the obsessively Oedipal structure of representation.

Since, as I have said, the relationship to the father can best be traced retrospectively, I wish to spend some time now examining the scene in which Marcello — as a young adult — accompanies his mother on a visit to his father in an insane asylum, a scene in which the question of fascism and historical neurosis is posed most acutely. This episode begins with a curious *Nachträglichkeit:* we learn that Marcello's ghoulish and "cadaverous" mother has a lover — her chauffeur, Alberi. Suddenly, the primal scene involving Marcello and Lino is displaced and reinterpreted by this anterior — though historically subsequent — relationship. The recurrent figure of the chauffeur clearly invites us to reinscribe the origin of Marcello's homosexual desire in terms of the Oedipal configuration: Alberi is/is not the father, and the "murder" of that other chauffeur, Lino, is therefore overdetermined. By "murdering" the chauffeur Lino, Marcello both acts out/represses his own desire and reinscribes that desire in terms of a traditional Oedipal (heterosexual) triangulation: he "kills" the chauffeur who will have been the lover of the mother—that is, the representation of the father.

Thus, the homo- and heterosexual discourses of desire intersect; or rather, homosexual desire seems to figure as a misplaced libidinal rein-vestment of the paternal relation. At the same time, however, the fact that the connection Lino/Alberi/Father is established only *subsequent* to the "murder" serves to question the possibility of postulating *any* desiring origin (necessary, I would contend, to apocalyptic thought), since the origin will always already have been reconfigured from the perspective of the mother's subsequent relationship. What would the mother's desire for this chauffeur have told us about Marcello's (repressed) desire for that other chauffeur? Are we to read Marcello's desire as a desire for him who possesses the mother? In fact, the figure of Lino seems to anchor a whole sexual and symbolic network that offers a glib libidinal framework for interpreting the novel: for example, Professor Quadri's wife (desirous of Giulia and desired by Marcello) is called Lina, as if she were a mere effeminization of the repressed first sexual partner. Again, Marcello's desire is for the desirer of the putative original object (the mother, the wife).

Instead of entering into a consideration of the possibilities latent within the Oedipal structure with regard to its feminine object, however, I wish to concentrate on the functioning of the patrilineal and historical continuum within that structure. I wish to demonstrate the way in which the Oedipal relation is deconstructed by this novel even where it seeks to maintain Oedipus as the interpretive touchstone for sexual normalcy.[19] In a gesture that is not unfamiliar from other attempts to restabilize the political edifice after the collapse of fascism, Moravia seems to be offering (in the asylum scene) the insanity of Marcello's father as a model for the political insanity of Italy under the fascists. Marcello's father imagines himself to be Minister of Foreign Affairs under the Duce (not, notably, the Duce himself—he has been displaced from the continuum of patriar-chal representations). The father's delusion leads his doctor to comment:

"But as far as the Duce goes, we're all just as mad as your husband, aren't we, Signora?—mad enough to need tying up, mad enough for treatment with the douche and the strait jacket. . . . The whole of Italy is just one big lunatic asylum, ha, ha, ha."

"In that way my son is certainly quite mad," said Marcello's mother, naively reinforcing the doctor's compliments; "in fact I was saying to Marcello, on our way here, that there were certain points of resemblance between him and his poor father." (144)

Of course the argument contains an apologetic assessment of fascism as a madness—a historical aberration—but in Moravia's presentation this madness is not a momentary or passing historical neurosis, but involves a radical rethinking of history itself. The mother's unwitting confirmation of the doctor's psycho-political diagnosis turns out to be all too glib, for in pointing out the similarities between Marcello and his father she asserts a continuity (a patriarchally inherited insanity) that insanity itself ruptures. This becomes clear when she explains the origins of the father's sickness: " 'The funny thing about it is,' she went on, 'that it was precisely with this idea of your being another man's son that your father's madness began . . . He had a fixed idea that you were not his son . . . And d'you know what he did one day? He took a photograph of me with you as a baby . . . ' 'And made holes through the eyes of both of us,' concluded Marcello" (145). The logic is confusing: Marcello's political "insanity" is predicated upon the fact that he has inherited it from his father; but this inherited paternal insanity originates in the idea that Marcello is *not* the father's son. The one insanity, in other words, obviates the cause of the other: if Marcello *is* insane because he is his father's son, then his father's insanity is groundless. One might say that Moravia replicates — at the micro-Oedipal level — that dilemma of proto-fascist patriarchalism outlined elsewhere by Wilhelm Reich: fascism (and, in this case, homosexuality too) is both a replacement for the de-potentialized Oedipal conflict and the result of that conflict. For Reich, however, the question of patriarchy turns on the identity of the father — is he, or is he not the *Führer?* Whereas for Moravia the ambiguity lies in the identity of the son — is he or is he not the son?[20]

In terms of the analysis offered by Lyotard, we are faced with a classic differend. How do we reconcile an interpretation of fascism that depends on the assertion of patrilineage ("I am insane politically because I am the son of an insane father") with an interpretation that asserts the illegitimacy of such a lineage ("The father is insane because I am not his son")? Returning to Lyotard's insistence on the particularly problematic notion of national phrasing, we might begin by registering a displacement that has taken place in the father's identification with the mechanisms of fascist state power: he does not imagine himself to be the Duce, but merely one of his minions.[21] As Minister of Foreign Affairs, indeed, the father has attempted to place himself in the position of watchdog and supervisor of his wife's "foreign affairs" and infidelities, regaining in insanity that power that he never held as a sane man. In this capacity, the Minister of Foreign Affairs oversees his own displacement from the center of power, from the patriarchal position. From the very origin, power is displaced: the father (even if he is the father) is not the patriarch. And I would argue that the Oedipal configuration no longer provides a framework for comprehension in *The Conformist* (as Moravia would like to pretend), that it is itself subtly deconstructed, though never destroyed.

Insanity results from the imagination of a break (in filiation) and per-
petuates itself (in fascistic political form) in the acknowledgment of a
continuity. In *The Conformist,* the law of the father — enacted in castration — itself becomes profoundly ambiguous in the case of the mutilated
photograph. The mutilation of the photograph demonstrates, I think,
the ways in which the law enacts itself in the very moment of its potentiary
abdication. Even where the gesture of violence seeks to express the *breakdown* of the patriarchal construct — a historical rupture — the aggression
itself reconnects the disaffiliated son with the structures of power.[22] The
symbolic castration enacted in the piercing of the eyes takes place precisely because the father does *not* acknowledge the potentially Oedipal
filiation of this non-son. In this sense, the mutilation is *not* a symbolic
castration, but a castration *from* castration, so to speak. Nevertheless, the
violence done to the son in the photograph — a gesture of *dis*-inheri-
tance — is yet a reenlistment of the son into the paternal symbolic order
that castration inaugurates. In other words, precisely by acknowledging
the rupture of the patrilineage (a purely imaginary rupture, since Marcello *is* his father's son) the father paradoxically reinstates it. The act of
mutilation that sought to exclude Marcello from the symbolic continuum
takes the form of a castration — an induction into precisely that symbolic
order.

Indeed, we should also note that the mutilation of a *photograph* — that
is, of an iconic representation of the child — is itself profoundly ambiguous, since this act of frustration at the collapse of the patriarchal and
symbolic continuum can only act itself out at the level of the imaginary.
Any rupture with the father, any rupture with fascism, any rupture with
history becomes ideological in its purely imaginary assault on the symbolic and social order. Moravia consistently suggests that both homosexuality and fascism result from distortions in the functioning of Oedipus:
yet the structure of *The Conformist* consistently demonstrates the ineluc-
tability of such malfunctionings as the condition of possibility of the
Oedipal order itself. Oedipus is shown to function precisely *by virtue of* its
breakdowns; and likewise, fascism (if it is, indeed, the effect of such
breaks) proves itself latent within the supposedly stabilizing, normaliz-
ing, *heterosexual* structures of Oedipus.

At issue, of course, is the possibility of bringing closure to the historical
phenomenon of fascism through the medium of a narrative genre that
seems to have become — in the insane "speech-making" of the father —
purely "rhetorical" rather than dialectical. Thus, the ambiguities in Moravia's Oedipalization of both fascism and homosexuality derive from a
desire, on the one hand, to posit a radical rupture, a narrative distance
that will allow for the representation of fascism, and the need, on the
other, for a continuous (patriarchal and heterosexual) historical meta-

narrative within which fascism would become explicable. The suggestion of a *failed* Oedipus serves to preserve an essential structure while asserting a fundamental critical distance. The failure to Oedipalize is the failure that leads both to fascism and to homosexuality.

This Oedipal ambiguity is mirrored in the fact that *The Conformist* is, one might say, a novel with two endings; or rather, a novel that articulates two senses of an ending, two senses (if this is possible) of the end. These two endings, moreover, rehearse the possibilities of historical ending already shown (through our consideration of Goux's work) to have been coded sexually: the practical coitus and apocalyptic destruction. The historical backdrop of the novel's conclusion is the fall of Mussolini's government in Rome — a patriarchal fall that obviously also bears catastrophic implications for Marcello and his family. Marcello seems at once resigned and euphoric at the collapse of the regime and, leaving his young daughter at home, takes his wife Giulia out onto the streets of Rome to "witness . . . the fall of a dictatorship" (296). Having left her home, Giulia seems oddly divorced from her fears for the future, and finally proposes:

"Come and let's make love here . . . on the ground. . . . Everyone thinks about war, and politics, and air-raids — when they could really be so happy . . . Come on . . . Why, I'd do it right in the middle of one of their public squares," she added with sudden exasperation, "if only to show that I, at least, am capable of thinking about something else . . . Come on."

She seemed now to be in a state of exaltation, and went in front of him into the thick darkness amongst the tree-trunks. "You see what a lovely bedroom," he heard her murmur, "Soon we shan't have a home at all . . . but this is a bedroom they can't ever take away from us . . . We can sleep and make love here as often as we like." (304)

The moment is one of sexual release, as well as of a release from the conjugal, socially reproductive implications of the sexual act. The coupling is nothing more than that — a sexual rather than reproductive act, the Hegelian coitus. Implicit in Giulia's sense of liberation, however, is an attempt to position the Hegelian imagination of an absolute, nonreproductive ending in opposition to a fascist ideology of *totalitarian* completion. This is a practical apocalypse, physical and partial rather than totalizing and transcendent, but it is, nevertheless, caught within the gendered heterosexual terms of the dialectic outlined by Goux. Indeed, Moravia seems to acknowledge the impossibility of a return to any such "beautiful death" (for is not the *petite morte* of orgasm the erotic expression of a beautiful death?) in the narration of a coitus interruptus. This time, it is Lino, the supposedly dead homosexual seducer from Marcello's past who accidentally stumbles upon the couple. The Hegelian idyll of a practical coitus is interrupted by the aberration of homosexuality no less than by the stifling conformity of fascist morality. The historical intervention of fascism has replicated itself in a model of desire — and a model of historicity — as homosexuality; that is, as a reversal — or inversion — more radical than the Hegelian practical coitus. It is "inversion," not "reversal" that displaces the apocalyptic dialectic: coitus reveals itself as mere reversal, the "internal external" of an imaginary system. Homosexuality is its anti-apocalyptic, unimaginable absolute external.

If Moravia implicitly acknowledges in this passage the impossible, ideological nature of a heterosexual reversal, the second ending of the novel is apocalyptic in a much more obvious and traditional sense, articulating a model of historical finitude that is less provisional, less momentary: "At that moment, from far away, the roar of the aeroplane as it turned became loudly audible again. He said to himself: 'Oh God, let them not be hit . . . they are innocent'; and then he waited, resigned, face down in the grass, for the plane to come back. The car, with its open door, was silent, and he had time to realize, with a sharp pang of pain, that no one would now get out of it. Then at last the plane was right above him; and it drew after it, as it receded into the burning sky, a curtain of silence and darkness" (317). In the shift from the first to the second ending, we have clearly moved to a more satisfactory apocalyptic finale. And this ending, I would contend, attempts to reinstate the possibility of a "beautiful death" in a much more recognizable form. Even as the innocence of the victims is proclaimed, there is talk of resignation, God, and burning skies — of a judgment, in short, that allows for an ethical transcendence even where it is unjust.

Both of the endings face the impossibility of thinking beyond apocalypse or beyond heterosexuality. The apparently nonapocalyptic ending of the coitus is, indeed, a form of beautiful death central to heterosexuality. Apocalyptic thought is heterosexual thought precisely because of its concern with historical continuity (the patriarchal, Oedipal configuration discussed with regard to Moravia) and with notions of ending derived from within that continuum. Homosexuality will always be the scandal of any such heterohistorical logic, a coitus interruptus. Both endings rehearse the possibility of an apocalyptic ending thought purely in terms of a closed heterosexual dialectic. Whereas *The Conformist* seeks thematically to identify homosexuality and fascism, its oscillation between the *petite morte* of coitus and the *deus ex machina* of total annihilation demonstrates the way in which its own (hetero-)sexual dialectic fails precisely because it cannot think beyond the apocalyptic logic that necessarily "makes sense" of fascism. "Sense" is heterosexual sense — production, pleasure, or death. It is a deathly logic. It is *homo*-sexuality — the coitus interruptus that defers endings by questioning origins (in this case, the false origin of Marcello's political neurosis) — that is alone capable of troping the postapocalyptic, postfascist possibility of narrative. The orgasmic logic of *jouissance* is indicative of precisely that dialectic of apocalypse we have attempted to foreground here: on the one hand, it indicates absolute presence, the uniqueness of the moment, but at the same time it annihilates consciousness of that moment.[23] Either way, it is caught within a philosophical problem of consciousness (and reproduction) alien to Moravia's presentation of homosexuality. Insofar as it will be possible to examine political, philosophical, and political configurations as interdependent, the "frivolous" phraseology of a postapocalyptic, postfascist aesthetic will be homosexual.

Notes

1. Jean-Joseph Goux, *Symbolic Economies: After Marx and Freud,* trans. Jennifer Curtiss Cage (Ithaca, N.Y.: Cornell University Press, 1990), 213 (italics Goux's).
2. Max Horkheimer and Theodor W. Adorno, *Dialectic of Enlightenment,* trans. John Cumming (New York: Continuum, 1987), 234.
3. Alberto Moravia, *The Conformist* (London: Secker and Warburg, 1952).
4. Jean-François Lyotard, *The Differend: Phrases in Dispute,* trans. Georges Van Den Abbeele (Minneapolis: University of Minnesota Press, 1988).
5. Without rehearsing the points of differentiation between the two political forms, I wish — in focusing on Italy — to resist the synecdochic reading of fascism that would take "Auschwitz" as the essential — modal — "experience" of fascism. In so doing, I by no means wish to invoke an alternate logic of accidence, in which fascism (in this case, Italian fascism) might be considered apart from the "excesses" or accidental appurtenances of genocidal Nazism. For a rudimentary introduction to the political forms of Italian Fascism and National Socialism, the following may be of help: Walter Laqueur, *Fascism: A Reader's Guide* (Berkeley: University of California Press, 1976), Ernst Nolte, *Three Faces of Fascism: Action Française, Italian Fascism, National Socialism* (New York: Holt, Rinehart, and Winston, 1966), Renzo DeFelice, *Introduction to Fascism,* trans. Brenda Huff Everett (Cambridge, Mass.: Harvard University Press, 1977).
6. Interpretations of fascism have long been divided between those that see in it an emanation of a fundamentally irrational tendency and those who see in it an expression of certain subterranean tendencies in the tradition of Western rationalism. *The Dialectic of Enlightenment* of Horkheimer and Adorno would be the *locus classicus* of this latter position while the former position is perhaps most stridently advanced in Gyorgy Lukacs, *The Destruction of Reason* (London: Merlin, 1980). More recently, we find a philosophical elaboration of some of the positions outlined by Horkheimer and Adorno in Philippe Lacoue-Labarthe, *Heidegger, Art and Politics,* trans. Chris Turner (Oxford: Blackwell, 1990). Interesting as a work that traverses this debate from the position outlined by the Frankfurt School to the conclusion that in fascism we encounter a lack rather than an excess of reason is Jeffrey Herf, *Reactionary Modernism: Technology, Culture and Politics in Weimar and the Third Reich* (Cambridge: Cambridge University Press, 1984).
7. The obvious starting point for the consideration of this apocalyptic tone in

philosophical writing would of course be Jacques Derrida, "Of an Apocalyptic Tone Recently Adopted in Philosophy," trans. John P. Leavey Jr., *Oxford Literary Review* 6, no. 2 (1984): 3–37.

8. What has been articulated most pointedly as a terminological debate — Holocaust or Shoah? — reflects, of course, fundamental differences of approach to the historical question of "Auschwitz." Perhaps the most concise opposition on this question can be drawn between Arno J. Mayer, *Why Did the Heavens Not Darken? The "Final Solution" in History* (New York: Pantheon, 1988), where the notion of a sacrificial holocaust is most decidedly rejected, and the review of this work in Jonathan LaCapra, "Review: *Why Did the Heavens Not Darken? The 'Final Solution' in History,*" *New German Critique* (Spring/Summer 1991).

9. This position is advanced most cogently and persuasively in Philippe Lacoue-Labarthe and Jean-Luc Nancy, "The Nazi Myth," *Critical Inquiry* 16 (Winter 1990): 291–312.

10. Lacoue-Labarthe and Nancy will recast this question of rhetoric in terms of a philosophical opposition of *muthos* and *logos* as alternative and supplementary systems of representation.

11. Lyotard offers the following definitions of his terminology:

In the deliberative politics of modern democracies, the differend is exposed, even though the transcendental appearance of a single finality that would bring it to a resolution persists in helping forget the differend, in making it bearable. The concatenation of genres of discourse and of phrase regimens at least allows itself to be taken apart, while in traditional narration the combination of various stakes — making believe, making known, convincing, making decide, etc. — defies analysis (so much is it inscribed in each phrase, and so much is the occurrence masked by the narrative form). (*The Differend* 147)

While:

Narrative is perhaps the genre of discourse within which the heterogeneity of phrase regimens, and even the heterogeneity of genres of discourse, have the easiest time passing unnoticed. On the one hand, narrative recounts a differend or differends and imposes an end on it or them, a completion which is also its own term. Its finality is to come to an end. . . . The narrative function is redeeming in itself. (*The Differend* 151)

12. Alberto Moravia, "Answers to Nine Questions on the Novel," *Man as an End: A Defense of Humanism. Literary, Social and Political Essays,* trans. Bernard Wahl (New York: Farrar, Straus, and Giroux, 1966), 190.

13. Walter Benjamin comments on a similar phenomenon in the emergence of fascism as an ideology in response to the traumatic experience of the First World War. The loss of the war — like the reversibility of Italian history — is finally ontologized as a specific national characteristic and the absence of a national subject hypostatized as a national characteristic: "What is special about the present and latest stage in the controversy over the war, which has convulsed Germany since 1919, is the novel assertion that it is precisely this loss of the war that is characteristically German." "Theories of German Fascism: On the Collection of Essays, *War and Warrior,* Edited by Ernst Jünger," trans. Jerolf Wikoff, *New German Critique* 17 (Spring, 1979): 120–128.

14. More specifically, Goux develops this line of thought in the following terms:

Now what seems at once the most noteworthy and least noted aspect of this process [i.e., Engels's anthropology] is that throughout the itinerary that concludes (which is not to say it culminates) the *history of man* in his reunion with nature, we find the same dialectic at work as in Freud — specifically, as in the *male* libidinal itinerary: the same severance from an original mother, made possible by phallic and paternal mediation; the same *opposition* culminating in the negation of the existence of another sex; then, finally, in a *negation of the negation of the mother,* the relation to the feminine, thanks to the interposition of a so-called paternal reference. This phallic dialectic shapes *the history of man* and the signifying position of the female sex considered apart from the mother. (*Symbolic Economies* 215)

15. Goux himself notes the limitations of the political structures of matriarchy: "Thus, far from constituting a historical alternative with respect to patriarchal society, the matrilineal family is its beginning" (218). Of course, Goux claims that this reconstituted feminine is precisely *non*-matriarchal, in that it disentangles the woman from the structures of maternal and material reproduction.
    16.
    Quali sono i fatti storici che stanno dietro a Il conformista?
    Il delitto Rosselli. In più volevo amalgamarvi quello che avevo conosciuto del fascismo. Il tutto retto sull'equazione: il protagonista è fascista perché omosessuale.
    L'equazione mi sembra vera ancor oggi: un fatto che ha un valore negativo su di un piano individuale si tramuta (o si crede che si tramuti) in positivo sul piano collettivo. Il decadentismo di d'Annunzio viene tramutato in patriottismo, per esempio.

Alberto Moravia: Vita, parole e idee di un romanziere, ed. Enzo Siciliano (Milan: Bompiani, 1982), 72. Translation is mine.
    17. In his "Theories of German Fascism" Benjamin comments on the function of the novel in the mastering and working through of the past. "Then came the attempt to forget the lost war. The bourgeoisie turned to snore on its other side — and what pillow could have been softer than the novel?" (123). It is ironic that Benjamin's analysis of the rhetorical and aestheticizing tendencies of the novel should prove so apt in the case of the antifascist novel of Moravia.
    18. Moravia states his case even more clearly elsewhere:

In *The Conformist*—whose origins were Freudian — I wanted to relate the case of a boy with early homosexual experience, who believes he has killed a man, who believes himself marked by this and therefore harbors an antisocial element that causes him to do everything to integrate himself into a society that seems to desire his expulsion. He wishes to cancel out—by himself—what he considers to be an original sin. To this end he accepts the criminality of his society. And if a crime is demanded of him as the price of this integration? He doesn't think twice: he pays for his integration with the crime.

Moravia quoted in *Alberto Moravia,* 71. Translation is mine.
    19. One critic has already commented on the question of the insufficiently Oedipalized hero of Moravia's novel; see S. L. Wood, "Religion, Politics and Sexuality in Moravia's *Il conformista,*" *Italian Studies* 44 (1989): 86–101. The theoretical elaboration of a similar position forms the basis of the seminal work of

Klaus Theweleit, *Male Fantasies,* 2 vols., trans. Stephen Conway in collaboration with Erica Carter and Chris Turner (Minneapolis: University of Minnesota Press, 1987–89). What I am suggesting here, in effect, is that this pre-Oedipal impulse in fascism is, in fact, both a ruse of the Oedipal configuration and a moment that undermines traditionally Oedipal readings of homosexuality and fascism such as those that Moravia seeks to encourage.

20. I refer to Wilhelm Reich, *The Mass Psychology of Fascism,* 3d ed., trans. Victor R. Carfagno (New York: Farrar, Straus, and Giroux, 1970). The central problem in this work is the interpretation of the role of the family in the emergence of fascism. Reich oscillates — as Moravia does here — between a *compensatory* relation of family and state, in which the leader replaces the defunct *paterfamilias,* and a *micrological* relation, in which the family serves as microcosm of the state superstructure.

21. The role of the father is replicated in Marcello's relation to his victim, Professor Quadri. Again, one suspects Moravia of a tendential Oedipalization of the conflict, but the analogies to the relationship to the father lie precisely in the ambiguity of the professor's patriarchal credentials. Marcello is hired to facilitate the assassination of Quadri supposedly because the latter was a former professor of his. In fact, Quadri never was his professor: we learn that Marcello met Quadri precisely on the day the latter left his position at the university to take up more practical antifascist activities. In other words, Marcello encounters in Quadri an abdication from the institutional framework of patriarchal power. The identity of Quadri and Marcello's father is established precisely on the basis of the nonidentity of each with his own supposed power.

22. The question of patriarchy in relation to fascism is a heated one, since the analyses of Reich and those who build upon him assert at one and the same time that fascism is a direct result of patriarchal familial relations and that it is the result of the *failure* of that familial structure. For an overview of this debate, see Jessica Benjamin, "Authority and the Family Revisited, or, A World without Fathers?" *New German Critique* 13 (Winter, 1978): 35–57. She responds in part to Alexander Mitscherlich, *Society without the Father: A Contribution to Social Psychology,* trans. Erich Mosbacher (London: Tavistock, 1969). In fact, I think her work responds to the broader *oeuvre* of Mitscherlich, specifically the problematics of mourning raised in Alexander Mitscherlich and Margarete Mitscherlich, *Inability to Mourn: Principles of Collective Behaviour,* pref. Robert Jay Lifton, trans. Beverley R. Maczek (New York: Grove, 1975). For a further consideration of fascism in the light of the issue of mourning and melancholia, see my forthcoming *Political Inversions* (Stanford University Press).

23. Implicit in my critique of an intrinsically heterosexual "orgasmic" logic, of course, is a parallel critique of the desire to retain *jouissance* as a model for a homotextual aesthetic. Such attempts find their classical justification in Roland Barthes, *The Pleasure of the Text,* trans. Richard Miller (New York: Hill and Wang, 1975).

At Last, All the *Goyim*: Notes on a Greek Word Applied to Jews

Jonathan Boyarin

"What are you doing out here in the ruins?"[1]

August 1, 1994

Dear Richard,

It will be immediately obvious that what follows is not the work of a specialist on Jewish apocalypse, but rather a set of reflections on the various associations that have come to hand in response to your request for an essay on Jewish apocalypse. In fact, though I'll have nothing more to say about them, the first thing that comes to my mind (still) when you say the word "apocalypse" is the figure of the Four Horsemen of Revelation. I know them, of course, not from having read that book but rather at the same level of popular imagery that leads, for example, to a further mental association with the Four Horsemen of Notre Dame.

Since it may seem at points in what follows that I'm straining to draw a sharper distinction between "Jewish" and "Christian" apocalypse than the textual history seems to warrant (which would necessitate exaggerating not only the differences between the two differences, but also the extent to which they are respectively internally coherent), let me state clearly that I do so only in order to reopen questions about notions of resolution and completion to which "we all" (by virtue not least of being people capable of reading this volume and inclined to do so) are heir. On the other hand I would not want the terms "Jewish" and "Christian" to dissolve into mere tokens of the twin horns of a Western dilemma about the particular and the universal. One indication of the continued or renewed distinctiveness of what we have learned to call textual communities is that this is virtually the first occasion on which I have opened, let alone cited, the Christian Bible! On the other hand, the Jewish prophetic texts I cite below are also new to me, since in the early modern "traditional Judaism" on which my own Jewish practice is loosely modeled, they are not a standard part of the curriculum.

Your expressed concern over your chronological plan for the volume produced some anxiety on my part over whether the Jewish subject matter dictating the essay's placement would also mesh with that plan. My guess is that it doesn't. Since much of the burden of the essay is to complicate chronological schemata of organization, I don't mind doing that as a trade-off for having ventured, at your invitation, where prudent scholars fear to tread.

Let me fortify myself for the journey with some definitions. One who has spent decades working on the Jewish apocalyptic texts of late antiquity and their early Christian heirs and contemporaries confirms the gloss of the term *apokalypsis* as "revelation."[2] What such texts purport to disclose is "a transcendent reality which is both temporal, insofar as it envisages eschatological salvation, and spatial insofar as it involves another, supernatural world."[3] It needs to be pointed out that this division into temporal and spatial is *our* grid,[4] but it nevertheless serves as a useful reminder in this context that the relation between revelation and resolution for "the Jews" and for the entire human species on earth is a question about both the time of the Jews and the place of the Jews.

As to the name apocalypse itself, the "genre label is not attested in the period before Christianity,"[5] and the first book designated as such is Revelation. From the beginning, however, the revelations the genre have in mind imply not only a Gnostic doctrine of the secret nature of the universe, but also always "the inevitability of a [future] final judgment."[6] Furthermore, there is an ancient type of apocalyptic literature that lays out a narrative of divine intervention giving sense and direction to human suffering and affording eventual redemption, and this "historical" type of apocalypse does contain an end-of-history scenario.[7] This scenario in turn entails the destruction of those who, depending on the ideological context of the particular apocalyptic text, either have unwarrantedly harrassed God's people and failed to acknowledge him, or failed to recognize the advent of his Son. In recent usages of the notion of apocalypse, this element of destruction has come to the fore, and thus in the present context it is not inaccurate to note that the two "dominant senses of *apocalypse* [are] revelation and destruction."[8]

Yet if the element of destruction is there from the "origin" of apocalyptic, as it were, it is also important to mark the slide from this original sense of uncovering, revealing a secret knowledge to the common modern notion of *the* apocalypse as a cataclysm leading to an "endtime." There is a near-reversal in the dramatic chronology of the dominant sense of apocalypse, from the emphasis on the first man enlightened, the first

"Christian" to whom the true and heretofore hidden promise of God's word has been revealed, to what Jacques Derrida calls a motif of "apocalypse without apocalypse,"[9] which here is not merely a rhetorical or philosophical figure of presence-in-absence, but is rather transcribable as endtime-without-revelation: the ultimate evacuation of any hope of meaning.

Since the "historical" ancient apocalypses, as suggested above, fundamentally include an aspect of judgment leading to reward and punishment, the notion of apocalypse without apocalypse could also mean endtime-without-judgment. Phrased this way we have, I suggest, a startling characterization of the postmodern turn, revealing both its Jewish and Christian roots in the vision of an endtime and how much of a break with the modern transformation of traditional hope it represents, since Jewish and Christian apocalypse both entail final judgment.

Here the first relevant distinction between Jewish and Christian ancient apocalypses comes into play. "In all the Jewish apocalypses the human recipient is a venerable figure from the ancient past, whose name is used pseudonymously."[10] The technique of assigning authorship to a revered figure from the past is actually a standard characteristic of Jewish writing down to the medieval mystical classic called the Zohar at least. It is consistent with the general Jewish tendency to view citation as more authoritative than originality. Thus there are noncanonized Jewish texts known as the Apocalypse of Abraham, the Apocalypse of Adam, and so on. This kind of "firstness" is quite different from the firstness of revelation to the self-named Christian authors, which proclaims the revelation as new and contemporary, the authority of its authorship not borrowed but boldly proclaimed. Thus "A man appeared, sent by God, whose name was John" (John 1:6). Susan Noakes has recently analyzed other scenes in the Gospel to show how this rhetorical habit of self-ascription as author/interpreter informs the Western Christian reading tradition down to the present.[11] We have tended therefore to take self-ascription as the norm, ourselves as the font of authentic interpretation, and the practice of ascription to a respected legendary ancestor as anomalous. At the same time we question our own authority now, when the confidence of modernity is exhausted, and seek to interrogate once again the legendary ancestors.

In the formative visions of the ancient apocalyptic, the meaning of life is to be found in a resolution after death. Our own sense of living in the shadow of apocalypse might be translated as a sense of being already located beyond or after death. The specific event I am thinking of as casting that shadow is indeed the Nazi genocide, the funeral pyre of the Enlightenment and of a certain culminating vision of Europe as the problem of difference resolved, the death of the attempt to solve the problem of the Other by the incorporation of this founding other. The future has collapsed upon itself, and we are burdened more by what we come after than by what awaits us. The postmodernist task is not so much any longer to offer hopeful or terrifying visions of the future (we, more conclusively than the moderns though perhaps as Derrida suggests not ultimately, having lost faith in retribution and reward), but to stand ourselves as the goaltenders, offering retribution and redemption to those who, before apocalypse / endtime / holocaust, that is before the time of the last of the just, of the last European, of the last man, of the last Jew, still lived their lives in some sense under the sway of faith in redemption and retribution. (And is it possible that I really do not?)

Hence the first broad theme of the essay focuses on a series of individual and implicitly pathetic, if not properly tragic, male figures, which will eventually be contrasted to a notion with very different affect and implications, the collective and quite properly and literally genealogical concept of the *genos*— or, as we will call it here following Derrida, the *goy*. Now I want to articulate a series of final figures that, I propose, serve as postmodern counterweights to the emphasis on originality, presence, and universality in Christian revelation.

The "last of the just" is the character of Ernie, the righteous son murdered by the Nazis in André Shwarz-Bart's novel of that name.[12] The title is drawn from the legend of the thirty-six concealed saints (in Yiddish, *tzaddikim* or, more specifically for the legend, *lamed-vovniks*, literally meaning "members of the thirty-six") on whose existence the continuity of the world depends. The figure has a particular valence vis-à-vis visions or ideologies of the endtime. Marking the novel's hero as the last in a line of such saints clearly does mean that his death is in some sense the end of a cultural world. More generally, since the designation of the thirty-six refers essentially to their saintly behavior toward others, the act of translating "just" back *into* Yiddish as *tzaddik* signals that the death of the last *tzaddik* is the end of a *moral* universe, the end of the time in which just behavior was the ultimate determinant of fate. To anticipate the discussion of another endtime fiction below, what makes *The Last of the Just* a novel not a legend and gives it an extraordinary human pathos is that it is also a family chronicle, the end of the world also the death of Ernie.

The "last European" comes from an even wispier source: Hannah Arendt's remark, in her introduction to the collection of Walter Benjamin's essays called *Illuminations,* that part of his ambivalence about coming to America to escape the Nazis (and hence one motivation for his suicide) was his fear that "people would probably find no other use for him than to cart him up and down the country to exhibit him as the 'last European.'"[13] With its echo of sad and isolated Eskimos, Indians, and pygmies caught on display and destined to die,[14] the phrase indicates an incredible flash of identification with the colonized in this indeed most European of thinkers. It reminds us, at least momentarily, that such figures of the end or of the last person are not limited to Europeans, to Christians and Jews — or at any rate, that the West has often pressed the Rest into the service of its apocalyptic vision. Furthermore, by envisioning the putative asylum of America as a sideshow in which he would be trapped, Benjamin marked this New World as an ironic anti-paradise, a place one goes to not so much to escape disaster, but *after* the catastrophe has already hit.

It is Maurice Blanchot who offers a portrait of the last man. The portrait begins with an acknowledgment of the startling and portentous responsibility of the title, and a suggestion that something has happened to make the narrator conscious that this is indeed the phrase he wants to use now: "From the time it was given to me to use this word, I expressed what I must always have thought of him: that he was the last man."[15] This person whom the narrator confronts and describes is a troubling, demanding, and uncertain presence, who always responds to every proffered idea with an understated demand, a tone of dissatisfaction: "Why do you only think thus? Why can you not help me?" There is something childlike about the last man's eyes. He has always been somewhat reclusive, "outside of us." Indeed his very existence is in doubt — which seems hardly surprising, for how certain could a narrator who comes after the last man, who is hence not a "man" himself, be of his own cognition? "I think today that perhaps he had never existed or perhaps that he no longer existed. . . . Perhaps he had changed everyone's condition, perhaps only mine."[16] What I find most striking, aside from the evocative mood of Blanchot's prose, is how easily it could be taken to be the words of a French intellectual, immediately after World War II, trying to figure a surviving Jew, surviving simultaneously as "the last Jew" and as "the last man," phantomlike. The point is not to establish whether Blanchot, in whose *oeuvre* the name "Jew" has occupied a significant place,[17] had a Jew in mind here, but to note that for a certain strand of high modernist European thought, it is after the great European catastrophe that the problem of Jewish difference can be resolved in its dissolution and idealization. Only after Auschwitz, as we say, has it been "given to" Blanchot's narrator "to use this word."

Regarding the last Jew, two texts draw my attention here. The most recent is Jacques Derrida's autobiography-cum-commentary, "Circumfession." Here, citing a diary excerpt from 1976, Derrida doubts the evidence of his own circumcision: "Last of the Jews, what am I [. . .] the circumcised is *the proper.*"[18] The "what am I" signals a profound puzzlement, already: can one be the last of the Jews, the last in a series and still a member of that series? The circumcised (male Jew, or Jewish penis) marks the property of generation. Thus when Derrida meditates on the meaning of that mark, as other Jewish critics have been doing recently, he does not see it as symbolizing a rounding continuity of generations.[19] For Derrida the circumcised penis is nothing so much as a point, a "head" or *cap* of individual finality associated (through the titillating mention of the practice of *metzitze*, or the sucking of the blood of circumcision [152]) with a generalized exchange of fluids, hence (inevitably now, and he refers to this elsewhere) to death through the exchange of a deadly virus. The finality is also expressed through a *reversal* of the emphasis on circumcision as continuation, fertilization, and generativity, a reversal through which circumcision becomes literal self-absorption, or as he coins the concept, "autofellocircumcision" (158). A further association of death with circumcision comes through his association of the cutting of the foreskin to the tearing of the clothes in mourning (specifically, here, for his mother, 167–168). That cutting away of the bond to his living mother is extended further into a death of collective identity; eventually, after hesitantly claiming the proud title of the last Jew, Derrida decides that he is "one of those *marranes* who no longer say they are Jews" (170). Denying the physical identification of circumcision and opting for a spiritualized carnal filiation, he insists that he "has a Christian body, inherited from Saint Augustine in a more or less twisted line" (170). Indeed.

How pretentious, properly speaking, to refer to oneself in writing as the last Jew, even when this identification is presented as an embarrassing revelation, the blow softened by distancing the author of "Circumfession" from it, citing it instead as a diary extract. But note well that to say "pretentious" is not to say phony or inappropriate. I would claim by way of anecdotal evidence that it is fairly common for (male?) Jewish intellectuals these days to fall occasionally into the apocalyptic mood of thinking themselves the last Jew. Yet this is the first time I have ever seen the sentiment, even equivocally, *written*.

The other case of the last Jew comes from Walter Miller's wonderful novel *A Canticle for Leibowitz*. The novel is set in and around a Christian monastery in the Southwestern desert, many decades after a nuclear holocaust. The collective identity of the monks centers around a shopping list attributed to the blessed "Saint Leibowitz," the kind of normal, middle-class American Jew who has been made legend by the likes of Bernard Malamud and Stanley Elkin. But the beginning of the book also presents another character, literally the last Jew — a hermit, living apart, and distinguished from the expectant and recuperative community of monks by his stance of crotchety survival.

The first major scene of the book describes a dramatic encounter between the novice Brother Francis, sent into the desert for a period of fasting and solitary, silent meditation as part of the process of initiation into his order, and the aging Jewish hermit. One gets ready for an allegory of the youth of Christianity versus the dried-up old age of Judaism. Miller might be said to be working off the legend of the wandering Jew — precisely a non-Jewish story about the Other — and this could be contrasted to Shwarz-Bart's deployment of the *Jewish* legend of the thirty-six hidden saints upon whom the world's existence rests. Indeed the picture of the Jew could be read as hostile: he is suspicious and ornery. Yet to this Jewish reader his very appearance in that postdisaster landscape — his remarkable survivorhood — comes across as affectionate, the "nasal bleat" in which he intones his recognizably Jewish blessing over his bread a moment of ethnographic familiarity rather than stereotyped caricature. Miller also grants the pilgrim a remarkable degree of cultural autonomy and even isolation, more than any American Jew today would be expected to have: "Still writing things backward,"[20] he says in response to Brother Francis, who chalks a note on a large flat stone to avoid speaking. When he finds just the stone that Brother Francis needs to complete his temporary shelter, he marks it with two Hebrew letters printed in the novel and left untranslated and untransliterated. The two letters spell the word *lets,* a term whose senses range from "clown" and "joker" to "trickster" and "devil." Miller even provides a gentle mockery of Christian suspicions of Jews; the hermit offers Brother Francis some bread and cheese (Miller does not say whether he knows Brother Francis is bound to fast). Brother Francis in turn sees this as the temptation of Satan and himself rescued by the vision of the Blessed Martyr Leibowitz, a parody of Christianity's historical demonization of Jews and deification of a Jew.

No clear difference in the experiences of nuclear holocaust of Christians and Jews is implied by Miller's characterizations. But in postmodern apocalyptic generally, there is a powerful imbrication of the feared *vision* of nuclear holocaust — that disaster that has indeed already happened, but in a place that is *elsewhere* for most Christians and Jews — and of the memory of the Nazi "Holocaust," as the genocide "here" is commonly styled. The conjunction of the two is most clearly present perhaps in Don DeLillo's bitterly funny novel *White Noise,*[21] which describes both a shameless professor who has made a name for himself by developing a Department of Hitler Studies, and a mushroom-like cloud of poison gas euphemistically referred to as "the airborne toxic event." The title of DeLillo's book could be taken to suggest precisely the absence of meaning that absence of a vision of ultimate judgment implies in our culture. Against this, *A Canticle for Leibowitz* seems to combine or in a kind of sad comedy almost resolve the genres of messianic vision and endtime apocalypse, inasmuch as there is a coming back together of the Jewish and the Christian, the abbey itself being named for Leibowitz,[22] significantly without the collapse of identity implied by Derrida's references to his circumcised yet "Christian" body.

The second question I want to raise concerns something like the double relation between visions of the end of the Jews and the end of the species or "world" on one hand, and between visions of the redemption of the Jews and the redemption of the species/world on the other.

When the question is phrased in this way, one would expect a neatly symmetrical, Aristotelian exposition of all of the various relations. But there is a very interesting disruption of the symmetrical balance between chosen people and "humanity," and between the right hand of reward and the left hand of punishment. That is, there is something that fundamentally cuts against the grain of anything that could roughly and broadly be conceived of as traditional "Judaism" in the notion of apocalypse as an end in oblivion. There seem to be powerful strains in Christianity that envision the destruction of all nonbelievers, all non-Christians. License for such rhetoric comes first of all from the Gospel of John, who states at the very beginning of his book that all those who receive the Light will be saved, but those who are sinners will be afraid to come into the light and, so to speak, "be revealed" and saved. (Hence the theme of revelation is double-edged, its very logic seeming to call forth interrogative impulses in Christian institutions, and it is tempting indeed to read back the origins of the Inquisition into this move of John's.) Jewish visions of endtime including the destruction of all non-Jews existed in the first century. The Rabbinic Judaism which has been "normative" for the past millennium and a half, however, rejects such notions. The issue of redemption is very much contested in Judaism — subject to both differing philosophical/speculative accounts at different times and places and to a wide variety of communal practices and disciplines very often closely akin to those of Christian or Islamic neighbors. Yet the idea of the extinction of the Jews (and *a fortiori* the extinction of the rest of the world) is explicitly refused consideration by the Bible, which would seem to preclude the possibility of the extinction of the world within the context of a recognizably Jewish thought system.

Scholars and others sensitive to the powerful ethnocentrism present in most of the Jewish biblical literature may doubt this claim. The prophet Zephaniah declares the imminent destruction of all the nations that surround Israel, who have brazenly defied God by harrying his people, along with most of the sinners in Israel who have in effect called forth such destruction upon themselves. Remarkably (or perhaps not so surprisingly, given the legacy of centuries of Diaspora and the lessons in discretion granted thereby),[23] only the last verse of his book is part of regular religious Jewish currency: "At that time will I bring you in, and at that time will I gather you; for I will make you to be a name and a praise among all the peoples of the earth. When I turn your captivity before your eyes, saith the Lord" (Zephaniah 3:20). Whereas the burden of the entire book has been focused "on the region," as it were — on the behavior of the people of Israel and its immediate foreign relations — this opens up to a vision of "all the peoples," oddly doubling back on everything the prophet has raged before, making it clear that *somebody* has to be left around to admire the saved and glorified remnant!

Still, if Zephaniah is a muted or "minor" Jewish canonical text, there is another brief passage that, for thousands of Jewish families, is a dramatic high point to the Jewish ritual calendar. The following verses from Psalms (79:6–7) are recited as part of the Passover seder: "Pour out Thy wrath upon the nations that knew Thee not, and upon the kingdoms that call not upon Thy name. / For they have devoured Jacob, and laid waste his habitation." The drama of this recitation and the anticipation of redemption that it carries are both accentuated by the custom of sending a child to open the door for the prophet Elijah, traditionally regarded as the harbinger of the Messiah, for whom an extra cup of wine has (always already!) been set out beforehand.

To whom do the verses refer? Precisely which "nations" (*goyim*) are Jews — some ignorantly, some triumphantly, some with profound ambivalence — praying God to punish at every Passover seder? A popular Yiddish encyclopedia states that "the content of the verses is a prayer that God take vengeance on the people who torment the Jews,"[24] which is indeed the conventional and colloquial understanding. A commentary to this passage based on the teaching of Reb Chaim Soloveitchik, the rabbi of Brisk, connects the presumably metaphorical "eating of Jacob" to the punishment meted out for those who improperly eat that which was set aside, made *kodesh,* separate, holy, to be eaten in the temple.[25] Through this expanded commentary, the conventionally understood historical plea for punishment of unjust historical action is reconnected to an emphasis on the *raising* and *separation* of Israel: the nation Israel is *kodesh.*

In any case, the "original" context of these two verses in the psalm powerfully attests to a particular situation where the land and the Jewish kingdom are being attacked. In a modern literary reading, the "devoured Jacob" there seems to be a metaphor of Jacob (a famous shepherd who identified with and protected his sheep) as a lamb being devoured by wolves coming out of the mountains. The language clearly does identify these people to be punished as those who do not acknowledge God (recalling John's admonitions against those who do not acknowledge his Revelation), but the emphasis is on the failure to respect Israel that comes out of that lack of acknowledgment. Furthermore, the context is a plea for God to stop punishing Israel for its sins, and the subsequent challenge to God, as it were, is a reminder that such devastation *encourages* the "goyim" to mock Israel's pretension to have a saving God.

It can safely be said of all these biblical texts that at least they know who Israel is, and who the *goyim*, the nations, are. Another text by Derrida suggests that such may not be clearly the case any longer. Certainly with the advent of Christianity, a troubling confusion — troubling to Jewish discourse as well as Christian — arises. Christian identity disrupts this dichotomy between inside and outside. Thus, especially perhaps vis-à-vis this theme of apocalypse, contrasting Jewish texts or ideas to Christian ones is not the same as contrasting Jews to the entirety of humanity!

The early Christian writers — often, as with Paul, addressing themselves to churches throughout the Empire modeled on the diasporic institution of the synagogue — borrow the insider's "we" of the Israelite self-conception, even while explicitly combating Jewish ethnocentrism. Hence perhaps the striking turn of phrase in the passage of Derrida's essay "Of an Apocalyptic Tone Recently Adopted in Philosophy" where he is paraphrasing the stance of John on the relation between his identity (his justification for being himself, as it were) and the revelation only some share with him as yet: "We are going to die, you and I, the others, too, the goyim, the gentiles, and all the others, all those who do not share this secret with us, but they do not know it."[26] The use of the consummately Jewish word *goyim* covertly but inescapably intimates an "us" that is the Jews, here not so much ancient Israel as contemporary, postgenocide Jews, and along with them — along with *us*, I, Jonathan Boyarin, can show off and say — any other literate person who is hip enough to have Jewish friends who will tell him what the word *goy* means.[27] But, precisely because it is the apostle John whom Derrida is ventriloquizing here, the "you and I" who are not "the *goyim*," who are not "the gentiles" cannot unambiguously be all Jews transhistorically, but rather the primitive Christian community. Derrida's words here would then be an ironic description of the unfulfilled apocalyptic aspirations of this primitive community, with its resentment at the failure of the gentiles to recognize "our" apocalyptic truth, compensated for by the booby prize of knowing the death-end, death sentence beforehand. Yet Derrida's catachresis — the semantic contradiction of borrowing an ethnic insider's term for an apostle of the bursting of the ethnic boundaries — remains unfulfilled and unexplored as well. At the very beginning of the essay in question Derrida refers to a (then) just-released new translation of the Hebrew Bible, affording him the opportunity to mention casually that it would be worthwhile comparing the range of meanings of the Hebrew *gala* to those of the Greek *apokalupsis,* but he hastens to add that he certainly has no intention or time or competence to carry this out.[28]

After this initial discussion of the difficult "task of the translator," "a task I shall not discharge,"[29] Derrida drops the Hebrew *gala* and proceeds using the Greek-derived and "European" *apocalypse.* His resort to the Hebrew *goyim* here is indeed significant, deliberately teasing, and provocative. It flaunts Derrida's own Jewishness (was he still taken by the notion of being "last of the Jews" when he wrote this?) to seduce a philosophical *community* or club — I write "seduce," because the word *goyim* is "taboo," impolite, obviously not totally so but sufficiently so to titillate when used outside a Jewish idiom. At the root of its inter-Jewish colloquial usage, its commonly but not inevitably dismissive *tone* does not refer to the gentiles' failure to possess an apocalyptic "secret" that we alone share amongst ourselves, but rather their failure to embrace and possess the Torah, which makes us smarter than they are, which lifts us into a more heightened, more fully realized *human* interaction with the world, God, and history.

There is yet further irony in Derrida's deployment of the Jewish term *goyim* just once, here, in this philosophical text. "You and I" not only *are* the community of early believers in Jesus's Godhead; we are also, manifestly and pointedly, not the collectivity of the people of Israel. In fact John expresses, right from the start, resentment at the failure of the Jews to recognize Jesus as the Messiah: "He came to what was his own, yet his own folk did not welcome him" (John 1:11). So the contrasting pair us / *goyim* could not for John mean Jews versus the other nations, but must always be translated into "we the believers" versus "everyone who is not Enlightened." Indeed, the covenant with God by birthright, the ethnic or tribal covenant, has been superseded in the vision of John: the new "children of God" are those "who owe this birth of theirs to God, not to human blood" (John 1:13). Genealogy, the connection of generation that underlies the contrast between Israel and the nations, is explicitly delegitimated as a mark of distinction here.

As the sentences above about present and ancient contexts of the term *goyim* intimate, Derrida's "goyim" shocks a(n apocalyptic?) constellation not only between Christian and Jew, but between "past and present." Even ripped out of their colloquial context, the "Jewish" associations of the word are strengthened by its deployment to emphasize insiderhood. Maybe Derrida uses the term because, imagining that we have spent enough time either being Jews or empathizing with Jews, he sees the term as offering us powerful empathetic access to John's paradoxical reinvention of a new, privileged and threatened insider identity. The catachrestical use of *goyim* reminds us once again that much of the murderousness between the two names, "Jew" and "Christian," has to do with the underlying awareness of their connection and fear of their mutual contamination.

Immediately preceding the paragraph in which Derrida speaks *goyim* as John's line is a discussion of the concept of *Verstimmung,* by which he means to identify all the hazardous chances and possibilities of intersubjective communication, especially here the interruption and potential disharmony of apocalyptic messages between sender and receiver. There is indeed a rich and troubling disruption of the potentially unproblematic reciprocity between "you and I" when the other terms are introduced: "the goyim, the gentiles." Who are all the others? I still don't have a clue; perhaps, as yet, a place marker for the recognition that dichotomies are not worlds.

Again Derrida is pretentious! Daring to speak as and for the apostle, daring to appropriate — *after all they've done to us,* the vernacular Jew in me mutters *sotto voce—* our word and try to make us sympathetic to a false Christian prophet! It works. He makes me interested in John. The word *goyim* sets in motion a sort of double helix here, one strand of which is the constellation joining past and present and the other, the intercontamination of the Jewish and the Christian.

The temporal strand is, of course, inadequately described as a linkage of past and present. Its complexity in this context is indicated by the multivalence of the term "recent" in Derrida's title. Since he chooses to substitute the word "apocalyptic" for the word "elevated" in the essay by Kant that he echoes and discusses, his "recent" could refer to the first blossoming of Christian apocalyptic — the time of the Book of Revelation to which, as cited above, the genre label was first applied, the time at which Jewish apocalyptic also blossomed. But since he alludes to Kant, he could refer to the period of the Enlightenment or more specifically the decline of high Enlightenment, the first period in which it was necessary to criticize popularized Enlightenment. And, since the paper was delivered during the second half of the twentieth century, "recent" could refer to the tone of philosophy since World War II. It might be objected that in the first case, the literature under question was not "philosophical." But this is not as powerful an objection as it might seem, because even in the third and most recent of the possible "recent" periods, philosophy is weakened and has little of the force it seems to have had in Kant's day.

Ironically, there is something in the new tone of the Christian apocalypse that works against the panchronic strand of all these pressing and urgent "recents." As I discussed toward the beginning, John's speaking of his apocalypse in his own name signals a *present* orientation. "Now," retrospectively as it were, two millenniums later as we are wont to say, this self-ascription makes John's apocalypse a *past* revelation, a revelation that happened in a certain sense "in history" and is repeated now. By contrast—although the point is difficult to articulate and I am not altogether certain of its validity—a pseudepigraphical Apocalypse of Abraham probably did not have the same quality of chronological pastness at the time it was first disseminated and, for whatever reasons, certainly has not taken on the quality of a "past" revelation two millenniums later. Apocalypse thus becomes not only a future-vision theme (a vision thing?), but an event in Western religious history, outside of whose shadow, Derrida suggests, we cannot stand to speak or write. Here the periodic necessity to question the inclusive "we" appears again, for since the revelation to John is one that non-Christian Jews obviously *missed,* their or rather *our* relation to the chronology of apocalypse is likely to differ from the dominant one, even if the ways that relation differs cannot be adequately specified yet.

One might begin specifying this different relation to apocalypse by noting that Jewish visions of the endtime tend to be associated with the vision of a future Messiah. Here we could rely on the scholarly distinction between apocalyptic literature proper and more general (and, for Jews, more canonical) prophetic visions of redemption and judgment. It is not obvious why, in our postcatastrophic situation, there has not been a greater turning toward an apocalyptic eschatology defined by Paul Hanson as

a religious perspective which focuses on the disclosure (usually esoteric in nature) to the elect of the cosmic vision of Yahweh's sovereignty—especially as it relates to his acting to deliver the faithful—which disclosure the visionaries have largely ceased to translate into the terms of plain history, real politics, and human instrumentality due to a pessimistic view of reality growing out of the bleak postexilic conditions within which those associated with the visionaries found themselves.[30]

One speculation this perhaps overly sharp contrast suggests is that a twentieth-century experience of Nazi genocide without the realization of Zionist dreams in a state might have produced a renewed emphasis on this sort of hermetic apocalyptic among a much more consciously isolated "remnant" of faithful and practicing Jews seeing themselves as the "elect." Such hypotheticals are too awesome for me to contemplate at length. Given the world as it is, the distinction between hermetic and prophetic apocalyptic is useful precisely in helping us to understand why, throughout the modern period and continuing into the last decade of the twentieth century, messianism has tended to be associated with Jews, apocalypse with Christian discourse. This tendency has been reinforced in twentieth-century literary criticism, which once again identifies millenarian, political, and public visions of the endtime with a primitive and outmoded Judaism, and sublime, inner-directed visions of redemption with Christianity.[31] Furthermore, inasmuch as "the canonical work of apocalypse persists in imagining the end of history to be the end of historical differences,"[32] such a characterization seems much more apt vis-à-vis Christianity than Judaism. While biblical visions of all peoples coming to acknowledge the God with whom the Jews already have a special relationship, and coming to bring sacrifices at God's Temple in Jerusalem may point toward a *reconciliation* of difference, once again the vision does not see the whole world becoming Jewish.

Not that even a public and this-worldly form of messianism has in fact gained hegemony in mainstream Jewish discourse after the genocide. As it stands, despite the messianic trends of movements such as Lubavitch and Gush Emunim (the Bloc of the Faithful who have struggled to gain the whole of the historical land of Israel for the Jews and for the Jews only), the dominant tendency has been to cast the events that shatter the Jewish world in the twentieth century in terms of a this-worldly, yet still progressive, secular history of nations — and on the popular level, as stated, to cast Jewish distinctiveness in terms of a privileged teaching and acuity rather than an esoteric revelation.[33]

By way not so much of a resolution or even restatement of the questions about authority, identity, ethnicity, and teleology I have raised in these pages but rather of an indication of the directions they might lead to in a dialogue with you and others, Richard, let me state in brief a notion that occurred to me years ago, but that I have never attempted to put in writing before. The question is whether it is possible to harmonize the notion of Nazi genocide as divine retribution against the Jews (a *Jewish* notion, let me hasten to clarify, that bears the weight of millennia during which a series of Jewish disasters were interpreted as the result of the collective convenantal failures of the people of Israel) with the notion of a secular history in which the Jews have no particularly important place. My bold proposal is to recast the notion of an inseparable link between moral action and historical fate, to rescue it as it were from an ethnocentrism which, at this level, has little purchase on me, by the move — odd perhaps for someone who sets such store by difference — of positing a *generalized* human moral responsibility for human history. In this way "humanity" (a term we have come to know and mistrust, rightly) would be responsible for what Blanchot calls "the disaster" that would include but not be limited to the Nazi genocide.[34] The problems with this suggestion are doubtless legion, but one of the reasons it appeals to me is its contingency. Unlike, for example, Hegel's progressive unfolding of the World Spirit, it does not posit any necessary *progress* in the relation-ship between morality and history.

In a sense that ironic resolution of the tension and confusion between Jewish and Christian identities that the very title of *A Canticle for Leibowitz* points toward is echoed here: *I* cannot live in a world that revolves so totally around the Jews, *nor* is all of me willing to accept a morally arbi-trary universe. It is not that I have "faith" that God doesn't play dice with the universe. Rather the nihilistic assumption seems to place too great a strain on my Jewishness.

Is that a good enough reason? Perhaps a further articulation of my investment in Jewishness is necessary in turn, by way of relating a post-genocidal mistrust of all pretenses to universal redemption, universal community, such pretenses having been shown, convincingly I think, to be intimately related to the possibility of a genocide rationalized in the Western terms of collective identities and destinies.[35] Yet it is significant that the very text I cite in support of this claim — Jean-Luc Nancy's *The Inoperative Community* — still insists on an articulation of the possibility of such community in universal terms that inevitably privilege clean slates and a lack of prior or outside commitments on the part of those "singular beings" who are to constitute and be constituted through the commu-nity. Nancy's emphasis on a lack of constraining or distorting formalized attachments recalls Paul's prejudice against marriage, an institution that only hampered the freedom of the believers to come together in the Spirit that has been revealed to them.

As Daniel Boyarin has argued, there is a link between Paul's sense of "speaking in an extreme eschatological situation"[36] and his criticism of those who "bear fruit for death" (Romans 7:5), that is, who bear children destined to die. Daniel Boyarin contrasts the link between the apocalyp-tic sense in Paul and Paul's opposition to generation to the quite norma-tive vision of established families in the land of Israel, which is a stock element of Jewish messianism — to which we might add Steven Gold-smith's dry observation that "after predicting imminent doom, Jeremiah, with his flair for symbolic action, buys land in Israel."[37] There is a sense in which, contrary to my identification of Blanchot's "Last Man" with the figure of the "Last Jew," the two tropes are in fact mutually contradictory. Unlike the romantic genre of "Last Man" poems written in England between 1823 and 1826, Mary Shelley's novel *The Last Man* denies "the mind's power to dictate its own transcendence."[38] This romantic notion of an all-encompassing male conscience that absorbs the universe in its transcendent solitude is the individual analogue of the apocalypse of Revelation, which, "by programmatically imagining a world rid of the *feminine* . . . imagines as its most general social ideal a community rid of *all* differences."[39] The Jewish vision of redemption referred to by Daniel Boyarin and by Goldsmith, on the other hand, entails precisely the continuation of Jewish specificity, grounded both territorially and generationally[40] — hence with the continuing presence of not just "the feminine," but women as well. Rabbinic Judaism cannot conceive a world rid of the feminine; because Judaism has so much difficulty containing a vision of nihilistic apocalypse, there is an inherent slippage between the vision of the last Jew and that of the last man, already conceived as autonomous and isolate. Outside of a secularized and individualized, modern or postmodern literary sphere, there can be no last Jewish man, and no last Jew, as intimated, "properly," by Derrida's "last of the Jews, what am I." To echo Kafka, who said that the Messiah would always come on the day before the last day, the "last Jew" can always only be the next-to-last Jew. Hence the refusal of nihilism, "realistic" or not, might serve to guard against the romantic impulse toward solipsism in this world, and the very *specificity* of the Jewish vision of redemption serve as a building block for that sense of generalized human responsibility I referred to above.

We are approaching what the West calls the millennium, all of us "last Europeans," but not with the anticipated sense of an event to come (*the millennium that, perhaps more than the Nazi genocide or the possibility of nuclear destruction, motivated you to gather this collection*). *After the last word has been said, can I hold out the vague notion of a provisional identity beyond a certain extinction?* Let me call it here post-Judaism, not only because it comes after Judaism in a way analogous to postmodernism following modernity, but more specifically because it comes after the catastrophe as the betrayal of the hopes for redemption central to Judaism. The question is not rhetorical, and I myself wonder at the paradoxical tone of apocalyptic resignation I seem to have worked myself into today. Too much reading Derrida!

Your response would be welcome of course, since any possible post-Judaism would apparently be articulated not only by "real Jews." Yet I would not yet relinquish the insistence that my question is most urgent to, and hence in the first instance addressed to, those of "us" who are still, rather dazedly, attempting to constitute ourselves as a *generation of Jews.*

> Warmly,
> Jonathan Boyarin

Notes

1. Walter M. Miller, Jr., *A Canticle for Leibowitz* (New York: J. B. Lippincott & Company, 1959).
2. John J. Collins, *The Apocalyptic Imagination: An Introduction to the Jewish Matrix of Christianity* (New York: Crossroad, 1987).

3. Collins, *Apocalyptic Imagination*, 4.

4. See my "Space, Time and the Politics of Memory," in *Remapping Memory: The Politics of TimeSpace*, ed. Jonathan Boyarin (Minneapolis: University of Minnesota Press, 1994), 1–37.

5. Collins, *Apocalyptic Imagination*, 3.

6. Collins, *Apocalyptic Imagination*, 7.

7. Collins, *Apocalyptic Imagination*, 9.

8. Peter Fenves, *Raising the Tone of Philosophy: Late Essays by Immanuel Kant, Transformative Critique by Jacques Derrida* (Baltimore: Johns Hopkins University Press, 1993), 3.

9. Jacques Derrida, "Of an Apocalyptic Tone Recently Adopted in Philosophy," trans. John P. Leavey, Jr., *Oxford Literary Review* 6, no. 2 (1984): 34.

10. Collins, *Apocalyptic Imagination*, 4.

11. Susan Noakes, "Gracious Words: Luke's Jesus and the Reading of Sacred Poetry at the Beginning of the Sacred Era," in *The Ethnography of Reading*, ed. Jonathan Boyarin (Berkeley and Los Angeles: University of California Press, 1993), 38–57.

12. André Shwarz-Bart, *The Last of the Just* (New York: Atheneum, 1960).

13. Hannah Arendt, introduction to Walter Benjamin, *Illuminations* (New York: Schocken Books, 1969), 17–18.

14. Theodora Kroeber, *Ishi in Two Worlds: A Biography of the Last Wild Indian in North America* (Berkeley: University of California Press, 1976); Phillips Verner Bradford and Harvey Blume, *Ota Benga: The Pygmy in the Zoo* (New York: St. Martin's Press, 1992).

15. Maurice Blanchot, *Le dernier homme* (Paris: Gallimard, 1957); my translation.

16. Blanchot, *Le dernier homme*, 8.

17. Jeffrey Mehlman, *Legacies of Anti-Semitism in France* (Minneapolis: University of Minnesota Press, 1983).

18. Jacques Derrida, "Circumfession," in Geoff Bennington, *Jacques Derrida* (Chicago: University of Chicago Press, 1993), 154 [emphasis and ellipses in original]. Further references are given in the text.

19. Cf. Jonathan Boyarin and Daniel Boyarin, "Self-exposure as Theory: The Double Mark of the Male Jew," in *The Rhetoric of Self-Making*, ed. Debbora Battaglia (Berkeley and Los Angeles: University of California Press, 1994); Gil Anidjar, "On the Cutting Edge? Sharpening Jewish Memory," in *Jews and Other Differences*, ed. Jonathan Boyarin and Daniel Boyarin (Minneapolis: University of Minnesota Press, forthcoming).

20. Miller, *Canticle*, 3, 5.

21. Don DeLillo, *White Noise* (New York: Viking, 1985).

22. Miller, *Canticle*, 14.

23. Jonathan Boyarin and Daniel Boyarin, "Generation: Diaspora and the Ground of Jewish Identity," *Critical Inquiry* 19:4 (1993): 693–725. (Scriptural quotes from *The Holy Scriptures According to the Masoretic Text*, vol. 2 [Philadelphia: Jewish Publication Society of America, 1955].)

24. Simkhe Petrushka, *Yidishe Folks-entsiklopedye, Vol. 2* (New York and Montreal: Gilead, 1949), 896.

25. Menachem Mendel Gerlitz, ed., *Hagode Shel Pesakh Mibeys Levi* (Jerusalem: Oraysoh, 1983).

26. Derrida, "Of an Apocalyptic Tone," 24.

27. Cf. Sander Gilman, *Jewish Self-Hatred: Anti-Semitism and the Hidden Language of the Jews* (Baltimore: Johns Hopkins University Press, 1986).

28. Unremarked by Derrida is how prominent translations are in the beginning of John (see for example the three terms, "rabbi," "messiah" and "cephas" translated in 1:38 and 1:41–42. Daniel Boyarin reminds me that *gala* means both "revelation" and "exile" (personal communication).

29. Derrida, "Of an Apocalyptic Tone," 3. Derrida's parenthetical citation of Walter Benjamin is omitted from the original English translation of the essay, and reinserted in the revised translation published in 1984 and republished in 1993.

30. Paul D. Hanson, *The Dawn of Apocalyptic* (Philadelphia: Fortress Press, 1975), 11–12.

31. Steven Goldsmith, *Unbuilding Jerusalem: Apocalypse and Romantic Representation* (Ithaca, N.Y.: Cornell University Press, 1993), 10.

32. Goldsmith, *Unbuilding Jerusalem,* 21.

33. Not that the idea has always been foreign to all Jews or to all ideological formations within Judaism. Daniel Boyarin has recently pointed to Paul's attack on "Jews who think that works are not necessary for salvation, since God saves Israel, and only Israel, by grace alone. Such chauvinist notions, by no means universal in first century Judaism, did exist" (Daniel Boyarin, *A Radical Jew: Paul and the Politics of Identity* [Berkeley and Los Angeles: University of California Press, 1994], 177).

34. Maurice Blanchot, *The Writing of the Disaster* (Lincoln: University of Nebraska Press, 1986).

35. Jean-Luc Nancy, *The Inoperative Community* (Minneapolis: University of Minnesota Press, 1991).

36. Daniel Boyarin, *Radical Jew,* 177.

37. Goldsmith, *Unbuilding Jerusalem,* 29.

38. Goldsmith, *Unbuilding Jerusalem,* 267.

39. Goldsmith, *Unbuilding Jerusalem,* 72.

40. See Boyarin and Boyarin, "Generation."

Part II
First-Generation
Postmodern Apocalyptics

Frye, Derrida, Pynchon, and the Apocalyptic Space of Postmodern Fiction

David Robson

> The end? Say it with missiles then . . .
>
> —James Joyce, *Finnegans Wake*

Thomas Pynchon's postmodern fiction *Gravity's Rainbow* (1973) repre- sents an apocalyptic space at once historical, imaginative, theoretical, and "fabulously textual."[1] Apocalyptic space is always textual, but never more so than in the American script. For the Puritan settlers, historical space was textualized because the experience of the New World had been typologically prefigured in the Bible. When the Puritans fled persecu- tion, they repeated Exodus: America was the "New English Canaan." But the Bible provided more than just textual types to be enacted or repeated in history; the biblical mythos completely *engulfs* history providing an account of primal origins and visions of the end. In the absence of either millennial or cataclysmic fulfillment, however, Puritan space remained the space of signification, where *more* discourse would predict, invoke, envision, explain, rationalize, or reevaluate the absence or imminence of apocalyptic fulfillment.

Even William Bradford's *Of Plymouth Plantation* (1630–50) — that semi- nal document that provides the American myth of origins of the Pilgrim Fathers — demonstrates the ever-present apocalyptic phenomenon of the *repetition* of the end: what Frank Kermode has referred to as "literal dis- confirmation . . . thwarted by typology."[2] Early in this historical docu- ment Bradford recounts how the community, facing persecution in En- gland and dissolution in Holland, decides to move "to some other place," not, of course, for reasons of "newfangledness . . . but for sundry weighty and solid reasons": the fulfilling of their Christian providential destiny.[3] This "other place" is named and colonized: it is America, "vast and un- peopled."[4] By the end of his account, however, it is clear that the millen- nial dream (as Bradford conceived it, at least) was not coming true. The pilgrim community had begun to scatter; the remnant, once again, "began seriously to think whether it were not better jointly to remove *to some other place*."[5] Thus the pattern repeats, but it is not a ritual repetition that subsumes historical difference into an archetypal sameness or identity (as in cyclical myths of eternal return of the sort Mircea Eliade has analyzed).[6] Rather, the typological repetitions that punctuate the more linear apocalyptic mythos entail a different sort of negotiation of identity and difference, one in which disconfirmation (or the failure of the attainment of apocalyptic closure), far from discrediting or invalidating the defining mythos or promise, serves to propel that mythos forward, often in a redefined and expanded form. Kermode remarks that the failure of apocalyptic promises does not mean those promises were false; they were merely true "in a different sense."[7] Literal disconfirmation thus becomes the opportunity for the recasting of the typological net: the intransigent otherness of history *must* be recontained. If New England failed to resolve into the Promised Land, "some other place" would be found, and the Puritan eschatological hopes would reconstitute themselves as America expanded across the continent invoking a more secularized but still universalist discourse of manifest destiny or progress, which, in time, would entail American returns to the Old World, forays into the Third World, and voyages to the Moon.

The way in which such pursuits of the millennium can become exercises in empire, power, and control is a central theme of Thomas Pynchon's *Gravity's Rainbow*. A character in the novel, one Major Weissmann (also known as "Blicero"), who commands a V-2 rocket battery during the closing months of the Second World War, meditates on America's ominous role in this unfolding apocalyptic mythos:

"America *was* the edge of the World. A message for Europe, continent-sized, inescapable. Europe had found the site for its Kingdom of Death, that special Death the West had invented. Savages had their waste regions, Kalaharis, lakes so misty they could not see the other side. But Europe had gone deeper — into obsession, addiction, away from all the savage innocences. America was a gift from the invisible powers, a way of returning. But Europe refused it. [. . .]

"In Africa, Asia, Amerindia, Oceania, Europe came and established its order of Analysis and Death. What it could not use, it killed or altered. In time the death-colonies grew strong enough to break away. But the impulse to empire, the mission to propagate death, the structure of it, kept on. Now we are in the last phase. American Death has come to occupy Europe. It has learned empire from its old metropolis. But now we have *only* the structure left us, none of the great rainbow plumes, no fittings of gold, no epic marches over alkali seas."[8]

Such is one vision of the negative pole of apocalypse in which the typological fulfillment of history is just another name for the endless series of acts of imperialism. But apocalypse means revelation, and although apocalyptic discourse aims to define, contain, and domesticate otherness, it also serves to *reveal* the other. It is this revelatory or irreducibly prophetic dimension of apocalyptic discourse that prevents its perfect coalescence with any particular historical, political, or institutional manifestation. Apocalyptic discourse is usually profoundly hostile to the status quo. Its meanings and referents always exceed what "is" and point toward what is "other" than what is, and this other dimension can be a source of prophetic hope of liberation: projected wish reflected back as the possibility of salvation.

Weissmann, to return to my example from the diegesis of *Gravity's Rainbow,* perceives the trajectory of death into which Western culture is locked and to which, as an SS officer, he contributes. But he desires to be something more than a functionary in this destructive apocalyptic mythos; he desires to escape the repeated patterns of conquest and embraces a more radical apocalyptic hope for a kind of dark transcendence: " 'I want to break out—to leave this cycle of infection and death. I want to be taken in love: so taken that you and I, and death, and life, will be gathered, inseparable, into the radiance of what we would become. . . .' " (724). He makes this "creative" affirmation at the moment just prior to the launching of a V-2 rocket, which he has specially modified to contain his lover, Gottfried, whom he is addressing. This launch is the culminating gesture in a relationship that has included sadomasochistic rituals— rituals that function to domesticate or master the larger horrors of the expanding deathkingdom that surrounds them. This launch presumably (and quite irrationally) will deliver them from the oppressions of the "real" into an "other" sort of hyperreal apocalyptic space. Gottfried seems to understand Blicero's desperate hope for salvation as he listens silently: "This is so more-than-real . . . he feels he must keep every word, that none must be lost. Blicero's words have become precious to him. He understands that Blicero wants to give, without expecting anything back, give away what he loves. He believes that he exists for Blicero, even if the others have all ceased to, that in the new kingdom they pass through now, he is the only other living inhabitant" (721–722). Beyond the repeated gestures of choreographed sex and violence, Gottfried has

also felt more, worshipfully more past these arrangements for penetration, the style [. . .] all become theatre as he approached the gates of that Other Kingdom [. . .] there have to be these too, lovers whose genitals *are* consecrated to shit, to endings, to the desperate nights in the streets when connection proceeds out of all personal control, proceeds or fails, a gathering of fallen—as many in acts of death as in acts of life—or a sentence to be alone for another night. . . . Are they to be denied, passed over, all of them? (722)

I doubt Pynchon endorses Weissmann's morbidly romantic desire for transcendence (and its bizarre technologically facilitated means), yet again and again within the diegesis characters express a wistful hope that apocalypse can be "worshipfully more" than just a synonym for the finality of destruction. The novel's obsession with technologies of destruction makes it seem nihilistic or fatalistic, but the acknowledgment of such grimly literal possibilities does not exclude other, romantic possibilities. As Northrop Frye reminds us — employing an especially apposite figure — "In romance violence and sexuality are used as rocket propulsions, so to speak, in an ascending movement" toward regained identity.[9] This necessarily entails a movement into figuration or, as Norman O. Brown has it, a movement "against gravity; against the gravity of literalism, which keeps our feet on the ground."[10] Weissmann is skeptical about the ability of the literal conquest of gravity via technology to usher in a new order: " 'Is the cycle over now, and a new one ready to begin? Will our new Edge, our new Deathkingdom, be the Moon?' " (723). Such a literal attainment of the apocalyptic referent (the Moon as the site of the millennium) would be just another instance of conquest and colonization. What *is* new, and what prompts another lyric celebration, is the possibility of inhabiting an apocalyptic space:

" . . . no, they weren't really spacemen. Out here, they wanted to dive between the worlds, to fall, turn, reach and swing on journeys curved through the shining, through the winter nights of space — their dreams were of rendezvous, of cosmic trapeze acts carried on in loneliness, in sterile grace, in certain knowledge that no one would ever be watching, that loved ones had been lost forever. . . . " (723)

The pastoralism of conventional Promised Land imagery gives way, here, to something much colder: a post-romantic, postmodern, post-Apollo space program version of the artifice of eternity (via Rilke's Tenth Elegy and Kubrick's *2001*).[11]

Frye acknowledges that the "creative" pole of apocalypse seems inevitably shadowed by what he calls the "paranoia principle": the lingering suspicion that any religious vision or imaginative hypothesis that transcends ideology really does nothing of the kind, but is merely subjective projection.[12] In *Gravity's Rainbow* the prophetic and the paranoid are invariably conflated. Certainly the apocalyptic dreams of Weissman betray a fair degree of psychopathology, although, Pynchon implies, in a culture for whom the crowning technological achievement is rocket-borne weapons, Weissmann is perhaps less abnormal than representative. By any standard, however, Weissmann's fusion of Eros and Thanatos in a glorious, phallic, techno-suicide could hardly be a universally valid symbol of apocalyptic fulfillment.

Gravity's Rainbow explicitly links the blend of paranoia and religion with the American strand of Puritanism. The ancestry of the novel's central character, Tyrone Slothrop, is traced "back to 1630 when Governor Winthrop came over to America on the *Arbella,* flagship of a great Puritan flotilla that year, on which the first American Slothrop had been a mess cook or something" (204). Like his ancestors, Tyrone Slothrop possesses "a Puritan reflex of seeking other orders behind the visible, also known as paranoia" (188). This reflex has a specifically hermeneutic orientation, and entails a hermeneutic problematizing of the given in an attempt to uncover its real (or at least, "other") meaning:

[Slothrop] will learn to hear quote marks in the speech of others. It is a bookish kind of reflex, maybe he's genetically predisposed—all those earlier Slothrops packing Bibles around the blue hilltops as part of their gear, memorizing chapter and verse the structures of Arks, Temples, Visionary Thrones—all the materials and dimensions. Data behind which always, nearer or farther, was the numinous certainty of God. (241–242)

Slothrop is a postmodern Puritan. Rather than entering the previously uncharted natural landscape and reading its significance via the Bible, Slothrop enters the Zone: the overdetermined or hyperreal space of "endless simulation" (489) that is the European theater of operations in the closing months of the Second World War; a space of shifting borders, multiple and overlapping jurisdictions (political, military, economic); a space where "nature" is merely one significant level among many. Slothrop has no master text through which he reads this postmodern landscape, but there is no question that the landscape signifies: "Signs will find him here in the Zone, and ancestors will reassert themselves" (281). It is not that Slothrop imposes his reading on the Zone; on the contrary, the Zone seems to read him.

Slothrop has an ambiguous attitude toward the proliferating intimations of the looming, ominous forces that surround him. At the recently liberated Casino Hermann Goering he backs away from the uncanny atmosphere of its Forbidden Wing, "retreating from yet facing the Presence feared and wanted" (203), and soon he is "snuggling up, masturbatorily scared-elated, to the disagreeable chance that exactly such Control might already have been put over him" (209). Slothrop is a sort of reluctant Puritan unwilling to decipher the extent to which he is inscribed and implicated in some larger defining mythos: "He gets back to the Casino just as big globular raindrops, thick as honey, begin to splat into giant asterisks on the pavement, inviting him to look down at the bottom of the text of the day, where footnotes will explain all. He isn't about to look. Nobody ever said a day has to be juggled into any kind of sense at day's end. He just runs" (204). Such unwillingness to read the signs of the times is a conventional element of biblical (or Bible-influenced) apocalyptic scenarios, since "the day of the Lord will come like a thief in the night" (1 Thess. 5:2 [Revised Standard Version]). In the context of *Gravity's Rainbow,* however, it is the V-2 rocket that functions as the apocalyptic Word: "the one Word that rips apart the day. . . . " (25).

Such an interdependence of technology and apocalypse is not a new phenomenon with postmodernism. The medium by which the Word is disseminated is never simply the "spirit" but always involves technologies of communication, transportation, commerce, and other manifestations of secular power — including weaponry — and this was certainly true of the Puritan New World adventure. The Protestant Reformation itself was facilitated in part by a development in what Walter Ong has called "the technologizing of the word."[13] In a very literal and practical way, the printing press allowed for the Christian Bible to be disseminated in a manner that allowed a closer and (the reformers believed) more immediate and spiritual interaction between individual believer and text, an interaction that prompted a questioning of the modes and forms of institutional and doctrinal mediation that for a millennium had been controlled by the Roman Catholic Church. Thus the essentially secular development of print technology — "the Word made printer's ink" (*Gravity's Rainbow* 571) — released a liberating and revelatory otherness in the official sacred Word and triggered a spiritual revolution. If, as Derrida suggests, the Bomb is also a technological incarnation of the word — with its "technologies of delivery, sending, dispatching, of the missile in general, of mission, missive, emission, and transmission"[14] — then it can be read as another unforeseen but nevertheless typologically explicable advance in the "Puritan hopes for the Word" (571).

This is precisely what Marcus Smith and Khachig Tölölyan suggest in their essay "The New Jeremiad: *Gravity's Rainbow.*" In their view, "the controlling idea of [the novel] is that the world's present predicament — the system of global terror dominated by ICBMs — threatens to fulfill in historical time the apocalyptic and millennial visions which prevailed in the Puritan culture of colonial New England." They suggest that, for Pynchon, "the rocket borne atomic dawn" is the most likely antitype to the Puritan type.[15]

Gravity's Rainbow, however, does not give us a literalistic account of nuclear war. While containing plenty of accurate historical detail, it is also surrealistic, rife with narrative disjunctions, dazzling in its range of tone, fabulously complex in plot, erudite beyond any reader, ontologically and epistemologically unstable, and pluralistic. It exemplifies what Jean-François Lyotard calls the postmodern "process of complexification"[16] associated with technoscientific development; in Fredric Jameson's terms, the novel is an example of "high tech paranoia" literature, which attempts "to think the impossible totality of the contemporary world system."[17] Or, as the novel's first page self-reflexively announces, "this is not a disentanglement from, but a progressive *knotting into*" (3). If this progress takes us toward a center — if there is a "still center of the order of words"[18] that is *Gravity's Rainbow*— that center can only be the problematic one evoked by the term "apocalypse."

Critics like Smith and Tölölyan deduce that *Gravity's Rainbow* is "all about" the Bomb, even if it does not deal directly with it. In this reading, the V-2 rocket, which is the central symbol of the novel, is a displacement of the Bomb: it is more comprehensible, something that can be negotiated by consciousness more easily than the thought of nuclear annihilation (so often associated with "the unthinkable" and which Derrida calls "that unassimilable wholly other").[19] The link, however, can be conceived of in less strictly metaphorical and more metonymic terms: the V-2 rocket is a stage in the chain of technological development culminating in nuclear missiles. Both "can penetrate, from the sky, at any given point. Nowhere is safe" (*Gravity's Rainbow* 728). Thus they have an almost divine omnipotence, and seem to violate limitations of space and time, projecting those beneath their trajectory into the space of the hear-after: "a rocket will hit before they can hear it coming. Biblical [. . .] spooky as an old northern fairy tale" (54). The brute repetition of rocket strikes suggests the dawning of a new order: "they will watch their system falling apart, watch those singularities begin to come more and more often, proclaiming another dispensation out of the tissue of old-fashioned time" (752). The bomb strikes that punctuate Part 1 modulate into celebratory champagne corks popping in Part 2, but the suggestion is made (by an unanchored paranoid voice), that "peace," announced with V-E Day, is no longer an accurate term to describe the situation: "There's *something* still on, don't call it a 'war' if it makes you nervous, maybe the death rate's gone down a point or two, beer in cans is back at last and there *were* a lot of people in Trafalgar Square one night not so long ago . . . but Their enterprise goes on" (628). This ominous "enterprise" is an aspect of the new dispensation born with the Second World War: the world of multinational cartels, the military-industrial complex, the Cold War, and perhaps most importantly, our nuclear predicament. This nuclear predicament intimates the grim closure of our historical trajectory and, like the Bible for the Puritans, inscribes everything leading up to the cataclysmic end within its mythos — a mythos of secular scripture, indeed. *Gravity's Rainbow* documents the launching point of this historical trajectory.

The novel does contain references to "the Bomb" but they are displaced, scattered, or fragmented. In a séance the spirit of Walter Rathenau — described as the "prophet and architect of the cartelized state" (164) — parenthetically refers to "cosmic bombs" (167), and in a particularly dense section later in the novel a punning reference to a priest's

"Critical Mass" is glossed for us: "get it? not too many did in 1945, the Cosmic Bomb was still trembling in its earliness, not yet revealed to the People, so you heard the term only in the very superhepcat-to-hepcat exchanges" (539). In the final section Slothrop glimpses "a scrap of newspaper headline, with a wirephoto of a giant white cock, dangling in the sky straight downward out of a white pubic bush" (693). This is a photo of a nuclear blast, and if we fill in the missing letters of the head-line — if we reassemble the shattered Word — it reads, "BOMB DROPPED HIROSHIMA." A Japanese ensign named Morituri, weary of the war, wants merely to return to his wife and kids, " 'and once I'm there,' " he says, " 'never [. . .] leave Hiroshima again' " (480) — a remark that un-dercuts the strategy of the retreat to the local as a response to the op-pressiveness of the totalizing closure of metanarratives.[20] An American colonel getting a haircut weaves into his monologue a reference to the altered quality of the sunsets: " 'Do you suppose something has exploded somewhere? Really — somewhere in the East? Another Krakatoa? An-other name at least that exotic . . . the colors are so different now. [. . .] Is there information for us? Deep questions, and disturbing ones' " (642). Finally, the closing moments of the novel seem to depict a nuclear rocket descending toward the Orpheus Theatre in Los Angeles during the Nixon years — a rocket that has metamorphosed from Weissmann's modified V-2 launched on the Luneburg Heath.

These oblique and fragmentary evocations of the nuclear bomb sup-plement and expand the ethos surrounding the V-2 rocket, which is the central historical focus of the narrative. No matter how self-referential and overdetermined *Gravity's Rainbow* might be it does not seal itself off completely from historical reference and enter some sort of realm of pure fantasy (as sci-fi novels can) or textual play (as does *Finnegans Wake*). Rather, as with typological interpretation, the historical (or "literal" level, as the medieval exegetes called it) becomes an integral level in the field of signification: not the ground of meaning, being, or reference, perhaps, but not unimportant or absent, either.

Northrop Frye, whose own critical system adapts the medieval prin-ciple of the four levels of interpretation, or "polysemous meaning," as Dante called it, associates the very fact of polysemy with the element of delight, pleasure, or exuberance in literature.[21] As he sees it, litera-ture has "a relation to reality which is neither direct nor negative, but potential" and thus "the reality-principle is subordinate to [and sub-sumed by] the pleasure-principle."[22] What literature yields ideally, then, is not knowledge of the real, but recreation, or re-creation according to the forms of human desire and imagination. Its limits are, like those of dream, "not the real, but the conceivable."[23]

Analogously, poststructuralism has much to say about the element of *play* in signification. The Derridean commentator Christopher Norris, however, cautions against misreading Derrida to make him the patron saint of the " 'anything goes' school of postmodern hermeneutic thought." Norris insists that "to deconstruct naive or commonsense ideas of how language hooks up with reality is not to suggest that it should henceforth be seen as a realm of open-ended textual 'freeplay' or floating signifiers devoid of referential content."[24] If there is an element of *jouissance* in the play of signification, there also exists something more ominous. In *Writing and Difference* Derrida poses the question, "Is not the center, the absence of play and difference, another name for death?"[25] If so (and Derrida's remarks on apocalypse confirm this), then the desire for a center is an aspect of a death wish. But such a desire is not easily escaped. As in Freud's psychoanalytic formulations, where the element of Thanatos is interwoven with the economies of desire (including the pleasure principle), so in Derrida's poststructuralist formulation the desire for a center is not merely an unhealthy aberration that contaminates the freedom of the play of signification; rather it is an important "function of play itself" possibly "the indestructible itself": "And in the repetition or return of play, how could the phantom of the center not call to us? It is here that the hesitation between writing as decentering and writing as an affirmation of play is infinite."[26] Such a space of hesitation, but with the stakes raised incalculably high by the Bomb, is the apocalyptic space of the nuclear epoch: "the *époché* suspending judgment before the absolute decision."[27] Thus, for both Frye and Derrida — and Pynchon — the play of signification has a limit, and that limit is apocalypse.

The following passage gives a good indication of the extent to which *Gravity's Rainbow* is thoroughly polysemous (if not polymorphously perverse) in its use of the symbol of the Rocket:

[T]he Rocket has to be many things, it must answer to a number of different shapes in the dreams of those who touch it — in combat, in tunnel, on paper — it must survive heresies shining, unconfoundable . . . and heretics there will be: Gnostics who have been taken in a rush of wind and fire to chambers of the Rocket-throne . . . Kabbalists who study the Rocket as Torah, letter by letter — rivets, burner cup and brass rose, its text is theirs to permute and combine into new revelations, always unfolding . . . Manichaeans who see two Rockets, good and evil, who speak together in the sacred idiolalia of the Primal Twins (some say their names are Enzian and Blicero) of a good Rocket to take us to the stars, an evil Rocket for the World's suicide, the two perpetually in struggle. (727)

In other contexts the Rocket is identified as the Word, "incoming mail" (6), information, spectacle, Presence, an icon, the Other, the phallus, Technology, the crowning achievement of the order of reason, a vehicle of romantic transcendence, a "terminal orgasm" (223), an image on a screen, a new star, a descending angel, a parable, Scripture, "a baby Jesus, with endless committees of Herods out to destroy it in infancy" (464), a "pyrotechnic Cross" (751), an equation ("that elegant blend of philosophy and hardware" [239]), and the Tower card in the Tarot pack, which signifies, we are told, "a system which, by its nature, must sooner or later fall" (747).

What can criticism do in the face of such wild overdetermination? Jacques Derrida, employing imagery that resonates nicely for anyone familiar with Pynchon's *The Crying of Lot 49* (1966), suggests that apocalyptic discourse "is a challenge to the established receivability of messages and to the policing of destination, in short to the postal police or the monopoly of posts." "By its very tone, the mixing of voices, genres, and codes, apocalyptic discourse can also, in dislocating destinations, dismantle the dominant contract or concordat."[28] In short, it poses a definitive if not subversive challenge to any critical approach, pushing it to an apocalyptic limit of its own.

Of course, a critic may simply refuse to take up the challenge and be dismissive. The critical response generated in the mid-sixties toward the "apocalyptism" of much contemporary fiction was often dismissive and occasionally quite hostile. For example, in his 1966 article "The Apocalyptic Temper," Robert Alter condemns the "apocalyptic postures" in the works of such writers as Ralph Ellison, John Barth, Joseph Heller, and Thomas Pynchon.[29] The pernicious progenitor of these works, in Alter's estimation, is the Book of Revelation — the most "inhuman" and "spiritually irresponsible" book of the Bible.[30] In a remark that reveals his bias toward realism in the novel, Alter decries the way in which these "comic-apocalyptic novelists . . . fill their worlds with the rattling skeletons of satiric hypotheses in place of fully fleshed characters."[31]

Far from seeing apocalypse as spiritually irresponsible, Northrop Frye sees it as constituting the spiritual and imaginative core of the Bible — and of literary experience. For Frye, "spiritual" always centrally means "metaphorical,"[32] and the metaphors employed in apocalyptic texts constitute "a form of imaginative comprehension."[33] Beyond this, Frye would regard the condemnation of any text because it is filled with "rattling skeletons of satiric hypotheses" as senseless because, from his point of view, literature *is* hypothesis, and his understanding of mimesis is of a more visionary and radical sort. For Frye, mimesis entails not an *imitation* of nature, but "an *emancipation* of externality into image, nature into art."[34] Beyond the descriptive, formal, and archetypal phases of literary symbolism is the anagogic phase in which this emancipation or transfiguration of nature is most obvious, and it is this phase that Frye specifically associates with apocalypse:

When we pass into anagogy, nature becomes, not the container, but the thing contained, and the archetypal universal symbols, the city, the garden, the quest, the marriage, are no longer the desirable forms that man constructs inside nature, but are themselves the forms of nature. Nature is now inside the mind of an infinite man who builds his cities out of the Milky Way. This is not reality, but it is the conceivable or imaginative limit of desire, which is infinite, eternal, and hence apocalyptic. By an apocalypse I mean primarily the imaginative conception of the whole of nature as the content of an infinite and eternal living body which, if not human, is closer to being human than to being inanimate. (*Anatomy* 119)

This Blakean apocalyptic man is at the center of Frye's controversial conception of literature as a "total form" or an autonomous "order of words" (118). It is identified with the Logos understood as "the universal creative word which is all words" and, in *The Great Code*, is associated specifically with Christ.[35]

It is suggestive to compare Frye's apocalyptic/textual space — a space that subsumes reference: "it does not describe or represent a separate content of revelation"[36] — with the poststructural textual space Derrida evokes in his famous affirmation, "*There is nothing outside of the text* [there is no outside-text; *il n'y a pas de hors-texte*]."[37] Derridean "writing" is apocalyptic since "what opens meaning and language is writing as the disappearance of natural presence."[38] Both theorists articulate notions of a sort of textual space (and textual temporality) that profoundly problematizes any simple conception of linguistic reference or literary mimesis. Both conceptions are useful for understanding the dynamics of apocalyptic texts, and especially in delineating the problematics of the apocalyptic referent.

Like Frye, Derrida makes use of a notion of "text in the unlimited sense,"[39] but he does so not to reveal the omnipresence or omnipotence of any Logos, but to reveal the radically contingent, unstable, self-subverting nature of "textuality" itself. Linguistic difference rather than the identity of the Word is the governing category. In a manner diametrically opposed to that of Frye, poststructuralist Derrida seems to take a fundamental centerlessness as the starting point for an examination of the dynamics of the textual field, which may indeed have more in common with "an endless series of free associations" than with a Fryean "real structure,"[40] and it is precisely the totalizing impulse within literary, aesthetic, philosophical or political constructs that Derrida programmatically deconstructs.

Derrida's antilogocentric orientation would make him anti-apocalyptic if apocalypse were considered only in Frye's terms (which clearly represent the positive pole). But how would the negative pole of apocalypse, associated with "literal" destruction, fit in to Derrida's "textualist" scheme? How does one take apocalypse literally? Derrida's 1984 essay

"No Apocalypse, Not Now" attempts to answer this question with particular reference to the possibility of nuclear war. As might be expected, the apocalyptic referent strains the theory of language that attempts to grasp it. For Derrida, all linguistic reference is problematic, the referent itself being an effect of the differential structure of language rather than a "given" that language mirrors. The apocalyptic referent, however, is so radically "other" that the very field of textuality itself — which is acknowledged as a field of difference, contingency, in short, the field of the play of the word and its other — cannot accommodate, negotiate, or otherwise trace the dynamic of *this* other. In simplest terms, nuclear war cannot be just another element within the textual play of signification. Derrida is thus forced into an astonishing reversal of terminology — a reversal that leads to pronouncements strangely analogous to those of Northrop Frye. Derrida characterizes the nuclear apocalyptic referent as "the absolute referent, the horizon and the condition of all the others."[41] For Derrida, however, if the center *is* to be thought, it would not be a Fryean vision of *infinite* form, but "a thought of *finitude*," specifically, "the total destruction of the archive, if not of the human habitat."[42]

Thus, the textual spaces articulated by both Frye and Derrida — the "real structure" of the order of words and the space of signification or *différance* — have apocalypse at their centers. A useful image, which embodies this contrast, is provided in Derrida's suggestion that the background against which the radical act of finitude (nuclear war) "cuts its figure . . . [is] the possibility of an infinite intellect which creates its own objects rather than inventing them."[43] This is Frye's Blakean "infinite man who builds his cities out of the Milky Way." Derrida deconstructs or ironically inverts this creature, substituting a figure who owes more to Beckett than to Blake: the nuclear space of hesitation, Derrida suggests, "occurs within a 'who knows?' without subject or knowledge,"[44] or, even more grimly and with a greater emphasis on finitude, apocalypse would be "the auto-destruction of the *autos* itself"[45] — Frye's infinite man blowing himself to bits. This contemporary theoretical configuration of the exploding word may be rooted historically in a post-Hiroshima world, but the roots run deeper than that: it is consistent with the double-edged symbolism of biblical apocalyptic revelations, including the smashed tablets of Sinai, the deferred Kingdom of Israel in exile, or Christ as the crucified Logos. The revealed Word, it seems, is always the shattered Word.

Both Frye and Derrida acknowledge that apocalypse, for the time being, at least, functions as an absent center. Frye's Logos of criticism clearly is religious in its scope, but Frye insists that it does not resolve into an ontological personality or religious presence: "Between religion's 'this is' and poetry's 'but suppose *this* is,' there must always be some kind of tension, until the possible and the actual meet at infinity."[46] It is precisely imaginative culture's power of hypothesis — the power it has to conceive and reveal a wholly other to juxtapose against any institutionally sanctioned Holy Presence — that prevents any sort of full closure (this side of infinity, at least). And for Derrida, since the irreversible destruction of nuclear war has not taken place, it exists only in discourse (broadly understood), and thus the essential feature of the nuclear epoch is "that of being *fabulously textual*."[47]

The apocalyptic/textual spaces delineated by both Frye and Derrida help map out the postmodern apocalyptic space of *Gravity's Rainbow*, a space centered on the quasi-theological, Holy/wholly other: "the one Word that rips apart the day" (25). *Gravity's Rainbow* encodes within itself both a thematic and formal awareness of both poles of apocalypse: the creative energies of desire that can transfigure the real (Eros-apocalypse), and the element of death within the play of signification (in the broadest sense) that potentially can obliterate the real (Thanatos-apocalypse).

I will conclude this discussion by examining a revelation experienced by another of the novel's central characters, Enzian, leader of the black rocket troops known as the Schwarzkommando, who is attempting to recenter his displaced people around the rather dubious Logos of a scavenged V-2 rocket. Enzian is a postmodern Moses leading his exiled people in the postmodern desert. He has a revelation while riding his motorcycle through the Zone: the apocalyptic space that is the devastated German industrial landscape.

Zoom uphill slantwise toward a rampart of wasted, knotted, fused, and scorched girderwork, stacks, pipes, ducting, windings, fairings, insulators reconfigured by all the bombing, grease-stained pebblery on the ground rushing by a mile a minute and wait, wait, say what, say *"reconfigured,"* now?

There doesn't exactly dawn, no but there *breaks*, as that light you're afraid will break some night at too deep an hour to explain away — there floods on Enzian what seems to him an extraordinary understanding. This serpentine slag-heap he is just about to ride into now, this ex-refinery, Jamf Ölfabriken Werke AG, is *not a ruin at all. It is in perfect working order.* Only waiting for the right connections to be set up, to be switched on . . . modified, precisely, *deliberately* by bombing that was never hostile, but part of a plan both sides — "*sides?*" — had always agreed on . . . (520)

Enzian had assumed that the "holy Text" for his messianic enterprise "had to be the Rocket," but wonders "if I'm riding through it, the Real Text, right now, if this is it":

— the bombing was the exact industrial process of conversion, each release of energy placed exactly in space and time, each shockwave plotted in advance to bring *precisely tonight's wreck* into being thus decoding the Text, thus coding, recoding, redecoding the holy Text . . . If it is in working order, what is it meant to do? The engineers who built it as a refinery never knew there were any further steps to be taken. Their design was "finalized," and they could forget it.

It means this War was never political at all, the politics was all theatre, all just to keep the people distracted . . . secretly, it was being dictated instead by the needs of technology . . . by a conspiracy between human beings and techniques, by something that needed the energy-burst of war [. . . .] (520–521)

Just as the deluge of the Old Testament entails a symbolic erasure and reinscription of nature such that nature becomes a signifier of something more radically other (the power and presence of Yahweh), so does the bombing of the industrial landscape — its literal destruction — actually constitute (as Enzian sees it) its deconstruction, part of an ongoing process of "coding, recoding, redecoding" of the "holy Text" (521). Politics and the political mode of understanding history are reduced to "theatre," and metaphors of theatre and film function throughout the novel as another mode of deconstructing or placing historical reference under erasure to reveal more expansive — and more paranoid — significance.

Enzian's attempt to read the text of his historical situation leaves him caught in a spiral of paranoid speculation, a seemingly endless attempt to seize and name the other. His paranoid "reasonings" are structured as a dialogue or pseudo-dialectical drive toward the "truth." Yet they culminate not in certainty but in something more like hysteria and collapse, a sort of final negation that leaves a blank where final revelation should be. Specifically, after political explanations of the war are negated, Enzian seems to reach a conclusion: the real impetus for war stems from the needs of technology, needs "which are understood only by the ruling elite . . . " (521). The subsequent paragraph, however, immediately negates this conclusion: "Yes but Technology only responds [. . .] 'All very well to talk about having a monster by the tail, but do you think we'd've had the Rocket if someone, some specific somebody with a name and a penis hadn't *wanted* to chuck a ton of Amatol 300 miles and blow up a block full of civilians? Go ahead, capitalize the T on technology, deify it if it'll make you feel less responsible — but it puts you in with the neutered, brother' " (521). The only thing that seems certain is that there is a plot to be deciphered, a plot that requires radically new modes of interpretation: "we have to find meters whose scales are unknown in the world, draw our own schematics, getting feedback, making connections, reducing the error, trying to learn the real function . . . zeroing in on what incalculable plot? [. . .] *the planetary mission* [. . .] waiting for its Kabbalists and new alchemists to discover the Key, teach the mysteries to others . . . " (521). But this Kabbalistic mood of resignation and dedication to the mystery is not the final word. It is still unclear to Enzian which ruin/text deserves his attention, that in Hamburg "or another make-

believe 'ruin,' in another city? Another *country*? YAAAGGGGHHHHH!"
(521).

If this is an apocalypse of the mind (to borrow Emerson's phrase) it is
not one that reveals the romantic coalescence, unity, and identity of
consciousness and nature in an apocalyptic harmony of the poetic Word.
Rather, it is almost the inverse of this: the mutual disunity of consciousness and landscape in an uncentered and highly unstable space of textuality. As always, the apocalyptic space of mediation is charged with both
apocalyptic poles. In this instance, the negative pole is associated with the
"literal" fact of wartime devastation. This devastation is not fully apocalyptic, in Derrida's sense, since it does not yet entail the total destruction
of the archive: there is still signification; total (nuclear) apocalypse may
perhaps be implicit in the logic of escalating technologies of weaponry,
but as yet apocalypse can only be "the signified referent" not "the real
referent."[48] We are still in the space of the "fabulously textual," and thus
Enzian can still "read" the devastation. Moving further up the positive
pole, we do not find, in this instance, an unequivocally "positive" affirmation or wish-fulfillment vision of the real transfigured by the energies of
imagination and desire. Instead we get paranoid fantasies of more expansive orders of control and significance, which, if not reassuring, at least
demonstrate a perversely creative power of speculation. The precise nature of the referent evoked remains highly ambiguous — as is always the
case with the apocalyptic referent.

Enzian speaks with the voice of the paranoid and the prophet. It is
also the voice of someone who has taken too many drugs. The paragraph
that follows immediately upon Enzian's barbaric yawp ("YAAAGGGG-
HHHHH!") tells us, in a more sober and seemingly omniscient narrator's voice, "Well, this is stimulant talk here, yes Enzian's been stuffing
down Nazi surplus Pervitins these days like popcorn at the movies" (521–
522). This observation is followed by the text of a song, one of many that
occur throughout the novel and routinely shatter whatever vestige of
novelistic realism might be emerging at any given point.

> Just a daredevil Desox-yephedrine Daddy
> With m'pockets full o' happee daze,
> Zoomin' through the Zone, where the wild dogs roam,
> Givin' all m'dreams away . . . (522)

Such a moment of glib playfulness completes the movement of supple-
mentation away from the literal (the devastated industrial landscape) to
the self-reflexively comic sphere of verbal play ("Don'tcha ephedrine of
me, my honey, / Swoon just to hear my name — " [522]). Playful and

humorous as these lines are, they also function to destabilize any sense of ontological grounding for the narrative (in the historically real, in Enzian as a coherent "round" character, in any of his visions or countervisions, or in a centered narrator's perspective). In Derridean terms this could be seen as a dissolve of the real in textuality; in Frye's terms, it could be an apocalyptic moment of the transfiguration of the real by the imaginative energies of language. It also exemplifies the stylistic means by which Pynchon's own text "permute[s] and combine[s] into new revelations, always unfolding" (727).

Notes

1. Jacques Derrida, "No Apocalypse, Not Now (Full Speed Ahead, Seven Missiles, Seven Missives)," *Diacritics* 14 (Summer 1984): 23.
2. Frank Kermode, *The Sense of an Ending: Studies in the Theory of Fiction* (New York: Oxford University Press, 1967), 9.
3. William Bradford, *Of Plymouth Plantation* [1630–50], ed. Samuel Eliot Morison (New York: Knopf, 1952), 23.
4. Bradford, *Of Plymouth Plantation*, 25
5. Bradford, *Of Plymouth Plantation*, 333; emphasis mine.
6. Mircea Eliade, *The Myth of the Eternal Return or, Cosmos and History* (Princeton, N.J.: Princeton University Press, 1954).
7. Kermode, *Sense of an Ending*, 29.
8. Thomas Pynchon, *Gravity's Rainbow* (New York: Viking, 1973), 722. Because this novel is full of ellipses, those that I have inserted into quoted passages are in square brackets.
9. Northrop Frye, *The Secular Scripture: A Study of the Structure of Romance* (Cambridge, Mass.: Harvard University Press, 1976), 183.
10. Norman O. Brown, *Love's Body* (Berkeley: University of California Press, 1966), 259.
11. Weissmann has had firsthand experience of colonialism at its genocidal worst: he served with the German forces that brutally quelled the Herero uprising in the colony of South-West Africa in 1922. And he brought his copy of Rilke with him: "Of all Rilke's poetry it's this Tenth Elegy he most loves" (98).
12. Northrop Frye, *The Critical Path: An Essay on the Social Context of Literary Criticism* (Bloomington: Indiana University Press, 1971), 130. Richard Hillman makes a similar point about the practice of criticism or analysis:

> Psychological endeavors are always partially paranoid because, as Jung says, the psyche offers no outside objective standpoint. We are always caught in our own vision of things. Moreover, our professional calling depends on the paranoid ability to detect, suspect, interpret, to make strange connections among events. . . . Each time we open a meaning we invite in the paranoid potential. Psychology walks the borderline between meaning and paranoia: psychologists, too, are borderline cases. (*On Paranoia*, [Ascona, Switzerland: Eranos Foundation, 1986], 34)

13. Walter Ong, *Orality and Literacy: The Technologizing of the Word* (London: Methuen, 1982).

14. Derrida, "No Apocalypse," 24.

15. Marcus Smith and Khachig Tölölyan, "The New Jeremiad: *Gravity's Rainbow*," in *Critical Essays on Thomas Pynchon*, ed. Richard Pearce (Boston: G. K. Hall, 1981), 169.

16. Jean-François Lyotard, "Note on the Meaning of 'Post-' " in *Postmodernism: A Reader*, ed. Thomas Docherty (New York: Columbia University Press, 1993), 49.

17. Fredric Jameson, "Postmodernism, or The Cultural Logic of Late Capitalism," *New Left Review* 146 (1984): 80.

18. Northrop Frye, *Anatomy of Criticism: Four Essays* (Princeton, N.J.: Princeton University Press, 1957), 117.

19. Derrida, "No Apocalypse," 28. Similarly, Peter Schwenger suggests that if *Gravity's Rainbow* can be read as a sort of dream, then the "latent content . . . is summed up in Hiroshima" (*Letter Bomb: Nuclear Holocaust and the Exploding Word* [Baltimore: Johns Hopkins University Press, 1992], 59).

20. Jean-François Lyotard, "The Postmodern Condition," in *After Philosophy: End or Transformation?* ed. Kenneth Baynes, James Bohman, and Thomas McCarthy (Cambridge: MIT Press, 1987).

21. Frye, *Anatomy of Criticism*, 93.

22. Frye, *Anatomy of Criticism*, 93, 75.

23. Frye, *Anatomy of Criticism*, 119.

24. Christopher Norris, *Uncritical Theory: Postmodernism, Intellectuals and the Gulf War* (Amherst: University of Massachusetts Press, 1992), 17.

25. Jacques Derrida, *Writing and Difference*, trans. Alan Bass (Chicago: University of Chicago Press, 1978), 297.

26. Derrida, *Writing and Difference*, 297.

27. Derrida, "No Apocalypse," 27.

28. Jacques Derrida, "Of an Apocalyptic Tone Recently Adopted in Philosophy," trans. John P. Leavey, Jr., *Oxford Literary Review* 6, no. 2 (1984): 29–30.

29. Robert Alter, "The Apocalyptic Temper," *Commentary* 41 (June 1966): 62.

30. Alter, "Apocalyptic Temper," 62.

31. Alter, "Apocalyptic Temper," 63. David Thorburn levels very similar criticisms against *Gravity's Rainbow* in "A Dissent on Pynchon," his *Commentary* review of the novel (September 1973). Both Alter and Thorburn follow the lead of Martin Buber's essay "Prophecy, Apocalyptic, and the Historical Hour," (in *Pointing the Way* [New York: Harper and Row, 1957]). Buber regards prophecy as a genuine call to responsible action in the face of the exigencies of history. Apocalyptic, as he sees it, is a rather decadent form that assumes an iron determinism that precludes the possibility of meaningful existential action. It is suggestive to contrast this Jewish critical response to apocalypse with that of Northrop Frye, whose radical Protestant inclinations lead him to focus much more on its emancipatory possibilities.

32. Northrop Frye, *The Great Code: The Bible and Literature* (Toronto: Academic Press, 1982), 56.

33. Northrop Frye, rev. of *The Rhetoric of Romanticism*, by Paul de Man, *Times Literary Supplement* (17 January 1986): 51.

34. Frye, *Anatomy of Criticism*, 113; emphasis mine.

35. Frye, *Anatomy of Criticism*, 125, and *The Great Code*, 166.

36. Frye, *Anatomy of Criticism*, 125.

37. Jacques Derrida, *Of Grammatology*, trans. Gayatri Chakravorty Spivak (Baltimore: Johns Hopkins University Press, 1976), 158.

38. Derrida, *Of Grammatology*, 159.

39. Derrida, "No Apocalypse," 26.
40. Frye, *Anatomy of Criticism,* 118.
41. Derrida, "No Apocalypse," 28.
42. Derrida, "No Apocalypse," 30, 28.
43. Derrida, "No Apocalypse," 30.
44. Derrida, *Writing and Difference,* 297.
45. Derrida, "No Apocalypse," 30.
46. Frye, *Anatomy of Criticism,* 127–128.
47. Derrida, "No Apocalypse," 23.
48. Derrida, "No Apocalypse," 23.

The Whiteness of the Bomb

Ken Cooper

> It is an atomic bomb. It is a harnessing of the basic power of the universe.
> The force from which the sun draws its power has been loosed against
> those who brought war to the Far East.
> — President Harry S. Truman, announcing the bombing of Hiroshima

> Get out the lunch-box of your dreams
> And bite into the sandwich of your heart,
> And ride the Jim Crow car until it screams
> And, like an atom bomb, bursts apart.
> — Langston Hughes, "Jim Crow Car"

Also sprach Harry Truman. During this transcendental moment, nuclear,
political, and divine power coalesce into an exclusively American possession: figuratively, the dawn of a new Atomic Age. Other Americans, however, emphasized continuities across the historical divide, such as an editorial cartoonist for the *Chicago Defender* who found it significant that
occupying forces aboard the *Mississippi* entered Japan with a Confeder-
ate flag flying and a band playing "Dixie."[1] Langston Hughes likewise
wondered, by way of a conversation with his alter ego Jesse ("Simple")
Semple, whether America would have dropped atomic bombs on "white
folks" like the Germans. Simple maintains that the United States has
waited "until the war is all over in Europe to try them out on colored
folks." "You are thinking evil now," Hughes replies in mock protest.
"Besides it is your government and mine using those atomic bombs,
so why do you say 'they'? Why don't you say 'we'? Huh?" Simple's re-
joinder — "I did not have nothing to do with them bombs" — raises fundamental questions about racial politics within the emergent Atomic Age.[2]
Consider, for instance, Simple's claim that there are connections between "atom-bomb-dropping in Japan and shin-kicking in Virginia." Can
it be dismissed as a non sequitur, as Hughes disingenuously suggests? And
Simple's argument that America's is not "an integrated bomb," that the
"atom belongs to white folks" — what would be the consequences of this
(dis)possession?[3]

I come to the issue of arms-racism not as a child of the Nuclear Age, but rather as its grandchild: for there, on a certificate for participation "in work essential to the production of the Atomic Bomb, thereby contributing to the successful conclusion of World War II," along with Secretary of War Henry L. Stimson's signature, is the name of my own grandfather, Earl J. Rae. The certificate, it turns out, is one of my few tangible legacies from his employment as a personnel manager at the Hanford Engineer Works between 1942 and 1945. Our conversations about the war years, inconclusive at best, have only recapitulated the difficulty of seeing the Manhattan Project as a whole from within the organizational flow charts of E. I. duPont Nemours & Co., which was the War Department's contractor for the Hanford reactor. My grandfather recalls that everyone working at Hanford knew something important was happening but not, paradoxically, what it was. This "compartmentalization of knowledge," according to Manhattan Project commander General Leslie R. Groves, was designed so that "each man would know everything he needed to know to do his job and nothing else,"[4] and my grandfather, along with some 60,000 other Hanford employees, did their jobs.

But I am here concerned with a very specific compartmentalization of knowledge, one that had separated my grandfather's wartime employment from the issues of race I was researching. The tens of thousands of construction workers needed to build the Hanford plant, I mentioned to him at one point — I hadn't realized that there were so many. Well yes, he responded, they'd come by the trainload full to the deserts of eastern Washington, a lot of them from Alabama and Georgia. It occurred to me that by this he meant many of Hanford's construction workers were African American, so I asked him. Yes, a lot of them, almost all in construction jobs. And were they segregated from the white workers, as in other branches of the U.S. military? Apparently they were, but the conversation, as with so many others that white Americans have about race, wandered off in another direction, although not before I had envisioned a very different atomic bomb. First as a student and then as a teacher, my history of the Manhattan Project was always that Los Alamos nativity of "Oppenheimer's Baby," with the corporate entities of Hanford and Oak Ridge as distant midwives; it never had occurred to me, frankly, that the tens of thousands of construction workers who built the laboratories, reactors, and processing plants were necessarily part of the bomb's history, because their presence, like the tent camps that temporarily housed them, had been effaced.

Like Ishmael's contemplation of Moby-Dick, my own scrutiny of the leviathan has come around to "the whiteness of the bomb," that is, to my inevitable (if unwanted) participation in the monstrosities of race.[5] The bomb appalls me, as the whale did Ishmael, because the properties of

idealized whiteness are inseparable from its power, whether as the apotheosis of Anglo-American scientific mastery or as the weapon of an
atomic elect described by President Truman: "We thank God that it has
come to us, instead of to our enemies; and we pray that He may guide us
to use it in His ways and for His purposes."[6] To put the matter bluntly, the
bomb was built by people like me for the protection of people like me;
it was not an integrated bomb any more than the U.S. Army was an
integrated army, although African Americans were a presence in both
hierarchies. So is there no room for apprehension, to echo Ishmael,
that possession of this cosmic force insinuated — among other things —
the "white man['s] ideal mastership over every dusky tribe"? Or that,
conversely, the dangerous proliferation of nuclear technology to "irrational," "immature," and "unstable" Third World countries (the term
Third World itself a postwar invention) was deemed somehow unnatural?[7]
And if the bomb was regarded as a properly (white) American possession,
to what lengths would we go in preserving a privilege that indirectly
secured many others? As far as an avowed racist like Senator Theodore
Bilbo of Mississippi, who said that he "would prefer to see my race and my
civilization blotted out with the atomic bomb than to see it slowly but
surely destroyed in the maelstrom of miscegenation, interbreeding, in-
termarriage, and mongrelization"?[8] Is the end of whiteness really that
terrifying, as *unthinkable* in its way as nuclear war?

No cultural history of the Cold War can be complete until it has addressed these kinds of questions, all of which entail a certain concep-
tual "mongrelization." The compartmentalized and essentially Olym-
pian story of Los Alamos is emblematic of a larger paradigm whereby
nuclear science and nuclear strategy have stood apart from — and indeed
above — racial politics. Nowhere has the color line more assiduously been
monitored than between the separate-but-equal histories of postwar
American politics, with the rubric of "Cold War" on the one hand and
"Civil Rights" on the other. To question the ways in which America's
racial history and racial tensions influenced Cold War policy, or to explore the deployment of nuclear menace amidst properly "domestic"
civil rights discourse, is to run against powerful disciplinary, theoretical,
and historiographical forces, all of which work to compartmentalize two
overlapping histories. But it seems clear that Hughes (or, for that matter,
Bilbo) did not view such formulations as non sequiturs; in fact, judging
from Hughes's poem "Jim Crow Car," the specters of nuclear and racial
apocalypse were somehow interrelated.

As someone who does not want to be implicated in the bomb's history
(but is), who does not want to be implicated in the windfalls of racism
(but is), I approach this provisional field of knowledge with an eye toward
a poem in Hughes's *Montage of a Dream Deferred* (1951):

You are white —
yet a part of me, as I am a part of you.
That's American.
Sometimes perhaps you don't want to be a part of me.
Nor do I often want to be a part of you.
But we are, that's true![9]

The postwar minority literature to be revisited here is both Other —
because it was culturally constituted that way — and intimately about the
two Americas created by that disavowal. While the bomb's historical association with whiteness (and vice versa) is my topic, I am hoping that it will
raise more contemporary and more difficult questions. With the collapse
of the Cold War paradigm, "we" are now in a better position to reevaluate
certain racial aspects of "our" Nuclear Age history that were long sub-
sumed under an apocalyptic or anticommunist rubric; the current political landscape, moreover, demands that America come to terms with this
legacy. But first, back to the future.

*   *   *

Long before 1945, as historian Spencer Weart has shown, the promise
of limitless atomic power was associated with "white cities of the future,"
technological utopias that would transcend the blights of war, over-
crowded slums, and industrial pollution.[10] But even this background
didn't prepare me for the early press coverage of both Richland, Washington (the site where most of Hanford's workers lived), and Oak Ridge,
Tennessee, much of which extravagantly praised the two cities not only
for their atomic achievements but for how they had "fended off crime,
slums and commercialized sin." In September of 1945, *New Yorker* reporter Daniel Lang enthused:

> The Army may not know it, but it is operating Oak Ridge on a downright radical
> principle. Only Manhattan Engineer district employees, and their families, are
> allowed to live in the area. Consequently, Oak Ridge is possibly the one American
> city in which there is full employment. . . . The Oak Ridge crime rate is one of the
> lowest in the country. There have been only three homicides since the project was
> started. There hasn't been one decent robbery, and what thieving goes on in-
> volves shirts, cigarette lighters, and Parker 51s. Needless to say, there are no
> panhandlers.[11]

A writer for *The Christian Century* was, if anything, even more complimen-
tary of the "magically multiplying city" of Richland and its ecumenical
"church of the future." Citing Richland's "neatly spaced homes" and
"well planned shopping centers," the writer also noted that "the Christian spirit and helpfulness of its churches constitute an important talking

point in persuading the highest type of people to come to the community to live."[12]

This discursive transformation of army bases into model "Atomic Cities" signals a crucial aspect of the larger reconversion from World War to Cold War, and it is precisely because the utopian portrayals are rather strained that they are so revealing. After all, a 1946 article on Oak Ridge noted that "control of the authorities over every phase of life is absolute" and that the town remained, "for practical purposes, a military reservation." There were also indications that older racial problems had not been transcended. At Oak Ridge, townspeople referred to the area where atomic scientists lived as "Snob Hill"; the reservation's 1,500 Negro workers still lived in "miserable Jim Crow hutments."[13] The wartime boomtown of Hanford—nicknamed the "tarpaper metropolis" by workers because of its thousands of temporary hutments and trailers—was razed upon completion of the nuclear reactors, with the remaining "permanent employees" moving to the more attractive town of Richland after World War II. Still, the uncompromising security measures of the Atomic Cities seems to have been an intrinsic part of their appeal, in some ways prefiguring the course of postwar suburbanization better than mass-produced tracts such as Levittown. Safeguarded by the U.S. military and substantial private police forces, here was security not only from communist spies but from "inner-city crime," "bad schools," "unhealthy neighborhoods," and similar code words for racial conflict. What is today physically explicit as walled communities (complete with armed guard stations, ten-foot-high fences, surveillance cameras, and battlement motif architecture) was, in the case of Cold War era suburbs, a more tacit complex of motivations that requires a place like Richland or Oak Ridge to recall the twofold nature of what one writer termed "the American quest for security."[14]

Among the many other candidates for this kind of racially symptomatic reading are civil defense plans for industrial and residential "dispersal," overlapping discourse about integration and national security in the forum of public education, and especially the curiously liberating genre of nuclear Armageddon novels and "scenarios." Read in the historical present tense, postholocaust narratives allow telling glimpses into the Cold War political unconscious. If, as Paul Brians has argued, imagining nuclear war liberated the libido, "justifying all manner of erotic behavior which would be otherwise taboo," then the same was true about repressed racial fantasies.[15] Postholocaust novels—fables, really—propagated flagrant, blood-will-tell stereotypes that were inflammatory even by the standards of civil rights discourse. Several novels, for example, show blacks reverting to cannibalism after nuclear war, while others envision Caucasian holocaust survivors joining noble bands of Native Americans and adopting their ways, frequently with sexual undertones.[16] Philip Wylie's 1954 novel *Tomorrow!* surmised that a nuclear attack would actually regenerate a Midwestern city by enabling a suburban "world brand-new" to rise from the ashes, but only after the bomb exploded—not coincidentally—above the Negro district "right on Ground Zero." Both Dean MacCannell and Martha A. Bartter have taken the symptomatic approach a step further, arguing that repressed fantasies of nuclear urban renewal add a chilling dimension to the "real-life" history of suburbanization and white flight.[17]

Substantially less has been done, within the academic disciplines, to approach the issue of arms-racism from the other side of the color line, that is, to read the bomb through minority writers.[18] While the overwhelming majority of nuclear scenarios, postholocaust novels, moral tracts, and critical essays about the bomb were (and are) the product of white writers, it would be the most insidious kind of racism to assume that exclusion from the nuclear power structure precluded the necessary concern or expertise to make valid statements about Cold War policy. An instructive exchange appears in Alice Childress's *Like One of the Family* (1956), a collection of monologues by a fictional Negro domestic named Mildred to her friend Marge. Serving at a white cocktail party when the topic turns to issues of war and peace, one of the guests has "the bright idea of tryin' to make a fool out of me by callin' me in and askin' my opinion." In contrast to what has apparently been sophisticated "chit-chattin' " about nuclear war, Mildred's inspired witnessing evokes a stunned silence: "I do not want to see people's blood and bones spattered about the streets and I do not want to see your eyes runnin' outta your head like water. . . . I don't want to see folks shakin' and tremblin' and runnin' and hidin' . . . but I do want to see the KINGDOM COME on *earth* as it is in Heaven and I do not think that bombs and blood and salty tears is a *Heavenly* condition." By dramatically changing the context in which opinions are to be considered, Childress both exposes the racial codes that are implicit in the insular "chit-chattin' " and imagines a kind of deliverance that will encompass both militarism and racial oppression. In another monologue, Mildred similarly expands the definition of "peace" to include matters of fair employment and housing, racial integration, and lynching.[19]

Hughes, as we have seen, likewise confronts the barrier of expertise in his Simple essays, where his persona as educated, integrationist liberal only serves up the toasts of his custodian friend, a self-avowed "race man" who counters with fanciful but politically radical rebuttals. Upon hearing Simple claim that the "atom belongs to white folks," Hughes deadpans: "My dear fellow . . . the Atom Age is intended to benefit all of mankind enormously. People will only have to work a few hours a day." "*White people*," replies Simple, "because Negroes will not be working *at all*. They will be laid off."[20] Thus are the Atomic Cities racially repopulated, and technological fantasies complicated by economic consequences. Simple argues that Cold War moralizing — over the conditions in Hungary or Yugoslavia, for example — is being used as a diversion from domestic apartheid; he notes that President Eisenhower's golfing vacation to Georgia is taking him "outside the Free World"; and he frequently wishes that, if the atom bomb really is for *his* protection, "my government would use one of them bombs in Mississippi."[21] In one amazing conversation, Simple imagines himself growing into a giant and administering a different sort of deterrence:

I would be the coolest, craziest, maddest, baddest giant in the universe. I would sneeze — and blow the Ku Klux Klan plumb out of Dixie. I would clap my hands — and mash Jim Crow like a mosquito. . . . And anybody in this world who looked like they wanted to fight or drop atom bombs, I would snatch them up by their collars and say, "Behave yourselves! Talk things out. Buy yourselves a glass of beer and argue. But he who fights will have *me* to lick!"[22]

It is against the background of his explicitly Cold War dialogues with Simple that Hughes's other postwar writings warrant reevaluation. *Montage of a Dream Deferred* in particular was impounded within the parameters of its Harlem setting, judged to be a lesser work by (white) critical preconceptions of "folk art." Yet the volume's oft-anthologized "Harlem," with its litany of "what happens to a dream deferred," alludes not simply to long-simmering anger but also, when paralleled with the similar "Jim Crow Car," to a kind of political action as unimaginable to whites, as apocalyptic as an atomic detonation: "*Or does it explode?*" (71). Such an eruption of race into the Cold War — which recognized and even encouraged fears about "enemies from within" or latent "time bombs," but within a national security paradigm — shows how intellectual compartments like anticommunism or McCarthyism can be misleading. What about the perceived *racial* enemy from within? In the poems "Island" and "Good Morning," Hughes embeds Harlem, "between two rivers, / North of the park," amidst the mythical land of opportunity as an American "Dream within a dream, / Our dream deferred," with Penn Station its symbolic Ellis Island for Puerto Ricans, Haitians, and African Americans from the southern states (75, 71–72). To a national culture speaking the language of democratic consensus — as much to itself as to potential allies — this "dark tenth of a nation" (71), both a part of America and something separate, becomes conflated with the threat to national security. In "Ballad of the Landlord," for example, the hysterical reaction to a disgruntled tenant blurs any distinction between Cold War politics and racist opportunism: "*Police! Police! / Come and get this man! / He's*

trying to ruin the government / And overturn the land!" (24). As Simple
succinctly puts it, "Who calls every black man *red* that wants a piece of
white bread?"[23]

Hughes's contention that there were really *two* Americas, separate and
unequal, that there were racial refugees in the land of the free, provoked
the kind of extreme reaction normally associated with treason. Called
before the McCarthy committee in 1953, Hughes was taken to task for his
Simple columns in the *Chicago Defender* and forced to renounce his leftist
views. An even more explosive encounter occurred when singer and political activist Paul Robeson appeared before the House Committee on
Un-American Activities in 1956. His presence abroad deemed "detrimen-
tal to the interests of the United States Government," Robeson's visa had
been revoked by the State Department until he would promise not to
make any speeches in foreign countries, since the treatment of blacks
in America was considered a "family affair." But appearing before the
HUAC, an unrepentant Robeson maintained that "I am not being tried
for whether I am a Communist, I am being tried for fighting for the rights
of my people, who are still second-class citizens in this United States of
America." This, and his related work for "the independence of the colonial peoples of Africa," was why the committee wanted "to shut up every
Negro who has the courage to stand up and fight for the rights of his
people, for the rights of workers."[24]

Beneath the catchall labels of Communism and "national security," it
seems clear, were racial dynamics explored only at one's own peril. The
political analysis by Hughes, Robeson, and especially W. E. B. Du Bois was
largely ineffectual during the 1950s not only because it had been isolated
from the sanctioned mainstream of black opinion, but also because racial
politics had been compartmentalized from foreign policy, nuclear strategy, the economics of defense contracting, and so on. Du Bois, well-
known in a variety of literary and political contexts, is only now being
fully appreciated for his critique of the military-industrial complex long
before President Dwight D. Eisenhower's cautionary farewell speech of
1959. In numerous essays and pamphlets, and in speeches during his
1950 campaign for the U.S. Senate on the American Labor Party ticket,
Du Bois argued that Americans were "ruled by Big Business and Big Brass
for profit."[25] He was instrumental in organizing important world peace
conferences during the late 1940s and early 1950s that led to the Stock-
holm Peace Appeal, the so-called "Ban the Bomb" petition eventually
signed by more than 2.5 million Americans and hundreds of millions
worldwide. All of this led to his 1951 indictment as an unregistered foreign agent, with the eighty-three-year-old Du Bois conducted to the hearing in handcuffs.

For Du Bois, the Cold War had to be understood in relation to centuries of colonial exploitation. "If tomorrow Russia disappeared from the face of the earth," he wrote in 1951, "the basic problem facing the modern world would remain," specifically, the reality that "most human beings are starving to death, dying of preventable disease and too ignorant to know what is the matter, while a small minority are so rich that they cannot spend their income." According to this view, nuclear saber-rattling was part of a larger mission "to maintain and restore where possible the essentials of colonialism under the name of Free Enterprise and Western Democracy." Du Bois was always careful to point out that African Americans had a personal stake in denouncing Cold War colonialism abroad (as exemplified by the war against Korea) because they occupied "a quasi-colonial status" at home; in other words, "as long as caste and race discrimination is by common consent practiced in colonial regions in Africa and Asia, it will be current in America." It was not enough, then, to view nuclear arms simply as a matter of "foreign" policy: the hundreds of billions diverted to national defense threatened people of color both outside the United States and, by impoverishing social and education programs enacted during the New Deal, "quasi-colonials" here at home.[26]

Now that the Soviet Union has, in a sense, "disappeared from the face of the earth," it is impressive to see the continued relevance of Du Bois to our post–Cold War landscape. A prophet without honor during his own lifetime (he died in Ghana after renouncing U.S. citizenship in 1961), Du Bois anticipates similar appraisals of "Domestic Law and International Order" by Eldridge Cleaver and Malcolm X during the 1960s and more recent assessments of Nuclear Age colonialism by Paul Virilio, Edward Said, Michael Paul Rogin, Gayatri Chakravorty Spivak, and Joseph Gerson.[27] For my purposes, however, it is crucial to focus not only on the manifest history of political actions, but the latent cultural, ideological, and religious paradigms that enabled such actions. Du Bois was certainly aware of this in suggesting that Americans seemed to be afraid of an idea:

Of what are we in such deathly fear? Have we been invaded? Has anyone dropped an atom bomb on us? . . . Is there any sign that the United States of America is victim, or can be victim of any foreign country? No! Then of what are we afraid, and why are we trying to guard the earth from Pacific to Atlantic and from the North to the South Pole, unless it be from ourselves?[28]

The great problem of evaluating the Atomic Age is that, in one sense, nothing happened: the bombs were never dropped, Armageddon was deferred. But in the realm of cultural discourse, the omnipresent menace of World War III—and the way in which it was depicted—had an important, if subtle, impact on how racial issues were situated. For this reason, works of fiction are crucial for exploring in detail the kind of speculations that were only alluded to elsewhere.

Ann Petry's *Country Place* (1947), for example, juxtaposes the fury of a returning African-American soldier with that of a catastrophic storm (186); Ralph Ellison's *Invisible Man* (1952) concludes with an apocalyptic race war that leaves its protagonist "underground" in a basement room that alludes simultaneously to Richard Wright's racial parable "The Man Who Lived Underground," Jonah's sojourn in the belly of the leviathan, and a bomb shelter. Norman Mailer's essay "The White Negro" (1957), which situates the "hipster" amidst a bizarre nexus of atomic war, blackness, sexual potency, "psychopathic brilliance," and existential rebellion, should be read in conjunction with Lorraine Hansberry's astute rebuttal, not to mention his novels *The Deer Park* (1955) and *An American Dream* (1965), whose protagonists are modeled on this hipster and are associated with atomic pyrotechnics. As for Hansberry, she would seem to be an ideal transitional figure between the "Fifties" of the Cold War and its quite different "Sixties." Friends with Hughes, Du Bois, and Robeson (she wrote for his newspaper *Freedom*), Hansberry was equally attuned to the emerging black power movement before her death in 1965. Her play *A Raisin in the Sun* (1959), which takes its title from Hughes's poem "Harlem," makes reference to atomic bombs being tested, but the *real* explosion on the horizon is the African tradition reemerging in America. Prophetically inspired, the play's protagonist conceives of himself as Flaming Spear, a tribal leader who is "a *descendent of Chaka*" and kin to Jomo Kenyatta, then leading the anticolonial resistance in Kenya. At this visionary moment, "the coming of the mighty war" anticipates a radical fusion of anticolonial revolution abroad and in America, the "big one" that whites had always feared.[29]

*   *   *

All of these texts speak to the Cold War imagination of apocalypse, but in officially *unacceptable* ways that only accelerated throughout the 1960s. A good place to see this systematic decompartmentalization is Ishmael Reed's ambitious 1972 novel *Mumbo Jumbo,* which locates nuclear weapons in a cultural context antedating Hiroshima not just by decades — as with histories of the bomb that "begin" with the discovery of radioactivity in 1895 — but by centuries. Reed, sometimes better known for his war of words with African-American feminists and New Black Aesthetic critics, will be discussed here for his innovative deconstruction of latent mythological, religious, and metaphysical formulations that empower armsracism. The word "deconstruction" is deliberately chosen, for I will later suggest that Reed's return to the very logos of whiteness parallels a similar journey undertaken by Jacques Derrida, from the other side of the color line, in response to the Vietnam War, student rebellions, and the assassination of Martin Luther King. Curiously, Derrida has been celebrated (or blamed) for the apocalypse of textual "meaning," but not for his astute political analysis regarding the collapse of whiteness as a metaphysical origin. The two catastrophes (from one point of view) or revelations (from another) are not unrelated.

Ostensibly set in 1920s Harlem, Reed's *Mumbo Jumbo* simultaneously looks forward to contemporary Amerika and back to mythical Egypt, drawing upon stories about the past "to prophesy about the future — a process our ancestors called 'Necromancy.' "[30] Thus, the narratives set in Egypt and Harlem are filled with proleptic and usually ironic glimpses of the future. Significantly, atomic bombs are mentioned in all three periods, not as the "subject" of the novel but rather as a shorthand for the violence implicit in Western Civilization's religious and cultural "crusades." Although it is extremely difficult to summarize the plot of *Mumbo Jumbo,* most of the novel concerns the "outbreak" of an entity called Jes Grew — a spirit or *Zeitgeist* that necessarily manifests itself in human forms like jazz music, drinking, dancing, and unabashed sensuality — and the hysterical reaction to its advent.

The spontaneous uprising of Jes Grew and its "carriers" augurs "the end of Civilization As We Know It" to the fervent adherents of the Atonist Path who are, one character explains, "all together on the sacredness of Western Civilization and its mission."[31] The Atonist Path (named after one of the first monotheistic sun-gods in Western history) is led by a conspiratorial group of insiders called the Wallflower Order, a term which seems to pun on "Ivy League."[32] The Wallflower Order is at once a secret society in the tradition of the Teutonic Knights, Knights Templars, and the Masonic Temple — all of which are mentioned in the novel — and a metaphor for the rites and rituals of power in America's purportedly classless society. Because of canonical history's power to turn narratives into "facts," revisionist interpretations such as Reed's are likely to be stigmatized as paranoid: they posit causality where none is supposed to exist. *Mumbo Jumbo* turns this predicament into an asset by using the trope of conspiracy to evoke the shadowy presence of culture across self-proclaimed origins like the Age of Reason or the Atomic Age; in other words, the *real* conspiracy pretends that nuclear weapons have nothing to do with a genealogy of religion, mythology, ritual, or conjuring.

From its top-secret headquarters, the Wallflower Order not only tracks the movements of Jes Grew, but actively plots to "curb" it: "To knock it dock it co-opt it swing it or bop it. If Jes Grew slips into the radiolas and Dictaphones all is lost" (64). The novel's conspiratorial version of history is manifested through proleptic glimpses of Wallflower works-in-progress: World War II, "being choreographed at this very moment," is termed "the next Crusade"; a promising Wallflower "candidate" in Germany prefigures Adolf Hitler (71, 155–156). As a last resort, the order engineers the Stock Market Crash of 1929 and subsequent Great Depression to limit radio sales and close dance halls, thus preventing the spread of Jes Grew. Significantly, Reed's historical necromancy extends well into the nuclear age, containing atavistic allusions to Malcolm X, John Wayne, Billy Graham, Ronald Reagan, the Beatles, and Northrop Frye, among others. This has the effect of radically compressing ten thousand years of history (if we include the lengthy section that takes place in ancient Egypt), but by using the device of secret societies, Reed avoids the simple platitude that history is cyclical — each generation is taught a culture's rituals, and has the power to change or reject them.

Against this historical background, nuclear weapons are less a technological device than a kind of spirit raised by incantation. If Jes Grew is written into existence, "an influence which sought its text," then so too can atomic bombs be the product of conjuring (211). This notion is addressed explicitly in two different episodes. In one, a character named Berbelang who repatriates sacred native art from "Centers of Art Detention" (i.e., museums) explicates the European Faust legend in terms that signify upon the Nuclear Age. According to Berbelang's interpretation, Faust is a charlatan who doesn't fully understand the implications of his conjuring: "China had rocketry, Africa iron furnaces, but [Faust] didn't know when to stop with his newly found Work" (91). In his heart, Berbelang says, Faust knows he is a *bokor,* even as his techno-sorcery "improves":

Soon he will be able to annihilate 1000000s by pushing a button. I do not believe that a Yellow or Black hand will push this button but a robot-like descendant of Faust the quack will. . . . We must teach you [Europeans and Americans] the difference between a healer, a holy man, and a duppy who returns from the grave and causes mischief. We must infuse you with the mysteries that Jes Grew implies. (91)

One of the most radical aspects of this passage is the way that nuclear weaponry — the very embodiment of Western technical mastery — is critiqued from the standpoint of an older, wiser culture, not, as some Americans would have it, a "developing," "Third World" culture. Berbelang's conviction that only a *white* finger would push the button goes to the heart of proliferation rhetoric, which intimates that non-Western societies are too unstable and emotional to possess nuclear weapons, or would use them in a ferocious holy war. Instead, Reed suggests that the bomb is itself a manifestation of conjuring by the dangerously messianic Judeo-Christian religion, a theme he revisits in *The Terrible Twos* (1982).[33]

To explain how Atonist culture reached this state, the novel returns to ancient Egypt for a tour-de-force episode about two brothers, Osiris and Set. Osiris is the god of agriculture and a phenomenal dancer, so arousing, in fact, that people performing his dances become possessed by loas; his friend Thoth persuades Osiris that the steps need to be written down, for there is no "litany to feed the spirits" which seize the people (164). The Book of Thoth is written and peace returns to the land. But Set, "the stick crook and flail man," is kept awake at nights by all the singing and dancing, making him tired and irritable in the mornings "when he went out on the field and drilled marched and gave commands to others" (162–163).

When Osiris leaves the country to tour the world with his "International Nile Root Orchestra," Set senses an opportunity. Jealous of his brother's popularity, he tries his hand at conjuring—as Faust will do thousands of years later—and accidentally creates "something resembling an A-bomb explosion" (173). Set flees to "Heliopolis City of the Sun" and other transformations occur:

Set began to develop a weird relationship with the Sun. If you can understand Los Angeles you can almost get the picture; imagine 2 or 3 Los Angeleses and you got Heliopolis. The legislators lay around in the Sun all day and developed a strange Body Building scene on the beach. Set decided that he would introduce a religion based upon his relationship to the Sun, and since he was a god then the Sun too would be a god. Of course this was nothing new because the Egyptians had worshiped the "heat, light, orbs, and rays," had worshiped the Sun in a pantheistic manner. With Set, the Sun's flaming disc eclipsed the rest of its parts. (173)

Using images that allude to contemporary America, Reed carefully juxtaposes solar worship with the nature religion of Osiris. Set, who had once been caught trying out Osirian dance steps in secret, subsequently becomes "Aton the 'burner of growing things,' the Egyptian Jehovah who causes famine pestilence and earthquakes" (174).

The Judeo-Christian connection is made with a related story about Moses, a well-meaning Osirian initiate who is nothing so much as a novice jazz musician trying to learn the famous "Black Mud Sound" of Osiris. Under the tutelage of Jethro, Moses learns to play "the sounds of the spirits," but in his ambition for power, his impatience, he receives only partial knowledge of the Book of Thoth. "He wouldn't listen," Jethro says ruefully, "and now he will be merely a 2-bit sorcerer practicing the Left Hand" (179). The debut of Moses as a "soloist" enacts the transformation from a participatory, pantheistic religion to the monotheism of Judeo-Christianity—"I'm the 1," he tells his audience (182). Despite assistance from applause signs and "Atonist thugs" with flails and crooks, the performance fails because it is not inclusive; a riot breaks out and in his anger Moses conjures a spell from the Book of Thoth: "Moses uttered The Work aloud. 1st there was silence. Then the people turned toward the Nile and they saw a huge mushroom cloud arise. A few minutes later, screaming of the most terrible kind came from that direction" (186). As with Set and Faust, the mushroom clouds conjured by Moses represent only a superficial technological "mastery" that results from a deeper self-delusion and paranoia.

Reconfiguring the military-industrial complex as a latter-day sun cult, Reed's counter-history presents an effective challenge to more conventional ways of thinking about nuclear arms. It is worth recalling, for instance, that Truman's announcement of the Hiroshima bombing claimed for America the same "force from which the sun draws its power" (197), and in fact the sun-bomb analogy was frequently mentioned both by Manhattan scientists and by journalists, often with millennial overtones.[34] That chilling sense of organizational mission surrounding the bomb — whereby scientists referred to an "atomic crusade" and defense strategists began calling themselves the "nuclear priesthood"[35] — is satirized in Reed's description of the Wallflower Order headquarters in New York City. Hierophant 1, ruler of the Wallflower Order, wears sandals and dresses "like a Cecil B. De Mille extra" (63); the order's secretly controlled mouthpiece is the *New York Sun*. The edifice itself seems to be a cross between Egyptian temple and nuclear war room, including a round, revolving chamber with "a dome of glass through which the Hierophant can keep track of the Heavens" (65). His surveillance of more earthly events is facilitated by dozens of video screens — this in the 1920s — and a huge map of the world that keeps track of animal species the Wallflower Order has successfully eliminated. With rows upon rows of "Like-Men" marching single file down the hallways (62), one is reminded of Lewis Mumford's argument that the "megamachine" of social hierarchy, beginning with solar theology, served as "the earliest working model for all later complex machines, though the emphasis slowly shifted from the human operatives to the more reliable mechanical parts."[36]

Mumbo Jumbo, as we have seen, interrogates the whiteness of the bomb by drawing parallels between the wrathful Jehovah of Mosaic law and the terrible fireball that watches over (and ultimately empowers) nuclear deterrence. As a corollary to this heliocentric model, Reed shows that political and cultural power during the Cold War were envisioned centripetally, that is, as a function of one's proximity to the nuclear center. I do not have space to discuss the many cultural documents that would bolster such a claim, but they would include: Arthur Schlesinger Jr.'s *The Vital Center* (1949), an influential manifesto that reinvented America's melting pot for the Cold War; Atomic Energy Commission chair David Lilienthal's remark, in 1947, that the "atom is the center of reality at

Figure 1. "The National Civil Defense Pattern." Illustration in *United States Civil Defense* (1950). Courtesy National Security Resources Board, Washington, D.C.

the council tables of chancelleries all over the world"; social-science discourse about the so-called *nuclear family* (a postwar term) in relation to "nontraditional" minority families; and widely distributed literature that celebrated white males as the "prime movers" of civil defense (Figure 1).[37] Most importantly, Reed shows how the paradigm of political centrality and marginality can be endlessly adapted and reformulated across historical boundaries. His narrator recalls that "I once leafed through a photo book about the West. I was struck by how the Whites figured in the center of the photos and drawings while Blacks were centrifugally distant. The center was usually violent: gunfighting lynching murdering torturing. The Blacks were usually, if it were an interior, standing in the doorway. Digging the center" (209–210).

While Reed was digging (at) the political center, others were registering its crisis from within. William Burroughs's *Nova Express* (1964), Thomas Pynchon's *Gravity's Rainbow* (1973), and Robert Coover's *The Public Burning* (1977), likewise undertaking a revisionary history of the Cold War, associated the bomb not just with "postmodern" forms of control but older, racist impulses toward Manifest Destiny.[38] Jacques Derrida's early formulations of deconstruction, in fact, include a specifically political impetus of using "against the edifice the instruments or stones available in the house" that has much in common with Burroughs, Pynchon, and Coover. His essay "The Ends of Man," which he dates "quite precisely from the month of April 1968," assumes a deliberately apocalyptic tone commensurate with the Last Days of "the unity of man." By this Derrida means that there has been a long "uninterrupted metaphysical familiarity with that which, so naturally, links the we of the philosopher to 'we men,' to the we in the horizon of humanity." So long as there remained a tacit and relatively transparent understanding about the constitution of this *we*, "however simple, discreet, and erased it might be," it was possible to inscribe "the question of Being within the horizon of metaphysics . . . to the possibility of which the origin of metaphysics is essentially linked." Through illustrative readings of Hegel, Husserl, and Heidegger, Derrida suggests that, because the "Western" metaphysical constitution of Being is structured in terms of proximity — "We who are close to ourselves, we interrogate *ourselves* about the meaning of Being" — a (political) challenge to who "we" are was shaking the foundational assumptions of Being and meaning.[39]

That this crisis in meaning coincides with the escalating crises of Vietnam (a paradigmatic Cold War "intervention" exceeding its Third World boundaries) and of civil rights (a "family affair" exceeding its domestic boundaries) is instructive: things fall apart, the (atomic) center cannot hold, and there are now *others* interrogating *us* about the formal structure of the question of being. Derrida's "White Mythologies" (1971) thus makes a wonderful companion piece to *Mumbo Jumbo*, for here too racial dynamics are strategically re-membered: "Metaphysics — the white mythology which reassembles and reflects the culture of the West: the white man takes his own mythology, Indo-European mythology, his own *logos*, that is, the *mythos* of his idiom, for the universal form of that he must still wish to call Reason. Which does not go uncontested." Arguing that "abstract notions always hide a sensory figure" Derrida observes that, as metaphysics relies on metaphor to naturalize its (patriarchal) hierarchy of ideas, the sun figures as the foundational "prime mover of metaphor, the father of all figures. Everything turns around it, everything turns toward it." He makes a similar observation about the patriarchal Sol-ar system in "Plato's Pharmacy" (1968): "The good (father, sun, capital) is thus the hidden illuminating, blinding source of *logos*. And since one cannot speak of that which enables one to speak (being forbidden to speak of it or to speak to it face to face), one will speak only of that which speaks and of things that, with a single exception, one is constantly speaking of."[40]

The deconstruction of Western foundational myths — a figurative "talking back" to the patriarchal white father whose presence has been effaced — is an endeavor common to all of these writers, which is why it seems to me that the bomb is so important for understanding the 1945 boundary of "Cold War" culture. Because any ideological system requires some kind of figurative origin to orient its hierarchical structure, the first atomic detonations simultaneously worked a historical effacement upon the earlier culture that had enabled them and located unlimited power at ground zero.[41] By way of example I would offer a passage from William Laurence, a *New York Times* science correspondent who was the only journalist allowed within the top-secret confines of the Manhattan Project. His privileged access amounted to a one-year head start on the competition, so his were the first detailed reports out of Los Alamos. Subtly influential during their time, they allow us to see in overdetermined form some of the cultural work that went into the creation of the "Atomic Age":

Everything relating to the gadget — the spot where it stood on its tower, the time scheduled for its blow-off, as well as the great god It of the occasion — were referred to as Zero, the code name for the test. For everyone concerned, Zero became the center of the universe. Time and space began and ended at Zero. All life centered on Zero. Everyone thought only of Zero and the zero hour, or rather the zero microsecond.[42]

We need not determine whether any of the writers discussed so far actually read this specific parable of political power: it was enough that influential politicians, nuclear scientists, military leaders, and the media were willing to accept the primacy of the bomb as "the center of reality," a new beginning, of national power and identity.

*   *   *

Given the intimate connections between the bomb and white male identity, it is perhaps not unexpected that the so-called C³I of defense operations (Command, Control, Communications, Intelligence) should privilege the postmodern nuclear war room: underground and invisible, yet extending its mastery over the global system. Nor, given the paradigm of nuclear centrality/marginality, should it be surprising that minority critiques of the bomb so often foreground the issue of colonialism. I want to close by mentioning three novels that not only reconfigure domestic politics as (nuclear) "colonialism," but imagine strategies of resistance from beyond the center: Paule Marshall's *The Chosen Place, the Timeless People* (1969), Toni Cade Bambara's *The Salt Eaters* (1980), and Leslie Marmon Silko's *Ceremony* (1977).[43] As with the texts discussed already, particularly Reed's *Mumbo Jumbo*, remembering beyond the 1945 boundary — or forgetting — is a political act.

Marshall's novel, which takes place on a fictional island in the Caribbean, includes a spectrum of responses to the legacy of colonialism. Readers catch glimpses of a U.S. airbase and missile-tracking station on the northern tip of the island (80), but the bomb figures primarily as a metaphor for one character's willful forgetting of the past. New Englander Harriet Shippen's involvement in an "aid-and-development program" for the island is enabled primarily by familial ties to a multinational corporation named Unicor, but she has spent most of her life denying any complicity in its history of West Indies exploitation. Whereas her new husband Saul Amron recognizes the historical continuities between a British lord in his "white-hunter outfit" and Americans in business suits — "Out to own and control the world, and determined to hold on no matter what means they have to employ" — Harriet refuses to think about her family's colonial past and "dislike[s] acknowledging to herself" that the problem of racism even exists (225, 200).

Still, Harriet has troubling nightmares involving her first husband Andrew Westerman, who is a nuclear scientist. In the middle of the most innocuous dreams, she will witness a nuclear explosion and mushroom cloud, realizing only later that it was not only "Andrew's hand on the lever which triggered the holocaust, that mass suicide in which its creators would be the first to go, but that her hand was also there, resting lightly on his, guiding it" (39). Marshall juxtaposes these nightmare-visions with Harriet's surreptitious desires, hidden even from herself, to control the nonwhite islanders. When the development project eventually slips beyond her influence, she arranges for its funding to be revoked. Saul learns of this and interrogates her in what is clearly Marshall's voice:

What is it with you and your kind, anyway? . . . If you can't have things your way, if you can't run the show, there's to be no show, is that it? . . . You'd prefer to see everything, including yourselves, come down in ruins rather than "take down," rather than not have everything your way, is that it . . . ?" (454)

Harriet's dream of a suicidal holocaust turns out to be ironically self-fulfilling, for not only does she do her best to end the "show" on the island, but she ultimately drowns herself in a tidal pool, the surf's "massive detonation . . . rising in the dazzling white toadstool of a cloud" (459). Unlike other characters such as Saul or Merle Kinbona, who openly acknowledge the cultural "diversity and disunity" within themselves and undertake a constant "struggle for coherence," Harriet's apparent serenity masks a violent fear of the racial Other (5, 401).

It would be a mistake to conclude that Marshall's novel has only limited applicability for a discussion of domestic politics; one character, in fact, makes a point of telling Harriet that he is fascinated by "those deeply rooted, almost mystical beliefs that appear to lie at the heart of your [American] racial dilemma. . . . They seem to suggest a terribly dark and primitive side to your troubled countrymen" (422). A Haitian in Reed's *Mumbo Jumbo* makes a similar observation within the context of America's obsession with highways: although Caucasians call it "destiny" or "progress," they are really being pursued by "Haints of their victims rising from the soil of Africa, South America, Asia" (135). Drawing a line at 1945 and proclaiming a new Atomic Age may have partially banished our nation's racial history from "mainstream" Cold War discourse, but these writers suggest that repressed memories in the political unconscious made an inevitable return in altered form, whether of cowboys-and-Indians metaphors during the Korean and Vietnam wars, or of fears about African Americans and "aliens" being national security risks. It is therefore both appropriate and psychologically necessary to confront a centuries-long history of slavery, Indian wars, and, as Bambara observes in *The Salt Eaters,* the internment of Japanese-Americans during World War II (222).

Possibly the most far-reaching exploration of nuclear colonialism *within* our national borders is Silko's novel *Ceremony.* Bambara's novel, it is true, has characters such as Velma Henry and Jan point out that radioactive waste is shipped through minority communities by minority workers, and that uranium is extracted from Native American lands to be used for "test-blasts" in those same locales (242–243). Silko takes this as a given and, like Reed, situates nuclear colonialism within a more comprehensive, frequently prophetic narrative that is centuries old. From Silko's explicitly Native American perspective, which constantly reaffirms the connectedness of this world and unseen others, Caucasians are participants in a ritual they do not fully comprehend, or willfully deny to themselves. Many readers of *Ceremony* are likely to draw a simplistic correspondence between whites and what Silko calls "the destroyers," but in actuality they—along with several of the Native Americans in the novel such as Leroy, Pinkie, and especially Emo—have been tricked by the destroyers, witches who "sent them to ruin this world, and day by day . . . were doing it" (204). The same subconscious fear of the Other noted by Marshall and Reed is, for Silko, embedded in American (racial) history, so that whites are "suffering as thieves do, never able to forget that their pride was wrapped in something stolen, something that had never been, and could never be, theirs"; this national "lie" is actually "destroying the white people faster than it [is] destroying the Indian people" (204).

The kind of symptoms that Silko uses to illustrate this point are wide-ranging. She notes the cultural imperialism of Caucasian art, and the "dissolution of their consciousness into dead objects" such as plastic and neon, concrete and steel; the whites try to "glut the hollowness with patriotic wars and with great technology and the wealth it brought" (204,

191). But most of all, Silko points to nuclear technology and the possibility of global holocaust as the inevitable conclusion of the witches'
ceremony:

> *They will take this world from ocean to ocean*
> *they will turn on each other*
> *they will destroy each other*
> *Up here*
> *in these hills*
> *they will find the rocks,*
> *rocks with veins of green and yellow and black.*
> *They will lay the final pattern with these rocks*
> *they will lay it across the world*
> *and explode everything.* (137)

We have already seen various constructions and deconstructions of the
bomb as a specifically Caucasian deity; here, Silko uses Native American
religion to interpret the ultimate purpose of uranium mining and thousands of missiles. Thoughtful readers of her novel will probably find it
difficult to return to familiar discourse concerning "escalation," "cities
targeting," and "overkill" without speculating about the underlying pattern of nuclear "national defense."

There is another component to the novel's supernatural connectedness, equally important, for a discussion of nuclear arms. If the world is
fragile as a spider's web (38–39), if the spiritual sickness of a single person
is "only part of something larger" (125–126) — as is the case with Silko's
protagonist Tayo — then it is also possible to visualize oneself as integral to
the larger designs of ceremonies, whether those of witches or otherwise.
Against the "final pattern" being enacted by the destroyers, Silko counter-
poises a web of healers who enact a ceremony of tentative reconciliation:
Ku'oosh, Betonie, Ts'eh, and, eventually, Tayo himself. The turning point
comes when Tayo realizes that "there were no boundaries; the world
below and the sand paintings inside became the same that night" (145).
The execution of Japanese soldiers that Tayo witnesses as an infantryman
in the Pacific is, after all, related to the death of his uncle Josiah on the
Laguna Pueblo thousands of miles away; the "dismembered corpses and
the atomic heat-flash outlines" of Hiroshima victims are connected to
witchery being practiced near Tayo's home (37).

In contrast to minorities being seen as merely peripheral or marginal
to America's nuclear center, Silko concludes her story by situating Tayo
himself at a uranium mine near Cebolleta, "the point of convergence
where the fate of all living things, and even the earth, had been laid"
(246). Trinity test site is located only three hundred miles to the south-

east, the laboratories at Los Alamos a hundred miles to the southeast. From this vantage, Tayo sees that "the lines of cultures and worlds were drawn in flat dark lines on fine light sand, converging in the middle of witchery's final ceremonial sand painting" (246). Consider for a moment the subtle differences between Silko's "ground zero" and more conventional associations. Tayo experiences a sense of unity ("human beings were one clan again"), but it is not the kind of Cold War "pulling together" or melting pot that positions America against the world; on the contrary, humans are united by "the fate the destroyers planned for all of them, for all living things" (246). Tayo stands in a position of power at the ritual center of the (five) world(s), but he recognizes it is really "a monstrous design" that is impelling him to commit violence against Emo, Leroy, and Pinkie. Instead of "jamm[ing] the screwdriver into Emo's skull the way the witchery had wanted" (253), Tayo rejects that power which is measured only by its ability to kill others, even if it means watching his friend Harley die. Harley, after all, had promised to deliver Tayo to this spot and, like Pinkie, is ultimately killed by Emo and Leroy when the witchery turns "upon itself" (247). More generally, Silko's reading of nuclear power uses a strategy I have emphasized throughout this survey of Cold War literature: the insistence that "old stories, the war stories, their stories" are all relevant to the Atomic Age, and that the bomb is itself part of a "story that [is] still being told" (246). Witches and destroyers, on the other hand, rely on a linear narrative of "progress" that moves toward the Christian Armageddon or nuclear holocaust or the "anger and hatred that would finally destroy the world" (191).

In order to confront what I have called the whiteness of the bomb, it is necessary for the white majority, myself included, that has experienced a half-century of nuclear *possession* to take responsibility for the racial history and latent cultural myths of the Atomic Age. And this means systematic divestment. Contemporary opinion, of course, has reached a point where some are claiming that the Cold War is "over," despite the continued presence of weapons and (post)colonial encroachment. The official victory announcement was made during President George Bush's 1990 State of the Union address, when he declared to Congress and a national television audience: "By the grace of God, America won the cold war . . . the cold war didn't 'end' — it was won."[44] Before assenting to what Robert Coover would call the latest "NEW New Enlightenment"[45] — provisionally labeled the "New World Order" — it is crucial to ask whether any of the fundamental assumptions have changed. Bush's success in mobilizing support for Operation Desert Storm was enabled by fears about Iraq obtaining nuclear arms,[46] and the more recent showdown with North Korea once again has the United States fearing the spread of (sacred?) nuclear technology to a nonwhite power. Only last week I saw

Arnold Schwarzenegger in the James Cameron film *True Lies,* playing a supermacho superdad who also happens to be a national security super-stud, single-handedly annihilate a group of stereotypical Arab terrorists who had managed to acquire four nuclear weapons. My response turns out to be a very old one, dating back to Jesse Semple, circa 1945: is America ready to accept anything other than a white finger on the nuclear button?

A Postscript: "This is the greatest thing in history!"

I began this survey of the Atomic Age with President Harry S. Truman announcing America's new sun-bomb and concluded by arguing that it has been intimately associated with white authority, often in unexpected venues. Truman himself seems to have been emboldened by possession of the sun-bomb, a suggestion persuasively argued by Robert Lifton. Inexperienced in the world of diplomacy and confronted with a menacing wartime ally, Truman thought the bomb might provide the "hammer" he needed for dealing with the Soviet Union. Both Secretary of War Henry Stimson and Prime Minister Winston Churchill remarked on Truman's sudden increase of vigor and self-assertion *after* he had learned of the successful Los Alamos test. Subsequently, Lifton argues, "that same euphoric sense of personal and national power was involved in Truman's disturbing comment upon hearing of the success of the Hiroshima mission: 'This is the greatest thing in history.' "[47] Truman's emphasis on the weapon's *newness* effectively disconnected it from prior history, reorganizing the bomb as a new *primum mobile,* a new origin, a new center for the Atomic Age. Thus did his brand of (a)historicism reinforce the workings of racial hegemony.

A cultural history of America's atomic sun suggests other possibilities. No fragment of evidence would be considered pre-nuclear or irrelevant, too "paranoid" to be of significance. Consider a 1949 portrait of Truman as Grand Master of the Missouri Masons that appeared in *Life* magazine, which he considered "the best ever done of him."[48] Truman, a thirty-third degree Mason, occupied this highest position in 1941, and the portrait shows him attired in the symbolic regalia of office: his hat and sash, the Jewel of Office, and apron with its all-seeing eye. According to one study of Masonry, the Jewel of Office was supposed to inspire its wearer

with profound veneration for that Incomprehensible Being at whose command the world burst forth from chaos into light, and all created matter had its birth; whose Infinite Wisdom directs, and whose unspeakable Goodness preserves and blesses every work that has proceeded from His Hands.[49]

The all-seeing eye (which appears, incidently, on the Great Seal of the United States, and is printed on the back of any dollar bill) likewise imparts to its possessor unspeakable power, the omnipresent eye of God emitting its divine light.

In a Masonic lodge, Truman would have occupied the position of Worshipful Master, which, according to one section of the initiation ritual, is a significant place indeed: "The three lesser lights are the three burning tapers which you see placed in a triangular form about this altar. They represent the sun, moon, and Master of the Lodge; and as the sun rules the day, and the moon governs the night, so ought the Worshipful Master to endeavor to rule and govern his Lodge with equal regularity."[50] Truman's chair as Worshipful Master would have been positioned on the east wall of the room, which explains one other detail in the portrait. Suspended behind Harry Truman, who would be / had been announcing the dawn of America's sun-bomb in 1945, is a solar disk with the letter *G* at its center. There are, even within the Masons, different opinions as to what this letter signifies. The *G* may refer to *Geometry*, the divine properties of the universe's Great Architect. It has also been taken to mean, more bluntly, *God*.

Notes

For their encouragement and suggestions, I would like to thank Caroline Woidat, Cecelia Tichi, Adam Meyer, David Guest, Richard Dellamora, and participants in the ACCUTE panel on Postmodern Apocalypse.

1. Editorial cartoon by Jay [?] Jackson, *Chicago Defender* (national edition), September 8, 1945: 12.

2. Langston Hughes, "Simple and the Atom-Bomb," *Chicago Defender,* August 18, 1945, p. 12.

3. Langston Hughes, *Simple's Uncle Sam* (New York: Hill and Wang, 1965), 123; and *Simple Stakes a Claim* (New York: Rinehart, 1957), 55.

4. Leslie R. Groves, *Now It Can Be Told: The Story of the Manhattan Project* (1962; reprint, New York: Da Capo, 1975), 140.

5. For detailed studies of Melville's response to race and the institution of slavery, see Michael Paul Rogin, *Subversive Genealogy: The Politics and Art of Herman Melville* (Berkeley: University of California Press, 1983), and Toni Morrison, "Unspeakable Things Unspoken: The Afro-American Presence in American Literature," *Michigan Quarterly Review* 28 (1989): 1–34. Their thoughts and Melville's on the "Whiteness of the Whale" have enabled my own thinking about the bomb.

6. Harry S. Truman, *Public Papers of the Presidents of the United States* (1945; Washington, D.C.: GPO, 1961), 213.

7. Herman Melville, *Moby-Dick* (1851; reprint, with a forward by Alfred Kazin, Boston: Houghton Mifflin, 1956), 157. Carl E. Pletsch argues that replacing the language of colonialism with social-science euphemisms—whereby "primitive"

cultures become "traditional," colonies become "developing nations," and so forth — does not impair the deep structure of ethnocentric hierarchies. His study of the "Three Worlds" paradigm, a model that seems to date from the early 1950s, shows it to be a response to Cold War policy objectives:

> The governing distinctions underlying the three worlds scheme — traditional/ modern and ideological/free — not only allocate the most diverse societies and cultures to the same categories, they also imply a pseudo-chronological or historical relationship among the categories themselves. . . . There are all sorts of problems with this faith in modernization, but perhaps the most basic is that modernity is as indefinable as tradition. The three worlds scheme locates the end of history in societies that are very much in flux. This arrogance of modernization theorists, locating the end of history in their own problematic societies, is particularly reminiscent of Hegel and his philosophy of history.

Pletsch, "The Three Worlds, or the Division of Social Scientific Labor, circa 1950–1975," *Comparative Studies in Society and History* 23.4 (1981): 576–577.

8. H. J. Duteil, *The Great American Parade*, trans. Fletcher Pratt (New York: Twayne, 1953), 104.

9. Langston Hughes, *Montage of a Dream Deferred* (New York: Holt, 1951), 40. All further citations are parenthetical.

10. Spencer R. Weart, *Nuclear Fear: A History of Images* (Cambridge, Mass.: Harvard University Press, 1988), 5–13.

11. "Model City," *Time*, December 12, 1949, 21; Daniel Lang, "The Atomic City," *New Yorker*, September 29, 1945, 54.

12. "Church of the Future," *The Christian Century* 69 (1952): 362, 365.

13. "Oak Ridge: Life Where the Bomb Begins," *Newsweek*, August 5, 1946, 33, 32.

14. Hanson W. Baldwin, "New Atomic Capital," *New York Times Magazine*, July 30, 1950, 19.

15. Paul Brians, *Nuclear Holocausts: Atomic War in Fiction, 1895–1984* (Kent, Ohio: Kent State University Press, 1987), 60.

16. See especially James Barton, *Wasteworld 1: Aftermath* (London: Granada, 1983) and *Wasteworld 3: Angels* (London: Granada, 1984); Robert A. Heinlein, *Farnham's Freehold* (New York: Putnam, 1964); Bruce Ariss, *Full Circle* (New York: Avalon, 1963); D. B. Drumm, *Traveler #3: The Stalkers* (New York: Dell, 1984); Howard Waldrop, *Them Bones* (New York: Ace, 1984); and Steve Wilson, *The Lost Traveller* (London: Macmillan, 1976). Andrew MacDonald's novel *The Turner Diaries* (Washington, D.C.: The National Alliance, 1978), in which blacks revert to cannibalism, became an influential text for the neo-Nazi group the Order.

17. Philip Wylie, *Tomorrow!* (New York: Rinehart & Company, 1954), 295; Dean MacCannell, "Baltimore in the Morning . . . After: On the Forms of Post-Nuclear Leadership," *Diacritics* 14.3 (1984): 33–46; Martha A. Bartter, "Nuclear Holocaust as Urban Renewal," *Science-Fiction Studies* 13 (1986): 148–158.

18. For more general studies of black writers and intellectuals in relation to the Cold War, see Mark Solomon, "Black Critics of Colonialism and the Cold War," *Cold War Critics: Alternatives to American Foreign Policy in the Truman Years*, ed. Thomas G. Paterson (Chicago: Quadrangle, 1971), 205–239; and Manning Marable, *Race, Reform, and Rebellion: The Second Reconstruction in Black America, 1945–1982* (Jackson: University Press of Mississippi, 1984), especially pp. 12–41.

19. Alice Childress, *Like One of the Family: Conversations from a Domestic's Life* (Brooklyn: Independence, 1956), 160–161, 151–153.

20. Hughes, *Simple Stakes a Claim,* 83.

21. Hughes, *Simple Stakes a Claim,* 126–130; *Simple Speaks His Mind* (New York: Simon and Schuster, 1950), 130–132; *Simple Stakes a Claim,* 143–146, 85; and *Simple's Uncle Sam,* 98–102.

22. Hughes, *Simple Stakes a Claim,* 26–27.

23. Hughes, *Simple's Uncle Sam,* 53.

24. Martin Bauml Duberman, *Paul Robeson* (New York: Knopf, 1988), 389; Eric Bentley, *Thirty Years of Treason: Excerpts from Hearings before the House Committee on Un-American Activities, 1938–1968* (New York: Viking, 1971), 778–779.

25. W. E. B. Du Bois, "I Speak for Peace" (New York: Peace Information Center, 1950; reprint, *Pamphlets and Leaflets by W. E. B. Du Bois,* ed. Herbert Aptheker [White Plains, N.Y.: Kraus-Thomson, 1986]), 290.

26. W. E. B. Du Bois, "I Take My Stand for Peace" (*Masses & Mainstream* 4, no. 4 [April 1951]: 10–16; reprint, *Pamphlets and Leaflets by W. E. B. Du Bois,* ed. Herbert Aptheker [White Plains, N.Y.: Kraus-Thomson, 1986]), 295–296; "Peace Is Dangerous" (New York: National Guardian, 1951; reprint, *Pamphlets and Leaflets by W. E. B. Du Bois,* ed. Herbert Aptheker (White Plains, N.Y.: Kraus-Thomson, 1986), 303; "Race Relations in the United States: 1917–1947" (*Phylon* 9, no. 3 [1948]: 234–247; reprint, *Writing by W. E. B. Du Bois in Periodicals Edited by Others,* vol. 4, ed. Herbert Aptheker [Millwood, N.Y.: Kraus-Thomson, 1982]), 73; "A Program of Emancipation for Colonial Peoples" (Merze Tate, ed., *Trust and Non-Self Governing Territories: Papers and Proceedings of the Tenth Annual Conference of the Division of the Graduate School Howard University,* April 8–9, 1947 [Washington, D.C.: Howard University Studies in the Social Sciences, vol. 6, no. 1, 96–104]; reprint, *Writings by W. E. B. Du Bois in Non-Periodical Literature Edited by Others,* ed. Herbert Aptheker [Millwood, N.Y.: Kraus-Thomson, 1982]), 263; "America and World Peace" (*New World Review,* November 1952: 49–52; reprint, *Writing by W. E. B. Du Bois in Periodicals Edited by Others,* vol. 4, ed. Herbert Aptheker [Millwood, NY: Kraus-Thomson, 1982]), 180–183.

27. For Cleaver's homage to Du Bois, see especially "Lazarus, Come Forth," "Rallying Round the Flag," "The Black Man's Stake in Vietnam," and "Domestic Law and International Order," all of which are collected in *Soul on Ice* (New York: Delta, 1968). In the *Autobiography,* Malcolm X observes that "the white man's working intelligence is hobbled" when dealing with nonwhites, committing "the most incredible spontaneous emotional acts." After dropping the A-bomb on Hiroshima and Nagasaki, he asks, "can the white man be so naive as to think the clear import of this *ever* will be lost upon the non-white two-thirds of the earth's population?" He observes that the same government that dropped the bomb had already herded Japanese-Americans into concentration camps while German-Americans remained free (268). See also Paul Virilio and Sylvère Lotringer, *Pure War,* trans. Mark Polizzotti (New York: Semiotext(e), 1983); Edward Said, *Orientalism* (1978; New York: Vintage, 1979), and "Representing the Colonized: Anthropology's Interlocutors," *Critical Inquiry* 15 (1989): 205–225; Michael Paul Rogin, "Make My Day!": Spectacle as Amnesia in Imperial Politics," *Representations* 29.1 (1990): 99–123; Gayatri Chakravorty Spivak, "Poststructuralism, Marginality, Postcoloniality and Value," *Literary Theory Today,* ed. Peter Collier and Helga Geyer-Ryan (Ithaca, N.Y.: Cornell University Press, 1990), 219–244; Joseph Gerson, ed., *The Deadly Connection: Nuclear War and U.S. Intervention* (Philadelphia: New Society Publishers, 1986); Joseph Gerson and Bruce Birchard, *The Sun Never Sets . . . : Confronting the Network of Foreign U.S. Military Bases* (Boston: South End Press, 1991).

28. Du Bois, "I Take My Stand," 295.

29. Ann Petry, *Country Place* (Boston: Houghton, 1947), 186; Ralph Ellison, *Invisible Man* (1952; reprint, New York: Vintage, 1972); Norman Mailer, "The White Negro: Superficial Reflections on the Hipster," *Dissent* 4.3 (1957): 276–293, reprinted in *Advertisements for Myself* (New York: Putnam's, 1959), 337–358, *The Deer Park* (New York: Perigee, 1955), *An American Dream* (New York: Dell, 1965); Lorraine Hansberry, *A Raisin in the Sun* (1959; New York: Signet, 1968), 65–66.

30. Ishmael Reed, "The Writer as Seer," *Black World* 23.8 (1974): 22.

31. Ishmael Reed, *Mumbo Jumbo* (1972; reprint, New York: Macmillan, 1989), 4, 136. All further references are parenthetical.

32. Henry Louis Gates Jr., *The Signifying Monkey: A Theory of Afro-American Literary Criticism* (New York: Oxford University Press, 1988), 225.

33. Set in Reagan's America of the 1980s — where it "feels good to be a white man again" (18) — and projecting into the future, *The Terrible Twos* (New York: St. Martins, 1982) likewise features a conspiratorial (and paranoid) band of insiders who see "the vital people" about to be overrun by "surplus people, reproducing like mink." The vital people have "[run] out of suburbs and high-rise buildings to flee to," and begin constructing deep-sea bubbles and space stations (54–56). To make matters worse, Nigeria and Uganda have developed their own nuclear weapons, and the vital people begin to circulate rumors about how the Africans "would fling them about every Saturday night after they got drunk on palm wine" (141). This is where Operation Two Birds comes in: U.S. missiles are to be launched on the major cities of America, exterminating the "surplus people" who live there; the attack will then be blamed on a hostile African country, "thereby providing a rationale for devastating that power, and the surplus people and the UDC's too. Operation Two Birds!" (133–134). Here is a more sweeping rendition of Berbelang's fears about a white hand pushing the nuclear button — even America's space program is implicated as the means by which executives of multinational cartels will "sit out the holocaust on another planet" (134). The novel is also noteworthy for a Dante-esque visit with Harry Truman, who is in hell for the bombing of Hiroshima.

34. Edward Teller, Philip Morrison, Ernest Lawrence, Gen. Thomas Farrell, and Joseph O. Hirschfelder all employed the language of solar splendor in recounting the first atomic explosions (Richard Rhodes, *The Making of the Atomic Bomb* [New York: Simon and Schuster, 1986], 672–673). We should also recognize the contributions of William Laurence, a science correspondent for the *New York Times* who was the only reporter allowed access to the top-secret Manhattan Project. Laurence told his editor to save front-page space for the forthcoming story, which was described as "a sort of Second Coming of Christ yarn" (Laurence, *Men and Atoms: The Discovery, the Uses, and the Future of Atomic Energy* [New York: Simon and Schuster, 1959], 112). In his narrative of the Trinity explosion, we find a tremendous effort to delineate the bomb's elemental power, and the images he calls upon are significant:

> It was a sunrise such as the world had never seen, a great green super-sun climbing in a fraction of a second to a height of more than eight thousand feet, rising ever higher until it touched the clouds, lighting up earth and sky all around with a dazzling luminosity. . . . For a fleeting instant the color was unearthly green, such as one sees only in the corona of the sun during a total eclipse. It was as though the earth had opened and the skies had split. One felt

as though one were present at the moment of creation when God said: "Let there be light." (Laurence, *Dawn Over Zero: The Story of the Atomic Bomb* [New York: Knopf, 1946], 10–11)

More than any other writer of the immediate postwar period, Laurence had time to formulate a mythology of the atomic bomb: not only did he have what amounts to a one-year head start, but relatively free access to the Manhattan scientists. Perhaps because a coherent narrative already emanated from official circles, the Hiroshima explosion and subsequent discourse about atomic technology were described in similar terms.

35. Arthur Holly Compton, *Atomic Quest* (Oxford: Oxford University Press, 1956); Carol Cohn, "Sex and Death in the Rational World of Defense Intellectuals," *Signs* 12.4 (1987): 702.

36. Lewis Mumford, *The Myth of the Machine*, vol. 1 (New York: Harcourt Brace Jovanovich, 1967), 188.

37. Arthur M. Schlesinger Jr., *The Vital Center: The Politics of Freedom* (Boston: Houghton Mifflin, 1949); Lilienthal quoted in Daniel Lang, "The Center of Reality," *From Hiroshima to the Moon* (1948; reprint, New York: Dell, 1961), 108.

38. Pynchon, who refers his readers to *Mumbo Jumbo*, likewise creates numerous proleptic glimpses of the bomb before it is formally deployed in Hiroshima, including one of the "famous Missouri Mason Harry Truman" who, by virtue of death in office, sits "with his control-finger poised right on Miss Enola Gay's atomic clit, making ready to tickle 100,000 little yellow folks into what will come down as a fine vapor-deposit of fat-cracklings." Later, their ashes produce striking new sunsets that literally "modulate" the postwar light of day. Pynchon intimates that a Caucasian fantasy of total control has propelled the union of German rocket and American bomb, creating a preemptive weapon that "can penetrate, from the sky, at any given point. Nowhere is safe" (Thomas Pynchon, *Gravity's Rainbow* [New York: Viking, 1973], 588, 642, 728). Coover's deified Uncle Sam makes a spectacular appearance "back from the ridge where the West commences: Yucca Flat, Nevada! — and bearing in his lean gnarled hands a new birth of freedom, a white-hot kernel of manifest destiny: a spark from the sacred flame!" His miraculous advent above Times Square taking the form of an atomic fireball, Uncle Sam claims to "chant the new empire," but within the context of Coover's novel he is a "wily Yankee Peddler" who simply reinvents the same old doctrine of "*uplift and civvylize*" for the Cold War (Robert Coover, *The Public Burning* [New York: Viking, 1977], 493, 6, 494–495). Burroughs's *Nova* trilogy has yet to be read as a political satire of the Cold War, but this horrific description of the insect planet Minraud is suggestive: "Controller of the Crab Nebula on a slag heap of smouldering metal under the white hot sky channels all his pain into control thinking — He is protected by heat and crab guards and the brains armed now with The Blazing Photo from Hiroshima and Nagasaki — The brains under his control are encased in a vast structure of steel and crystal spinning thought patterns that control whole galaxies thousand years ahead on the chessboard of virus screens and juxtaposition formulae." At the exact center of the city, where the American melting pot is reconceptualized as ground zero, "vast communal immersion tanks melt whole peoples into one concentrate — It's more democratic that way you see?" (William S. Burroughs, *Nova Express* [1964; New York: Grove, 1965], 67, 132).

39. Jacques Derrida, "The Ends of Man," *Margins of Philosophy*, trans. Alan Bass (1972: Chicago: University of Chicago Press, 1982), 135, 114–116, 125–126.

40. Jacques Derrida, "White Mythology: Metaphor in the Text of Philosophy," *Margins of Philosophy,* trans. Alan Bass (1971; Chicago: University Press, 1982), 213, 210, 230–245; "Plato's Pharmacy," *Dissemination,* trans. Barbara Johnson (1968; Chicago: University of Chicago Press, 1981), 82–83.

41. See Peter Schwenger for a similar discussion of attempts to locate epistemological presence around a point that is characterized by its utter absence. Using Russell Hoban's postholocaust novel *Riddley Walker* as his exemplary text, Schwenger parallels the protagonist's failure to locate ground zero of the "1 Big 1" that exploded somewhere near Canterbury. Instead, Schwenger argues that Riddley's journey, both physical and psychic, consists of a "circle [that] does not originate in a governing center but in a line that is continuously deflected from itself." Any beginning or center can only be the result of "inferring an origin from signs viewed as traces" (Schwenger, "Circling Ground Zero," *PMLA* 106 [1991]: 258, 254).

42. Laurence, *Dawn Over Zero,* 189.

43. Paule Marshall, *The Chosen Place, the Timeless People* (New York: Harcourt, 1969); Leslie Marmon Silko, *Ceremony* (1977; New York: Penguin, 1989); Toni Cade Bambara, *The Salt Eaters* (New York: Random House, 1980). All references to these texts are parenthetical.

44. George Bush, *Public Papers of the Presidents of the United States: 1990,* vol. 2 (Washington, D.C.: GPO, 1991), 16.

45. Coover, *The Public Burning,* 494.

46. David Albright and Mark Hibbs offer an intriguing account about how the Bush administration used fears of an Iraqi bomb to galvanize support for Operation Desert Shield/Storm. A CBS/*New York Times* poll on November 20, 1990, revealed "that a majority of Americans would not go to war in the Gulf to protect access to Middle East oil, but would support a military effort to prevent Iraq from getting the bomb" (Albright and Hibbs, "Hyping the Iraqi Bomb," *Bulletin of the Atomic Scientists* [March 1991]: 27). Two days later, Bush told troops stationed in the Gulf that Iraq might be only months away from nuclear weapons, a theme that dramatically changed the tone of subsequent public debate and press coverage. Albright and Hibbs conclude, even after later revelations about Iraq's top-secret uranium enrichment program, that estimates of nuclear capability were consistently inflated or even willfully misleading in order to justify certain political objectives in the Middle East (Albright and Hibbs, "Iraq's Nuclear Hide-and-Seek," *Bulletin of the Atomic Scientists* [September 1991]: 14–23).

47. Robert Jay Lifton, *The Broken Connection: On Death and the Continuity of Life* (1979; New York: Basic Books, 1983), 380.

48. The illustration, by Greta Kempton, appears in "The Truman Memoirs, Part V: 'The Greatest Thing in History,' " *Life,* October 24, 1955: 105.

49. Walton Hannah, *Darkness Visible: A Christian Appraisal of Freemasonry* (1952; reprint, Devon: Augustine, 1984), 184.

50. William Joseph Whalen, *Christianity and American Freemasonry* (Milwaukee, Wis.: Bruce, 1958), 29.

Representing Apocalypse: Sexual Politics and the Violence of Revelation

Mary Wilson Carpenter

The End drove up to their doorstep in a tank, spitting gas, fulfilling prophecies. *And if anyone wants to harm them,* says the Book of Revelation, *fire pours from their mouth and consumes their foes.*

Buzzards circled overhead and the wind blew hard on the day the Branch Davidians died. Before the sun came up, state troopers went door to door to the houses near the compound, telling people to stay inside, there might be some noise. Over their loudspeakers, the tired negotiators called one last time for David Koresh and his followers to surrender peacefully. Then they got on the phone and told him exactly where the tear gas was coming, so he could move the children away. The phone came sailing out the front door. *They will make war on the Lamb, and the Lamb will conquer them.*

The pounding began a few minutes after 6 a.m., when an armored combat engineer vehicle started prodding a corner of the building. Shots rang out from the windows the moment agents began pumping in tear gas. A second CEV joined in, buckling walls, breaking windows, nudging, nudging, as though moving the building would move those inside. "This is not an assault!" agent Byron Sage cried over the loudspeakers. "Do not shoot. We are not entering your compound." Ambulances waited a mile back; the local hospital, Hillcrest Baptist Medical Center, was on alert. But no one was supposed to get hurt. "You are responsible for your own actions," agents called out. "Come out now and you will not be harmed." *Do not fear what you are about to suffer . . . Be faithful unto death, and I will give you the crown of life.*[1]

Nancy Gibbs's May 3, 1993, *Time* magazine account of the Branch Davidians' fiery end writes that "end" intertextually with the words of the book thought to have inspired the cult members' apparently unprotesting acceptance of a violent death: the last book of the Christian Bible, the Book of Revelation. The *Time* cover pictures the cult leader David Koresh, his face tilted upward in a smile of ecstasy, flames roaring up behind him, the words of the sacred text emblazoned beneath him: " 'His name was Death, and Hell followed with him.' Revelation 6.8." Gibbs's narrative compellingly posits a direct link between the violent words of the apocalyptic text and the violent death of the apocalyptic sect. She writes the history of the cult members' death as if informed by a Foucaultian, academic notion of "history": history is the text, the text is history.

Yet the news media today more typically assumes a radical separation between the general public fascination with apocalyptics and a supposedly disinterested and secularized academic discourse. Peter Steinfels, writing in the *New York Times* eight days before Gibbs's *Time* account, had commented that "the power of the book, also known as The Apocalypse and The Revelation of John the Divine, is obvious . . . millions of American Christians are preoccupied with deciphering Revelation, often seeking clues in books and broadcasts so numerous that they comprise an industry of apocalypse." He noted that Hal Lindsey's 1970 book, *The Late Great Planet Earth,* a fundamentalist Christian interpretation of the prophecies in Revelation and other biblical texts, had sold 28 million copies from 1970 to 1990. (It was, in fact, the single best-selling nonfiction work of the entire decade of the 1970s.) "But," Steinfels continued, "where interpreting apocalyptic texts like Revelation once occupied the best minds of an era — St. Augustine, John Milton, Isaac Newton and Jonathan Edwards, among others — today it flourishes on a popular level distant from academic life or cultural centers like New York and Washington."[2]

Steinfels's statement represents a popular misconception about the separation between "prophecy" and the study of "secular" literature. From about the mid-sixties to the mid-eighties, or the same period in which he noted the remarkable florescence of popular apocalyptics, academic scholars and critics were also turning out a flood of writings on the Book of Revelation, on "apocalyptic," and on "prophecy" and "apocalypse" in literature. Bernard McGinn commented in his essay in the 1984 collection edited by C. A. Patrides and Joseph Wittreich, *The Apocalypse in English Renaissance Thought and Literature,* that "the volume of materials published on Jewish and early Christian apocalypticism over the past twenty years has been impressive." These materials, he noted, fell within the purview of many disciplines, including "Biblical studies, Judaica, Patristics, the History of Religions, to name just the major areas."[3] McGinn didn't include literary studies, although the collection in which he made his observation had been occasioned by the tide of interest in the "prophetic" or "apocalyptic" tradition in literature. Lindsey's 1970 mass-market paperback, for example, was bracketed by two academic best-sellers in the field of what might be called literary apocalyptics: Frank Kermode's *The Sense of an Ending* (1967) and M. H. Abrams's *Natural Supernaturalism* (1971).[4] Joseph Wittreich concludes *The Apocalypse in English Renaissance Thought and Literature* with a detailed bibliography of writings on and about Apocalypse, including a final section

titled "Literature as prophecy, especially literature and the Book of Revelation" (369–440). Although the last-named section includes works from
early in the twentieth century, the majority of the titles appeared in the
1960s and 1970s. Wittreich's bibliography documents a flourishing academic "industry of apocalypse" that began growing in the early sixties,
was particularly prolific in the seventies, and only began to recede during
the eighties, when academic interest in issues of gender, sexuality, and
race became increasingly prominent.

Scholars appear to have been unconscious of the continuities between
literary apocalyptics and contemporary popular apocalypticism. Even in
his essay "Apocalypse: Theme and Variations," which concludes *The Apocalypse* collection, Abrams makes no connection to late twentieth-century
manifestations of popular apocalypticism in American society.[5] Yet Ronald Reagan's political rhetoric was sufficiently infused by allusions to Revelation that a group of Christian and Jewish leaders felt it necessary to
condemn his "ideology of nuclear Armageddon" in October 1984.[6] Reagan's rhetoric, in fact, could have been written intertextually with Lindsey's book, which articulates a program of imperialist, militarist, and
profoundly racist policy as prophesied in the visions of Revelation. Apocalypticism was not distant from the centers of academic and cultural
power in the 1980s — it was not even at the doorstep, it was inside the
compound.

What makes the reading of these "representations of apocalypse,"
whether academic or nonacademic, urgent is the question of their link
with violence. The Branch Davidians' reading of Revelation appears to
have inclined them to anticipate, and perhaps to provoke, a violent
death, and scholars have demonstrated the historical association of apocalyptic sects with violence of varying kinds and degrees.[7] The 1960s–80s'
"industry" of literary apocalyptics emphasized the transformation of the
militaristic vision of apocalypse in Revelation into an "apocalypse of the
imagination," an aestheticization of apocalypse that, as Steven Goldsmith
has argued, constitutes a motivated erasure of the history and politics of
millenarianism, and therefore cannot be exonerated of complicity in the
politics of representing apocalypse.[8]

Nevertheless, for some of the 1960s–80s writers of literary apocalyptics,
I will argue, the "apocalypse of the imagination" was held to underwrite a
program of political change and cultural reform — an oppositional politics — while for others it represented an investment in lack of change,
stability, and containment, a politics of the status quo. The literary apocalyptics of this period, in other words, spanned the spectrum of male
homosocial relations from a "patriarchal apocalyptic" invested in male
supremacy and the maintenance of gender hierarchy to an antipatriarchal and countercultural apocalyptic allied with feminism that I shall

call a "gay apocalyptic." Meanwhile, feminist literary scholars often appropriated the language of apocalypse, but in a rhetoric that explicitly underwrote a program of change and reform in *gender* politics. And during the same period (1960s–80s), studies of the Book of Revelation by feminist theological scholars began to acknowledge and try to explain the text's obsession with violence.

Yet even these feminist theological readers of Revelation do not posit any crucial link between the violence of the book and its sexual politics. I will argue that Revelation's violence is a representation of a continuing power dynamic of gender and sexuality in Western culture, or as Michel Foucault puts it, of "the way in which sex is 'put into discourse.'" The important questions to ask about both the Book of Revelation and its representations by late twentieth-century readers are Foucault's questions about the discursively constructed history of sexuality: "What were the effects of power generated by what was said? What are the links between these discourses, these effects of power, and the pleasures that were invested by them? What knowledge (*savoir*) was formed as a result of this linkage?."[9] Or, in Judith Butler's formulation, "Sexuality is an historically specific organization of *power,* discourse, bodies and affectivity."[10] The text of Revelation constructs such a historically specific organization of sexuality as power, discourse, bodies, and affectivity. What even recent twentieth-century "representations of apocalypse" have consistently overlooked is that the violence of Revelation is *male* violence, and that it is a violence *between* men and *to* women. The Book of Revelation does not represent violence between women, as it does not represent bonds between women, nor violence by women to men. The violence of Revelation is a gendered violence that puts a certain kind of sexual politics into discourse and effects a certain kind of sexual power.

In addition, I want to emphasize that this is a text that, as Eve Kosofsky Sedgwick has demonstrated in the case of certain Gothic novels, makes instrumental to power the male homosocial bond that is maintained by culture.[11] The author of Revelation may have wanted to encourage Christians who faced persecution, though biblical scholars have pointed out the dubiety of this belief, but the text of Revelation offers more than faith and hope — it offers access to power based on the manipulation of a cultural system of gender and sexuality.[12] The words of Revelation transfer to the female body the horror of sexuality, consuming that body both by eating and by fire. But the words of Revelation also write a paranoia about the persecution and pursuit of males by another male (or males): the text may be read as an early Christian version of what Sedgwick calls "the Gothic paranoid."

To problematize the links between gender, sexuality, and power in Revelation is also to problematize the links between readers of Revelation and their historically specific relations to power. After first reading the text of Revelation in a way that attempts to expose the sexual politics traditionally suppressed by biblical and literary exegetes, I will then demonstrate how the 1960s–80s' genre of "literary apocalyptics" constructed a discourse "between men" that represents apocalypse both as a "patriarchal apocalyptic" and as a "gay apocalyptic." Finally I will examine certain feminist attempts at apocalyptics, both in this century and in the nineteenth, to pose the question as to whether a "feminist apocalyptic" may be a textual/sexual impossibility given not only the existence but the canonized status of the Book of Revelation in our Western, Christianized culture. If Revelation puts sex into discourse as gynephobia and homophobia, then sexual and gendered violence may be integral to "apocalypse" as we know it: the sexual politics of "apocalypse" may be unable to dispense with violence because that violence — a *gendered* violence — may be what is at stake in the vision of apocalyptic power.

A Reading of the Book of Revelation

In her extensively researched and carefully argued study of Revelation, *Crisis and Catharsis: The Power of the Apocalypse* (1984), Adela Yarbro Collins solemnly concludes:

> The movement from a precritical to a critical reading of the Apocalypse involves the experience of its vision as a broken myth. The critical reader can no longer simply live and move and have one's being within the "world" of the text. A critical reading also leads to an awareness of how the text is flawed by the darker side of the author's human nature, which we, like all the readers, share.[13]

Not only is power a major issue in Revelation but "Christ as lamb is overshadowed by Christ as judge and warrior" (173). Finally, Yarbro Collins acknowledges, the very "symbols" of Revelation — the dragon, the beasts, and the harlot — suggest that "there are trends, social structures, ideas, and institutional processes which are human creations, but which get out of human control and turn against their creator, like a Frankenstein monster" (173). Collins exposes her own experience of loss in the course of her movement from a "precritical" to a "critical" reading of Revelation: what was once a "vision" has become a "broken myth"; what were once literary "symbols" have taken on a monstrous corporeality. The aesthetically pleasing and consoling conception of Revelation as vision of a meaningful End has disintegrated into an abortive assortment of "violent images, symbols, and narratives" from which she labors to extract some "constructive way of dealing with these feelings" (173).

Yarbro Collins's critical progress maps the opposite of the one Goldsmith traces out in the "tradition" of literary readings of Revelation.

Starting with the blunt observation that, "the Book of Revelation is a violent book," Goldsmith ponders the question, "under what extraordinary circumstances, then, might a reader come to see the apocalyptic text as the very antithesis of impending, violent change, indeed, even as a model of order, harmony, stability?" Ultimately, Goldsmith indicts the politics of literary analysis itself: "the emergence, or perhaps I should say creation, of Revelation as an object of formal literary analysis occurs in part as a concerted effort to occlude the book's relation to violence — that is, both its own graphic depiction of acts of violence and its long historical association with violent, revolutionary movements." Yet finally Goldsmith concludes his stunning analysis of the "disarming" of Apocalypse from the Reformation to present-day criticism with the comment that Revelation "will not go gently into that good night of aesthetic harmony. There remains the thorny problem with which the chapter began, the graphic and nearly continuous textual violence that even the most mesmerizing formalist criticism cannot make go away."[14]

The irony here is that something *has* made the violence of Revelation go away. One might better ask the question suggested by Yarbro Collins's unhappy conclusions: under what circumstances does a reader become able to "see," to attend to, to *read* the "palpable, visceral violence" of Revelation?[15] If even "the most mesmerizing formalist criticism" cannot make that violence go away, why has it been so difficult to stage an encounter with it? Why, in particular, has it been so difficult to attend to the most blatantly gendered aspect of that violence, the detailed account of the physical destruction and consumption of the Whore of Babylon? Even Yarbro Collins, for example, simply dispenses with the Whore as a "traditional" prophetic image for Rome.[16] Elisabeth Schüssler Fiorenza, despite her recognition that power is the main concern and kingship the main motif of Revelation, very temperately concludes that because "we have become conscious of androcentric language," we can "detect" that Revelation encourages the reader "to perceive women in terms of good or evil, pure or impure, heavenly or destructive, helpless or powerful, bride or temptress, wife or whore."[17]

While Goldsmith's analysis tends to unmask those strategies by which exegetes and literary critics alike have colluded with institutional power, Yarbro Collins's difficult struggle from precritical to critical reading suggests the collusion of the *text* with institutional power. To exploit a Foucaultian perspective on this issue, we should ask not what cause or origin preceded the text, but what effects of power were generated by it, what pleasures invested by it, what knowledges formed by it? Instead of assuming that, because Revelation constitutes its readers as anticipating persecution, "persecution" must have preceded the writing of the text, the critical reader of both text and institution examines the effects generated by the text's constitution of the reader's subjectivity as "paranoid." Such an examination suggests that the "pleasure" invested by the interpellation of a paranoid (male) subjectivity is the transfer of that anxiety to the body of the Other — the female body — and the climactic gratification of spectacularizing the destruction of that body. The "knowledge" formed by such a narrative is the always uncertain and vulnerable nature of male sexuality, its "blackmailability" and, by contrast, female sexuality as its binary opposition, as "known" and manipulable sexuality, available for consumption either as "madonna" or "whore."

Sedgwick develops the theory of male "blackmailability" in relation to the "molly houses" or male brothels in eighteenth-century England, on the one hand, and the emergence of the Gothic novel on the other. She postulates that the English state's intermittent pogroms on the molly houses, interspersed with periods of tolerance, produced a far more powerful instrument of social control than either total destruction or complete tolerance could have. At the same time the Gothic novel could exploit the uncertainty of distinguishing male homosocial from male homoerotic bonds as the narrative of paranoia, or the pursuit and persecution of a male by another male. The effect produced by such a "Gothic paranoid" is the *blackmailability* of all men in a society dependent on male homosocial bonds.[18]

Sedgwick carefully situates her analysis of the construction of "homophobic thematics" in the literature of a certain historical period and national culture, and it is crucial to remember that the Book of Revelation was not written and read in eighteenth-century England but in first-century C.E. Mediterranean culture. The structures of gender, sexuality, and power are presumed not to be ahistorical but contingent on local effects and therefore variable. But biblical scholarship has long continued in the opposite error, assuming that the structures of gender and sexuality so important in our cultural texts were of little significance in the construction of textual power in the first century, whereas religious persecution and the fear of imperial power were of major significance.[19] Yarbro Collins, however, demonstrates that the evidence for persecution of Christians under the Roman emperor Domitian is very slight and suggests instead that "a more plausible view of its [Revelation's] function is that it was written to awaken and intensify Christian exclusiveness, particularly vis-a-vis the imperial cult."[20] Elisabeth Schüssler Fiorenza discusses the process of structural consolidation in the early Christian community in the second half of the first century C.E. and asks "whether it is legitimate to speak of Christianity in the singular or whether we have to speak of Christianities or Christian communities." Mentioning especially the manner in which the author of Revelation "abuses" the prophetess he names Jezebel, she suggests that "her authority seems to have at least equaled that of John whom, in turn, she might have perceived as a false prophet."[21] Both Yarbro Collins and Fiorenza, then, suggest that the apocalyptic text might have promoted political interests *within* the Christian movement to at least as great an extent as serving to strengthen Christians against the probably unlikely prospect of imperial religious persecution. The strongest motive for constituting the reader's subjectivity as paranoid might simply be that some members' fear of "persecution" could be mobilized in the interests of other members of the group.

Sedgwick's criteria for the Gothic texts she identifies as sites for the construction of male homosexual panic as well as homoerotic desire name those narrative fictions that hold out the allure of "secret truths," that hint of all kinds of sinfulness, abominations, and violence, and that construct a plot of paranoia, usually about a male "who not only is persecuted by, but considers himself transparent to and often under the compulsion of, another male."[22] It is remarkable how completely the epistolary introduction to Revelation's visions of destruction conforms to these criteria for the "Gothic paranoid."

Speaking through the magnificent and fear-inspiring figure of the "Son of man" — the first of several such figures of great male power and beauty in the text — John writes that though he knows the work, labor, and patience of the church of Ephesus, "Nevertheless I have somewhat against thee because thou hast left thy first love" (2:4).[23] This menacing but mysterious message appears to refer in coded terms to some unspecified heresy. But, the message continues, "this thou hast, that thou hatest the deeds of the Nicolaitans, which I also hate" (2:6). The Ephesians are praised for their "correct" political hatred of a particular faction. With the phrase, "He that hath an ear, let him hear . . . " (2:7), the speaker emphasizes a context of secrecy and partisanship. Some will know what is meant by leaving "thy first love" — and some will not.

To the church of Smyrna, the Son of man states ominously, "I know the blasphemy of them which say they are Jews, and are not, but are the synagogue of Satan" (2:9). The suggestion that Satan might be "inside" as well as "outside" is made even more confusingly in the message to Pergamos: "I know thy works, and where thou dwellest, even where Satan's seat is: and thou holdest fast my name, and hast not denied my faith, even in those days wherein Antipas was my faithful martyr, who was slain among you, where Satan dwelleth" (2:13). Satan appears to be everywhere here, including in the very midst of the faithful. Continuing that "I have a few things against thee," the text indicts Pergamos for holding to the doctrine of Balaam, for eating food sacrificed to idols, for committing fornication, and for holding to the doctrine of the Nicolaitans. If they do not repent, they are warned, "I will come unto thee quickly, and will fight against them with the sword of my mouth" (2:14–

16). But "to him that overcometh will I give to eat of the hidden manna, and will give him a white stone, and in the stone a new name written, which no man knoweth saving he that receiveth it" (2:17). To the compulsion of surveillance and threats is added the incentive of access to secret knowledge: a white stone on which a secret name is written.

The message to the church of Thyatira again begins with "knowledge" of the church's works, charity, service, and faith but continues, "Notwithstanding I have a few things against thee." The "few things" in this church refer to its practice of allowing a woman, "Jezebel, which calleth herself a prophetess," to teach in the community. Jezebel has been given "space" to repent, but since she hasn't she is threatened with violent consequences: "Behold, I will cast her into a bed and them that commit adultery with her into great tribulation, except they repent of their deeds. And I will kill her children with death; and all the churches shall know that I am he which searcheth the reins and hearts . . . " (2:20–23). The text continues, "and he that overcometh . . . to him will I give power over the nations: And he shall rule them with a rod of iron . . . " (2:26–27). The church of Thyatira is thus threatened for its tolerance of a woman preacher, and in return for giving up this egalitarianism is specifically promised the reward of a phallic power over the nations — a power to rule with a "rod of iron."

The epistolary messages emphasize not only constant surveillance and an intimate knowledge of the subject, but the continual uncertainty of exposure and reprisal. To the church in Sardis John writes, "I have not found thy works perfect before God," and that "If therefore thou shalt not watch, I will come on thee as a thief, and thou shalt not know what hour I will come upon thee" (3:2–3). In a message that surmounts all the others for its mystification, the Laodiceans are warned that "I know thy works, that thou art neither cold nor hot: I would thou wert cold or hot. So then because thou art lukewarm, and neither cold nor hot, I will spue thee out of my mouth" (3:15–16). Only Philadelphia is spared the warnings, threats, and reminders of surveillance because, "thou hast a little strength, and hast kept my word, and hast not denied my name" (3:8). But the issue of power is inserted even into this nonthreatening and nonthreatened church: Philadelphia is to be *rewarded* with a gift of power, for those who are of the "synagogue of Satan" will be forced to "come and worship before thy feet" (3:9).

Fiorenza reads the epistolary introduction to Revelation as evidence that the "main objective" of the writer is the "prophetic communication of the revelation . . . to the seven communities in Asia Minor." Resorting to traditional categories of literary analysis, she postulates that Revelation is "a work of visionary rhetoric" that successfully intertwines "poetic and rhetorical elements," and that the writer's aim is "to motivate and encourage Christians in Asia Minor who have experienced harassment and persecution."[24] Fiorenza's interpretation of the writer's "main objective" here overlooks the pervasively constituted paranoia of the introductory letters to the seven churches. Encouragement is entirely secondary to *warnings* that the church members are under constant surveillance, that judgment could come at any moment, and, most frightening of all, that they can never be sure what behavior or which members belong to "Satan."

The introductory epistles are, then, like Gothic texts, replete with "hints" of all kinds of sinfulness, abominations, and violence, with the allure of "secret truths," and with the perpetual constitution of subjectivity as "transparent to and often under the compulsion of, another male."[25] They thus construct an appropriate staging for what Elizabeth Cady Stanton called "visions which make the blood curdle."[26] The catalog of horrifying visions of judgment and vengeance is subsequently introduced: the four horsemen of the Apocalypse, the three woes, the murder of the two witnesses, the threatening of the woman clothed with the sun, the rise of the beast, the pouring out of the seven vials of the wrath of God, the hideous plagues of poisonous blood and "unclean spirits." Suddenly, as if in the midst of these, the terrifying warning reappears: "Behold, I come as a thief. Blessed is he that watcheth, and keepeth his garments, lest he walk naked, and they see his shame" (16:15). The language of the warning explicitly invokes the shame of bodily or sexual exposure: the "thief" is constructed as a voyeur, as one who may "see" that which should not be seen.

Immediately following this warning, the Whore of Babylon with her cup of "abominations and filthiness of her fornication" is incarnated as the textual locus of sexual evil. She rides a great scarlet beast, "full of names of blasphemy," and having many heads and horns. She is arrayed in purple and scarlet, decked with precious stones, and carries a golden cup "full of abominations and filthiness of her fornication" (17:4). Whereas only secret and undisclosed "names" and "marks" have been alluded to previously, the text "spells out" the nature of the Whore's evil on her forehead: "MYSTERY, BABYLON THE GREAT, THE MOTHER OF HARLOTS AND ABOMINATIONS OF THE EARTH" (17:5). She is a drunken woman, a figure of intoxication and fleshly indulgence, drunk with that most prohibited substance in Judaic law—blood.[27] After this creation of the Whore as "spectacle," the text intervenes with mystical speculations about the beast: "the beast that thou sawest was, and is not . . . the beast that was, and is not, and yet is" (17:8). "The mind which hath wisdom" interprets the heads and horns on the beast as mountains and kings who will make war with the Lamb. Then the sexualized body of the Whore is consumed by the "horns" of the beast: "these shall hate the whore, and shall make her desolate and naked, and shall eat her flesh, and burn her with fire" (17:16). The whole of chapter 18 consists of an exultant celebration over the destruction and burning of the Whore. "Babylon" has not only fallen, but has become "the hold of every foul spirit, and a cage of every unclean and hateful bird" (18:2). From her beginning to her end, the Whore is the locus of every bodily perversity, every sexual sin.

My reading of the text deliberately emphasizes the physicality of its metaphorical reference. Biblical scholars have traditionally insisted that the corporeal reference of the language constructing the Whore is "immaterial" because she, like the New Jerusalem, is only a metaphor. Fiorenza explains that "both the oppressive and eschatologically redemptive communities are female because cities were personified as women."[28] Collins describes the Whore as simply "another prominent and striking image" for Rome, and is chiefly concerned about the violence with which "Rome" is attacked.[29] Indeed, the text itself informs the reader that "the woman which thou sawest is that great city, which reigneth over the kings of the earth" (17:18), and that the waters "where the whore sitteth, are peoples, and multitudes, and nations, and tongues" (17:15). The text and its readers perform a maneuver identical to that of the Lacanianist defense of the "phallus" as having no reference to the "penis." The Whore is not a whore but a city and therefore it has no reference to whores or to sexuality constructed as deviant, polluting, and, above all, as female. But as Jane Gallop has remarked, "Of course, the signifier *phallus* functions in distinction from the signifier *penis. But* it *also* always refers to *penis*" (126).[30] The text tells us that the woman is not a woman but a city, that the woman is not what we can "see" that she is — a whore — but something else. But just as the very insistence that the phallus is not a penis but a phallus means that the phallus always has reference to the penis, so the repeated insistence that the Whore of Babylon is not a whore but a city only reinstates our understanding that the "city" is not a city but a whore.[31]

I would suggest that it is the foregrounded and yet denied reference of the Whore to the female body that confers power on the spectacle of the destruction and consumption of "Rome/Babylon." In the narrative of male sexual paranoia, "Woman" must be constructed as that known object to which male anxiety can be transferred, either to secure male power or to be utterly destroyed — and consumed. Marilyn Frye notes that "masculist literature is abundant with indications of male cannibalism, of males deriving essential sustenance from females."[32] The image of the phallic "horns" devouring the naked body of the Whore is surely one of these instances of "male cannibalism." Frye attributes this to male "parasitism" on women, but the text here suggests not so much a metaphorical representation of male social dependency on women as the precariousness of male sexual subjectivity as constituted in the text. In a symbolic universe where a "thief" may come at any moment and expose one's "nakedness," a voracious desire to project, consume, and utterly destroy that "nakedness" has been generated. The burning of the Whore is a necessary apocalyptic climax in Revelation — a required "catharsis" of a carefully constructed anxiety and aggression.

It does not seem coincidental that of the two female figures introduced prior to the Whore, one is a "false prophetess" threatened with silencing and death and the other takes up the classic position of the woman exchanged between men, who serves to facilitate male power and bonding. "Jezebel" functions as the most explicit location in the text of what appears to be an antifeminist backlash. A woman or some women have dared to speak as prophets in the early Christian community or communities, to do what the text obviously perceives as *usurping* a masculine prerogative. The focus here seems to be on silencing Jezebel, on keeping her from preaching or teaching or having verbal or intellectual authority in the church. But she is also constituted in sexual terms, spoken of as fornicating and seducing men to go to bed with her. Nevertheless, the fact that Jezebel "prophesies" has been acknowledged in the text. Only later, in the figure of the Whore, is female power successfully reduced to the single element of sexuality, which can be represented as wholly foul and polluting, and then wholly destroyed.

The woman clothed with the sun has sometimes been read as figuring feminocentric, if not feminist, power.[33] But in Revelation she functions to provide a male heir who is to rule with a "rod of iron," and who is immediately caught up to God, after which the woman retreats to the wilderness and is not heard from again in the text. She serves, then, not as a figure of maternal but *paternal* power. The text silences her more effectively than it does Jezebel by consigning her to a single bodily function, that of facilitating the exchange between men through her reproductive capacity.

The "New Jerusalem," on the other hand, though named and dressed as the bride for the Lamb, is almost wholly lacking in bodily or sexual reference. The New Jerusalem has nothing to say, neither partakes of the marriage supper of the Lamb nor is eaten, and lacks either a maternal or a prostituted body. "She" figures, I believe, only the triumph of a universally constituted subjectivity, one that has successfully subsumed the feminine Other. There is now no difference of gender or sexuality, and there is no anxiety, but it is because the Other has been destroyed, consumed, and incorporated. The knight called "Faithful and True" appears, clothed in "a vesture dipped in blood." The name that, until now, no man knew is written on his "vesture and on his thigh" (19:11–16). The writing on the forehead of the Whore has been superseded by the writing on the thigh of the knight. The supper that is now consummated is not the marriage supper of the Lamb, but the "supper of the great God": an angel summons the fowls to eat the flesh of kings, captains, mighty men, "and the flesh of all men, both free and bond, both small and great" (19:17–18). The way is now cleared for the descent of the New Jerusalem, since the Whore has been destroyed, and in the wake of her destruction, all deviant male flesh can also be consumed. Violence is a necessary part of the apocalyptic vision, for without it some "difference" may creep in, may already have crept in, like a thief in the night, exposing that most private "shame."

Apocalyptics of the Closet

The reading I have offered of the Book of Revelation represents this first-century text as an instance of the "Gothic paranoid": the text effects its power, my reading suggests, by the exploitation of male sexual anxiety and the expurgation of that anxiety through its location in the body of the sexual Other, which is then exultantly destroyed and consumed. In this reading, the sexual politics of the Book of Revelation itself are not theorized as dependent on the "now chronic modern crisis of homo/ heterosexual definition," which, Sedgwick argues in her *Epistemology of the Closet,*

has affected our culture through its ineffaceable marking particularly of the categories secrecy/disclosure, knowledge/ignorance, private/public, masculine/feminine, majority/minority, innocence/initiation, natural/artificial, new/old, discipline/terrorism, canonic/noncanonic, wholeness/decadence, urbane/provincial, domestic/foreign, health/illness, same/different, active/passive, in/out, cognition/paranoia, art/kitsch, utopia/apocalypse, sincerity/sentimentality, and voluntarity/addiction.

But I will propose that the literary apocalyptics of the 1960s–80s constitute one of those discursive sites "for the contestation of meaning in twentieth-century Western culture," which Sedgwick argues are "consequentially and quite indelibly marked with the historical specificity of homosocial/homosexual definition, notably but not exclusively male, from around the turn of the century."[34] This chronologically "postmodern" (but not poststructuralist) genre of literary apocalyptics may be characterized as an apocalyptic of the closet, an apocalyptic intensely invested in some of the binarisms listed first by Sedgwick — secrecy/disclosure, knowledge/ignorance, private/public, and masculine/feminine.[35]

In this critical production of the "open secret" of apocalypse, we post-Stonewall readers may trace not only the ineffaceable though "invisible" markings of the crisis of homo/heterosexual definition but the emergence of a gay apocalyptic.[36] The pervasive twentieth-century cultural anxiety of marking the line between homosexual and heterosexual predictably fuels heterosexist readings of the "poet-prophets" and of their representations of "Apocalypse." In these patriarchal apocalyptics, "Apocalypse" not only valorizes male divinity but is secured through the subordination or incorporation of the feminine, demonstrating a vested interest in maintaining the gender status quo. These apocalyptics also manifest a pervasive concern with the issues of secrecy/disclosure, knowledge/ignorance, private/public, always insisting on the "openness" of "prophecy" — by which is meant the denial of any occluded or obscure meaning — while at the same time underlining the singularity of its authority, or restriction to the individual prophet.

But the events of the revolutionary sixties also gave rise to an oppositional apocalyptic: readings of Revelation that valorize a line of prophets linked in a common opposition to "culture," and that celebrate apocalyptic vision as a rapturous opening of the seals of prophecy or the doors of perception, a longed-for "coming out." In this "gay apocalyptic," representations of Revelation take on the structure of a visionary "coming-out" narrative, a prophecy of something to be revealed at the end of History but not *in* history. Here the emphasis lies on the "secrecy" side of the binary, on the need for specialized knowledge to "release" the prophet's vision, but at the same time on locating the vision in a more public, democratic arena — in the *line* of prophets, the *pair* of witnesses, the *community* of poets.

Although Northrop Frye's book on William Blake, *Fearful Symmetry*, was first published in 1947, I shall begin my discussion of the sexual politics of the "patriarchal apocalyptic" with this work rather than the later *Anatomy of Criticism* (1957), not only because Frye provides explicit commentary on the Book of Revelation in *Fearful Symmetry* but because so many of the writers of the literary apocalyptics of the sixties and seventies look back to this work as seminal to their own.[37] Moreover, in his preface to the 1969 re-edition of the work, Frye relates it directly to the 1960s:

I wrote *Fearful Symmetry* during the Second World War, and hideous as that time was, it provided some parallels with Blake's time which were useful for understanding Blake's attitude to the world. Today, now that reactionary and radical forces alike are once more in the grip of the nihilistic psychosis that Blake described so powerfully in *Jerusalem*, one of the most hopeful signs is the immensely increased sense of the urgency and immediacy of what Blake had to say.[38]

Dated March 1969, Toronto, Canada, this preface clearly suggests that Frye felt what he had to say in his World War II work was even more "immediate" in the days of antiwar protests, the U.S. civil rights movement for blacks, and the North American feminist movement.

In *Fearful Symmetry,* Frye asserts that it is "quite impossible to understand Blake without understanding how he read the Bible, and to do this properly one must read the Bible oneself with Blake's eyes" (11). Accordingly, Frye presents many passages of biblical exegesis in which he does not distinguish his own position from that of "Blake," thus leaving the matter of his own acquiescence in the supremely sexist religious politics he attributes to the poet open to question.[39] In his discussion of Blake's ethical and political ideas in a chapter titled "Beyond Good and Evil," for example, we are informed that

> In many religions God is certainly worshiped as a trinity of father, mother and child, as in Beulah, but in the more highly developed ones God is always the Supreme Male, the Creator for whom the distinction between the beloved female and created child has disappeared. The reappearance of the Madonna in Christianity is thus a corruption of that religion, and is in direct contradiction to Jesus' own teachings. Mother-worship is womb-worship, a desire to prolong the helplessness of the perceiver and his dependence on the body of nature which surrounds him. (75)

Is it Blake who believes that in the more highly developed religions God is always the Supreme Male, or is it Frye, himself an ordained Protestant minister, who believes not only this but that "the reappearance of the Madonna" is always a corruption of Christianity?

But if it's hard to know whether Frye or "Blake" is vouching for male supremacy, Frye gives himself away in his reading of the meaning of "apocalypse" in the Book of Revelation. After explaining early in his text that "John's symbol" for the final apocalypse is "the burning of the Great Whore who is called Mystery" (44), Frye later identifies the Whore with Blake's principle of the "female will," but then goes on to characterize the "female will" as the principle not only of eternal but of *modern* feminine evil:

> The Great Whore of the Bible is the Medusa who turns men to stone, the *femme fatale* of the romantic poets whose kiss is death, whose love is annihilation, whose continual posing of the unanswerable riddle of life in this world is reflected in the mysterious female smiles of the Sphinx and Mona Lisa; and whose capacity for self-absorption has haunted art from ancient Crete to modern fashion magazines. (140)

Frye's reading of Revelation "with Blake's eyes" thus unequivocally identifies "apocalypse" with the burning of the Whore, and the Whore with the general deadliness of the female to the male. It was the same in Blake's time as in these days of "modern fashion magazines," Frye tells us, and it is right and reasonable that the end of mystery will only come with the destruction of Whoredom, in all its manifestations.

In *Fearful Symmetry*, Frye also situates the reading of Blake in the "apocalyptics of the closet," vigorously insisting that there is no arcane mystery to be deciphered in the works of this poet, yet that "enthusiasts of poetry," like the readers of mystery stories, may "enjoy sitting up nights trying to find out what the mystery is" (7). The "mystery" in Blake is not to be "pursued by a band of superstitious dilettantes into the refuge of a specialized cult"; his prophecies "may need interpretation, but not deciphering"; the "ordinary reader" must not be scared away from him (7). Frye's attempt to define the difference between acceptable and unacceptable mystery ultimately devolves on the term "mysticism," which Frye posits is "a form of spiritual communion with God which is by its nature incommunicable to anyone else," and therefore incompatible with poetry (7). There may be such things as "mystical poets" but "they are very rare birds, and most of the poets generally called mystics might better be called visionaries, which is not quite the same thing" (8). Frye's definition of the "visionary," however, seems indistinguishable from that of the mystic: "[a] visionary creates, or dwells in, a higher spiritual world in which the objects of perception in this one have become transfigured and charged with a new intensity of symbolism" (8).

In his "General Note: Blake's Mysticism," appended to the end of the critical work, Frye acknowledges that the "confusion" about Blake's mysticism has not been cleared up, and here he makes the startling statement that "the real apocalypse comes, not with the vision of a city or kingdom, which would still be external, but with the identification of the city and kingdom with *one's own body*" (431, my emphasis). And in a final reversal of his own earlier attempt to expurgate "mysticism" from the reading of Blake's work, he concludes that "if mysticism means primarily the vision of the prodigious and unthinkable metamorphosis of the human mind just described, then Blake is one of the mystics" (432). Frye thus italicizes the binary "visionary/mystic," simultaneously intensifying and mystifying this crisis of definition, and finally linking it to a body identified as "one's own" as well as to the universalized "human mind."

The line between "secrecy/disclosure" continues to be charged in Harold Bloom's *Blake's Apocalypse* (1963) with reference to the body and the urgency of its "definition." Bloom everywhere undercuts the need for any specialized interpretation or elucidation of Blake's texts: "Blake does not need anybody to elucidate his ideas for the alert reader. What the critic can do for that reader is to increase his alertness, to help him recognize much that is left implicit." Bloom's secularized reading of Blake aims at an uninhibited appreciation of Blake's representation of "the human truth of sexual freedom." Yet this alignment of Blake with Freudian "truth" inevitably determines that "truth" to be heterosexual. Commenting on Blake's lines

Till I turn from Female Love,
And root up the Infernal Grove,
I shall never worthy be
To Step into Eternity

Bloom feels it necessary to "alert" the reader to the fact that "[t]his of course does not mean that the speaker is going to be either ascetic or homosexual, but only that he is going to give up love as the Female Will understands it."[40]

Similarly, Bloom's earlier work, *The Visionary Company* (1961), supplies a sexualized reading of Wordsworth's image of apocalyptic marriage, but the notion of an apocalyptic sexuality is defined by its "common," that is, its *one* sexuality:

> For Wordsworth the individual Mind and the external World are exquisitely fitted, each to the other, even as man and wife, and with blended might they accomplish a creation the meaning of which is fully dependent upon the sexual analogy; they give to us a new heaven and a new earth blended into an apocalyptic unity that is simply the matter of common perception and common sexuality raised to the freedom of its natural power.[41]

Although Bloom always appears to avoid reference "outside" the text — begging his reader, for example, to forgive him for the necessity of reference to the Bible in his reading of Blake — his critical practice of helping the reader to recognize what is "implicit" in the text tends to mark the obscured line between "common sexuality" and any other kind.[42] He points out the difference between Wordsworth's "apocalyptic unity" of man-and-wife-like Mind and World and Blake's insistence that the visible body of Nature is "the barrier between us and the God within ourselves."[43] He does not point out that both apocalyptic visions are equally dependent on the subordination of the feminine, one through marriage in which the lesser, feminine "nature" is subsumed and the poet takes over the function of creation, and the other through destruction, in which the "Female Will," identified with the Whore of Babylon, must be expurgated or destroyed.

The figure of "apocalyptic marriage" becomes most prominent in M. H. Abrams's *Natural Supernaturalism: Tradition and Revolution in Romantic Literature* (1971). Although Abrams describes Revelation as "the most detailed, terrifying, and compelling of all the descriptions of the last days," he concludes that "the fierce destruction is a cleansing one," and he chooses to stress just two images from the book: the creation of a new heaven and a new earth, or "apocalypse," and the marriage of the Lamb.[44] The two images, however, are merged together in a single, coherent image of "holy marriage":

The vision is that of the awesome depths and height of the human mind, and of the power of that mind as in itself adequate, by consummating a holy marriage with the external universe, to create out of the world of all of us, in a quotidian and recurrent miracle, a new world which is the equivalent of paradise. (28)

As Abrams makes quite explicit in his final chapter, he means to deliberately oppose the Romantic poets' celebration of the "great positives of the Western past" to those authors of "our own age" who "have turned against the traditional values of the civilized order" and who "voice the negatives of what Lionel Trilling has called an 'adversary culture' " (430). His selection of "holy marriage" and the apocalyptic creation called forth by it as the two "key images" in Revelation is therefore a motivated one, calculated to affirm the "traditional values of the civilized order," among which must be included the privileging of heterosexuality and gender hierarchy.

But Abrams's emphasis on marriage is clearly a two-edged sword: while ostensibly inscribing the apocalyptic vision with the narrative of heterosexuality, the transformation of marriage into a metaphor for "a culminating and procreative marriage between mind and nature" effectively evacuates the body of woman from the transaction and authorizes a union between man and his feminine nature (28). Abrams's insistence on limiting the marriage metaphor to the biblical text and its Christian exegesis suggests his anxiety about the excess meaning that may spill from the figure, but does not succeed in controlling it, as in his example of early Christian interpretation of the cross as the bed on which Christ consummated his marriage with humanity (45).[45] The "key" image of apocalyptic marriage is indeed a keystone of male homosocial desire, articulating the incorporation of the feminine with the evacuation of the female body, complying with compulsory heterosexuality but celebrating a union with "nature."

These instances of a "patriarchal apocalyptic," while betraying their construction as "apocalyptics of the closet" in their pervasive anxiety about what can and cannot be defined about apocalypse, all make that definition dependent on the opposition and subordination of the feminine. Gender hierarchy appears essential to "apocalypse," whatever it may be. But in other instances of the 1960s–80s literary apocalyptics, figures of gender opposition or difference are strikingly absent, and the meaning of apocalypse is even more heavily invested in the secrecy/disclosure, knowledge/ignorance, private/public binaries. The generic distinction, not between Sedgwick's "utopia" and "apocalypse" but between "epic" and "prophecy," is also heavily freighted, culminating in the distinction between the epic narrative that enshrines culture and history and the apocalyptic narrative that constructs a visionary coming-out story, a coming out that is a Pisgah vision of a Promised Land not to be entered in history but only in imaginative "apocalypse."

Not all of the apocalyptic studies that appeared in academia during the 1960s to 1980s endorsed, as Abrams does, the "traditional values of the civilized order." Others assumed, on the contrary, that the genre of apocalypse had always been in opposition to the prevailing order of the contemporary society. In *The Dawn of Apocalyptic* (1975), the theologian Paul D. Hanson argues

> The continued dedication of the majority to Progress contradicts not at all the assertion that the dawn of a new apocalyptic era is upon us, for the crisis which sociologists find at the root of every apocalyptic movement is a minority phenomenon. This crisis is the collapse of a well-ordered worldview which defines values and orders the universe for a group of people, thrusting them into the unchartered waters of chaos and anomie. While the majority continues on the course defined by past norms, the apocalyptic minority calls attention to signs indicating that the course leads to perdition and offers in its place a new vision of life's values.[46]

In the same year in which *The Dawn of Apocalyptic* was published, Joseph Anthony Wittreich Jr. locates the distinction between the majority dedicated to "Progress" and the apocalyptic minority in a distinction between the literary genres of "epic" and "prophecy":

> The epic poet enters into a contentious relationship with his precursors and into a harmonious one with his culture; he transcends their achievement by enshrining the value systems of his own time, which themselves transcend the less adequate systems celebrated by his predecessors. On the other hand, the prophet asserts discontinuity between himself and his culture, whose collective mind he is assaulting, and continuity between himself and his precursors, whose visions he releases and then expands.[47]

Both the theological and the literary formulations of "apocalyptic" (which for Wittreich is here synonymous with "prophecy," though he will elsewhere distinguish between them) resonate with the fervor of the radical political movements of the seventies and the preceding sixties. There is nothing new in the academic characterization of countercultural movements as "apocalyptic" — in 1964, for example, Ross Grieg Woodman wrote that "[a]s an apocalyptic poet, Shelley sought to reveal the archetypal form of a certain set of radical beliefs by releasing them from the limitations of time and space with which, he felt, moral reformers as 'promoters of utility' were largely concerned."[48] But Wittreich's formulation here suggests something new about the conception of the "prophet" in literary apocalyptics: the prophet does not stand alone — a single, supremely authoritative figure of male divinity — but is continuous with a "line of vision." The construction of the prophet's discontinuity from his culture as simultaneous with his continuity with other prophets points to his location in a marginal politics.

Wittreich's formulation appears in a collection edited by him, *Milton and the Line of Vision* (1975), in which other critics join him in a common emphasis on the poet-prophet as part of a tradition of prophecy, an "intrapoetics" that links the line of poet-prophets with the biblical prophecies, especially the Book of Revelation.[49] Kathleen Williams, for example, speaks of "a poetic line, a community of poets extending through time and engaging, as often as not, in a kind of dialectic with the tradition of which they so strongly feel themselves a part."[50] The entire collection is intended to demonstrate a theory of influence that takes issue with Harold Bloom's *The Anxiety of Influence: A Theory of Poetry* (1973).[51] To Wittreich, Bloom's theory is wrongheaded not only because it insists on conflict between poets (and prophets) but because it *privatizes* that conflict, thus "translating revolutionary ideology into mental perversity."[52] But that "revolutionary ideology" is itself part of a common "line of vision": each poet-prophet releases and expands the vision of other prophets, developing an unbroken line of prophecy that assaults the inadequate value systems of cultures.

Significantly, the image from the Book of Revelation that Wittreich sees as central to Blake's work is not the Whore of Babylon but the "two witnesses." In *Angel of Apocalypse: Blake's Idea of Milton,* also published in 1975, Wittreich states that Blake interpreted the poet-prophets as "the fullest approximations of John's two witnesses." From here he goes on to interpret the two witnesses as those who testify to

the truth of a new birth, opening and expounding the Bible, especially the New Testament, and thus precipitate a revolution that reforms the world. The witnesses are alive, reborn, only when their visions are turned into life and practice in us, only when the reigning orthodoxies, the false doctrines, cease to slay man and are instead slain by him.[53]

The two witnesses recall the "pairs of prophets" in the Old Testament, such as Moses and Aaron or Elijah and Elisha. The line of vision is thus constituted "between men," rather than in the visionary authority of any single prophetic figure. And Wittreich "expands" the meaning of the two witnesses to a rebirth in "us" that will slay the "reigning orthodoxies" and "false doctrines" of our time. The two witnesses figure not only a generally countercultural but a specifically countertheological apocalyptic to be reborn in a community.

At the same time, Wittreich's articulation of the meaning of "prophecy" underlines the "secrecy/disclosure," "knowledge/ignorance," "public/private" binaries, repeatedly insisting on the *necessary* "obscurity" of prophecy and consequently, on the specialized knowledge necessary for "opening the seals." Because prophecy is a literature of multiple contexts, it inevitably produces obscurity: "Blake creates a poetry of contexts, and thus his poetry remains sealed until the contexts around it are penetrated."[54] Quoting Don Cameron Allen's *Mysteriously Meant: The Rediscovery of Pagan Symbolism and Allegorical Interpretation in the Renaissance* (1970), he suggests that the creator of prophetic poetry " 'eschews various symbols, which are without value, and employs those darker conceits, which circle and wind the meaning into obscurity' — into an obscurity that hides the poet's vision from 'Corporeal Understanding,' protecting it from vulgarization, but that is still comprehensible to the initiated."[55]

"Prophecy" is then a closeted literature, and "opening the doors of perception" or the windows of eternity is the interpreter's visionary goal, as "*opening our eyes*" is "finally the objective of all prophecy and the obligation of all prophets."[56] Wittreich elaborates the meaning of the "two witnesses" into a liberatory testimony against injustice that becomes a visionary coming-out narrative: "Now the witnesses of Christ, liberated from injustice and cruelty, from the abuses of institutionalized religion, rise up, like Milton's uncouth swain, doffing their sackcloth and donning the garments of the resurrection, to testify to God's providence."[57] In his *Visionary Poetics: Milton's Tradition and His Legacy* (1979), Wittreich underlines the meaning of this visionary narrative even more as a "coming-out" narrative, an escape from one confine after another: "the breaking of each seal denotes a new discovery, an unfolding of visionary meaning, the breaking of yet another manacle as the mind moves progressively toward total consciousness . . . yet any vision, once penetrated, moves the reader closer to the city; and progressing from vision to vision, the reader finds himself continually bursting confines, breaking seals."[58]

Ultimately, Wittreich indicates that this final coming out can only be accomplished outside history in the liberation of the mind: "When the prophet looks at history he finds only a paradigm for tyranny, but when he turns inward he discovers, in his own psychic history, the possibility for becoming liberated from oppression."[59] Goldsmith proposes that whereas "the classical prophet prophesies because he can influence the course of history . . . the discrediting of history and the subsequent turn to mythical visions of cosmic redemption tend to occur only when an apocalyptic writer perceives no viable means of self-determination for the community."[60] In his *Angel of Apocalypse*, Wittreich makes a similar distinction between "prophecy" and "apocalyptics": "the one converts downward into history, the other outward into eternity; the one takes as its objective the reformation of man, the other, upon man's reformation, the creation of Jerusalem."[61] Even in the post-Stonewall days of the seventies, only the most limited "means of self-determination" were available to the gay community. Looking "downward into history" could promise no more than continued opposition to continuing oppression, while looking "outward into eternity" voiced the one hope for real freedom — the apocalypse in one's own "psychic history."

In his *Apocalyptic Overtures: Sexual Politics and the Sense of an Ending* (1994), Richard Dellamora observes that "among dominant groups apocalyptic narratives have often been invoked in order to validate violence done to others," while "among subordinate groups apocalyptic thinking is frequently an effect of the pressure of persecution."[62] The literary apocalyptics of the 1960s to 1980s suggest the production of both kinds of apocalyptic narratives: the "master narrative" of individual male prophetic authority and the erection of that authority on the necessary subordination of women and the assumption of inevitable conflict between men; and the visionary narrative of "pairs of prophets" whose apocalyptic goal is to "open the doors" of both institutional and imaginative oppression. The "line of vision" writes a gay apocalyptic that looks to an end of violence between and in men but does not expect to see it till the end of "history."

When We Dead Awaken, or Of A Feminist Apocalyptic Tone

Looking back, now, from the fin de millennium, it doesn't seem surprising that what I have learned to think of as "second-wave feminists" should have spoken, in the 1970s, in apocalyptic tongues. Kate Millett ends her revolutionary *Sexual Politics* (1970) with a paean to "the spontaneous mass movements taking place all over the world," and envisions a "second wave of the sexual revolution" as at last accomplishing "its aim of freeing half the race."[63] Adrienne Rich's 1971 Modern Language Association talk, "When We Dead Awaken: Writing as Re-Vision," ends with a prophetic dream about singing a blues song that she interprets as signifying the "awakening of consciousness" among women.[64] Elaine Showalter, in her 1979 "Toward a Feminist Poetics," compares feminist criticism to the Old Testament and gynocritics to the New Testament, and posits that both kinds are necessary to lead us to "the promised land of the feminist vision."[65] Sandra M. Gilbert and Susan Gubar's *The Madwoman in the Attic* (1979) reads in the sibylline leaves a prophetic parable of the woman artist.[66]

But by the time of her 1981 "Feminist Criticism in the Wilderness," Showalter is already uneasy about apocalyptic rhetoric. Rather than seeking a promised land of texts "like angels," sexless and equal, she suggests that feminist critics must seek truth in "the tumultuous and intriguing wilderness of difference itself."[67] Feminist criticism was beginning to discover that it could not speak with a single voice nor prophesy a single "vision." Elizabeth Abel pinpoints 1985 as "a watershed year that marked the simultaneous emergence of what has been called postfeminism and, not coincidentally, of pervasive white feminist attention to texts by women of color."[68] For feminist critics, the mid-eighties were the time of a second "Great Awakening," this time to the "blind spots" in their own apocalyptic discourse: the prophetic parable of "the woman artist" told the story of a white, middle-class, heterosexual woman — *only*. The figure of the woman clothed with the sun receded as the features of the "wilderness of difference" began to emerge.

In the 1984 version of his essay "Of an Apocalyptic Tone Recently Adopted in Philosophy," Jacques Derrida suggests why philosophers take on an apocalyptic "tone": "Whoever takes on the apocalyptic tone comes to signify to, if not tell, you something. What? The truth, of course, and to signify to you that it reveals the truth to you: the tone is the revelatory of some unveiling in process."[69] The apocalyptic tone makes the claim of some implicit access to universal truth. Derrida's elegant reading of the functions of apocalyptic in Western discourse, especially in relation to biblically constructed meanings of the term, and even more especially in relation to "apocalypse" in the Book of Revelation, makes the point, however, that this rhetoric can be used for other ends:

> No doubt one can think—I do—that this demystification must be led as far as possible, and the task is not modest. It is interminable, because no one can exhaust the overdeterminations and the indeterminations of the apocalyptic strategems. And above all because the ethico-politics motive or motivation of these strategems is never reducible to simple. I recall thus that their rhetoric, for example, is not only destined to mislead the people rather than the powerful in order to arrive at retrograde, backward-looking, conservative ends. Nothing is less conservative than the apocalyptic genre. And as it is an apocalyptic, apocryphal, masked, coded *genre,* it can use the detour in order to mislead another vigilance, that of censorship. (29)

Derrida thus postulates that an "apocalyptic tone" can be exploited to mislead the "censorship" of the apocalyptic tone. There is no reason to believe, from the perspective of his argument, that an apocalyptic tone might not be able to mislead *any* censoring authority.

But in the earlier part of his argument, Derrida endorses André Chouraqui's thesis that "apocalypse," in its construction in the tradition of Hebrew and early Christian literature, has no reference to violence. In the Apocalypse of St. John, Derrida argues, "apocalypse" means an uncovering, unveiling, or disclosure, particularly with reference to the uncovering of the man's or woman's sex and, here quoting Chouraqui, " 'nowhere does the word *apocalypse* . . . have the sense it finally takes on in French and other languages, of fearsome catastrophe. Thus the Apocalypse is essentially a contemplation . . . ' " (4). Derrida (following

Chouraqui) here participates in what Goldsmith has called the "disarm-ing" of Revelation: his reading of Revelation ignores the indisputable violence of its narrative, and while it plays with the notion of veiling and unveiling the woman, it has nothing to say about the graphic narrativiza-tion of violence to the prostituted body of the woman in "the Apocalypse of John." While his analysis may be said to develop an affirmative as well as a deconstructive analysis of Revelation useful to some marginalized political groups, it does not address the question as to whether—in its violent complicity with male violence to women — there can be such a dis-cursive possibility, in this "Western philosophical tradition" so repeti-tively linked to the Book of Revelation, as a feminist "apocalyptic tone."[70]

In closing, I would like to refer to certain earlier women writers who preceded second-wave feminists in their attempt to appropriate the au-thority of the apocalyptic tone for feminist purposes, but whose narrativ-ization of apocalypse suggests the inescapability of gendered violence in the heterosexual tradition of reading Revelation. Both Charlotte Brontë, in *Jane Eyre* (1847), and Elizabeth Barrett Browning, in *Aurora Leigh* (1857), write the endings of their narratives as "apocalyptic marriages." The last words of *Jane Eyre*, after Jane has described her apocalyptic union with Rochester and envisioned St. John's equally apocalyptic death as an unwed missionary—"he never will marry now"—are the last words of Revelation: "Even so, come, Lord Jesus."[71] Jane quotes these words from what she prophesies will be St. John's last letter. Jane thus allows *her* St. John to write *his* story—and hers—intertextually with Revelation.[72] But Jane's St. John will be killed off while she herself takes up the position of the New Jerusalem, joined with the now lamb-like Rochester, partially blinded and maimed. And it is Jane who is now the "visionary," for Roch-ester can see "nature" and books only through Jane's eyes (476). Jane appropriates the words of both St. John Rivers and St. John of Patmos to write the "end" of her narrative—but what a curiously violent end! Not only does Jane seem to exult over St. John's impending martyr's death, but her union with her blind and one-handed bridegroom is dependent on the violent death by fire of the sexualized and racialized Other in the text, the "creole" Bertha Mason. Jane's assumption of the prophetic mantle is thus contingent on her text's repetition of the burning of the Whore, and its infliction of violence on both the potential bridegrooms.

The narrative project of Elizabeth Barrett Browning's *Aurora Leigh* is precisely that of positing the formation of a *female* poet-prophet and a feminist apocalyptic, yet the apocalyptic "end" of this narrative is sim-ilarly predicated on both repetition and inversion of gender violence. The "other woman," Marian Erle, is first "murdered" symbolically by being raped, and she is then symbolically "saved" or resurrected through becoming the mother of a male child.[73] At the end of the text Aurora takes up her position as visionary, reciting the jewels of the New Jerusalem for the benefit of her thoroughly subordinated bridegroom, who has been blinded and almost killed in the burning of his philanthropic institution. Barrett Browning's *Künstlerroman* thus makes the "birth" of her female visionary contingent, once again, on violence to the male.

Is a feminist "apocalyptic tone" thus structured by heterosexualized reference to the Book of Revelation a discursive possibility, assuming that "feminist" implies both the recognition of differences between women and the institution of nonhierarchical, nonviolent relations with men? Or is gender opposition in this tradition always a matter of the gendering of violence, the violencing of gender? Is apocalyptic "marriage" only a metaphor for the violent consumption of the gendered Other and the subsequent elevation of a sovereign Self, such that a narrativization that privileges the feminine only succeeds in reversing the direction of violence? The nineteenth-century women writers' texts I have cited here suggest that a "feminist apocalyptic" situated within the discursive field of "apocalyptics" constructed by readers of the Book of Revelation may not be even a visionary possibility. The "disarming" of Revelation by its readers inevitably leads to a re-arming of the apocalyptic narrative, another burning of the Whore. "This is not an assault!" the agent cried, as the long nose of the tank penetrated the wall of the compound and pumped the tear gas in.

Notes

1. Nancy Gibbs, "Fire Storm in Waco," *Time* (U.S.), May 3, 1993, 29–30.
2. "Bible's Last Book Was Key to Cult," *New York Times*, April 25, 1993, 32. Stephen Stark had earlier made the same point: noting that "sales of religious and prophecy books are going through the roof," and that Lindsey's book had seen its sales almost double since July, apparently in anticipation of the Gulf War threatened by George Bush, Stark commented that "to be sure, the religious movements that spawn these theories are virtually invisible to East Coast intellectuals . . . " ("Apocalyptic Fervor," *Boston Globe*, November 11, 1990, 20).
3. Bernard McGinn, "Early Apocalypticism: The Ongoing Debate" in *The Apocalypse in English Renaissance Thought and Literature*, ed. C. A. Patrides and Joseph Wittreich (Manchester: Manchester University Press, 1984), 2. All further references in my text are to this edition.
4. Frank Kermode, *The Sense of an Ending: Studies in the Theory of Fiction* (New York: Oxford University Press, 1967); M. H. Abrams, *Natural Supernaturalism: Tradition and Revolution in Romantic Literature* (New York: W. W. Norton & Co., 1971).
5. M. H. Abrams, "Apocalypse: Theme and Variations," in Patrides and Wittreich, *Apocalypse*, 342–368.
6. John Herbers, "Armageddon View Prompts a Debate," *New York Times*, October 24, 1984, A12.
7. See Norman Cohn, *The Pursuit of the Millennium* (London: Secker and War-

burg, 1957), and also Bernard Capp, "The Political Dimension of Apocalyptic Thought" in Patrides and Wittreich, *Apocalypse*, 93–124. A *New York Times* report after the trial of eleven Branch Davidians concluded that "the trial never conclusively provided answers for key question [*sic*] like who fired first on Feb. 28, whether the Branch Davidians would have eventually surrendered had the Federal authorities not rushed their home with tear gas, or just how the deadly fire that turned the compound into ashes got started on April 19" (Sam Howe Verhovek, "Questions Linger After 11 Cultists' Trial," *New York Times*, February 28, 1994, A14).

8. Steven Goldsmith, *Unbuilding Jerusalem: Apocalypse and Romantic Representation* (Ithaca, N.Y.: Cornell University Press, 1993), 1–5.

9. Michel Foucault, *The History of Sexuality*, vol. 1 (New York: Vintage Books: 1978), 11.

10. Judith Butler, *Gender Trouble: Feminism and the Subversion of Identity* (New York: Routledge, 1990), 92, my emphasis.

11. Eve Kosofsky Sedgwick, *Between Men: English Literature and Male Homosocial Desire* (New York: Columbia University Press, 1985), 1–20, 85–96.

12. See below ("A Reading of the Book of Revelation") for discussion of the question of imperial persecution of Christians at the time of the writing of Revelation.

13. Adela Yarbro Collins, *Crisis and Catharsis: The Power of the Apocalypse* (Philadelphia: Westminster Press, 1984), 172. All further references in my text are to this edition.

14. Goldsmith, *Unbuilding Jerusalem*, 86, 90, 128.

15. Goldsmith, *Unbuilding Jerusalem*, 86.

16. Collins, *Crisis and Catharsis*, 121.

17. Elisabeth Schüssler Fiorenza, *The Book of Revelation: Justice and Judgment* (Philadelphia: Fortress Press, 1985), 24, 199. Susan R. Garrett is almost as temperate in her criticism of the "stereotyped feminine images" in Revelation, noting that the author's use of feminine "symbols reflects the male-centered culture of the first century," and that "the dehumanizing way in which he phrased his message will remain deeply troubling." She does lament that "the author seems especially to delight in describing the gory destruction of the woman Babylon" and that "the author's exultation over the mutilation, burning, and eating of a woman — even a figurative one — tragically implies that women are sometimes deserving of such violence" ("Revelation" in *The Women's Bible Commentary*, ed. Carol A. Newsom and Sharon H. Ringe [London: SPCK; Louisville, Ky.: Westminster/John Knox Press, 1992], 377, 381).

18. Sedgwick, *Between Men*, 86–89.

19. See Collins's extensive review of the evidence, both external and internal, for the scholarly consensus that the Book of Revelation was probably written at the end of the first century C.E., and that it was the work of a single author (*Crisis and Catharsis*, 25–83).

20. Collins, *Crisis and Catharsis*, 73. In an earlier essay, Collins states that the theory that apocalypticism "arises in social settings of crisis or alienation" does hold for Revelation but that "the crisis is much more a matter of perspective than of an objective reality about which various observers would agree" (Adela Yarbro Collins, "Persecution and Vengeance in the Book of Revelation" in *Apocalypticism in the Mediterranean World and the Near East: Proceedings of the International Colloquim on Apocalypticism, Uppsala, August 12–17, 1979*, ed. D. Hellholm [Tübingen, 1983]).

21. Elisabeth Schüssler Fiorenza, *In Memory of Her: A Feminist Theological Reconstruction of Christian Origins* (New York: Crossroad, 1984), 78, 55.

22. Sedgwick, *Between Men*, 91.

23. All references to the Book of Revelation are to the Authorized Version (King James).

24. Fiorenza, *Book of Revelation*, 140, 187.

25. Sedgwick, *Between Men*, 91.

26. Elizabeth Cady Stanton and the Revising Committee, *The Woman's Bible* (Seattle: Coalition Task Force on Women and Religion, 1974; orig. pub. 1895), 179.

27. On the priority of prohibitions concerning blood, especially as elaborated in the Book of Leviticus, see Mary Douglas, *Purity and Danger: An Analysis of Concepts of Pollution and Taboo* (London and Boston: Ark Paperbacks, 1984; c1966).

28. Fiorenza, *Book of Revelation*, 199.

29. Collins, *Crisis and Catharsis*, 121.

30. Jane Gallop, *Thinking Through the Body* (New York: Columbia University Press, 1988), 126.

31. Goldsmith's analysis of the Whore downplays the sexual reference of the language in which she is constituted, finding himself more interested in "the way misogyny is bound to an attack on a certain idea of fallen language." Although I find no error in his thesis here that the Whore is explicitly tied to "the fallen history of social and linguistic differences," I think he has failed to see that the "tie" is part of the text's strategy to substitute interpretation of language conceived as transparent for attention to the opacity of the language (Goldsmith, *Unbuilding Jerusalem*, 62, 67). The "Whore" is a "whore," whatever the "mind of wisdom" may have to say about her.

32. Marilyn Frye, "Some Reflections on Separatism and Power" in *The Lesbian and Gay Studies Reader*, ed. Henry Abelove, Michèle Aina Barale, David M. Halperin (New York: Routledge, 1991), 91–98.

33. See, for example, my own earlier readings of the significance of this figure for Victorian writers in *George Eliot and the Landscape of Time: Narrative Form and Protestant Apocalyptic History* (Chapel Hill: University of North Carolina Press, 1986), 74, and also in "The Trouble with Romola," in *Victorian Sages and Cultural Discourse: Renegotiating Gender and Power*, ed. Thäis E. Morgan (New Brunswick, N.J.: Rutgers University Press, 1990), 107–120. In the latter essay I discuss the extraordinary violence to *men* that marks George Eliot's "historical romance" about the prophet Savonarola—a novel that, as I argue in *George Eliot and the Landscape of Time*, she attempts to structure as a "feminist" apocalypse.

34. Eve Kosofsky Sedgwick, *Epistemology of the Closet* (Berkeley: University of California Press, 1990), 11, 72.

35. Richard Dellamora comments on the "vexed" status of this term, specifically in relation to such participants in literary apocalyptics as M. H. Abrams and Frank Kermode. Although it seems fairly obvious, for example, that M. H. Abrams's work is not characterized by the typically antihumanist politics of "postmodernism," it comes as something of a surprise to discover that in *The Sense of an Ending* Frank Kermode carries on a defense of "traditionalist modernism" against what he evidently regards as the cultural decadence of certain "avant-garde" writers such as William Burroughs (*Apocalyptic Overtures: Sexual Politics and the Sense of an Ending* [New Brunswick, N.J.: Rutgers University Press, 1994], 101–102, 104).

36. Kermode's *The Genesis of Secrecy: On the Interpretation of Narrative*, published in the same year as Joseph Wittreich's *Visionary Poetics: Milton's Tradition and His Legacy*—1979—would appear to be a particularly prominent confirmation of the

investment of this critical genre in the "secrecy/disclosure" binary. Although *The Genesis of Secrecy* takes one of the gospels rather than Revelation as its focus, Kermode's "interpretation of interpretation" theorizes hermeneutics as always dependent on a distinction between "initiates" and "outsiders," or on those whose ears are "circumcised" and those whose ears are not (*Genesis of Secrecy* [Cambridge, Mass.: Harvard University Press, 1979], 2, 3, 18; *Visionary Poetics* [San Marino, Calif.: Huntingdon Library, 1979]).

37. Northrop Frye, *Fearful Symmetry: A Study of William Blake* (Princeton, N.J.: Princeton University Press, 1947; 1969); Northrop Frye, *Anatomy of Criticism: Four Essays* (Princeton: Princeton University Press, 1947). All further references to *Fearful Symmetry* in my text are to this edition.

38. The new preface has no pagination.

39. In his discriminating study of Frye, A. C. Hamilton notes that "his ambition as a critic may be expressed in what he says of Blake by substituting his name for Blake's, and 'criticism' for 'poetry' " (*Northrop Frye: Anatomy of His Criticism* [Toronto: University of Toronto Press, 1990], 204).

40. Harold Bloom, *Blake's Apocalypse: A Study in Poetic Argument* (Garden City: Doubleday & Company, Inc., 1963), 191, 100, 287.

41. Harold Bloom, *The Visionary Company: A Reading of English Romantic Poetry* (Garden City: Doubleday & Company, Inc., 1961), 123.

42. Bloom, *Blake's Apocalypse*, 260.

43. Bloom, *Visionary Company*, 124.

44. Abrams, *Natural Supernaturalism*, 37, 40–42. All following references will be noted parenthetically in the text.

45. Although acknowledging that the biblical imagery of marriage and whoredom might have origins in pagan religious rites, Abrams insists on the absolute priority of its biblical origins, for "the long evolution of the figure, from its rudimentary form in the early books of the Old Testament through the prophets to the Book of Revelation, is coherent, full, and explicable without reference to anything outside the Biblical texts themselves" (*Natural Supernaturalism*, 44).

46. Paul D. Hanson, *The Dawn of Apocalyptic* (Philadelphia: Fortress Press, 1975), 2.

47. Joseph Anthony Wittreich Jr., " 'A Poet Amongst Poets': Milton and the Tradition of Prophecy" in Joseph Anthony Wittreich Jr., ed., *Milton and the Line of Vision* (Madison: University of Wisconsin Press, 1975), 104.

48. Ross Greig Woodman, *The Apocalyptic Vision in the Poetry of Shelley* (Toronto: University of Toronto Press, 1964), vii.

49. Wittreich, *Milton and the Line of Vision*, xv.

50. Kathleen Williams, "Milton, Greatest Spenserian" in Wittreich, *Milton and the Line of Vision*, 26.

51. Harold Bloom, *The Anxiety of Influence* (New York: Oxford University Press, 1973).

52. Wittreich, " 'A Poet Amongst Poets,' " 104 n16.

53. Joseph Anthony Wittreich Jr., *Angel of Apocalypse: Blake's Idea of Milton* (Madison: University of Wisconsin Press, 1975), 227, 228.

54. Wittreich, *Angel of Apocalypse*, xiii.

55. Don Cameron Allen, *Mysteriously Meant: The Rediscovery of Pagan Symbolism and Allegorical Interpretation in the Renaissance* (Baltimore: Johns Hopkins Press, 1970), as quoted in Wittreich, *Angel of Apocalypse*, 186.

56. Wittreich, *Angel of Apocalypse*, 187; " 'A Poet Amongst Poets' ": 125.

57. Wittreich, " 'A Poet Amongst Poets' ": 118.

58. Wittreich, *Visionary Poetics*, 33.

59. Wittreich, *Visionary Poetics*, 52.

60. Goldsmith, *Unbuilding Jerusalem*, 32.

61. Wittreich, *Angel of Apocalypse*, 193.

62. Dellamora, *Apocalyptic Overtures*, 3.

63. Kate Millett, *Sexual Politics* (Garden City: Doubleday, 1970), 507.

64. Adrienne Rich, "When We Dead Awaken: Writing as Re-Vision" in *The Norton Anthology of Literature by Women: The Tradition in English*, ed. Sandra M. Gilbert and Susan Gubar (New York: W. W. Norton & Co., 1985), 2055.

65. Elaine Showalter, "Toward a Feminist Poetics" in Elaine Showalter, ed., *The New Feminist Criticism* (New York: Pantheon, 1985).

66. Sandra M. Gilbert and Susan Gubar, *The Madwoman in the Attic: The Woman Writer and the Nineteenth-Century Imagination* (New Haven, Conn.: Yale University Press, 1979), 93–104.

67. Elaine Showalter, "Feminist Criticism in the Wilderness" in Showalter, *The New Feminist Criticism*, 267.

68. Elizabeth Abel, "Black Writing, White Reading: Race and the Politics of Feminist Interpretation," *Critical Inquiry* 19:3 (Spring 1993): 478.

69. Jacques Derrida, "Of an Apocalyptic Tone Recently Adopted in Philosophy," trans. John P. Leavey Jr., *Oxford Literary Review* 6, no. 2 (1984): 24. All further references in my text are to this edition. A note to the 1984 essay comments that "an earlier version of this translation appeared in the journal *Semeia*" (3).

70. It seems relevant that in his *Feminist Milton* Wittreich argues that early female critics of Milton read Milton's work as transformative of gender paradigms, but he does not argue here, as in his earlier works, that Milton's "feminism" takes the form of "apocalypse" (Joseph Wittreich, *Feminist Milton* (Ithaca, N.Y.: Cornell University Press, 1987).

71. Charlotte Brontë, *Jane Eyre*, ed. Q. D. Leavis (London: Penguin Books, 1966), 477. All further references in my text are to this edition.

72. Carolyn Williams elaborates much more fully than I have on the nature of this "contradictory and double-binding" intertextuality in "Closing the Book: The Intertextual End of *Jane Eyre*," in *Victorian Connections*, ed. Jerome J. McGann (Charlottesville: University Press of Virginia, 1989).

73. Elizabeth Barrett Browning, *Aurora Leigh*, ed. Kerry McSweeney (New York: Oxford University Press, 1993).

Queer Apocalypse: Framing William Burroughs

Richard Dellamora

When James Creech comments that "deconstruction is nothing if not a general economy of queering," he has in mind the idea that "all identity, any sexuality, all presence to self of whatever kind are equally queer in that they are all undecidable when — as deconstruction allows us to do — we view them against the ceaseless and irreducible movements of *différance* and rhetoricity."[1] Creech's remark makes clear the point that this economy operates at the expense of the specific economy of sexual dissidence, whether gay, lesbian, or "queer," in various significations of that currently fashionable term. Despite this fact, Creech argues that deconstruction has played an important part in contemporary queer theory by demonstrating that supposedly natural norms of gender and sexuality are power-effects produced within the institution of compulsory heterosexuality.[2]

The following essay is a contribution to the genealogy of the queer. With respect to the introduction to the United States of poststructuralism in the guise of French deconstruction, I argue that deconstruction is connected with "queering" in yet another way. In the opening skirmishes between modernist and postmodernist literary critics and between poststructuralists and academic humanists, humanists contended (as they still do) that there was something perverse about deconstruction. This slur has been an ambiguous gift to deconstruction. In the 1970s, it impelled American deconstructionists toward a textualist mode that turned deconstruction into a yet more refined practice of the so-called New Criticism, the dominant mode of literary analysis at the time. When J. Hillis Miller, for instance, engages in analysis of the subject, he confines his efforts within the conventional terms of Freudian or Lacanian interpretation. On the other hand, a number of theorists have subsequently embraced both deconstruction and its queerness. Writers such as Judith Butler, Lee Edelman, and Eve Kosofsky Sedgwick invoke deconstruction to interrogate both "Freud" and "Lacan" and likewise the doxa of lesbian and gay identity. As practiced by Cathy Caruth, psychoanalytic deconstruction provides important means toward understanding the gaps, erasures, and blockages that characterize individual and group history among male sexual minorities.[3] And, in *Apocalyptic Overtures,* I exploit the deconstruction of a binary model of sexual difference in Derridean apocalyptic theory in order to articulate a genealogy of male sexual dissidence.

In the 1960s, the opening salvos of the modernism versus postmodernism debate tended to focus on the repudiation of humanism. When literary critics such as M. H. Abrams and Frank Kermode responded to this attack, they took the author of *Naked Lunch* to task as the exponent of disorder. In the opening section of the essay, I explore the construction of masculinity implicit in this panicked invocation of "Burroughs" as a sign of the collapse of Western civilization. In the middle section, I turn to the analysis of apocalyptic narrative and tone in William Burroughs's work of the preceding decade. Burroughs's aesthetic of silence, which is in homage to John Cage, offers an example of deconstruction *avant la lettre* in the context of hip queer culture of the 1950s. As has become increasingly clear, this position had already been theorized when Burroughs began to write. Caroline A. Jones, for example, finds a point of origin in the "Lecture on Nothing" that Cage delivered in 1949 to the Artists Club, a bohemian group in New York City. Although the new aesthetic has several contexts, including Burroughs's resistance to the military-industrial nation-state, a central aspect is the critique of the heroic (re)presentation of the male heterosexual ego in the postwar aesthetic of Abstract Expressionism.[4] The recovery of Cage's theory in the context of the rather different forms of queer theory that exist today is a significant project. Jones suggests that Cage attempted to withdraw "the body" from what Foucault would later refer to as the "body politic," that is, the "discursive construction of the body, its affects and desires."[5] For Burroughs such a withdrawal entails what he describes as "a shocking disintegration."[6] In contrast to queer existence today, which is predicated on disidentification from both normalcy and minority sexual identities,[7] Burroughs was a queer without benefit of knowledge of what a sexual minority might be. For him, the consequences of this absence were apocalyptic.

Narrative structure in *Queer,* the autobiographical fiction that he wrote in the 1950s but withheld from publication until 1985, takes the particular form of queer apocalypse, in which an errant "I" stumbles to exotic locales in search of an elusive, ultimate intoxication. The subject is condemned to psychic and physical disintegration since, disidentified from the Oedipal contract, he lacks as well any alternative psychological or social structure in relation to which he might constitute himself.[8] Although this absence is usually represented in terms of a hopeless dependence on a straight-identified object of desire, what is lacking is not a norm of the male couple but rather norms of sociality in relation to which male couples and coupling might become significant. In the final section of the essay, I turn to David Cronenberg's 1991 film version of *Naked Lunch,* which draws on fictional, biographical, and autobiographical texts in order to conflate Burroughs with his fiction. Cronenberg's adaptation offers a cautionary example of the recuperation of queer difference within modernist paradigms in contemporary filmmaking. In Cronenberg's film, queer apocalypse is translated into the familiar narrative of the heroic male artist that Cage reacted against when he lectured at the Artists Club.

Culture Clash

The Burroughs of *Naked Lunch* plays a brief but important role as *the* exemplar of postmodern fiction in Frank Kermode's *The Sense of an Ending* (1967). Ignoring novelists such as Ralph Ellison, John Barth, Joseph Heller, and Thomas Pynchon, whom Robert Alter in 1966 attacked for the "apocalyptic postures" of their fiction,[9] Kermode instead focuses on Burroughs. Identifying his work with what Kermode refers to as "*avant-garde* writing," Kermode describes "the language of his books" as "the language of an ending world."[10] Against this backdrop of cultural disintegration, Kermode carries on an urgent defense of what he refers to, in contrast, as "traditionalist modernism" (103). Choosing *Ulysses* as his exemplary text, Kermode positions himself as a leading proponent of a modernism that, in becoming institutionalized within undergraduate curricula in anglophone universities, had truly become "traditionalist." At the same time, he lodges "Burroughs" and, more generally, postmodernist fiction and poststructuralist theory in a critical metanarrative, homophobically charged, of reaction against cultural innovation. When Kermode describes the lineage in which Burroughs writes as one that "destroys the indispensable and relevant past,"[11] apocalypse becomes a set of metaphors that shape Kermode's historical and critical analysis.

Burroughs's textuality acquires further significance in relation to the contest over the legal definition of pornography that centered on *Naked Lunch* in the mid-1960s. In this context, *Naked Lunch* was validated within liberal discourse as an exemplary instance of juridically defined free speech. As for Kermode, in enlisting *Ulysses* against "*avant-garde* writing," he draws for support upon a text, at one time excoriated for its literary experimentation, that was involved in a major obscenity ruling in a United States court in 1933.[12] In the renewed struggles of the 1960s, Kermode places himself on the side of freedom of literary expression; he limits the range of acceptable expression not on legal but on cultural grounds.[13]

The crises of the 1960s prompted the development of the neoconservative cultural critique that climaxed during the second Reagan administration. Literary humanists reacted against "avant-garde" practice and other forms of cultural dissidence, some of which challenged the universities in which these men taught. Many had formerly been liberals. Whether liberal or conservative, many were associated in their critical writing and teaching with the high modernist classics. The debate between "modernism" and "postmodernism" was waged on other bases too, including resistance to the incursion of poststructuralist theory from abroad, particularly France. What is easily forgotten today is the sexualized rhetoric and apocalyptic narrative within which these arguments were carried on. In light of this history, subsequent episodes in cultural politics, such as the decision taken early in the Bush presidential campaign of 1992 to target male homosexuals, become more comprehensible.[14]

In *Natural Supernaturalism: Tradition and Revolution in Romantic Literature* (1971), M. H. Abrams translates the current debates into an argument about literary periodization. Abrams differentiates "romanticism" from "modernism" in a way that corresponds with the modernist/postmodernist, humanist/poststructuralist oppositions of contemporary polemic. It is this context that made the consequent argument between Abrams and J. Hillis Miller so highly charged. Apocalyptic pattern can be transferred into critical discourse as a framing narrative. This is the case with Abrams, who deploys an apocalyptic metanarrative in his clashes with Miller, Paul de Man, and other so-called Yale Critics. Abrams articulates his readings of English romantic poetry within a narrative of fallen and restored consciousness. In this construct, displaced from Christian belief, an original sense of being at one with oneself and nature is succeeded by a period of divided self-awareness and alienation from the external world. Abrams contends that romantic poems function so as to restore to the lyric persona a sense of unity with self and "the order of the living universe."[15] When Abrams first put forward this narrative in the 1950s in an influential book, *The Mirror and the Lamp,* it underlined the ethical seriousness of literary studies. In that decade of Cold War struggle, literary criticism acquired a level of prestige hitherto unknown in the United States.

Though the terms, texts, and dates are different, in *Natural Supernaturalism* Abrams's dyad of "romanticism" and "modernism" carries the same phobic charge that Kermode attaches to what he describes as "anti-traditionalist modernism."[16] Abrams contrasts a catastrophic narrative of the "end" of culture to the millennial vision that he ascribes to romanticism. In the ensuing clash, he makes clear his identification with the romantics' attempt to adopt "the traditional persona of the poet-prophet" in order "to speak with an authoritative public voice" at a time of "crisis of civilization and consciousness": "I decided to end *Natural Supernaturalism* by identifying, in my chosen authors, those Romantic positives which deliberately reaffirmed the elementary values of the Western past, and to present these values in a way directly addressed to our own age of anxiety and of incipient despair of our inherited civilization."[17] Abrams's text expresses what Derrida refers to as a "unity of the apocalyptic tone" that results in monotonous iteration of the apocalyptic pattern of redeemed selfhood.[18] The experience of an original state of unity "between self and nature" is followed by a solipsistic fall, which is followed in turn by a "personal secular redemption" that issues in an experience of restored unity.[19] This pattern provides by implicit analogy a model of social and cultural unification.

Abrams represents late 1960s culture in contrast as a time of catastrophic decline. While he limits his specific reference to literature and the visual arts, critical culture, especially emergent deconstruction, is implicitly targeted as is a wide range of cultural dissidence that at the time threatened the unity of tone of a wide range of institutions, including the Department of Defense, the Democratic national party, and elite East and West Coast universities such as Cornell, where Abrams taught. By the late 1960s, gay liberation had also emerged as a significant element within this dissidence. Deploying a gnostic apocalyptic narrative in which the forces of Life are poised against the forces of Eros *à rebours*, Abrams writes:

Salient in our own time is a kind of literary Manichaeism—secular versions of the radical *contemptus mundi et vitae* of heretical Christian dualism—whose manifestations in literature extend back through Mallarmé and other French Symbolists to Rimbaud and Baudelaire. A number of our writers and artists have turned away, in revulsion or despair, not only from the culture of Western humanism but from the biological conditions of life itself, and from all life-affirming values. They devote themselves to a new Byzantinism, which T. E. Hulme explicitly opposed to the Romantic celebration of life and admiringly defined as an art which, in its geometrized abstractness, is "entirely independent of vital things," expresses "disgust with the trivial and accidental characteristics of living shapes," and so possesses the supreme virtue of being "anti-vital," "non-humanistic," and "world-rejecting." Alternatively, the new Manichaeans project a vision of vileness, or else the blank nothingness of life, and if they celebrate Eros, it is often an Eros *à rebours*—perverse, hence sterile and life-negating.[20]

Abrams's disparagement of those who revolt against "the biological conditions of life itself" is a not very covert allusion to subjects of male-male desire—such as Rimbaud, mentioned by Abrams, and Beat writers, including Burroughs, attacked by Kermode.

The passage occurs in a context in which Abrams responds to recent critiques of the poetry of William Wordsworth that negate Abrams's earlier emphasis on the "integral unity of thought and feeling" in Words-worth's aesthetic.[21] Although Abrams directs his comments toward these critics, the implicit target of his remarks is de Man. In an important essay, "The Rhetoric of Temporality" (1969), de Man critiques Abrams's argument about the unification of consciousness with language and nature by means of the romantic symbol.[22] In the second part of the essay, where he discusses romantic irony in Baudelaire, de Man repudiates "the inherent violence" of normal sociality while defending the decision to fashion an ironic fiction of personal madness even if, in doing so, the artist risks the loss of sanity.[23] Abrams's stricture on Baudelaire in the passage cited above glances at the prominent place of Baudelaire in the ethic of de Man's essay. In singling out French aestheticism and decadence for criticism, Abrams tars with a single brush both the proponents of French post-structuralism and the Beats. Irony as validated by de Man is antipathetic both to Abrams's injunction to "qualified hope" and to the norm of "consonance" that Kermode identifies with "traditionalist modernism."[24]

Sexual Politics and *The Sense of an Ending*

Kermode's career and ideological stance are symptomatic of changes in higher education in the United States and Great Britain following World War II. In the United States, the GI Bill dramatically increased opportunities for former members of the armed services to enroll in colleges and universities. In Britain, change occurred more slowly. Passage of the (Butler) Education Act in 1944 promised "Free Secondary Education for All." But this goal was achieved only by means of a compromise that resulted in a class-segregated model that preserved the traditional public schools alongside grammar and secondary modern institutions.[25] Following publication in 1963 of the Robbins Report on higher education, the government embarked on a major effort to convert university-level education from "a minority's privilege" into "a universal right."[26] Democratization did not include transforming the organization and curricula of universities. As John Sutherland has argued, university expansion conserved "the traditional nature of the British university (above all its small size, autonomy, pastoral relationships between staff and student, liberal Newmanesque ethos, and close tutorial teaching method)."[27] Through secondary and higher education and institutions such as the Arts Council (1945) and the BBC Third Programme (1946), a much wider portion of the British populace enjoyed access to high culture. But culture also assimilated lower-middle- and working-class citizens to middle-class values. In the universities, the study of English literature served an important function in consolidating a cultural consensus that validated conventional culture while affirming efforts to democratize British society. By the 1960s, "EngLit" had become the central humanistic course of study. But lags in curricular and administrative reform undermined the centrality of literature as a locus of cultural values and as a way of inculcating civility among upwardly mobile students. The new demographic mix undercut the very consensus upon which government financing of increased access to higher education depended.

Kermode's peripatetic career, which brought him to many universities in England and the United States, is an index of the expansion of personal and professional opportunities that took place at this time. Sutherland argues that Kermode played a "crucial" role in widening the critical and theoretical range of English studies from the late 1950s to the 1970s.[28] By the time that he presented the lectures at Bryn Mawr College that were to appear two years later in book form as *The Sense of an Ending* (1967), cultural dissidence among students and members of minority groups in Britain and the United States had become a disturbing phenomenon. Within this context, the politics of Kermode's book is complex. In the dawning battle between modernists and postmodernists, he provides a moderate defense of literary modernism against what Leslie Fiedler and Ihab Hassan were beginning to celebrate as postmodernism.[29] Kermode defends the autonomy of literature against the politics of both academic conservatives and radicals. But he depends on the very principles of aesthetic form that he defends in making his own political intervention. In his argument, modernist literary form, especially in the novel, validates the norms that he and other liberal academics have traditionally found in literature.

In *The Sense of an Ending*, Kermode focuses on the paradigms that human beings invent in order to give meaning to what would otherwise be "purely successive, disorganized time." Apocalypses or "fictions of the End" distinguish *saeculum* or ordinary chronicity from a sense of time that "ends, transforms, and is concordant." Between these two times occurs a third, a "period of Transition," in which the character of the end, whether millennial or catastrophic, is determined or revealed. Kermode argues that while predictions of the end are continually being made, they are counterbalanced just as frequently by what he refers to as a "clerkly scepticism," reminding the faithful "that arithmetical predictions of the End are bound to be disconfirmed."[30] When skepticism fails, apocalyptic paradigms degenerate into what Kermode refers to as "myths," explanatory fictions whose hypothetical character has been ignored or forgotten. To illustrate this point, he contrasts the use of mythic form in high modernist poetry to the right-wing political mythmaking that occurs in the obiter dicta of modernists such as Wyndham Lewis, D. H. Lawrence, William Butler Yeats, Ezra Pound, and T. S. Eliot (110).

Kermode finds in apocalyptic thinking "clues to the ways in which fictions, whose ends are consonant with origins, and in concord, however unexpected, with their precedents, satisfy our needs" (5). Despite his criticism of the extreme right-wing political views expressed by a number of male modernist writers, Kermode revalidates "traditionalist modernism" (103) as exemplified by *Ulysses*. According to Kermode, narrative form in Joyce's novel acknowledges both the inconsecutive character of daily existence and the impulse to organize human experience in myth. Joyce deploys both mythic and random temporal structures in *Ulysses*. In this way, he avoids the Scylla of irrational belief, on the one hand, and the Charybdis of *chronos*, mere "passing" or "waiting time," on the other. According to Kermode, Joyce achieves this end by means of aesthetic *form*, which serves a further function by providing a fictive model of order in a world that suffers from being either too organized or not organized enough. "Alone" among the "great works" of traditionalist modernism, *Ulysses* "studies and develops the tension between paradigm and reality, asserts the resistance of fact to fiction, human freedom and unpredictability against the plot. Joyce chooses a Day; it is a crisis ironically treated. The day is full of randomness. There are coincidences, meetings that have point, and coincidences which do not. We might ask whether one of the merits of the book is not its *lack* of mythologizing" (113). In this composite form, partly realist, partly mythic, Joyce is able to contain the full range of existence.

Kermode interprets *Ulysses* as fashioning a norm of realism appropriate to modern life. In doing so, he reasserts the traditional idea that aesthetic *form* can have a regulative cultural significance. This affirmation is doubled by an implicit analogy between literary form and the forms of bureaucratic rationalism in the modern industrial state. In the 1960s, liberal intellectuals were confident that these forms could be used to protect "human freedom" both from the effects of political mythmaking on the Left and the Right, from the consequences of random events, and from the destabilizing effects of the social reforms that they fostered. Yet even within the limits of cultural politics, Kermode's use of *Ulysses* begs the question of the extent to which *literary* fictions can serve to satisfy a general need within culture for a sense of order. Kermode overvalues the capability of aesthetic form to give a sense of consonance to human existence. He makes this commitment at the expense of "clerkly scepticism" when, as in the passage quoted above, he falls into blank assertions about what is "reality" and "fact." Kermode's analysis of apocalyptic pattern should preclude his forgetting that "reality" is shot through with fictive and mythic structures and that "fact" acquires significance within narratives.

Kermode's critique of mythical thinking is further directed against two of the leading critical theorists of the decade: Northrop Frye, who, in the words of Jan Gorak, proffers a "myth of an undissociated past," and Marshall McLuhan, who provides a "myth of an undissociated future."[31] Both myths are apocalyptic. Invoking "clerkly scepticism," Kermode dismisses the Frye of *A Natural Perspective* as "the critic of regress towards myth and ritual, writing regressive criticism about plays he finds to be regressive."[32] Kermode invokes the norm of reality/realism against myth as it structures critical discourse. Kermode would have found particularly disturbing Frye's description of apocalypse in *Anatomy of Criticism* (1957).[33] Frye concludes his theory of symbols with a discussion of what he refers to as the anagogic or universal phase of symbolic meaning.[34] In this phase, representational elements are organized within literary form so as to express untrammeled human desire. In Frye's words:

> When we pass into anagogy, nature becomes not the container, but the thing contained, and the archetypal universal symbols, the city, the garden, the quest, the marriage, are no longer the desirable forms that man constructs inside nature, but are themselves the forms of nature. Nature is now inside the mind of an infinite man who builds his cities out of the Milky Way. This is not reality, but it is the conceivable or imaginative limit of desire, which is infinite, eternal, and hence apocalyptic. By an apocalypse I mean primarily the imaginative conception of the whole of nature as the content of an infinite and eternal living body which, if not human, is closer to being human than to being inanimate.[35]

Frye's tracking of desire to its "conceivable or imaginative limit" is in sharp distinction from Kermode's endorsement of aesthetic form as a reality principle governed by compromise between sense-making and sense-resisting aspects of representation. Although Frye reminds his readers of the "hypothetical" relation between imaginative modeling and the external world, Kermode ignores this insistence.[36] In relation to 1960s youth culture, Frye's utterance was liable to be construed as an endorsement of the most extravagant fantasies of liberated desire. That a basis for such delusions could be found in the work of a leading theorist, who drew his critical citations from the most revered texts of the English canon, made his position that much more unacceptable to some.

Kermode expresses his most serious misgivings over the tendency in "adversary culture" to subvert the very possibility of producing consonant fictions of contemporaneity. Locating such work in the line of "anti-traditionalist modernism" or dada, he names as current practitioners American writers of the Beat Generation such as Jack Kerouac, Allen Ginsberg, and Burroughs.[37] In making this criticism, Kermode resists American incursions into British culture as well as the dissidence among blacks, students, antiwar demonstrators, feminists, and gays, which threatened liberal consensus in the United States during the years following Lyndon Johnson's election to the White House in 1964. Kermode's attack on Burroughs in particular may be contrasted to "a symptomatic occasion" held at the Albert Hall in London in June 1965, where "a reading of Beat and Underground poetry for 6,000 people" occurred "in an atmosphere . . . of 'pot, impromptu solo acid dances, of incredible barbaric colour, of face and body painting, of flowers and flowers and flowers, of common dreaminess in which all was permissive and benign.' "[38]

Kermode opposes academic or "traditionalist" modernism to emergent postmodernism. In his view, postmodern culture (which he describes as "*avant-garde*" or "anti-traditionalist") is marked by apocalyptic illusions, the demise of literary form, and the glorification of substance abuse. To this litany, he adds obsession with sexual perversity. He finds all the elements of this bizarre concatenation in Burroughs, whose work he appears to know primarily by way of an essay by Ihab Hassan titled "The Subtracting Machine."

His is the literature of withdrawal, and his interpreters speak of his hatred for life, his junk nihilism, his treatment of the body as a corpse full of cravings. The language of his books is the language of an ending world, its aim, as Ihab Hassan says, is "self-abolition." *The Naked Lunch* is a kind of satura, without formal design, unified only by the persistence in its satirical fantasies of outrage and obscenity.[39]

Kermode may fail to cite the title of *Naked Lunch* accurately, but that does not stop him from objecting to Burroughs's subversion of narrative by means of the "cut up method" in writing.[40] He likewise objects to Burroughs's prophecy of "the cold apocalypse of the race." Recoiling from Burroughs and falling into the critical embrace of Wyndham Lewis, Kermode cites approvingly Lewis's analogous censure of Marcel Proust's " 'cheap pastry of stuffy and sadic romance,' " his " 'sweet and viscous sentimentalism.' " "Imagine Lewis on the cult of orgasm, or on Allen Ginsberg," exclaims Kermode.[41]

While the homophobia of these references is, if anything, even more evident today than when they were first written, Kermode's antipathy is ostensibly directed against Burroughs's antihumanism. In his writing, Burroughs attacks the rhetorics of domestic and public responsibility that he sees as a prime means whereby identity is constituted. Like Oscar Wilde before him, Burroughs says: "To speak is to lie." He focuses attention on language (or the word) as the chief instrument in the hands of the powers to which, in his fiction, he refers as the Novia Guard: "Picture the guard as an invisible tapeworm attached to word centers in the brain on color intensity beams. The Head Guards are captives of word-fallout only live in word and image of the host." In a favored metaphor uncannily prescient of the specter of HIV infection, Burroughs projects human subjection in terms of a universal viral incursion.[42] This invasion can be dispelled only by undoing the verbal codes that constitute consciousness and identity. "Rub out your stupid word," says Burroughs. "Rub out

separation word 'They' 'We' 'I' 'You' 'The!' Rub out word 'The' forever. . . . Go back to Silence. Keep Silence. K. S. K. S. . . . From Silence rewrite the message that is you."[43] Only by an imaginative escape from
discourse, only by entry into silence can cultural prescriptions be de-
railed.[44] Burroughs's critique of the linguistic construction of subjectivity
is congruent with the critique of the subject under way in structuralist
and poststructuralist theory in the 1960s, including writing by Foucault
and Derrida.[45] Writing in mid-decade, Kermode found Burroughs's position unacceptable because it devalidated the authority of the interpreta-
tive community in which Kermode played a modestly oppositional role.
He complains that Burroughs's writing ignores the need to address "a
public of a certain kind, a public which cannot visualize the conditions
which might obtain after its own extinction" (*Sense of an Ending* 118). Yet
in challenging Burroughs, Kermode's anxiety betrays him into projecting the very end of the culture beyond which he and others "cannot
visualize."

Apocalyptic Burroughs

Like the Derrida of *The Post Card* (1980; trans. 1987), Burroughs has
long been preoccupied with the "reality engineering" made possible by
twentieth-century technology. This concept has an important locus in
the development of American commercial culture from the 1920s to the
present. Burroughs's analysis of the construction of identity depends on
what Michael R. Solomon and Basil G. Englis have referred to as "the
conventional communications model" used in traditional marketing
strategy. In this model communication is represented in terms of "a
message transmitted from a source to a receiver via some medium."[46]

In *Queer,* the autobiographical fiction that Burroughs wrote in Mexico
shortly after he shot and killed his wife, transmission is often represented
as having the unified tone described by Derrida. The meaning of the
message is determined by the prescribed identities of sender and receiver. Burroughs uses metaphors of consumption (of junk and sex, especially homosexual) to describe the subject under control. These metaphors refer to the engineering of consent in the market economy as well
as in command economies such as the USSR.[47] According to Burroughs,
control is "one-way telepathy," whereby the agents of those with a monopoly of knowledge and technology dominate the general population.
"I have a theory," says Bill Lee, *Queer's* protagonist, that "the Mayan
priests developed a form of one-way telepathy to con the peasants into
doing all the work." In *Queer,* power is exercised within the context of the
Cold War. Reporting on a magazine article that he has read, Lee says:
"The Russians are using Yage [a consciousness-altering drug] in experi-

ments on slave labor. It seems they want to induce states of automatic obedience and ultimately, of course, thought control. The basic con. No build-up, no spiel, no routine, just move in on someone's psyche and give orders."[48] The most inward aspects of consciousness are subject to manipulation:

Automatic obedience, synthetic schizophrenia, mass-produced to order. That is the Russian dream, and America is not far behind. The bureaucrats of both countries want the same thing: Control. The superego, the controlling agency, gone cancerous and berserk. Incidentally, there is a connection between schizophrenia and telepathy. Schizos are very telepathically sensitive, but are strictly *receivers*. Dig the tie-in? (91)

Invoking American-Soviet conflict, Burroughs extends the reference of "control" to the social conformity that characterized American culture in the 1950s.

Burroughs writes in a genre of dualistic apocalypse that posits the possibility of a cosmic conflict between the powers of the Angel of Darkness and of the Sons of Light. He represents material existence as a set of signs that conceal/reveal malign powers that can take possession of the human mind. His favored image of such signs are hieroglyphs: "In 1939, I became interested in Egyptian hieroglyphics and went out to see someone in the Department of Egyptology at the University of Chicago. And something was screaming in my ear: 'YOU DON'T BELONG HERE!' Yes, the hieroglyphics provided one key to the mechanism of possession. Like a virus, the possessing entity must find a port of entry" (xix–xx). Burroughs insists on the possibility of demonic possession: "My concept of possession is closer to the medieval model than to modern psychological explanations, with their dogmatic insistence that such manifestations must come from within and never, never, never from without. (As if there were some clear-cut difference between inner and outer.) I mean a definite possessing entity" (xx). The point of this mythology is not Burroughs's belief in it. If the reader were to be convinced that he does believe in it, the myth would be yet one more "con," one more way of foreclosing questions of agency and representation. Rather, the model puts in question the reduction of signs to their referents and the reliance within humanist ideology on binary pairs such as inner/outer. There is no interiority reserved from manipulation. Hence the emphasis on signs as hieroglyphs that contain coded instructions, of which receivers are unaware. Because hieroglyphs traditionally were taken to signify the secret knowledge of an Egyptian priestly elite, they are metaphors of control. But as material signs, hieroglyphs are liable to reversible, plural, and contradictory significations. The hieroglyph can program, but in the process of reception it can be recontextualized.

Burroughs sees Freudian analysis as yet another mode of technology. Accordingly, he resists the psychoanalytic explanations of homosexuality that passed for scientific knowledge in the United States during the 1950s. But he also lacks a concept of minority sexual identity. And he lacks an erotics, which might provide a locus at which ethical and social relations could be developed. In short, he has no readily available way in which to validate desire for sexual and emotional ties with other men.

Homosexual activity becomes literally hieroglyphic late in the novel. Traveling in Ecuador, Lee comes across "ancient Chimu pottery, where salt shakers and water pitchers were nameless obscenities: two men on all fours engaged in sodomy formed the handle for the top of a kitchen pot" (94–95). Burroughs has no knowledge of the cultural context in which these objects were produced.[49] Instead, in a moment of symbolization that Cronenberg later literalizes in the most extravagant special effect of his film, Lee asks:

What happens when there is no limit? What is the fate of The Land Where Anything Goes? Men changing into huge centipedes . . . centipedes besieging the houses . . . a man tied to a couch and a centipede ten feet long rearing up over him. Is this literal? Did some hideous metamorphosis occur? What is the meaning of the centipede symbol? (95)

In this passage, symbol functions in what Frye describes as the anagogic phase, in which it acquires universal significance. Symbols in this mode become representational elements within an apocalyptic narrative that describes "the conceivable or imaginative limit of desire." But Frye's "infinite and eternal living body" of desire is in Burroughs a waking nightmare.

Burroughs's commentary on hieroglyphics is yet more unsettling in that he adduces it in addressing the anxiety he continues to experience over his fatal shooting of his wife in the early 1950s. Burroughs contends that his inability to construe this act within conventional ethical terms motivated his turn to writing:

I am forced to the appalling conclusion that I would never have become a writer but for Joan's death, and to a realization of the extent to which this event has motivated and formulated my writing. I live with the constant threat of possession, and a constant need to escape from possession, from Control. So the death of Joan brought me in contact with the invader, the Ugly Spirit, and maneuvered me into a lifelong struggle, in which I have had no choice except to write my way out. (xxii)

Burroughs distinguishes a number of different relations between writer and text. First, writing can provide a means of mastering prior experience through verisimilar representation. He describes the autobiographical fiction of his first novel, *Junky* (1953), in these terms. Secondly, writing can be a process that produces an "I." Burroughs says: "While it was I who wrote *Junky*, I feel that I was being written in *Queer.*" Such a process can be useful, even necessary, when the subject experiences itself as unintegral. In terms of apocalyptic thinking, writing can provide a means of staving off or recovering from "possession." "I was also taking pains to ensure further writing . . . : writing as inoculation. As soon as something is written, it loses the power of surprise, just as a virus loses its advantage when a weakened virus has created alerted antibodies" (xiv).

As I mention above, Burroughs writes in a genre of gnostic apocalypse that projects a shadowing world of malign significance. The obverse of the genre is the quest for illumination. In *Queer*, this apocalyptic quest is figured by the fictionalized account of a South American journey in search of yage. While living in Mexico City, Burroughs undertook such a search together with a young straight-identified man with whom he was infatuated. In the novel and in Morgan's biography, this man goes by the pseudonym Eugene Allerton. In the novel, Lee and Allerton are unable to locate the hallucinogen. The book shifts into yet a third apocalyptic mode when the pair arrive at the town of Puyo: "Dead end. And Puyo can serve as a model for the Place of Dead Roads" (xvii). In the failure of Puyo to be disclosed as either heaven or hell, arrival there can also be seen as anti-apocalyptic. So can the narrative of *Queer* generally. *Queer* is a novel about Lee's attempt to achieve "contact" with Allerton, yet Lee chooses as the object of intimacy a straight-identified man (2). In this choice, Burroughs/Lee negates the conventional narrative trajectory that ends in marriage. But he also perversely confirms it by placing himself in the position of the "woman" who frustratedly yearns for a man. This path, like the search for yage, is headed nowhere. As if in acknowledgment of that fact, between the end of chapter 9 and the beginning of the epilogue, Allerton disappears from the book. There is no account of his departure. He is simply gone.

In the introduction to *Queer*, Burroughs describes the writing of the book as a "performance" played out to a chosen audience of one, in which a painfully dispersed "I" devises rhetorical routines to "mask, to cover a shocking disintegration" (xv). This pattern becomes the definitive one in Burroughs's fiction, especially *Naked Lunch*, his "vision of the post-Bomb society," which is comprised literally of a set of performances or "routines," though with the difference that they are no longer directed to a single addressee from among Burroughs's acquaintance.[50] The motive of this textual performance is not to achieve self-integration but rather to achieve "contact or recognition, like a photon emerging from the haze of insubstantiality to leave an indelible record" (xvi). The photon leaves a trace.

Burroughs's abandonment of notions of integral or even heterono-
mous selves in favor of a metaphor of the self as trace invites the analysis
not of an individual consciousness but of queer culture in the postwar
years. Although the theory of possession can be read as providing a con-
venient way of transferring responsibility for Burroughs's act onto some
alien thing, his account has parallels with the experience of many subjects of same-sex desire. Anxieties about control make sense in relation to
dominant structures of gender and sexuality that are phobic about contamination occurring across genders and that define same-sex desire as
outside the realm of the human. The tendency to introject this view of
same-sex desire is exacerbated in hip and Beat culture by the absence of
public modes of expression that could have provided alternative narratives of personal experience. Yet the intersection of perverse sexual behavior with bohemian existence in the 1940s and 1950s contributed to
the development of gay male politics. The historian John D'Emilio has
argued that, rubbing shoulders with the Beats, "gays could perceive
themselves as nonconformists rather than deviates, as rebels against stul-
tifying norms rather than immature, unstable personalities."[51] Nonetheless, there is a tendency, both in gay social history and other accounts, to
play down the significance of the homosexual hipster between 1945 and
the advent of Jack Smith and Andy Warhol and the early 1960s.[52] Reading
Burroughs provides an opportunity to begin to rewrite the relations of
desire in hip culture.

Burroughs, c'est moi

The early 1990s marked the return of William Burroughs as an icon
within high culture and the mass media as a result of the release of
Naked Lunch, directed by the Canadian filmmaker David Cronenberg. In
writing the script, Cronenberg fashioned a postmodern metafiction that
combines aspects of Burroughs's autobiographical writing, including
Queer; Ted Morgan's biography, *Literary Outlaw: The Life and Times of William S. Burroughs* (1988); and *Naked Lunch*. The result is a carefully controlled, psychologically coherent narrative in which Cronenberg conflates Burroughs with Bill Lee, the protagonist of *Queer* and *Naked Lunch*.
The closure that Cronenberg effects in this way paradoxically renders the
thematic of the film not postmodernist but modernist. He produces a
mythic figure of the artist-in-revolt with which he and the young men who
admire his films can identify. But Cronenberg's apocalypse is very different from the formal and thematic apocalypse of Burroughs's fiction.

In producing the screenplay for the film version of *Naked Lunch*
(1991), which he also directed, David Cronenberg frames the novel
within a heterosexual reading of Burroughs's biography. This misrepre-

sentation demonstrates anew how the narratives in which queer existence is represented within hegemonic culture subordinate being-queer to heterosexual truth.[53] Cronenberg's framing of Burroughs, moreover, indicates how metaphoric substitutions in fictional narrative can allay cultural anxieties at a particular time and place. The insistence on control in thematic and formal terms, the emphatic closure of the script, and the decision to coalesce biography and fictional text into a unified allegory of the creative process make the film, for all its "special effects" and "difficult" material, an exercise in what Kermode refers to as traditionalist modernism.

Cronenberg has long had a reputation as a director who exercises an unusual degree of independence by writing his own scripts and by financing his films outside the usual channels. The latter has been made possible by public funding and favorable tax legislation in Canada and by the development of technical resources for filmmaking in Toronto, where *Naked Lunch*, including the scenes set in Tangiers, was shot. Cronenberg draws on Toronto's financial and production facilities in adapting genres more usually associated with low budget, exploitation films made in Hollywood, particularly sci-fi and horror shockers.[54] His northern location has enabled him to resist pressures to mainstream his work, even after the release of conventionally financed, commercially successful films like *The Fly* (1986). In this way, he has managed the cross between high and low culture that is usually associated with postmodern art.

In addition to affinities with pop art, Cronenberg from the start has shown a strong attraction to the work of the Beats, especially Burroughs, who came to prominence with the publication of *Naked Lunch*, first in Europe in 1959 and then in the United States three years later. From the beginning, Cronenberg's films have shown marked affinities with Burroughs's outlook. Like Burroughs, Cronenberg is obsessed wth bodily metamorphoses produced by mysterious invasive organisms. His scripts, like Burroughs's novels, are dominated by conspiratorial institutions. Both are also preoccupied with a play of "masculine" and "feminine" difference within masculinity that threatens the stability of the ego, though in one case the masculinity is homosexual and in the other it is heterosexual. These obsessions have also proved to be attuned to the hysteria around AIDS of the mid-1980s. Cronenberg's most successful commercial release to date, *The Fly*, appeared at the height of AIDS paranoia in 1986.[55] In a characteristic gesture, Cronenberg has distanced the film from that moment: "The AIDS connection is very superficial. I see it [*The Fly*] as talking about mortality, about our vulnerability, and the tragedy of human loss." Despite the universal rhetoric of this response, the editor of a collection of commentaries by Cronenberg notes that the context in which the film was released inevitably linked it with AIDS.[56]

Cronenberg's career has long been implicated in the increasingly overt struggle between gay artists and the remnant of the alienated East Coast male intellectual elite who once dominated liberal thinking in the United States.[57] The rightward shift of this group has resulted in the emergence of Jewish neoconservative journalists, such as Hilton Kramer, who have long been outspoken antagonists of postmodern art. Cronenberg has eschewed this position, as he also has the views of Jewish "hawks" on national security issues and the defense of high culture by academic polemicists such as Allan Bloom. *Naked Lunch* was released during the course of a continuing crisis generated by outraged conservative and Christian responses to the funding of a Robert Mapplethorpe exhibition by the National Endowment for the Arts.[58] Cronenberg includes in the film a prolonged shot of a sculpture in a pawnshop window. The figure is of a nude male hanging suspended by his arms and with a Mugwump on his back. Foreshadowing a scene of sexual assault that occurs near the end of the film, the figure refers secondarily to an image that has been exploited by political and religious fundamentalists in the recent moral panic: namely, Andres Serrano's *Piss Christ* (1987), a sixty-by-forty-inch Cibachrome photograph of a wood-and-plastic crucifix immersed in urine (Figure 2). In public appearances accompanying release of *Naked Lunch,* Cronenberg has strongly opposed current antipornography moves, whether emanating from the Supreme Court of Canada, from rightwing bigots such as Patrick Buchanan and Jesse Helms in the United States, or from feminists such as Andrea Dworkin and Catherine MacKinnon.[59] In these interventions, Cronenberg always speaks within the terms of a general humanism. Despite this fact, his commitments have significant connections with cultural politics as it involves sexual and ethnic minorities.

Cronenberg's relationship to the politics of sexual representation in American culture has a defining significance for his position as a Toronto artist who is also Jewish. True to the liberalism of American and Canadian Jewish intellectuals of the 1960s, Cronenberg has consistently linked his choice of subject matter with the assertion of freedom of speech. His decision to film *Naked Lunch* is motivated as much by the special significance of this novel in the development of American jurisprudence as it is by cathexis with Burroughs. The obscenity trials that followed publication of the book in the United States in 1962 resulted in exoneration of the book and clarification of the Brennan Doctrine, new at the time, which held that a book could be declared legally obscene only if it was "utterly without redeeming social importance. The portrayal of sex in art, literature, and scientific works is not in itself sufficient reason to deny material the constitutional protection of freedom of speech and press."[60] The decision by the Massachusetts Supreme Court on July 7, 1966, that

Figure 2. Andres Serrano, *Piss Christ* (1987). Cibachrome photograph of a wood-and-plastic crucifix immersed in urine. Courtesy Paula Cooper Gallery.

Naked Lunch is not obscene made Burroughs's novel the benchmark for what is and is not legally obscene in the United States. In view of continuing efforts today, by political and moral conservatives and by some feminists, to widen the definition of obscenity, renewed attention to the novel is specifically political.[61]

Since visual representations are especially vulnerable to political attack, Cronenberg puts himself at risk in making the film, but the risk is limited in a number of ways. For instance, Cronenberg treats homosexual relations obliquely when sympathetic and with comic disgust when direct. In the one scene of anal penetration, the active partner metamorphoses into a huge centipede-like creature that fuses with its passive victim. In converting the scene of sex into the film's most sophisticated special effect, Cronenberg overstamps sexual violation (which he tropes as murder) with his signature as a master of FX filming. Combined with the male protagonist Bill Lee's horrified revulsion from the scene, technological control distances the viewer from the action, especially the young, heterosexual male Cronenberg fan, who is preoccupied with the technology of special effects. The fan is given the thrill of sexual danger while secured by (his) identification with Bill Lee's reaction and by the control exercised over the scene by means of puppetry and film edits.[62]

The representation of male homosexual difference in the film substitutes for the representation of ethnic difference, especially Jewish ethnic difference. This particular substitution is grounded in the history of representing minorities. Writers like George Mosse and Sander Gilman argue that anti-Semitic prejudice has long been associated with effeminacy and sexual perversity. The stigmatized body of members of this ethnic group has been used as a surface on which sexual meanings can be written across "racial" ones.[63] The prosecution and imprisonment of Oscar Wilde, for instance, provided opportunities for Jewish artists and intellectuals of the fin de siècle to identify *with* an innovative artist who had been subjected to attack by members of the philistine majority. At the same time, men like Karl Kraus and Gustav Mahler were able to identify *against* sexual aspects of Wilde that resembled those routinely projected upon despised subgroups among Jews. In the aftermath of the Wilde trials, this double movement permitted assimilated "German" Jews to identify with advanced artistic and intellectual positions while simultaneously resisting Aryan chauvinism and distancing themselves from association with recent Jewish migrants from Eastern Europe.[64] Cronenberg's fixation on Burroughs works similarly. He identifies with Burroughs as an artistic iconoclast in revolt against the commercial and political pieties of American culture at the same time that he dissociates himself from the "womanly" Burroughs who is a sexual pervert. In the process, Cronenberg asserts his superiority to bigotry while defending himself and other Jews against derogatory stereotypes.

In assimilating himself to an idealized version of the best aspects of American and anglophone Canadian liberalism, Cronenberg disavows affiliation with minority subject positions.[65] For example, in *Cronenberg on Cronenberg*, he attacks the doctrine of "political correctness." "Bullshit" is his word for any attempt, from feminist, gay, or other positions, to censor a script during the production process.[66] While I agree with the stance on prior censorship, the aggressiveness of Cronenberg's reaction registers a recoil from minority identification that is necessary in order to enable him to identify with anglophone culture's best self. Cronenberg, who speaks of his "fusion" with Burroughs, has repeatedly identified his repertory of imagery with the aesthetic articulation of the symbolic in Burroughs's writing.[67] At times, Cronenberg recognizes that his Burroughs is a translated one: "I was forced . . . to fuse my own sensibility with Burroughs and create a third thing that neither he nor I would have done on his own. It's like the Rubaiyat of Omar Khayyam." But there are moments in writing the script when the fusion is complete: "When I transcribed word for word a sentence of description of the giant centipede, and then continued on with the next sentence to describe the scene in what I felt was a sentence Burroughs himself could have written, that was a fusion. I . . . almost felt for a moment, 'Well, if Burroughs dies, I'll write his next book.' "[68] The final comment recalls a "cynical joke" that Freud recounts in the course of discussing what he refers to as "the law of ambivalence of feeling" that individuals experience in relation to their intimates. In Freud's telling, a husband remarks to his wife: "If one of us two dies, I shall move to Paris."[69] Cronenberg's joke indicates how intensely ambivalent his connection with Burroughs is.

Fusion, which is an instance of accentuated transference and countertransference, paradoxically gives Cronenberg a way of mastering his imaginary investment in Burroughs.[70] Not only because what is unique in Burroughs is rewritten under the signature "Cronenberg," but also through the shaping of the script and by means of film technique. Cronenberg combines details from the biography of Burroughs, particularly the shooting of his wife, which occurs twice, at the beginning and at the end of the film, with surreal elements adapted from the fiction such as the Mugwumps. The combination, which fuses fact, fiction, and motive in "Burroughs," produces a reversible, metonymic chain of cause and effect between "art" and "life," but the chain is very much that of Cronenberg's script.

Although Burroughs does see his life after the killing of his wife as a series of efforts to gain control over the significances of that extreme act, Cronenberg represents Burroughs's relationship to the shooting as one of repetition. In other words, "shooting" Joan in life and in obsessive rerun is an example of the sort of acting out to which the psychoanalyst draws attention in the course of an analysis.[71] At the end of the film, Burroughs receives permission to continue to practice his art only after he kills his wife (once more). "Shooting" is a term used more in relation to filming than to writing, with the result that the shooting of Joan op-

Figure 3. Judy Davis plays a double role in David Cronenberg's *Naked Lunch* as wife to
Bill Lee (Peter Weller) and as Joan Frost, a character based on Burroughs's friend in
Tangiers, Jane Bowles. Photo: Attila Dory and Brian Hamill. Courtesy Alliance Releas-
ing, Toronto; Twentieth-Century Fox, Los Angeles.

erates as a switch point for representing processes having to do primarily with Cronenberg. Burroughs shot once; Cronenberg "shoots" twice.
Moreover, it is Cronenberg who casts Judy Davis to play the parts both of
Joan Lee and Joan Frost (the latter character a translation of Burroughs's
Jewish friend in Tangiers, Jane Bowles). (See Figure 3.) This conflation
heterosexualizes and anglicizes the narrative while draining both women
of specificity, converting them into Woman or Mother as in the most
predictable gesture of the psychological thriller.[72]

Soon after Bill Lee becomes addicted to the black powder, his Clark-
Nova typewriter, metamorphosed into an insect with a talking asshole,
tells him to type "homosexuality" because homosexuality is a good cover
for an "agent." Lee starts typing. The transaction suggests that perversity
is discursively produced, an act of writing that is a being-written. Yet
agency of the sort that most interested the Beats and that they drew upon
in *à rebours* tradition is also involved: the typist makes a deliberate choice
to take upon him or herself the burden of perversity. This commitment
attracts Cronenberg to Burroughs, but the ability for homosexuality to

Figure 4. Weller as Bill Lee in Cronenberg's *Naked Lunch*. Photo: Attila Dory and Brian Hamill. Courtesy Alliance Releasing, Toronto; Twentieth-Century Fox, Los Angeles.

exceed its discursive boundaries requires the setting of a contractual limit. Hence Cronenberg, in a line virtually the same as one of Lee/Burroughs's in the film, says: "I'm not afraid of the homosexuality, but it's not innate in me."[73] Yet at times Cronenberg uses the camera subjectively, seeing through Lee's eyes, so as to identify the (implicitly straight male) viewer's emotional reactions with Lee's — especially in the scene of sexual introjection. The identification of Lee with young straight male viewers is further underwritten by Cronenberg's choice in casting Peter Weller (Figure 4), an actor best known for his roles as the cyborg protagonist of *RoboCop* and *RoboCop 2*. The shared viewpoint works to confirm the actor, the character, the viewer, and the writer-director in a sense of difference that is still normal enough to recoil from male-male sex. The murder of Kiki conflates sodomy, sexual assault, and murder — a set of conventional associations in the heterosexual imaginary that resonates with the intensified anxieties about "unsafe sex" that have attended AIDS. By intensifying this affect in a scene whose literal referents are not to AIDS, Cronenberg types the effect even more indelibly onto the white surface of the viewer's consciousness.

It is also pertinent that a Moroccan is the object of this violence, a specificity negated by Cronenberg's insistence when interviewed that the entire action of the film occurs in New York. Similarly, the "Arabian" and "African" character of Fadela, the object of Joan Frost's cathexis, is erased when she turns out to be, *in effect,* a white man. Jewish cathexis in Arabs is a point that is both expressed and erased in *Naked Lunch.* Converted into Davis/Frost, the Bowles character ceases to be Jewish. Kiki, the young Moroccan, is played by Joseph Scorsiani. The conflation of southern[74] European with Moroccan ethnicity reinscribes the traditional racist dichotomy between northern Europeans and "Orientals," a divide that apparently begins at Locarno. When Oriental or Jewish referents surface in the film, they are unflattering. In the bug powder shop, the dispenser, who apparently eats the stuff, is an East Asian. The owner is A. J. Cohen. In a scene early in the film that is set in the shop, Lee sits as far as possible from the exterminators, who are eating lunch. The men look like inmates of a concentration camp.

Typewriting and hallucinating (sometimes the two processes fuse) are scenes that conform to an orthodox psychoanalytic model in which the (male) analyst witnesses the signs of a perversity that belongs to the analysand while leaving the analyst's subjectivity intact. Transferred to the film, the paradigm, which is characteristic of Freud's analytic practice, absolves Cronenberg (and the viewer) from implication in Burroughs's deviance despite the acknowledged exploitation of transference.[75] A have-your-cake-and-eat-it-too approach is also evident in the Freudian metanarratives in which Cronenberg somewhat sententiously couches his project. Accepting "the Freudian dictum that civilization is repression," he argues for the liberating effect of artistic desublimation in work like his own. At the same time, the location of perversity in specifically *aesthetic* discourse absolves Cronenberg of "social responsibility" while likewise abstracting homosexuality into a generalized linguistic transgression.[76] Even the choice of homosexuality as the privileged sign of transgression is Freudian. In the Dora case, for instance, Freud remarks: "I have never yet gone through a single psychoanalysis of a man or a woman without having to take into account a very considerable current of homosexuality."[77] Comments like this one, which he repeats in the postscript at the end of the case, can be read as signaling an obsessive interest in (male) homosexuality, an interest involved in Freud's friendship with Wilhelm Fliess.[78] But these comments can be read just as plausibly in another way. When homosexuality is used as a generic index of psychological unease, it ceases to have significance in relation to a set of social forms. Precisely this effacement of the social reference of homosexuality makes it possible to use the term to signify many other referents.

In an interview in the gay press, Cronenberg describes the "talking

asshole" not as the loquacious site of sodomy but as "the one underneath, from the dark place who says stuff that nobody wants to hear but
will not be denied and they can shove candles up and all that stuff, but
still it's going to be heard."[79] Cronenberg describes *Naked Lunch* as a
"coming out" movie, but, as usually occurs when adapted by heterosexuals, the phrase is recontextualized: Cronenberg comes out— *as a writer.*
Well, not something one can be imprisoned for in the United States or
Canada, though one could lose one's job, one's medical insurance, one's
spousal benefits, or one's visitation rights if one were to come out as a
homosexual. Furthermore, Cronenberg's "take" on Lee/Burroughs's
perversity naturalizes Burroughs's homosexuality by psychologizing it.
The social significance of sexual perversity is left, at best, implicit. Thus, a
timely opportunity is lost to analyze queer culture among the Beats in
relation to the very different queer culture that has developed since
lesbians and gay men constituted visible subcultures. The displacement
of social motives and effects to psychological ones is routine in Hollywood
production; and in this respect, despite auteurist aggrandizement, *Naked
Lunch* is as much subject to de facto control as are other commercial
films.

The effacement of sexual and gender difference in *Naked Lunch* is a
reminder of how dehistoricizing Cronenberg's approach is. In an interview published in a Toronto gay newspaper, Cronenberg asks rhetorically
about the shooting of Burroughs's wife: "Is he killing the heterosexual
part of himself to realize himself? Is he killing the female part of himself,
or is he killing the creative part?"[80] The answer to these questions is "No":
he is killing Joan Vollmer, who, shortly before this incident had left Mexico City to file for a divorce in Cuernavaca.[81] In Cronenberg's questions,
this woman, her history and situation, are translated into the metaphor
of an internalized femininity. Cronenberg's interest is in "the woman
within" the man. Female difference is significant insofar as it refers to an
Other within. Similarly, in one of the film's effects, Joan Frost's Moroccan
"dominatrix," Fadela (Figure 5), rips off a plastic body suit to disclose
underneath Dr. Benway (Figure 6), the chief executive officer of Inter-
zone Inc.[82] So much for lesbian difference, represented here as a delu-
sive projection of desire toward the simulacrum of a female body that
conceals a "real man" underneath. Similarly, in the scene of anal rape,
Cloquet's metamorphosis functions as a sign of Cronenberg since the
production of such effects is typical of his work. This moment of demonstrated technical mastery is also the moment, as Danny O'Quinn has
argued, when a metanarrative of "control" subsumes all the differences
and perversities (of gender, sex, race, art-making, crime, and drugs) thus
far registered.[83] After the visit to Cloquet, Lee is in position to become
Benway's chief "agent"/pusher. At the end of the film, he leaves in a van

Figure 5. Monique Mercure as Fadela in Cronenberg's *Naked Lunch*. Photo: Attila Dory and Brian Hamill. Courtesy Alliance Releasing, Toronto; Twentieth-Century Fox, Los Angeles.

for Annexia (which Cronenberg identifies with "Canada" in one interview)[84] together with Frost, then shoots her when the border guards demand to see an example of his writing.

One could multiply the number of times that referents disappear into artistic phantasmagoria in the film. Cronenberg, for instance, argues that Tangiers, the colonial setting of much of the film's action and all its homosexual sex, is a wholly imaginary place: "One understands by the end of the film that Lee never really leaves New York City."[85] This effacement of the material conditions in which Burroughs lived, wrote, and shot his wife is necessary to produce the myth of the artist in which Cronenberg/"Burroughs" is lodged and to constitute that myth as reality. Nonetheless, both in *Queer* and in the appended introduction (1985), Burroughs gives the name of "Mexico" to "The Land Where Anything Goes." It is to Mexico that he fled with his wife and two children in order to avoid prosecution for possession of heroin and marijuana in the United States. And it was in Mexico, where, according to his report, women were radically devalued and in Mexico City, at the time "the murder capital of the world," that he says "the accidental shooting of my

Figure 6. But what is Roy Scheider doing in a female body suit? Roy Scheider as Fadela/ Dr. Benway in Cronenberg's *Naked Lunch*. Photo: Attila Dory and Brian Hamill. Courtesy Alliance Releasing, Toronto; Twentieth-Century Fox, Los Angeles.

wife, Joan," occurred.[86] The framing myth of addiction and control that gives the film its political allegory, though it has referents in Burroughs's experience and writing, is a portentous simulacrum that blocks the sorts of analysis of race, class, and gender relations that Burroughs's biography and fiction might prompt. Gender relations are not always violent. Sex (including homosex) is not always addictive nor are drugs. What, then, are the conditions of violence and abuse?

Cronenberg's "fusion" with Burroughs/Lee is apocalyptic in the catastrophic sense that Derrida finds in male homosocial tradition, where a precursor is made to say what a younger man wants him to say. The script is also apocalyptic in the more familiar sense of retelling the modernist artistic myth of the Dionysian male artist who needs to undergo a kind of death in order to be born into artistic creativity.[87] But the film is not apocalyptic in the sense of opening new possibilities of meaning by unsettling the norms of representation.

Oliver Stone's *JFK* (1991), released shortly before *Naked Lunch*, shares with it a number of attitudes: a sense of apocalyptic menace, a predilection for conspiracy theories, the projection of an enemy within — named by President Eisenhower in a clip at the beginning as "the military-industrial complex." Like Cronenberg, Stone also takes an unflattering view of homosexual snobs and lowlifes, whom he contrasts to the home-loving though increasingly obsessive New Orleans district attorney Jim Garrison, played by Kevin Costner. Gay reviewers have attacked Stone and Garrison for "making gays the scapegoats" of the Kennedy assassination, a plausible complaint since the one person ever to stand trial for his alleged share in a conspiracy to kill the president is Clay Shaw (played by Tommy Lee Jones), who is portrayed in the film as a prominent New Orleans businessman and homosexual.[88] Garrison's wife (played by Sissy Spacek) accuses him of hounding Shaw because of his homosexuality. Yet homosexuality in Stone's film functions as an unstable signifier. The break in the case is provided by Willie O'Keefe (Kevin Bacon), a gay hustler and prison convict. True, he turns out to be a right-wing wacko; but he is also a Teiresias-figure, the person, both woman and man, who can unravel the secret of corruption stalking the land. In one scene, Lee Harvey Oswald (Gary Oldman), the assassin-who-is-not-one, masquerades as the queer he-may-or-may-not-be. A defrocked priest, eventually murdered, is the only one among the conspirators who shows signs of remorse. He and Garrison's wife become passion bearers, who carry the emotional stigmata of Garrison/Costner's effort to find out the truth about the shooting. (The autopsy scene, the most shocking in the film, is a gruesome parody of the laying to rest of the sacrificed leader.) All these types have a place in the history of homosexual representation, but in *JFK* they exceed these limits. No single gendered or sexual position sets the standard of normative subjectivity in this film nor can any particular position be quarantined from infection. Similarly, the cutting of *JFK*, the repetition and mixing of documentary with fictional footage, in 8 millimeter, 16 millimeter, and 35 millimeter, color and black and white, splices together the pieces of Stone's conspiracy theory at the price of showing the viewer that crucial evidence is lost and that no single narrative of the assassination can be believed with confidence. In this way, the film negates the desire for apocalyptic closure that appears to motivate it.

In contrast, Cronenberg's screenplay mixes biography, autobiography, conventional story, and hallucinatory narrative in a seamless whole that turns out to be the familiar narrative of the artist who sacrifices life (read wife or inamorata) to art and whose art becomes his life. In this sense, Cronenberg takes Burroughs's defamiliarizing representation of routines of addiction and control and refamiliarizes them. The narrative fuses Burroughs and Cronenberg with the romantic stereotype of the artist as antihero that the Beats drew from the nineteenth-century tradition of Poe and Baudelaire, Rimbaud and Verlaine. In this aesthetic discourse, art becomes the regulative norm that validates the extremity of Burroughs's experience while justifying Cronenberg's choice of subject matter. Now that Po Mo is the mode, Burroughs, the academy's onetime anarchist nemesis, has become the patron saint of Soho and the East Village. Asserting that *Naked Lunch* is "the first truly postmodern literary text," Gary Indiana makes Burroughs not only the source of the New Narrative but a leading progenitor of virtually all postmodern cultural practice with the exception of architecture. Converted into an icon, what remains unaddressed is the significance of Burroughs's queerness to the history of sexual minorities.[89] In his introductory remarks to *Everything Is Permitted,* Burroughs lays emphasis on Cronenberg's decision to approach "homosexuality as a somewhat unwelcome accident of circumstance and plot." Not wearily but dryly, Burroughs observes: "Probably he simply did not, as an artist, find that aspect of 'Lee' to be significant to the story he wanted to tell in the film."[90] Yes, precisely.

Notes

1. James Creech, *Closet Writing/Gay Reading: The Case of Melville's* Pierre (Chicago: University of Chicago Press, 1993), 192.

2. Creech, *Closet Writing,* 8–9.

3. See Cathy Caruth, "Introduction," *American Imago* 48 (Winter 1991): 417–423; "Unclaimed Experience: Trauma and the Possibility of History," *Yale French Studies* 79 (1991): 181–192; and, with Thomas Keenan, " 'The AIDS Crisis Is Not Over': A Conversation with Gregg Bordowitz, Douglas Crimp, and Laura Pinsky," *American Imago* 48 (Winter 1991): 539–556.

4. Caroline A. Jones, "Finishing School: John Cage and the Abstract Expressionist Ego," *Critical Inquiry* 19 (1993): 654.

5. Jones, "Finishing School," 655.

6. William S. Burroughs, *Queer* (Harmondsworth: Penguin, 1987), xv.

7. Michael Warner, "Something Queer about the Nation-State," *Alphabet City* 3 (October 1993): 14–16.

8. Teresa de Lauretis, "The Female Body and Heterosexual Presumption," *Semiotica* 67, no. 3/4 (1987), esp. pp. 260, 277 n. 1; Monique Wittig, *The Straight Mind and Other Essays,* foreword by Louise Turcotte (Boston: Beacon Press, 1992), 24–25. See also de Lauretis, "Eccentric Subjects: Feminist Theory and Historical Consciousness," *Feminist Studies* 16 (Spring 1990): 128–129.

9. Robert Alter, "The Apocalyptic Temper," *Commentary* 41 (June 1966): 62. I would like to thank David Robson for providing me with a copy of this essay. I am likewise in the debt of his expert knowledge of Fryean apocalypse in relation to straight-identified male postmodernist fiction in the U.S. during the 1960s.

10. Frank Kermode, *The Sense of an Ending: Studies in the Theory of Fiction* (New York: Oxford University Press, 1967), 116, 117.

11. Kermode, *The Sense of an Ending,* 123.

12. James Joyce, *Ulysses* (New York: Random House, 1934), vii–xiv.

13. Kermode appeared as a witness for the defense in the successful prosecution on obscenity charges of the English publishers of Hubert Selby Jr.'s novel,

Last Exit to Brooklyn (Kermode, "Obscenity and the Public Interest," in *Modern Essays* [London: Fontana, 1971], 71–89).

14. Paul Cellupica, "The Political Dawn Arrives for Gays," *New York Times,* November 7, 1992, L21.

15. Abrams, *The Mirror and the Lamp: Romantic Theory and the Critical Tradition* (New York: Norton, 1958), 225. See also Donald Pease, "J. Hillis Miller: The Other Victorian at Yale," in *The Yale Critics: Deconstruction in America,* ed. Jonathan Arac, Wlad Godzich, and Wallace Martin (Minneapolis: University of Minnesota Press, 1983), 70.

16. Kermode, *The Sense of an Ending,* 103.

17. Abrams, "Rationality and Imagination in Cultural History: A Reply to Wayne Booth," *Critical Inquiry* 2 (1976): 462.

18. Jacques Derrida, "Of an Apocalyptic Tone Recently Adopted in Philosophy," trans. John P. Leavey Jr., *Oxford Literary Review* 6, no. 2 (1984): 23.

19. Dominick LaCapra, "The Temporality of Rhetoric," in *Chronotypes: The Construction of Time,* ed. John Bender and David E. Wellbery (Stanford, Calif.: Stanford University Press, 1991), 120, 122.

20. M. H. Abrams, *Natural Supernaturalism: Tradition and Revolution in Romantic Literature* (New York: Norton, 1971), 445–446; quoted by LaCapra, "The Temporality of Rhetoric," 125.

21. Abrams, *The Mirror and the Lamp,* 102.

22. De Man singles out Abrams for a view of the romantic symbol that "resembles a radical idealism" (Paul de Man, "The Rhetoric of Temporality," in *Interpretation: Theory and Practice,* ed. Charles S. Singleton [Baltimore: Johns Hopkins Press, 1969], 180).

23. De Man, "The Rhetoric of Temporality," 198, 199.

24. Abrams, *Natural Supernaturalism,* 447.

25. Alan Sinfield, *Literature, Politics, and Culture in Postwar Britain* (Berkeley: University of California Press, 1989), 55–56.

26. John Sutherland, "The Politics of English Studies in the British University, 1960–1984," in *Historical Studies and Literary Criticism,* ed. Jerome J. McGann (Madison: University of Wisconsin Press, 1985), 127.

27. Sutherland, "The Politics of English Studies," 128.

28. Sutherland, "The Politics of English Studies," 131.

29. Ihab Hassan, "The Question of Postmodernism," in *Romanticism, Modernism, Postmodernism,* ed. Harry R. Garvin (Lewisburg, Pa.: Bucknell University Press, 1980), 118.

30. Kermode, *The Sense of an Ending,* 45, 5, 12, 10.

31. Jan Gorak, *Critic of Crisis: A Study of Frank Kermode,* (Columbia: University of Missouri Press, 1987), 32, 32–33, 33.

32. Frank Kermode, *Continuities* (London: Routledge, 1968), 119.

33. Michael Payne compares and contrasts Kermode and Frye in his introduction to Frank Kermode, *Poetry, Narrative, History* (London: Basil Blackwell, 1990), 1–4.

34. Northrop Frye, *Anatomy of Criticism: Four Essays* (Princeton, N.J.: Princeton University Press, 1957), 116.

35. Frye, *Anatomy of Criticism,* 119.

36. Frye, *Anatomy of Criticism,* 74.

37. Kermode, *The Sense of an Ending,* 95, 103.

38. Sinfield, *Literature, Politics, and Culture,* 187.

39. Kermode, *The Sense of an Ending,* 117.

40. Ihab Hassan, "The Subtracting Machine: The Work of William Burroughs," *Critique* 6 (Spring 1963): 6. Burroughs's friend, the Swiss-Canadian painter Brion Gysin, describes the method as follows:

> Method is simple: Take a page or more or less of your own writing or from any writer living or dead. Any written or spoken words. Cut into sections with scissors or switch blade as preferred and rearrange the sections. Looking away. Now write out result. . . .
> Applications of cut up method are literally unlimited cut out from time limits. Old world lines keep you in old world slots. Cut your way out. (Quoted in Hassan, 9)

41. Kermode, *The Sense of An Ending*, 117, 122.
42. Quoted in Hassan, "The Subtracting Machine," 5, 16, 10. More literally, elsewhere in *Naked Lunch*, Burroughs "predicts the coming of a viral venereal disease that originates in Africa, as AIDS is believed to have done: . . . 'Males who resign themselves up for passive intercourse to infected partners . . . may also nourish a little stranger' " (Ted Morgan, *Literary Outlaw: The Life and Times of William S. Burroughs,* [New York: Avon Books, 1990], 355).
43. Quoted in Hassan, "The Subtracting Machine," 16.
44. See Tony Tanner's discussion in *City of Words: American Fiction, 1950–1970* (New York: Harper and Row, 1971), 109–140. Tanner finds a context for Burroughs's validation of silence in the work of the composer John Cage (122, 128–129). Cage, who was gay, has influenced the work of many gay artists, including Andy Warhol.
45. For the "crisis" in American criticism in the mid- to late-1960s, see "Criticism and Crisis," in Paul de Man, *Blindness and Insight: Essays in the Rhetoric of Contemporary Criticism* (New York: Oxford University Press, 1971), 3–19.
46. Michael R. Solomon and Basil G. Englis, "Reality Engineering: Blurring the Boundaries Between Commercial Signification and Popular Culture," 6. Unpublished paper. Presented at a Roundtable, Rutgers Center for Historical Analysis, Rutgers University, November 3, 1992.
47. William S. Burroughs, "Interview," *The Paris Review* 35 (1965): 47.
48. Burroughs, *Queer,* 50, 49–50 (brackets mine). Subsequent page references to this work are provided in the text.
49. See Oscar Urteaga-Ballón, *Interpretacion de la sexualidad en la ceramica del antiguo Peru* (Lima: Museo de Paleo-patologia, 1968).
50. Morgan, *Literary Outlaw,* 350. In the film *Naked Lunch,* Lee performs the "queer" routine and the "talking asshole" routine.
51. John D'Emilio, *Sexual Politics, Sexual Communities: The Making of a Homosexual Minority in the United States, 1940–1970,* (Chicago: University of Chicago Press, 1983), 181.
52. For the work of Jack Smith, see Michael Moon, "Flaming Closets," *October* 51 (Winter 1989): 19–54. Andrew Ross articulates "hip" in relation to music, class, and race while leaving gay sexuality out of account in *No Respect: Intellectuals and Popular Culture* (New York: Routledge, 1989), chap. 3. For underground filmmaking in the postwar period, see Richard Dyer, *Now You See It: Studies on Lesbian and Gay Film* (New York: Routledge, 1990), 111–173.
53. For a discussion of the term "queer" within theory, see the special issue of *Differences* titled *Queer Theory,* esp. Teresa de Lauretis, "Queer Theory: Lesbian and Gay Sexualities: An Introduction," *Differences* 3 (Summer 1991): iii–xviii.

54. Chris Rodley, introduction, *Cronenberg on Cronenberg* (Toronto: Knopf Canada, 1992), xvii.

55. Rodley, *Cronenberg on Cronenberg*, 134; Nik Sheehan, "Naked Lunch: Coming Out with Talking Assholes," *Xtra!*, no. 188, January 10, 1992, XS15.

56. Rodley, *Cronenberg on Cronenberg*, 128, 127.

57. Ross has traced this struggle in part in *No Respect*, chap. 5.

58. Carole S. Vance, "The War on Culture," *Art in America* 77 (September 1989), 39+. In the final week of February 1992, President Bush fired John Frohnmayer, chairman of the National Endowment for the Arts. Bush took action after Patrick Buchanan, his opponent in the Republican presidential primary in the state of Georgia, began to show a television advertisement linking the Bush administration with financial support for the activities of leaping, muscle-bound leather queens. In a parting statement, Frohnmayer said: "I leave with the belief that this eclipse of the soul will soon pass and with it the lunacy that sees artists as enemies and ideas as demons" (Brian Wallis, "Pandering to Conservatives, Bush Dumps Frohnmayer," *Art in America* 80 (April 1992): 36; see also in the same issue, "Gay Images Haunt Campaign," 35).

59. David Cronenberg, interviewed by Michael Ondaatje, Premier Dance Theatre, Toronto, March 11, 1992. Early in 1992, the Supreme Court of Canada ruled, in the Butler decision, that material can be declared obscene if it "raises a reasonable apprehension of harm." This test is liable to result in arbitrary and variable obscenity standards across the country. On the topic of women and obscenity, Cronenberg recommended an article by Sallie Tisdale, "Talk Dirty To Me," *Harper's* 284 (February 1992): 37–46.

60. Morgan, *Literary Outlaw*, 346.

61. Homosexuality surfaced as a security issue in national party politics during the presidential campaign of 1964. Less than three weeks before the election, Walter Jenkins, President Johnson's chief of staff, was arrested "with another man . . . and charged with performing 'indecent gestures' in a basement restroom of the Y.M.C.A. two blocks from Jenkins' office in the White House" (Lee Edelman, "Tearooms and Sympathy, or, The Epistemology of the Water Closet," in *Nationalisms and Sexualities*, ed. Andrew Parker, Mary Russo, Doris Sommer, and Patricia Yeager [New York: Routledge, 1992], 263). For a discussion of recent controversies over obscenity legislation, see Judith Butler, "The Force of Fantasy: Feminism, Mapplethorpe, and Discursive Excess," *Differences* 2 (Summer 1990): 105–125.

62. The picture book published simultaneously with release of the film includes seven pages of photographs of this effect (Ira Silverberg, ed., *Everything Is Permitted: The Making of* Naked Lunch (New York: Grove Weidenfeld, 1992).

63. George L. Mosse, *Nationalism and Sexuality: Middle-Class Morality and Sexual Norms in Modern Europe* (Madison: University of Wisconsin Press, 1985), 36; Sander L. Gilman, "Opera, Homosexuality, and Models of Disease: Richard Strauss's *Salome* in the Context of Images of Disease in the Fin de Siècle," in *Disease and Representation: Images of Illness from Madness to AIDS* (Ithaca, N.Y.: Cornell University Press, 1981), 155–181; Sander L. Gilman, "Karl Kraus's Oscar Wilde: Race, Sex, and Difference," in *Inscribing the Other* (Lincoln: University of Nebraska Press, 1991), 173–190.

64. Mahler was Bohemian, and Kraus, an Austrian.

65. Cronenberg remarks on the subject of being an anglophone Canadian: "I'm very balanced. I'm cursed with balance, which is to say I immediately see all sides to the story. And they are all equal. That can be a curse, maybe it's very

Canadian too. This has been noted by some critics like Carrie Rickey, who humorously said that my political stance, since it seems to come down on all sides at once or none at all, seems to be very Canadian" (Rodley, *Cronenberg on Cronenberg*, 118).

66. Rodley, *Cronenberg on Cronenberg*, 159.

67. On the Lacanian symbolic, see Jean Laplanche and J.-B. Pontalis, *The Language of Psycho-Analysis*, trans. Donald Nicholson-Smith and introd. Daniel Lagache (New York: Norton, 1973), 439–440.

68. Rodley, *Cronenberg on Cronenberg*, 162.

69. Sigmund Freud, "Thoughts for the Times on War and Death," in *The Standard Edition of the Complete Psychological Works*, trans. and ed. James Strachey in collaboration with Anna Freud, vol. 14 (London: Hogarth Press, 1974), 298.

70. I use imaginary here as "from the intersubjective point of view, a so-called *dual* relationship based on — and captured by — the image of a counterpart (erotic attraction, aggressive tension)" (Laplanche and Pontalis, *Language of Psycho-Analysis*, 210). For transference and countertransference, see 455–461, 92–93.

71. Laplanche and Pontalis, *Language of Psycho-Analysis*, 460.

72. Burroughs's biographer, Ted Morgan, does not suggest that Jane Bowles and Burroughs were sexually intimate. Feminist analyses of Cronenberg's preceding film, *Dead Ringers* (1988), focus on separation anxiety in male psychology. See Barbara Creed, "Phallic Panic: Male Hysteria and *Dead Ringers*," *Screen* 31 (Summer 1990): 125–146; Marcie Frank, "The Camera and the Speculum: David Cronenberg's *Dead Ringers*," *PMLA* 106 (May 1991): 459–470.

73. Rodley, *Cronenberg on Cronenberg*, 162.

74. In contrast, Jackie Burroughs, in her performance piece, the Jane Bowles Project, acknowledges Bowles's ethnicity. Bowles was highly ambivalent about her Jewish heritage. (Jackie Burroughs, *Jane Bowles Project*, Factory Theatre Studio Cafe, Toronto, March 13, 1992.)

75. I am indebted to Sherwood William for these observations on Freud's practice of analysis. Sherwood William, "The Gay Science: Paradox and Pathology in Wilde and Melville," paper presented at the conference, Pleasure/Politics, Harvard University, Cambridge, Massachusetts, October 27, 1990, 14–16.

76. Rodley, *Cronenberg on Cronenberg*, 169, 158.

77. Cited in Judith Roof, *A Lure of Knowledge: Lesbian Sexuality and Theory* (New York: Columbia University Press, 1991), 178.

78. Roof, *A Lure of Knowledge*, 181–183.

79. Sheehan, "Naked Lunch: Coming Out with Talking Assholes," XS15.

80. Sheehan, "Naked Lunch: Coming Out with Talking Assholes," XS15.

81. Morgan, *Literary Outlaw*, 177.

82. "Dominatrix" is Danny O'Quinn's word in a paper, "War on . . . ," delivered at the Colloquium of the English Graduate Students Association, York University, North York, Ontario, March 5, 1992.

83. O'Quinn, "War on . . ."

84. O'Quinn, "War on . . ."

85. Brian D. Johnson, "Sex, Drugs and Bugs," *Maclean's*, January 20, 1992, 50.

86. Morgan, *Literary Outlaw*, 172; Burroughs, *Queer*, v, vii, xviii.

87. I discuss *fin-de-siècle*, male homosexual versions of the myth in Richard Dellamora, *Masculine Desire: The Sexual Politics of Victorian Aestheticism* (Chapel Hill: University of North Carolina Press, 1990), chap. 9.

88. Brett Stewart, "Sissies and Superman," *Xtra!*, no. 190, February 7, 1992, 11.

89. Silverberg, *Everything Is Permitted*, 122.

90. Silverberg, *Everything Is Permitted*, 15.

Part III
Contemporary
Apocalyptics

Can the Apocalypse Be Post?

Teresa Heffernan

At the end of the century, at the close of the millennium, Jean Baudrillard announces "the year 2000, in a certain way, will not take place."[1] For Baudrillard the proliferation and (re)producibility of the apocalypse are signals that the world has already ended. "Everything has already become nuclear, faraway, vaporized. The explosion has already occurred; the bomb is only a metaphor now."[2] From the Last Judgment to the nuclear holocaust, the drama of the end has played itself out; emptied of meaning, the end of the world is now only a spectacle in reruns. In this postapocalyptic period, the real has imploded and the subject has disappeared; history, culture, and truth are absorbed by the simulated image.[3] Everything has already happened, "been liberated, changed, undermined."[4] In this Nuclear Age we have been (over)exposed, rendered transparent; in the reign of the obese, the obscene, the visible, the ecstatic "pure and empty form" dominates, leaving no resonance, no remainder, no archive.[5] In this "material paradise," this "timeless area," disconnected from but nostalgic for the past, we inhabit a future that has no future. We are beyond history and at the end of difference.

At this point, it is perhaps important to slow down and interrupt Baudrillard's seductive call to suicide with a few questions: What is at stake in this narrative of a future without a future? And have we heard this prophecy before? Baudrillard looks to America as the land of the postapocalypse, of exposure, speed, space, fluid capital, simulation, the bomb, star wars, a "paradise," a "desert for ever" — the site of the end of the end. He writes, in *America*, "We [Europeans] philosophize on the end of lots of things, but it is here [America] that they actually come to an end. It is here, for example, that territory has ceased to exist (though there is indeed a vast amount of space), here that the real and the imaginary have come to an end (opening up all spaces to simulation). It is here, therefore, that we should look for the ideal type of the end of our culture."[6]

As Jacques Derrida writes, and as Baudrillard's writing demonstrates, even announcements on "the end of the end [la fin de la fin], the end of ends" partake of an apocalyptic tone;[7] and thus Baudrillard continues an apocalyptic tradition. Joining a long line of Europeans, Baudrillard leaves behind the Old World and voyages to the New World; he leaves behind history for the end of history; leaves behind the past for an eternal future, he leaves behind darkness for light—"America is a giant hologram . . . it has the coherent light of the laser, the homogeneity of the single elements scanned by the same beams."[8] In 1630, John Winthrop, on a ship traveling from England to America, delivered a sermon in which he also envisioned the New World in apocalyptic terms as a land of homogeneous light: "for wee must Consider that wee shall be as a Citty vpon a hill,"[9] echoing Matthew 5:14: "You are the light of the world. A city on a hill cannot be hidden." Europeans have a long tradition of looking to America as the land of apocalypse forever—as "a heaven on earth," "utopia achieved," the land of the "chosen." David Ketterer writes: "Although all apocalyptic writers might be said to inhabit an America of the mind, the central tradition clings to American soil."[10] In the crossing of the Atlantic, the gap between the world and paradise, the sign and the referent, the old and the new, the saved and the damned closes; or as Douglas Robinson argues, in his reading of Michael Wigglesworth's Puritan apocalypse *The Day of Doom* (1662), fixity or stasis are imagined in the notion of crossing—"the transference or translation across the gaps of spatial difference (earth-heaven) and temporal deferral (now-then) that would heal the negative dialectic of differance."[11]

Disconnected from history and its "destination," Baudrillard sets off into space at the end of his piece entitled "The Anorexic Ruins" in a ship where all life has ceased but vital functions continue ("Anorexic," 39). Driving through the desert of America, aiming for the "point of no return," Baudrillard envisions "the extermination of meaning" and the "end of the scene of the journey" (*America*, 10). Rocketing into space or traveling through the "desert forever," Baudrillard, however, is trapped by a past he thought he had escaped. Like the Europeans who preceded him, he becomes entangled in a rhetoric of ruins and speed.

In "The Anorexic Ruins" and *America,* which both invoke a dialectic of absence and presence, incompletion and completion, Baudrillard as the narrator of the end of the end, in his memory of a history that had a destination, of a world that did have meaning, of a self that was unified, of a real that was transcendent, perseveres in the postholocaust. Richard Klein, in his article on "The Future of Nuclear Criticism," asks an important question about the interests that are served, "the pleasure being taken," or "the profit being made—here now" by the adoption of a tone of the nuclear sublime, which he describes as "that all too familiar aesthetic position from which one anticipatorily contemplates the end, utter nuclear devastation, from a standpoint beyond the end, from a posthumous, apocalyptic perspective of some future mourning, which, however appalling, adorably presupposes some ghostly survival, and some retrospective illumination."[12]

   The Europeans who arrive in America leaving behind the Old World and imagining a radically new beginning also confront the problem of ruins. The Europeans find they have voyaged not to a "new" land, but to one already populated with other people, and have voyaged into a land beginning to be populated, by force, by another people who think of America as the end of their world. The Europeans are stuck in a confusion of multiple beginnings and endings that makes it difficult to determine where (and what) old world stops and what new one begins, a confusion that complicates their desire to name themselves as the "chosen" people. As Douglas Robinson, exploring some of these problems, queries:

If America is the New Israel, who are American Jews, those representatives of the Old Israel who dwell in the New? Are Americans Europeans, or are they a new breed of men? Are the descendants of Protestant Europeans the only true Americans? Who are African-Americans, Asian-Americans, Catholic Americans? What is to be done with a white Anglo-Saxon Protestant who declares himself a Communist? And, most troublesome of all, who are the "Indians," projected in name by white settlers to another continent — those "native Americans" whose discomfiting appellations as the *first* Americans relegates the American remnant itself to secondariness?[13]

   In the European tradition of violently imposing "origins" in the so named New World, which in turn gives rise to such myths as the Founding Fathers giving birth to the Land of the Free, Baudrillard, as a European, persists in reading America as "completely original."[14] In this utterly "original" land, Baudrillard announces the end of the end; however, even as he desires to be beyond the end of man, he remains mired in the middle ground: announcing that the world has already ended, he carries and preserves (in memory) what has ended.

   "At the beginning" writes Derrida "there will have been speed."[15] In "No Apocalypse, Not Now (Full Speed Ahead, Seven Missiles, Seven Missives)," Derrida distinguishes between individual death and the apocalypse by pointing to the difference between the remainder of cultural and social memory that limits the reality of individual death and the total obliteration of the archive in the apocalypse. Nuclear obliteration, at this point, can only be a fiction and "literature has always belonged to the nuclear epoch."[16] Hence, the name can only meet its referent at the moment of the catastrophe, which is also the moment of unveiling, of truth. The war then would be fought in the "name of nothing," the "pure name," the "naked name."[17]

   In the war, the word speeds toward its referent and the referent speeds toward the word. The early Europeans, who imagined America to be the fulfillment of the Divine Order, and envisioned, in the movement from the Old to the New World, a movement out of decay and into innocence, a movement from prophecy to revelation, from sign to referent, were confronted with a dilemma. Imagining themselves, as Cotton Mather wrote, "a colony of chosen people" in the New World,[18] they continued to battle over signs as they tried to read, in accordance with Calvinist doctrine, the evidence of election. Derrida has argued that signs, even as they emerge from the desire to repair a sense of loss, stand in for a presence and thus necessarily testify to the absence of that presence. The Puritans come up against a problem that plagues literal predictions and originates in the very book that often inspires them: "the Book of Revelation is a semiotic of completion that contains within itself the telling trace of incompletion."[19] Still reading and arguing over the interpretation of signs, the pilgrims had to confront, to some degree, the absence of Divine Order.

Searching for a resolution to this dilemma and hurtling into space at an accelerating velocity, Baudrillard speeds (according to the theory of relativity, which proposes that time slows down as speed increases) toward immortality as time decelerates, "as it nears its end." In the postlapsarian world of simulation (after the fall from the real), Baudrillard posits the possibility of resurrection in the absolute victory of the sign. In the inert world "it is useless to dream,"[20] announces Baudrillard, and, yet, caught in a rhetoric of ruins and speed, he dreams of survival and immortality and of a world that escapes death.

Simulating but also interrupting the discourse of the postapocalypse, Don DeLillo's novel *White Noise* comments on the interests of this skeptical and melancholic narrative. In a world of flickering television screens, of tabloids, of floating toxic clouds and postmodern sunsets, of children with receding hairlines who volunteer to play victims in simulated disasters and who chant advertising slogans in their sleep, Jack Gladney, in his choice of spouse and career, turns toward the solid, the stable, the serious.

Babette, unlike his former wives, several of whom were employed by the secret service or engaged in espionage, trusts in "the tangible and real."[21] "She was not a keeper of secrets" (213); her ample size suggests a presence and a "seriousness" (5). Jack is not naturally endowed with what he reads as Babette's "seriousness," but he works hard to generate the "aura." When Jack proposes the establishment of a Hitler Studies department, the chancellor warns Jack about his "tendency to make a feeble presentation of self" (16–17). In response to the chancellor's concerns, Jack gains weight, changes his name, and adopts glasses with thick frames and dark lenses. When Babette asks him about the naming of his son, Heinrich, Jack responds: "I thought it was a forceful name, a strong name. It has a kind of authority. . . . I wanted to shield him, make him unafraid. . . . There's something about German names, the German language, German *things*. I don't know what it is exactly. It's just there. In the middle of it all is Hitler, of course" (63).

On an outing with Murray, a professor of American Environments who wants to do with Elvis what Jack has done with Hitler ("He is now your Hitler, Gladney's Hitler" [11]), Jack visits the most photographed barn in America. Murray lectures on the barn while Jack remains silent. Frank Lentricchia engages in an interesting reading of this passage that points to the common but problematic assumption that Murray's "miniature essay" on postmodernism transparently reflects DeLillo's own views on the subject. Lentricchia points out that Murray's lecture is filtered through Jack, who reports on "long silences and background noises."[22] Murray argues in his lecture that, " 'Once you've seen the signs about the barn, it becomes impossible to see the barn. . . . We're not here to capture an image, we're here to maintain one. Every photograph reinforces the aura. Can you feel it, Jack? An accumulation of nameless energies' " (12). Jack's silence suggests his discomfort with a world in which signs dominate and Hitler is interchangeable with Elvis. His attraction to his corporeal wife and in things German mark his nostalgia for the real, the tangible, the certain. However, given that Jack's nostalgia is rooted in Nazi Germany, can the real really stand as a site of resistance to the sign? Or is there a similarity between these two discourses?

While Baudrillard in his crossing of the Atlantic finds the true experience of America in "the feeling that Europe ha[s] disappeared"[23] (and Europe in *America* stands in for meaning, ideas, history), *White Noise* reflects back on the "old" world opening up the gulf between the old and the new—whether the crossing (and closing) is imagined in the name of the sign and the end of meaning or in the name of the end of the sign and the fulfillment of meaning—in order to explore the interests at stake in closing the gulf.

There have been several critical works on Don DeLillo's *White Noise* that have noted similarities between Baudrillard's theory and the novel. For instance, Leonard Wilcox, reading the novel in light of Baudrillard, describes the world of *White Noise* as a world of surfaces, simulation, and signs that ensure the erasure of the real world and the dispersal of the self.[24] Wilcox tries to salvage the novel from Baudrillard's position of "radical scepticism," where there is "no real in which a radical critique of the simulational society might be grounded."[25] Wilcox argues that, in Gladney's persistent attempts to recuperate a heroic narrative that works itself out in terms of boundaries and ends, which in turn allow for the possibility of "self-knowledge" and "vision," the hero battles postmodern discourse:

The passion for meaning that animates readers is the desire for the end; to eradicate a sense of ending in life or narrative is to extinguish meaning. Yet the sense of boundaries and endings that define the self and give life or narrative meaning (or "heroic" possibilities, moments of self-knowledge, moments of vision) are erased in postmodern society.[26]

Wilcox concludes: "DeLillo's sympathies surely must be with his protagonist as Gladney holds tight to his fear of death in a society where the fear of death, like other aspects of the deep structures of subjectivity, is being transformed into images and codes, simulations, and charismatic spectacle."[27]

Ignoring for a moment those of us who do not wish for a return of what could be called patriarchal modernist narratives (even though they might well guarantee a certain kind of agency for a select few), we might explore whether restoring a "meaningful" end that secures narrative (or life) is a viable option given the thinking about life in a Nuclear Age. In DeLillo's novel, Jack Gladney, as a "doomed man," terrified of dying, listens to a great deal of advice on how to meet the end. This advice ranges from Murray's "disease of the week" scenario (" 'I'm saying you can't let down the living by slipping into self-pity and despair. People will depend on you to be brave. What people look for in a dying friend is a stubborn kind of gravel-voiced nobility, a refusal to give in, with moments of indomitable humor' " [284]) to Winnie's Hemingway-like scenario involving a macho confrontation with nature as a heroic moment of self-discovery (" 'It is a grizzly bear, enormous, shiny brown, swaggering, dripping slime from its bared fangs. . . . You see yourself in a new way and intense way. You rediscover yourself. You are lit up for your own imminent dismemberment. The beast on hind legs has enabled you to see who you are as if for the first time, outside familiar surroundings, alone, distinct, whole.' " [229]).

In a novel that offers a variety of narratives on the end and in which "all plots tend to move deathward," it is difficult to read Gladney's attempts to hold on to a sense of an end as meaningful as anything but ironic, given Baudrillard's reading of the catastrophe as the loss of the end or Derrida's reading of a nuclear end as loss of the possibility of loss. The discourse of opposition that Wilcox sets up — the real as a sight of resistance to simulation — an opposition which is necessary in his attempt to recuperate a sense of death (real meaningful death versus simulated tabloid death), is problematic given the fables of a nuclear end, which document a future without a past, a future that cannot make sense of or give meaning to the past.

Because, as Derrida suggests in his article on the nuclear apocalypse, in this absolute absence there could be no record, no archive of the history of presence or even a history of loss of presence, nuclear destruction (even as a fiction) disrupts the binary of death/life or absence/presence in the here and now and forces us to think of the future differently. In this disruption, how can the real take precedence over or be distinguished from the simulated? If the hierarchy is leveled, how do we know whether we are witnessing the real imagined or the simulated image? The scenes in *White Noise* that are populated by the SIMUVAC (short for simulated evacuation) people point to this dilemma; as they regularly stage impressive rehearsals for real disasters, they in turn use the real event, the airborne toxic event, to practice their simulation:

> "But this evacuation isn't simulated. It's real."
> "We know that. But we thought we could use it as a model."
> "A form of practice? Are you saying you saw a chance to use the real event in order to rehearse the simulation?"
> "We took it right to the streets."
> "How is it going?" I said.
> "The insertion curve isn't as smooth as we would like. There's a probability excess. Plus which we don't have our victims laid out where we'd want them if this was an actual simulation. In other words we're forced to take our victims as we find them. We didn't get a jump on computer traffic. Suddenly it just spilled out, three-dimensionally, all over the landscape. You have to make allowances for the fact that everything we see tonight is real. There's a lot of polishing we still have to do. But that's what this exercise is all about." (139)

What is real and what is simulated? Which is the act and which is the image? Michael Valdez Moses, in his paper, "Lust Removed from Nature," argues, further supporting a view of the complicity between the real and the simulated, that corporate America and the environmentalists share a common language that is evident in this passage in which the SIMUVAC people use the real disaster as a dry run for their simulations: "The absurdity of this bizarre reversal reveals that these organizations operate according to the same logic as do those cultural and economic forces they ostensibly oppose." In other words, Moses argues, nature is for both the pro-business and the environmentalists a thing "to be managed and controlled."[28]

Caught between a world of advertising logos and Nazi nostalgia, *White Noise* suggests that perhaps we have never known the difference between the true and the false, the saved and the damned, the sign and the referent; perhaps, in all our attempts to dramatize an end, the difference has never become clear. Maybe we are asking the wrong question and instead should ask a different one: What is at stake in the relationship between the real and the image?

The pilgrims think of themselves as the chosen in a millennial city but are caught in the dilemma of reading the signs of election. Confused about their arrival in a not so new land and trapped in a rhetoric of ruins and speed, they become more intent on proving that they are the light and truth of the world. In spreading the light, Jonathan Edwards was inspired to distinguish the saved from the damned, "the aliens from the common wealth of Israel," so "that every tree which brings not forth good fruit, may be hewn down and cast into the fire."[29] After clearing the forest and standing among the remaining good trees, Edwards imagined that his was "most properly the time of the kingdom of *heaven upon earth*."[30] Baudrillard, in his vision of America as "paradise,"[31] the land of simulation and "coherent light," is also excited by "this overall dynamism, this dynamic of the abolition of differences."[32]

In *White Noise*, crowded in the barracks where the town has gathered to escape the toxic cloud, a Jehovah's Witness converses with Jack:

"You're either among the wicked or among the saved. The wicked get to rot as they walk down the street. They get to feel their own eyes slide out of their sockets. You'll know them by their stickiness and lost parts. People tracking slime of their own making. All the flashiness of the Armageddon is in the rotting. The saved know each other by their neatness and reserve. He doesn't have showy ways is how you know a saved person." (136)

In an indirectly reflexive moment, Jack thinks: "He was a serious man, he was matter-of-fact and practical, down to his running shoes. I wondered about his eerie self-assurance, his freedom from doubt. Is this the point of Armageddon? No ambiguity, no more doubt" (137).

Jack's fascination with an earlier Holocaust, in which the line between good and evil was also neatly drawn, suggests that "freedom from doubt" is what drives him in his attraction to things German, in his resistance to Babette's dark secret, and in his unwillingness to face mortality. Jack chooses German studies as a way of shielding himself from fearful thoughts about his own death; after his presentation about the crowds that gather around Hitler in the name of death "to form a shield against their own dying" (73), Jack thinks: "Death was strictly a professional matter here. I was comfortable with it, I was on top of it" (74). Following Jack's exposure to the toxic cloud, Murray comments on Jack's interests in Hitler Studies: " 'Some people are larger than life. Hitler is larger than death. You thought he would protect you' " (287). When Babette finally reveals her dark secret, her own fear of death, Jack, in an absurd and desperate moment, tries to convince her that she is really afraid of something else, perhaps weight gain, arguing that: " 'There must be something else, an underlying problem' " (197). Although Jack is plagued by doubt, he needs to read Babette as true, transparent, exposed.

The world of the sign and the real collide in Jack's confrontation with Dylar, a drug that proposes to alleviate the fear of death. In Jack's plot to kill Mr. Gray, the seducer of his wife, the foreigner in Germantown, Jack plays out a Hitlerian narrative of eradicating the other. In the act of murder, he searches for the authentic moment as a "cure for death." " 'Be the killer for a change. Let someone else be the dier,' " says Murray, invoking a strategy with a long tradition. He advises Gladney, " 'You can't die if he does. He dies, you live' " (291).

Leonard Wilcox convincingly argues that Gladney, in the passages that deal with his plot to kill Mink/Gray, rewrites "a present which seems without link to past and future. . . . Yet in spite of this heightened intensity, the encounter suggests not the existentialist sense that pure existence looms up as artificial words and constructs drop away, but rather the postmodern awareness that words themselves construct reality."[33] Wilcox points to the failure of Gladney in his attempt to escape the world of signs. More importantly, this passage also points, in the search for the authentic moment, to the desire for the collapse of time, an escape from the past, and a future without future. Yes, we *have* heard this prophecy before.

Faced with the infeasibility of transcending the sign (and the end), Jack is drawn to another "cure" in the form of Dylar. Almost mimicking a Baudrillardian strategy, the drug implodes in the body. Like the implosion of the real, the drug collapses the difference between the word and the referent, so that when Jack says "plunging aircraft," Mink, who ingests Dylar pills by the handfuls, overcome by panic, jumps into crash position (309). As is clear from Mink's terror, Dylar, like Baudrillard's narrative, is not very successful in its attempt to move beyond the end of the end.

Fueled by a faith in exposure and clarity, Jack imagines the possibility of the real and the authentic, while Baudrillard announces the triumph of the sign. Whether the subject engages in the discourse of the real or in that of simulation, there is no unspoken; everything is transparent; the strong subject and the dissolute subject fully know presence and absence, respectively. In the comfortable arena either of the real or of the image, the world is fully readable; even the apocalypse is domesticated; catastrophe happens elsewhere and is exposed, framed, and contained by the television set and tabloids. Although he employs different strategies, Jack, like Baudrillard, dreams of a world beyond death, a world without difference and without a future: "Don't let us die. . . . Let us both live forever" (103) is his frequent refrain to Babette. Whether death is approached as the last frontier of rational knowledge, an experience waiting to be conquered, as Babette approaches it (she tells Jack, " 'You know how I am. I think everything is correctible. Given the right attitude and the proper effort, a person can change a harmful condition by reducing it to its simplest parts. You can make lists, invent categories, devise charts and graphs' " [191]) or we are living death, as Baudrillard announces, death is assumed to be knowable.

So, what has been exposed in our hero's exposure to the toxic airborne event and in this novel about death? The impossibility of final exposure. When Jack reveals the circumstances of his exposure to the toxic cloud to the SIMUVAC man, Jack is in turn exposed on the man's computer screen. However, despite the "pulsating stars" that show up on the computer screen and the mass that is traceable on the X rays, death resists examination and categorization. For all the technology that is working toward mastering death, Jack's mortality remains vague, ambiguous, and indeterminate:

> "Am I going to die?"
> "Not as such," he said.
> "What do you mean?"
> "Not in so many words."
> "How many words does it take?"
> "It's not a question of words. It's a question of years. We'll know more in fifteen years. In the meantime we definitely have a situation."
> "What will we know in fifteen years?"
> "If you are still alive at the time, we'll know that much more than we do now. Nyodene D. has a life span of thirty years. You'll have made it halfway through."
> "I thought it was forty years."
> "Forty years in the soil. Thirty years in the human body."
> "So, to outlive this substance, I will have to make it into my eighties. Then I can begin to relax."
> "Knowing what we know at this time."
> "But the general consensus seems to be that we don't know enough at this time to be sure of anything." (140–141)

Rather than looking to the end to stabilize meaning, to draw the division between absence and presence, the real and the simulated, we might look at the end or death as the impossibility of the stabilization of either the referent or the sign, as a "viral agent." And you well might ask, as Jack asks of the foreigner: " 'Are you saying death adapts? It eludes our attempts to reason with it?' " (308).

Notes

1. Jean Baudrillard, "The Anorexic Ruins," in *Looking Back on the End of the World,* ed. Dietmar Kamper and Christoph Wulf, and trans. David Antal (New York: Semiotext(e), 1989), 39.

2. Baudrillard, "The Anorexic Ruins," 34.

3. See for instance Jean Baudrillard, *Simulations,* trans. Paul Foss, Paul Patton, Philip Beitchman (New York: Semiotext(e), 1983).

4. Baudrillard, "The Anorexic Ruins," 34.

5. See for instance Jean Baudrillard, *Fatal Strategies,* ed. Jim Fleming, trans. Philip Beitchman and W. G. J. Niesluchowski (New York, London: Semiotext(e) / Pluto, 1990).

6. Jean Baudrillard, *America*, trans. Chris Turner (London: Verso, 1988), 98.

7. Jacques Derrida, "Of an Apocalyptic Tone Recently Adopted in Philosophy," trans. John P. Leavey Jr., *Oxford Literary Review* 6, no. 2 (1984): 21.

8. Baudrillard, *America*, 29.

9. John Winthrop, "A Modell of Christian Charity," quoted in James G. Mosely, *John Winthrop's World: History as a Story, the Story as History* (Madison: University of Wisconsin Press 1992), 44. Scriptural reference quoted in *The Thompson Chain Reference Bible, New International Version* (1989).

10. David Ketterer, *New Worlds for Old: The Apocalyptic Imagination, Science Fiction, and American Literature* (New York: Anchor Books 1974), 332.

11. Douglas Robinson, *American Apocalypses: The Image of the End of the World in Literature* (Baltimore: Johns Hopkins University Press, 1985), 59.

12. Richard Klein, "The Future of Nuclear Criticism," *Yale French Studies* 77 (1990): 77.

13. Robinson, *American Apocalypses,* 61.

14. See for instance Baudrillard's interview with Suzanne Moore and Stephen Johnstone in which he says "American culture or rather non-culture is in itself completely original." "The Politics of Seduction," *Marxism Today* (January 1989): 54.

15. Jacques Derrida, "No Apocalypse, Not Now (Full Speed Ahead, Seven Missiles, Seven Missives)," trans. Catherine Porter and Philip Lewis, *Diacritics* 14 (Summer 1984): 20.

16. Derrida, "No Apocalypse," 27.

17. Derrida, "No Apocalypse," 31.

18. See, for instance, Cotton Mather, *Magnalai Christi Americana or the Ecclesiastical History of New England,* ed. Raymond J. Cunningham (New York: Frederick Ungar Publishing Co., 1970).

19. Robinson, *American Apocalypses,* 35.

20. Baudrillard, "The Anorexic Ruins," 34.

21. Don DeLillo, *White Noise* (New York: Penguin, 1986), 185. All further references in my text are to this edition.

22. Frank Lentricchia, "Tales on the Electronic Tribe," in *New Essays on White Noise,* ed. Frank Lentricchia (Cambridge: Cambridge University Press, 1991), 90.

23. Baudrillard, *America*, 105.

24. Leonard Wilcox, "Baudrillard, DeLillo's *White Noise,* and the End of Heroic Narrative," *Contemporary Literature* 33, no. 3 (1991): 346–347.

25. Wilcox, "Baudrillard," 363.

26. Wilcox, "Baudrillard," 361.

27. Wilcox, "Baudrillard," 364.

28. Michael Valdez Moses, "Lust Removed from Nature," in *New Essays on White Noise,* ed. Frank Lentricchia (Cambridge: Cambridge University Press, 1991), 66.

29. Jonathan Edwards, "Sinners in the Hands of an Angry God," in *The Works of Jonathan Edwards,* vol. 2, revised and corrected by Edward Hickman, 2 vols. (1834; reprint, Carlisle, Pa.: The Banner of Truth Trust, 1974), 12.

30. Jonathan Edwards, "The End of Time," in *The Works of Jonathan Edwards,* vol. 1, revised and corrected by Edward Hickman, 2 vols. (1834; reprint, Carlisle, Pa.: The Banner of Truth Trust, 1974), 609.

31. Baudrillard, *America*, 98.

32. Baudrillard, *America*, 89.

33. Wilcox, "Baudrillard," 356.

Cyborg Economies: Desire and Labor in the *Terminator* Films

Kevin Pask

Science fiction, the popular genre most clearly associated with modern attempts to imagine the future, provides an interesting gloss on the pervasive characterization of the "postmodern" condition that we inhabit as the *ne plus ultra* in disenchantment with the "grand narratives" of the past. In its early formulation as the description of scientific and technological utopia, science fiction was a pendant to such "grand narratives," and in fact "cyberpunk," a popular mode of science fiction in the past decade, announces its break with earlier versions of the genre as the decommissioning of a utopian vision of the future. Dystopia has long played a role in science fiction, but it is difficult to imagine cyberpunk without it. In this sense, then, cyberpunk is the dystopian alternative to a considerably more cheerful vision of history, which, despite its Hegelian sweep, also conditions the experience of postmodernity — Francis Fukuyama's version of an "end of history" in which liberal capitalism emerges as the final form of human society. Fukuyama's essay "The End of History?" was first published in 1989, but its essential assumption that "we cannot picture to ourselves a world that is essentially different from the present one, and at the same time better," "a future that is not essentially democratic and capitalist," was already widespread.[1] In the absence of any generally persuasive challenge, notably in the perceived failure of socialism as an alternative to liberal capitalism, Fukuyama's must be allowed to hold the field. This metanarrative of the *present* as the decisive conclusion of history ("apocalypse now"), moreover, structures what postmodern theorists celebrate as the cessation of all such narratives. What they share with Fukuyama's grand narrative is a sense of the impossibility (or undesirability) of formulating an alternative to liberal capitalism. "Le capital fait jouir" is Jean-François Lyotard's formula for the libidinal dynamics of postmodernism.[2] As the cultural expression of "post-Fordist" capitalism, a connection insisted on by both Fredric Jameson and David Harvey,[3] postmodernism's theorization of the liberating pleasures of consumer capitalism accommodates itself readily enough to the metanarrative in which there is no "post" to the order characterized by the Group of Seven, GATT, and the International Monetary Fund, only its indefinite extension throughout the globe.

If the present is also the future, what is the role of science fiction in imagining that present-future? Science fiction, like any imagining of the future, has always and necessarily reflected the time of its production. Jameson argues that the function of the genre is "not to give us 'images' of the future . . . but rather to defamiliarize and restructure our experience of our own *present,* and to do so in specific ways distinct from all other forms of defamiliarization."[4] Thus, the optimistic technocracy of early science fiction is partly the celebration of the possibilities opened by industrial capitalism — an epistemic progressivism shared by capitalism and socialism. Cyberpunk is manifestly embarrassed by this aspect of its generic ancestor, but, of course, its dystopian future is equally symptomatic of the era in which it is produced. The latter point is made by Andrew Ross in the course of arguing against what he perceives as the defeatist vision of the future offered by recent science fiction.[5] Ross's leftist plea for the reappropriation of the progressive political possibilities available in earlier modes of science fiction is rather strikingly endorsed by a mainstream product of science fiction, *Star Trek VI: The Undiscovered Country* (1991). This "undiscovered country," the film informs us, is history itself, which remains available to be "made." Like most of the conservative critiques of Fukuyama, however, its vision of this "frontier" appears as simply an intergalactic extension of a "Pax Americana" (a "Confederation" of planets strikingly similar to NATO or the current incarnation of the United Nations whose domains are patrolled by the USS *Enterprise*) envisioned by Fukuyama himself. This essentially *nostalgic* mode in science-fiction films and criticism is an attempt to return "back to the future," a future much like the Reaganite "fantasy of technological omnipotence" (the "Star Wars" militarization of space), which served as the end game of the Cold War imaginary.[6]

In this context, the refusal to imagine a progressive future carries a political weight that need not be simply condemned. The "New Bad Future" that Fred Glass describes in recent science-fiction films simply represents the underside of the indefinite extension of the present world order imagined in the "End of History."[7] As necessarily popular and populist products of Hollywood, such films usually gesture, often quite lamely and usually at the last possible moment, to the reappropriation of a progressive future. Both *The Terminator* (James Cameron, 1984) and *Terminator 2: Judgment Day* (Cameron, 1991), the films under consideration in this essay, are the most popular examples of this subgenre. Since in both films the future is fought out in the "apocalyptic" (as the subtitle of *Terminator 2* indicates) *present,* they insist on a close affinity between a "New Bad Present" and the "New Bad Future." It might be useful, at this point, to juxtapose Donna Haraway's insistence in her "Manifesto for Cyborgs" (first published in 1985) that "the boundary between science fiction and social reality is an optical illusion"[8] with the opening declaration of *The Terminator:* "The machines rose from the ashes of the nuclear fire. Their war to exterminate mankind had raged for decades, but the final battle would not be fought in the future. It would be fought here, in our present. Tonight. . . . "[9] The paradoxical time-loop logic of both films, which Constance Penley has emphasized,[10] moreover, undercuts every explicit insistence on the individual's ability to change this present-future. *Terminator 2,* for instance, reveals that Sarah Connor's apparent victory over the Terminator at the end of *The Terminator* leaves the remains that allow for a significant breakthrough in the defense technologies that makes possible the dystopian future. In *Terminator 2* Sarah Connor carves the words "no fate" into a picnic table before having a nightmare about the future nuclear apocalypse and then deciding to change that future. Her son, John Connor, discovers, or rather recognizes, the carving: "No fate. No fate but what we make. My father told her this. I mean, I made him memorize it up in the future as a message to her."[11] This articulation of individual can-doism is itself a time-loop paradox, a "memory" of the *future* that in turn serves as the basis for that future. The *Terminator* films ask their audience to imagine the remaking of the future even as they reveal a future that is also the *past* in their narrative logic. Such paradoxes are, however, tremendously productive sites of cultural fantasy, which is part of the critical interest of the *Terminator* films.

The most interesting readings of the *The Terminator* and its sequel are readings of the sexual politics of the films.[12] This fact registers the importance of feminism and queer studies in the current practice of cultural studies. The most recent studies, moreover, have acutely located technology, rather than human sexuality, as the site of libidinal liberation in the films.[13] This development corresponds to J. G. Ballard's elegant formula for recent science fiction: "sex times technology equals the future."[14] My own reading relies on such deployments of sex and gender, but it also attempts to locate the libidinal economies of the films in the context of a political economy that has been absent from most readings of the films. Here it is necessary to recall that Haraway's "Manifesto," the crucial text for most recent celebrations of cyborg sexuality, is an explicitly socialist one, which locates its "cyborg feminism" in the context of the international division of labor in which the burden of exploitation is borne by Third World women. This global context is the underutilized aspect of Haraway's work that informs my own reading of the contradictory sexual politics of the films. Briefly, I propose that both films deal with the consequences of this international division of labor — the replacement of rel-

atively high-paying unionized jobs in North America by low-wage manufacturing work throughout the Third World — as a gender crisis: the
disappearance of the father (Reese), the "cyborgization" of the mother
(Sarah Connor), and even the "recuperation" of the nuclear family in
the return of the Terminator as a mechanically programmed father figure in *Terminator 2*.

This reading also requires some consideration of the contradictions in
the political messages of the films — contradictions that are probably
linked to the need for Hollywood spectacles to appeal to a multiplicity of
audiences. *The Terminator* itself announces its subject, as we have already
seen, as technology's war upon human beings. This war between humans
and machines is the basis of the film's explicitly progressive politics; that
is, its anticorporate, antimilitarist politics. The machines in question are
the products of a deranged national security state, "Defense Network
Computers," as Kyle Reese calls them, which literally take on a life of
their own, coming to consciousness at some moment in the future and
declaring war on human beings. In the film, a cyborg (Arnold Schwarzenegger), a machine covered by human skin and external organs, is sent
back in time from the year 2029 in order to "terminate" Sarah Connor
and thus prevent the birth of her son, John Connor, who by 2029 has
become the leader of the human resistance. John Connor, meanwhile,
sends back a human, Kyle Reese, both to protect Sarah and, it turns out,
to impregnate her. Both the Terminator and Reese arrive in Los Angeles
in the year 1984, the year of *The Terminator*'s release, which was also one of
the peak years of Reagan's military buildup in the United States.[15] Plans
for a "Star Wars" defense initiative had been announced only the year
before, and a "free enterprise" Olympics, one relying entirely on private
financing and thus serving as an international spectacle of the free market, was held in Los Angeles that summer. Los Angeles was also one of the
chief beneficiaries of the military Keynesianism that characterized the
American economy between World War II and the end of the Cold War, a
fact that has become retrospectively all too apparent in its inordinate job
loss in the recession and restructuring of the early 1990s.[16] Los Angeles,
then, is not simply Hollywood; it is the site (and was particularly so in
1984) at which the "pure war," the permanent war economy described by
Paul Virilio, converges with the spectacular entertainments of postmodern capitalism. Modern war, according to Virilio, is about "setting in
place a series of automatisms, reactionary industrial and scientific procedures from which all political choice is absent."[17]

The film's *explicit* politics, then, its progressive humanist (i.e., anti-
machine) politics meant to be juxtaposed to the Reaganite defense
buildup, is also decisively aligned with its less explicit politics, which are
reactionary humanist. As Margaret Goscilo has argued, the film articulates

its progressive humanism by making Sarah Connor preeminently the mother-to-be, fighting to save her unborn child.[18] The police psychologist called in to analyze Kyle Reese, for instance, dismissively refers to the Terminator's mission as a "retroactive abortion." It is also the case, moreover, that even the film's progressive humanism evades any *human* responsibility for its nightmare of the future. Machines, which are the products of human labor, simply become the binary opposite of the human, coming to "life" and making war upon their creators. This binary opposition allows Reese to evade any human agency in his description of the deranged security state of the future. "It was the machines, Sarah," says Reese, explaining the origin of the nuclear war. "Defense Network Computers. New. Powerful. Hooked into everything. Trusted to run it all. They say it got smart. A new order of intelligence. Then it saw *all* people as a threat, not just the ones on the other side." The grammatical confusion of Reese's lines — is it "they" ("computers" is pluralized) or "it" which is responsible for nuclear annihilation? — reflects an even greater evasion of agency: It certainly *was not* "we" or "you." Much as in Oliver Stone's recent *JFK,* Reese conjoins this populist humanism with a vision of political action based on both conspiracy theory and the intervention of the great man: "But there was one man who taught us to fight, to storm the wire of the camps. To smash those mutant motherfuckers into junk. He turned it around. He brought it back from the brink. His name was Connor. John Connor. Your son, Sarah. Your unborn son." Even the film's "progressive" politics surreptitiously register what in the early 1980s was already a growing political alienation of Americans. The film locates that development in the burgeoning apparatus of the national security state, while simultaneously refusing any complicity or responsibility in that development. Even as it criticizes the permanent war economy, then, the film also accepts the logic of the "automatisms" that such an economy deploys.

A close examination of the romance between Sarah Connor and Kyle Reese, however, reveals the contradictory relationship between the film's explicit humanism and its construction of a classically Oedipal nuclear family romance that is meant to sustain that humanism. The terms of that romance evacuate its human family in the course of celebrating its apotheosis, and this evacuation in turn reveals the characteristic anxieties and cultural fantasies of postmodern capitalism.

In the second of three romance scenes Sarah asks Kyle, "What's it like when you go through time?" and he replies, "White light. Pain. It's like being born maybe." It is, not coincidentally, at this moment that Sarah's affection for Reese enters the register of the maternal, and she begins to bandage Reese's wounded arm. She then asks Reese to tell her about her son. "He's about my height. He has your eyes," Reese replies. "What's he like?" Sarah wants to know. "You trust him. He's got a strength. I'd die for John Connor," says Reese. The emerging clarity of the romantic/erotic interplay between Reese and Sarah is thus fixed by the phantasmatic presence of their future son as well as Reese's new position as her *present* son. As Jonathan Goldberg points out ("Recalling Totalities," 182), Reese's love for John Connor, his willingness to die for him, structures his attraction to Sarah. In the same scene, moreover, Reese explains that he volunteered for the time-travel mission in order "to meet the legend: Sarah Connor. Taught her son to fight. Organize. Prepared him when he was a kid." It is her status as the *mother* of John Connor that attracts him to her while it is from the position of mother that she is attracted to him. Thus, it is a homosocial bond between father and son, one that the film displaces onto the relationship between a charismatic leader and a young fighter, which is represented as preceding the heterosexual bond between mother and father.

The climactic scene between Sarah and Reese, the one that concludes with them in bed, relies again on Sarah's maternal concern for Reese's experience of pain. "The women in your time. What are they like?" asks Sarah.

"Good fighters."
"That's not what I meant. Was there someone special?"
"Someone . . . ?"

Reese is plainly confused.

"A girl, you know?"
"[Decisively] No. Never."
"Never? I'm sorry. I'm so sorry."

Sarah begins stroking his wounds, saying "So much pain." Reese's pain, which recalls that of time travel and thus birth, is also associated with his virginity. His virginity, however, is also connected to his status as a warrior, and he must lose *both* virginity and virility in order to become a father. Reese's double bind is the double bind of homosocial masculinity more generally: his virginity is aligned with his strength as a warrior, but it is also a sign of not having attained the position of patriarch. The film relies on the time-honored misogynist tradition in which sex with a woman inevitably drains a man's *potentia*.[19] Reese's declaration of love for Sarah, which also informs us that a picture of Sarah given to him by their son, John Connor, is responsible for that love, gets them in bed for a bout of lovemaking featuring frequent cuts to slow-motion shots of Reese's hand clenched in hers, signaling, apparently, the exquisite pain through which the sensations, painful or otherwise, of the masculine warrior are super-seded by those of the lover.

Reese afterward loses his status as the good warrior, but he makes no compensatory gain as patriarch. His sexual encounter leaves him vulner-able to the Terminator, who, not surprisingly, wounds and eventually kills him in the succeeding chase sequence. As Constance Penley points out, the fantasy governing the series of exchanges between Sarah and Reese is that of the primal scene, the male fantasy of being one's own father, of making one's father into a son. As the film's time loop allows John Con-nor to occupy that fantasy position and insists on his phantasmatic pres-ence as the object of desire that mediates Sarah's and Reese's desire for each other, it also enforces the elimination of the biological father, Reese. To alter the terms somewhat, John Connor (and of course his initials are no accident) can occupy the position both of Christ *and* God the Father only if Reese is reduced to the status of Joseph.[20] As we have already seen, John Connor refers to the future "up" there — a heavenly rather than temporal location. *Terminator 2*'s invocation of religious apocalypse in its subtitle, "Judgment Day," again highlights the reliance on Christian nar-rative. The film's derogation of Reese proceeds directly from his hetero-sexual encounter with Sarah, which, in the logic of the film saps his warrior's power, a power that Reese connects to his homosocial devotion to John Connor. Reese is thus caught in the paradoxical (and aggressively Oedipal) logic of the film's time loop. His biological paternity of his own role model and source of strength is also the condition of his loss of that strength. The lesson is unintentionally registered by Sarah's tape-recorded message to her son at the end of the movie: "Maybe it will help if you know that in the few hours we had together, we loved a lifetime's worth." If this is a "pro-life" film, it is one in which the fetus's life exists at the expense of the biological father, "terminated" immediately upon the performance of his biological mission.

For Sarah, on the other hand, the sexual encounter sets her on the road to realizing her destiny as one of the "good fighters" that women of the future will be. After a wounded Reese collapses in their final refuge, a factory run by robotics, Sarah screams at him as his commanding officer, "Move it, Reese! On your feet, soldier!" Here, we only need recall Reese's first exchange with Sarah after rescuing her from the Terminator at Tech Noir, in which he barks out the imperative assertions of male authority, "Do exactly what I say. Don't move unless I say. Don't make a sound unless I say," to register the extent to which Reese and Sarah change positions in the course of the film. While this exchange marks the film's explicit feminism, Sarah's transformation from passive victim to militant fighter only occurs after the conception of her child, John Connor; motherhood regulates, and therefore legitimates, that transformation. It is, moreover, a message from her adult (in the future) but unconceived (in the present) son that informs her of the necessity for that transformation into a fighter: "You must be stronger than you imagine you can be. You must survive, or I will never exist." Her own survival, like Reese's sacrificial mission, is subordinated to the existence of the great man.

It remains, however, distinctly the case that Arnold Schwarzenegger's Terminator, rather than Reese, occupies the center of the film. The film's repressed, but entirely legible, alternative narrative to that of the Holy Family is one in which the Terminator doubles both Reese and Sarah, providing a space in which the film confuses its own explicit insistence on the absolute distinction between human and machine. With the Terminator and Reese at the beginning of the film, this doubling relies on the spectator's uncertainty recapitulated by Sarah's conviction that Reese is a psycho killer: the spectator knows that both the Terminator and Reese stalk Sarah; Reese is less violent than the Terminator, but he has also stolen clothes and guns.[21]

The doubling of Sarah and the Terminator, on the other hand, is of much greater interest to the film, and it is this relationship that challenges the populist humanism enunciated by Reese. In the series of shots that establish Sarah's life at home, we first see Sarah and her roommate, Ginger, grooming themselves at the mirror. Mobilizing the feminist critique of classical Hollywood film, Goscilo writes that Sarah "appears now as object of her own look as well as ours, in anticipation of the objectifying male gaze" ("Deconstructing *The Terminator,*" 40). Ginger, however, looks into the mirror, hugs Sarah and declares, "Better than mortal man deserves." In fact, Sarah's own relationships with "mortal" human beings are consistently promised *and* deferred by the medium of the telephone. She picks up the ringing telephone to receive an obscene phone call from Ginger's boyfriend, who halts his description of progressive sexual entanglement when he discovers that he is talking to Sarah. Playing back her message machine, Sarah ignores a message from her own mother while searching for her pet iguana named Pugsley, whom she addresses as "young man" and tells to "mind your mother." Her next message informs her that her date for the evening has backed out on her. Goscilo, again, reads this as evidence of the film's traditional sexism: a "void . . . in Sarah's life and in the narrative that a man must fill" (40). The film certainly seems to be preserving Sarah from any sexual entanglements before Reese, but it also establishes her position within a kind of alternative family (iguana over mother) and alternative sexuality ("better than mortal man deserves") that makes her a potential match for the Terminator even more than for Reese. In the shots that introduce us to Sarah working at a "Big Boy" restaurant, her first line is spoken to the Big Boy mannequin, asking it to look out for her motorcycle. That, of course, is the world in which she is represented to us as victim. Only by becoming like the "Big Boy" (the Terminator) can she overcome him. As we discover later, Ginger's taped voice on the answering machine reinforces this potential connection: "Hi there. . . . Ha ha ha, fooled ya. You're talking to a machine. But don't be shy, it's okay, machines need love too. So talk to it." The human voice, itself mediated by a machine (like every human voice in a film, for instance) invites its audience (including, of course, the film's audience) to love the machine. The film appears to ironize this affection for machines in accord with its own stated technophobia, but the film's technophilia is just as great. The second time we hear this message on the machine, we hear it *with* the Terminator, and the subsequent message, left by Sarah herself, enables the Terminator to encounter Sarah for the first time. This meeting occurs at the disco whose name might also be said to name the genre of the movie itself, Tech Noir, and names it, furthermore, as the Terminator's place. This is also, significantly, where the Terminator's murderous hunt for Sarah turns into a kind of slow-motion cruise to the tune of the insistent disco chorus, "You got me burnin'." Reese's intervention rescues Sarah from this "burnin' " encounter with the Terminator, but it would perhaps be more accurate to say that it merely defers that encounter.

Throughout, *The Terminator* constantly produces analogies between contemporary human dependence on machines and the cyborgs of the future: the message machine with the human voice, the stereo earphones worn by Ginger, which prevent her from hearing both a telephone call from the police and her boyfriend being killed by the Terminator, the paging beeper worn by the criminal psychologist, which goes off just as he is passing the Terminator coming into the police station. In these instances, however, the attachment to machines only seems to weaken humans and make it impossible to recognize the threat posed by the Terminator. Goscilo accurately remarks that machines seem to fail people, particularly women, in the movie ("Deconstructing the Terminator," 42), but only until the moment at which women themselves *become* cyborgs. As I tried to suggest earlier, the man who, in Goscilo's terms, fills the "void" may not, in fact, be a man at all. Another telephone call, this one placed by Sarah to her mother but *displaced* to the Terminator, now perfectly mimicking her mother's voice, concludes with a declaration of love between the two. For Sarah, becoming, finally, a "good warrior" means leaving behind the warrior, Reese, whose failure *is* his heterosexuality, and becoming instead a female Terminator. This certainly seems to be the force of her final line to the Terminator, "You're terminated, fucker," just before unleashing the power of the mechanical compressor upon it. At this point in the film, moreover, the doubling of Sarah and the Terminator has also assumed the hint of sexual consummation. Reese's last act is to blow the Terminator in half. The explosion, however, leaves a metallic shard of the Terminator lodged in Sarah's left thigh, which she must extract before fleeing. In the ensuing scene, leading to the Terminator's termination, the machine, now mobile only through its arms, crawls after Sarah, who is also forced to rely on her arms for movement. The climactic sequence of the film, then, relies on both the visual and diegetic consummation of the relationship between Sarah and the Terminator.

This reading of the film's climactic sequence clarifies the necessity of the epilogue, in which Sarah records a message for her son while preparing to drive off into the Mexican desert. It functions to reassert Reese's, rather than the Terminator's paternity of the child, John Connor. "Should I tell you about your father? Boy, that's a tough one." Although the epilogue reassures us that Reese is the father, Penley reminds us that Reese's own last words to the Terminator, "Come on, you motherfucker," apply also to the terms of his own mission, traveling through time in order to both protect and inseminate the "legend," the mother of John Connor.[22] The question, then, is a genuinely tough one, as *Terminator 2* recognizes. Both Reese and the Terminator are "motherfuckers." *Terminator 2* provides John Connor with a surrogate father none other than the same model of Terminator, played by the same Arnold Schwarzenegger, that threatens the Holy Family of *The Terminator.* The two films would seem to require a strong machine, rather than a sensitive man, as the appropriate father for the hero-to-be. In this respect, *Terminator 2* attempts to rescue the cyborg for the normative nuclear family, transforming the Terminator as death drive into a paternal function. In *The Terminator* Reese insists of the Terminator, "It doesn't feel pity or remorse or fear. And it absolutely will not stop. Ever! Until you are dead." In *Terminator 2,* on the other hand, Sarah reflects: "Watching John with the machine, it was suddenly so clear. The Terminator would never stop. It would never leave him. And it would never hurt him. . . . Of all the would-be fathers who came and went over the years, this thing, this machine was the only one who measured up." The Terminator's "death drive" has been retooled as its "daddy drive." *Terminator 2* announces this transition in the classical terms of the outlaw biker movie and the Western, now fused into a single genre. Early in the movie, Schwarzenegger enters a biker bar called "The Corral" and proceeds violently to outfit himself in biker regalia. When we next see Schwarzenegger in action, he is wielding a rifle like Chuck Connors (the imaginary progenitor of the Connor clan?) in the television series *The Rifleman,* and we understand that, like the Rifleman, his prowess is now deployed for the benefit of his "son."[23]

For Sarah the lesson at the end of *The Terminator* seems to be that one must become a Terminator in order to defeat the Terminator. We see her driving a jeep, wearing sunglasses, like the Terminator, and placing a large revolver upon her pregnant belly. The movie's "pro-life" message is decisively "contaminated" by the necessary mediation of the technology of the Terminators. A kind of cyborg feminism coexists with the peculiar blend of political messages characteristic of American right-wing populism: Sarah's preparation for an apocalyptic, total state requires a survivalist pro-gun, "pro-life," anti-state stance.

Haraway concludes her "Manifesto" with the declaration, "I would rather be a cyborg than a goddess" (204). Sarah, on the other hand, appears to become *both* cyborg and goddess, a development made much clearer by *Terminator 2*, in which she becomes both a bodybuilder (that is, more like Schwarzenegger) and an ecofeminist. In *Terminator 2* Sarah rearticulates the earlier film's humanism in explicitly feminist terms, snarling at Dyson, the scientist responsible for the horrific future, "You think you're so creative. You don't know what it's like to really create something, to create a life, to feel it growing inside you. All you know how to create is death and destruction." Her own maternal function, however, is also militarized, and we discover that she has spent some time running guns with an ex–Green Beret. "One thing about my mom," says John Connor upon viewing the weapons cache she has prepared, "she always plans ahead." We first see John himself wearing a Public Enemy T-shirt, which he retains throughout the film, a visual message that associates his own petty crimes of the early sequences with his future status as an anti-state revolutionary. His nemesis, the new-model Terminator, appears most frequently in the guise of a Los Angeles cop. (The film was released less than a year before the riots in Los Angeles.) Only a romance of the American ideal of individualism appears to unite these apparently contradictory political valences.

Perhaps, however, a return to the question of machines, and more generally technology, will help to displace the films' individualism in order to reveal the anxieties that it covers over. If the governing fantasy of the Holy Family sequences in the film is that of a boy's becoming his own father and thus short-circuiting the progression of human generations, generations of technology progress quite rapidly in both films, a mark of Hollywood's own large investment in special effects. "The six hundred series had rubber skin. We spotted them easy," Reese says, telling Sarah about the development of the Terminator. "But these are new. They look human. Sweat. Bad breath. Everything. Very hard to spot." By *Terminator 2*, of course, even Schwarzenegger's Terminator has been displaced by another generation, the T-1000, much as the very expensive special effects of *Terminator 2* (a film that cost close to $70 million) are meant to displace those of *The Terminator*, a movie, after all, that was produced for about $6.4 million. The T-1000 may represent the polymorphous sexuality ("liquid metal") that trumps the phallic sexuality of the Schwarzenegger model, but he is just as importantly a nostalgic figure. Although he can shift his appearance at will, his preferred form is that of a jug-eared Los Angeles cop who appears to have just stepped out of an episode of *Adam 12*. He thus represents the fusion of high-tech special effects with the cultural memory of television police serials, and in this fusion of past and future he is a perfect emblem of the film itself.

Hollywood's reliance on its own technological innovations to bring audiences to the cinema thus ensures that the simplistic technophobic message of the movie never succeeds in overcoming its equally powerful technophilia, which is thematized in the relationship between the represented technology and that of the film apparatus itself.[24] The dystopian *present* represented by *The Terminator* is one in which technological reproduction (generations of machines) outstrips and even forecloses human reproduction. This is perhaps clearest in the case of Ginger, punished for both her sexuality and her reliance on technology. The insistence upon the mediation of the human voice through recording devices is one site of this relationship. Perhaps even more powerful is the equation between the most advanced technology of the future, the Terminator, and the camera. One of the most popular and remembered moments in the film is, not coincidentally, the Terminator's most self-reflexive moment. He stands in front of a mirror (not unlike Sarah and Ginger earlier in the film), repairing his wounds, and finishes up by removing his human eye in order to closely examine his mechanical eye. This "eye," we discover in the course of the film, also provides him with a menu from which he can choose various verbal responses, including, at one moment, the great crowd pleaser, "Fuck you, asshole." That is, the Terminator functions as a kind of mobile film production unit masking itself as the human. In Jean-Louis Baudry's terms then, the Terminator represents, but also exposes, the ideological effects of the film apparatus. "The 'reality' mimed by the cinema is thus first of all that of a 'self,'" writes Baudry, adding that cinema usually works "as if, the subject himself . . . unable . . . to account for his own situation, [needs] to substitute secondary organs, grafted on to replace his own defective ones, instruments or ideological formations capable of filling his function as subject. In fact, this substitution is only possible on the condition that the instrumentation itself be hidden or repressed."[25] It is precisely this ideological function of classical Hollywood cinema, the elision of its function as a kind of mechanical prosthesis to human seeing and hearing, that *The Terminator* calls into question by aligning the film's viewing apparatus and locating it in the domain of the "termination" of human beings. "Can you even see anything?" John asks Schwarzenegger in *Terminator 2*. "I see everything," he replies, and the film cuts to a point-of-view shot, with the message, "Image Enhance" on the Terminator's screen. These moments in the two films thematize the "objectifying male gaze," but they also thematize the gaze as itself mechanical.

The film's thematization of its own technology, I think, is responsible for the short-circuiting of its own explicitly antitechnological, "pro-life" message. Special effects, after all, drive big-budget action films, and perhaps the secret of Schwarzenegger's success as an actor is his ability to mimic a special effect, a machine. *The Terminator* thematizes the generational drive transposed from human reproduction to machines by setting the climactic action scene in a factory run by robotics. The choice of location is apt insofar as it is the place where machines build other machines without the apparent intervention of the human, much as they are understood to do in the dystopian future. It is also the site that can carry the weight of the displacement of once (relatively) privileged American workers by worldwide technological innovation and the shift from mass production to "flexible accumulation."[26] McKenzie Wark terms this the passage from "Fordism to Sonyism."[27] This globalization and restructuring of capitalism, already as early as 1984 misrecognized by the American media as an epic struggle between Americans and Japanese, is often accompanied in the media by the representation of Japanese (and Asian workers generally) as lifeless automatons, incapable of any action not directed by the monstrous corporations to which they remain attached for life.[28] The film's explicit political message simply echoes that populist and racist representation, insisting on the distinction between displaced humans (i.e., American workers) and machines (i.e., Japanese workers). The impossibility of that distinction in the film, however, is, as I have tried to demonstrate, most fully acted out in the domain of the robotics factory. The Terminator can only be conquered when Sarah herself becomes a kind of cyborg.

The decline of the power of industrial unions in the United States after the successive economic shocks of the early 1970s and the rapid globalization of capitalism may very well help to explain some of both films' operative contradictions. Distinguishing between American workers and foreign workers considered somehow less than human has become increasingly difficult, and the anxieties about such indistinctions and hybridities are the basis of a resurgent hostility to immigrants throughout the advanced capitalist countries. It is, however, capitalism itself that fuels the immense and unparalleled migrations of people throughout the world.[29] Peter Fitting observes that William Gibson's cyberpunk fiction portrays a future in which a "polyglot mix of styles and cultures is the result of the convergence and globalization of national economies" and the urban "sprawl" in which "living conditions approximate our ideas of

some Third World city"[30] — a "future," in other words, entirely continuous with the present. Here, I think, Haraway's "Manifesto" is of tremendous importance for a description of not just women workers laboring in
the Third World, her privileged example of a cyborg feminism and socialism, but also of male American workers, whose relatively privileged position was already, in 1984, understood as a threatened one. The robotics
factory, then, operates as the site of Reese's disappearance, but also as the
representative site of the disappearance of male American industrial
workers through the loss of their jobs to various "maquiladora" zones
(clusters of American-owned assembly plants in northern Mexico using
inexpensive labor) throughout the world. Certainly the intervening years
between *The Terminator* and *Terminator 2* have only served to highlight
these developments, especially in Los Angeles itself, with the loss or de-
skilling of defense manufacturing jobs and the arrival of great numbers
of Third World immigrants.[31] As Haraway points out in her "Manifesto,"
the resurgence of the homework and sweatshop economy in the United
States creates a situation in which workers are "feminized" (to use her
term) in the sense of "made extremely vulnerable; able to be disassembled, reassembled, exploited as a reserve labor force" (190).[32] Haraway
brilliantly connects the new character of multinational capitalism with
the development of new types of families connected to the homework
economy, "with its oxymoronic structure of women-headed households
and its explosion of feminisms and the paradoxical intensification and
erosion of gender itself" (191). The Connors represent one such family.
Sarah Connor is a single mother engaged in serial monogamy. In the first
film, she is introduced as a waitress, who, as she says, "can't even balance
my checkbook." The position of the working human father, of course,
disappears altogether, only to be replaced by a machine.

This does not prevent *Terminator 2*, however, from returning to a factory as the site of a struggle that is now focused on the struggle between
the different generations of technology. Unlike the final scene of *The
Terminator*, this factory is not a high-tech robotics factory, but a steel mill,
one of the traditional sites of American mass production — and the place
that produces "liquid metal." This nostalgic invocation of American industrial "brawn" as fatal to the "higher-tech" Terminator certainly con-
cords with the film's attempt to recuperate the nuclear family. The Terminator's "daddy drive" is thus connected to an attempt to compensate
for the crisis of demilitarization and general restructuring that hit the
American economy at the end of the Cold War. Schwarzenegger's declaration, "I need a vacation," after the labor of defeating the T-1000 in this
factory is the comic relief that aligns him with American factory workers.
He is, however, triumphant only at the moment of his own dissolution as
a functional machine.

Sarah's voice-over at the end of *Terminator 2* "returns" us "back to the future," which is guaranteed by Schwarzenegger's triumph: "The unknown future rolls toward us. I face it for the first time with a sense of hope. Because if a machine, a Terminator, can learn the value of human life, maybe we can too." This return to the future, however, is a nostalgic one, shaped by a return to the nuclear family and to the factory that once supported its American incarnation. To the extent, moreover, that the film also evacuates the human family—the cyborg father, the mother both Terminator and generator, the demigod son—it also indicates that the explicit morality overcompensates for a perceived loss, much as Schwarzenegger overcompensates for the loss of a father-dominated nuclear family. That perceived loss is the growing insecurity of the patriarchal nuclear family in an economy increasingly defined by female-headed households and a female or "feminized" workplace. Such a reading of the cyborg family provisionally *historicizes* the apocalyptic "future" to which it responds.

Notes

1. Francis Fukuyama, *The End of History and the Last Man* (New York: Free Press, 1992), 46. The book expands Fukuyama's original essay, "The End of History?" *The National Interest* 16 (Summer 1989): 3–18.

2. Jean-François Lyotard, *Economie Libidinale* (Paris: Minuit, 1974), 117ff.

3. Fredric Jameson, "Postmodernism, or The Cultural Logic of Late Capitalism," *New Left Review* 146 (1984): 59–92; David Harvey, *The Condition of Postmodernity* (Oxford: Blackwell, 1990).

4. Fredric Jameson, "Progress Versus Utopia; or, Can We Imagine the Future?" *Science Fiction Studies* 9 (1982): 151.

5. Andrew Ross, "Getting Out of the Gernsback Continuum," *Critical Inquiry* 17 (1991): 411–433.

6. Introduction, Les Levidow and Kevin Robins, eds., *Cyborg Worlds: The Military Information Society* (London: Free Association, 1989), 10. Ross himself is quite aware that the future has become "the favored environment for corporate and military forecasting" ("Getting Out," 433).

7. Fred Glass, "Totally Recalling Arnold: Sex and Violence in the New Bad Future," *Film Quarterly* 44 (1990): 2–13.

8. Donna Haraway, "A Manifesto for Cyborgs: Science, Technology, and Socialist Feminism in the 1980s," in *Coming to Terms: Feminism, Theory, Politics*, ed. Elizabeth Weed (New York: Routledge, 1989), 174.

9. All citations are from *The Terminator* (dir. James Cameron; written by Cameron and Gale Anne Hurd, 1984).

10. Constance Penley, "Time Travel, Primal Scene and the Critical Dystopia," in *Alien Zone: Cultural Theory and Contemporary Science Fiction Cinema*, ed. Annette Kuhn (London: Verso, 1990), 119–120.

11. All citations from *Terminator 2: Judgment Day* (dir. James Cameron; written by Cameron and William Wisher, 1991).

12. Penley, "Time Travel"; Margaret Goscilo, "Deconstructing *The Terminator*,"

Film Criticism 12 (1987–88): 37–52; Jonathan Goldberg, "Recalling Totalities: The Mirrored Stages of Arnold Schwarzenegger," *Differences* 4 (1992): 171–204.

13. Goldberg reads the Schwarzenegger-machine as a gay male icon, the "leatherman," which escapes the nominal humanist-heterosexual ideology of *The Terminator.* Albert Liu attempts to take a post-humanist, post-Oedipal sexuality one step further in his celebration of the new model Terminator, the T-1000, of *Terminator 2* as the "postcybernetic body" of the "metalmorph." "Theses on the Metalmorph," *Lusitania* 1, no. 4 (1993): 135.

14. Interview with Peter Linnett, *Corridor* no. 5 (1974); cited in Claudia Springer, "The Pleasure of the Interface," *Screen* 32 (1991): 303.

15. This permanent war economy also featured the military funding of bio-cybernetic research that aimed to supplement the manifest vulnerabilities of human warriors. Chris Hables Gray reports that "[s]ince the Spanish-American War more US soldiers have been lost to psychiatric collapse than are killed in action" and that the percentage of such losses have been growing in recent wars. "The Cyborg Soldier: The US Military and the Post-Modern Warrior," in Levidow and Robins, *Cyborg Worlds,* 59.

16. See Joan Didion's perceptive description of the social consequences of this restructuring, "Trouble in Lakewood," *The New Yorker,* July 26, 1993, 46–65.

17. Paul Virilio, *Speed and Politics: An Essay on Dromology,* trans. Mark Polizzotti (New York: Semiotext(e), 1986).

18. Goscilo argues that legitimate female aggressivity still exists for Hollywood only under the sign of outraged motherhood. Her example is another James Cameron film, *Aliens* (1986), a film that was viewed by many as the triumph of a new representation of women in Hollywood. In that movie, as Goscilo notes, Ripley's (Sigourney Weaver) "maternal instinct" as a mother attempting the rescue of an endangered child legitimates her confrontation with the monstrous alien mother. "Deconstructing *The Terminator,*" 49–50.

19. This convention appears to have a place of honor in the classical articulation of science fiction. Vivian Sobchack writes that "our public astronauts reek of locker-room camaraderie, but hardly of male sweat or semen. As if in training for the big game, they have rejected their biology and sexuality—pushed it from their minds and bodies to concentrate on the technology required to penetrate and impregnate not a woman, but the universe." "The Virginity of Astronauts: Sex and the Science Fiction Film," in Kuhn, *Alien Zone,* 108.

20. Several reviewers of the film noticed the evocation of the Holy Birth, and Goscilo reads this Mariolatry as another aspect of the film's sexual conservatism. "Deconstructing *The Terminator,*" 48.

21. Goldberg calls Reese the "sensitive" version of the Terminator and speculates that Reese is coded as gay. "Recalling Totalities," 183.

22. "[I]n the narrative logic of this film it is Kyle who is the mother fucker." Penley, "Time Travel," 121.

23. Cameron's reactionary *True Lies* (1994) brings the full force of the national security state to bear on the problem of restoring the nuclear family.

24. Liu observes that because "T-1000 can be resurrected in any way and at any time, then the narrative connection between *T2* and its projected sequel *T3* will be completely arbitrary, but therefore unlimited in its range of possibilities. The future of the Terminator films is now as open and fateless as the world they finally depict." "Theses," 141. Of course, one fate continues to govern this apparently "fateless" world—the need to produce an even more spectacular (and profitable) sequel.

25. Jean-Louis Baudry, "The Apparatus: Metapsychological Approaches to the Impression of Reality in Cinema," in *Narrative, Apparatus, Ideology: A Film Theory Reader,* ed. Philip Rosen (New York: Columbia University Press, 1986), 295.

26. See Harvey, *The Condition of Postmodernity,* 141–172.

27. McKenzie Wark, "From Fordism to Sonyism: Perverse Readings of the New World Order," *New Formations* 15 (1991): 43–54.

28. This, of course, ignores the movement of American, European, and Japanese capital to newer zones of production in the Pacific as well as numerous workers in Japan who fall outside the protected spheres of the corporations. The recent *Tetsuo* ("Iron Man") films in Japan (written and directed by Shinya Tsukamoto) further complicate any monolithic picture of the Japanese economy. Tetsuo is a human who painfully re-constructs himself using materials from the scrap heap of Japanese industrial might — a waste product of the Japanese economy.

29. Benedict Anderson's "New World Disorder" provides a brilliant description of this situation. *New Left Review* 193 (1992): 3–13.

30. Peter Fitting, "The Lessons of Cyberpunk," in *Technoculture,* ed. Constance Penley and Andrew Ross (Minneapolis: University of Minnesota Press, 1991), 300.

31. Didion's description of defense plants as the "cathedrals of the Cold War" underscores their status as artifacts of the past:

> Since this was an industry in which machine parts were drilled to within two-thousandths or even one-thousandth of an inch, tolerances that did not lend themselves to automation, the people who worked in these plants had never, as they put it, gone robotic. They were the last of the medieval handworkers, and the spaces in which they worked, the huge structures with the immaculate concrete floors and the big rigs and the overhead cameras and the project banners and the flags of the foreign buyers, became the cathedrals of the Cold War, occasionally visited by but never entirely legible to the uninitiated. ("Trouble in Lakewood," 62)

32. A few months after the release of *Terminator 2, The Montreal Gazette* featured a headline announcing, "Human material being retailored to fit the times" for an article on the retraining of Montreal's workforce (January 14, 1992, A1).

The Cyborg Manifesto Revisited: Issues and Methods for Technocultural Feminism

Linda Howell

Since its debut in 1985, "A Manifesto for Cyborgs" has undergone what writer Donna Haraway calls a "surprising half-life." The radioactive metaphor aptly summarizes a varied and widespread fallout of critical response to Haraway's polemical critique of "science, technology, and socialist-feminism in the 1980s."[1] Widely reprinted and extensively criticized, the manifesto continues to enliven cultural studies of science and technology, science-fiction criticism, and feminist political theory.[2] Here, in the context of postmodern apocalypse, it serves as a provisional map through which to chart the emergence of a relatively new field of inquiry within feminism, postmodernism, and cultural studies. A dynamically charged element of its surprising half-life, technocultural feminism inherits from the cyborg manifesto the legacy of its specifically feminist vision of apocalypse.

As its hybrid names suggests, technocultural feminism understands technologies not as inanimate machines, but as lively, historically significant, and highly social actors in twentieth-century culture. Indeed, to the extent that machines both enable and represent cultural practices, they also redefine culture as something more and less than a high-minded realm of aesthetic pursuit. The works discussed here share a concern with popular technoculture such as television, film, and video. They shift the stakes in traditional "images of women" criticism by perceiving images of women not as stereotypes or progressive role models, but rather as focal points for rearticulating traditional women's issues.

The issues this essay considers are violence against women, pornography, reproductive rights, and the gendered construction of racial difference. Neither they nor the essay's focus on visual representation exhaust the field of technocultural feminism. Nevertheless, by comparing treatments of these issues in the context of the cyborg manifesto's apocalyptic vision, I hope to show how technocultural feminism has transformed that vision — for the 1990s and beyond.

A preliminary comparison of the manifesto with Jacques Derrida's "No

Apocalypse, Not Now" helps to describe what I mean by Haraway's feminist apocalypse.[3] Another name for feminist in this context might be "post-humanist," for in several ways the manifesto describes the position of women and feminists after Jacques Derrida's perceived crisis in the humanities has already happened. Writing of "painful fragmentation among feminists," as a result of conflicts within feminism in the 1980s, Haraway announces the end of traditional humanist categories on which much feminist epistemology and methodology have been based:

> With the hard-won recognition of their social and historical constitution, gender, race and class cannot provide the basis for belief in "essential" unity. There is nothing about being "female" that naturally binds women. There is not even such a state as "being" female, itself a highly complex category constructed in contested sexual scientific discourses and other social practices. (179)

Haraway charges dominant feminist theory with dependence on humanist plots of innocence lost through a fall into language and difference. To the extent that feminist theory imitates these humanist plots, it also participates in a tradition of dominance through strategies of appropriation, incorporation, or erasure. The monstrous figure of the cyborg, an emblem of that dominating tradition, thus serves partly as a *memento mori* for the "fractured identities" of Western feminism in the mid-1980s.

Hence, whereas "No Apocalypse, Not Now" seeks to defend humanist thought by turning it into rhetorical "missiles," the cyborg manifesto assumes that such missiles have already been deflected. The collapse of unified feminist theory is no isolated accident, but rather a symptom of numerous, simultaneous boundary breakdowns in the "integrated circuit" of multinational capitalism. For Haraway, the simultaneity of these breakdowns holds promise for progressive, anti-apocalyptic redefinitions of humanity, nature, machines, and culture.

Haraway's understanding of a cultural politics arising in this context is premised on what Mary Carpenter calls the "second 'Great Awakening' " of feminist critics: "the prophetic parable of the 'woman artist' told the story of a white, middle-class, heterosexual woman — *only*."[4] Basing political struggle not in naturalized identities, but in consciously constructed "political kinship"[5] promoted among women of color, the manifesto sees the work of feminist cultural studies as the work of redefining women's experience in a global context that can account for differences of race, gender, and class without essentializing or subordinating them.

Emerging from collapsed distinctions between animal, human, and machine identities in postwar technoscience, cyborg images are potent tools for this work of cultural redefinition. Like Derrida's combination of epistolary missives and nuclear missiles, they are in part coded weapons of "Star Wars" proportions. However, unlike Derrida's "tiny, inoffensive missiles," cyborgs are highly offensive monsters. Their collective voices are raised in blasphemy "from within the secular-religious, evangelical traditions of United States politics, including the politics of socialist feminism" ("Manifesto" 173). Emerging from the apocalyptic feminist consciousness of the 1980s, blasphemy becomes a way to protect "one from the moral majority within, while still insisting on the need for community" (173).

Nevertheless, cyborgs also signify the most vulnerable targets of the Moral Majority and its Star Wars teleology: finite, vulnerable, mortal bodies. Haraway points out that these bodies are increasingly understood in science and medicine as biotic components or cybernetic communications systems; as a result of the increased use of visualization technologies in medicine, they are also targets of the "cultural practice of hunting with the camera and the deeply predatory nature of a photographic consciousness" (193). Combined with their status as laborers and boundary transgressors, cyborg bodies form a monstrously perverse, yet largely peaceful collectivity, which Haraway describes as "a kind of disassembled and reassembled, post-modern collective and personal self. This is the self feminists must code" (187).

While Haraway's cyborg imagery and rhetoric of blasphemy pave the way for some of the surprising political bedfellows produced in techno-cultural feminist studies, they also emphasize the material stakes in apocalyptic rhetoric. Structured, like Derrida's rhetorical missiles, on thin distinctions between fantasy and belief, the utopian cyborgs of the manifesto shift the stakes in postmodern discourses of the body by grounding them in the materiality of everyday life. Encompassing sites of profound change such as home, school, workplace, church, and clinic/hospital, everyday life also entails changes in the ways that people negotiate the eroding distinctions between public and private, production and reproduction, work and leisure in a high-tech world.

The multiple, overlapping experiences of everyday life at these sites are not representable by humanist literature. Hence, the cyborg body eludes the trajectory of Derrida's work of nuclear criticism, aimed at an audience of humanities scholars. Derived from the annals of science fiction — a genre considered by Derrida less capable than Mallarmé, Kafka, or Joyce for dealing seriously with the nuclear epoch — cyborgs are situated outside Derrida's prospect of "an irreversible destruction, leaving no traces, of the juridico-literary archive."[6] The survival of literature, libraries, or the legal rights of authors is not at stake in "A Manifesto for Cyborgs"; the survival of women and writing is.

In its concern with the power of popular culture to mobilize collective action around belief, the cyborg manifesto revalorizes socialist-feminist constructions of "women's experience" in a postmodern mode. That experience, including the experience of complicity with humanism — becomes "a fiction and fact of the most crucial, political kind."[7] The alignment of theory between fiction and fact is a significant point for technocultural feminism, for as Constance Penley and Andrew Ross broadly define technoculture, it "is located as much in the work of everyday fantasies and actions as at the level of corporate or military decision making."[8] The cyborg manifesto does not throw out the category of women's experience, but rather asks its readers to reconsider it as one of several tools for redefining the boundaries between nature and culture in anti-apocalyptic ways.

More specifically, in its understanding of literacy as a historical mode of survival, as well as its acknowledgment of popular culture as an important site for renewed feminist criticism, the manifesto encourages readers to rethink writing as a deconstructive technology. "Deconstruction" is considered in the manifesto in the nonspecialized sense of intervention and disruption, jamming the dominant circuits through which information does or does not flow. Hence, cyborg writing is expressly committed to interrupting the extended chat between God and Man that Derrida holds out as an anti-apocalyptic strategy. Cyborgs and women would probably want to participate in Derrida's "long colloquy with warriors in love with life, busy writing in all languages in order to make the conversation last."[9] Yet the restriction of that colloquy to God and Man would not only exclude cyborgs and women, but probably escalate the warriors' conflicts by securing their identities in masculinized theology. While Derrida's warriors continue their conversation, Haraway's cyborgs are elsewhere, "speaking in tongues to strike fear into the circuits of the supersavers of the new right."[10]

The manifesto's principle message to feminists of the 1980s was to take responsibility for the social relations of science and technology. Such responsibility is well illustrated by the work of technocultural feminists in recent years. However, although most critics agree with the manifesto's message of social responsibility, fewer have agreed that the image of the cyborg can be deployed for progressive ends in a renewed socialist feminism. As Kevin Pask notes in his discussion of *The Terminator,* popular cyborg images register apocalyptic anxieties about shifting definitions of labor and gender in late capitalism.[11] For Canadians especially, the 1989 mass murder of fourteen women engineering students is a horrific example of such shifting definitions at work. Targeted as "feminists" by a man who couldn't (or wouldn't) tell the difference between women engineering students and feminists, the women who died in the Montreal Massacre remind us that technocultural redefinitions are matters of life and death.[12]

The Montreal Massacre also brings to light an intensified struggle for survival amid various instances of antifeminist backlash today. One element of the manifesto's half-life has been its positioning in relation to popular instances of this backlash, many of which seek to relegitimate masculine authority through ostensibly liberated versions of cyborg women. In *The Terminator*, for example, the authority of a dead father is recuperated in the figure of a messianic fetus that lives to extend that authority across the boundaries of mortal time and space. Lodged in the belly of working woman Sarah Connor, the fetus becomes Sarah's principle reason for survival, rather than protection of her own life. In *Terminator 2*, the continuous troping of Sarah Connor as hysterical mother combines with the androgynous fluidity of a new generation of cyborgs to situate apocalyptic threat at the level of feminist, gay, and lesbian gender-bending practices.[13] One of the important stakes in the manifesto's surprising half-life has been the possibility of visually representing women using technologies in peaceful, empowering, and nonmilitaristic ways. Haraway's *written* cyborg body, for all its blasphemy and its ironic sense of boundary confusion, still stands in opposition to the visual spectacle of right-wing mothers who wear army boots, or doll-like figures of submission to masculine expertise.

Constance Penley's recent contributions to the discourse of technocultural feminism shift the stakes in cyborg representation away from traditional "images of women" territory. Perhaps the most surprising part of that shift is its focus on a practice that reimagines men, rather than women. In "Brownian Motion: Women, Tactics and Technology," Penley reports on a widespread community of *Star Trek* fans who produce amateur romantic pornography about the relationship between all-too-human Captain Kirk and Vulcan Commander Spock. This technique is called slashing by the many women in the United States, Britain, Canada, and Australia who have been boldly taking *Star Trek* where its producers never (consciously?) wanted it to go. Dislocating the term "slashing" from the context of horror films, the practice of these fans is not about the mutilation of bodies. It has more in common with the cyborg manifesto's definition of writing as a practice for subverting origin myths. By revising the official version of the Kirk-Spock (or "K/S") relationship, slashing reconstructs the objects of heterosexual women's desire along the lines of gay masculinity.

For Penley, slashing is a significant technocultural practice not only because it redefines dominant images of heterosexual masculinity. It also similarly redefines technology in user-friendly terms. Slashing is "Brownian Motion" because of the apparent randomness of its tactics: what looks like escapism, or what the slashers call "just having fun," also works to provide "a comfortable yet stimulating social space in which women . . . stage a popular debate around issues of technology, fantasy, and everyday life."[14]

But as Penley reports, "just having fun" means a highly sophisticated private publishing apparatus expressly concerned with accessibility and democratic use. It means women using skills developed in their everyday jobs to produce, advertise, and publish their work. Having fun means encouraging others, with workshops on desktop publishing, VCR editing, and the production of song tapes. It means annual meetings, juried prizes, charity fund-raisers, and absolutely no monetary profit, because the nonprofit nature of this enterprise protects it from copyright suits (139–141). In continuous debates about their divided loyalties to the official *Star Trek* universe, and in their erotic parodies of its homosocial continuum, slashers articulate their collective desire for recognition as contributors to that universe.

To think of homoerotic pornography as a progressive tactic for gaining recognition obviously challenges an understanding of pornography as universally demeaning to women. Penley's description of K/S writing challenges such a totalizing view. She claims that these women produce "a unique hybridized genre which ingeniously blends romance, pornography and utopian science fiction" (137). In stories of Kirk and Spock "learning to overcome the conditioning that prevents them from expressing their feelings" (156), slashers avoid the romance formula of masculine dominance and feminine submission. By choosing a relationship between two adventurers as their focus, they also explore possibilities for remaking manliness without replicating the wimpy "sensitive man" of the eighties (155).[15] Running parallel to their commitment to accessible technologies in practice is a commitment to retool the masculine psyche in conscious affinity with gay men.

That the pleasures of this commitment are limited for present-day women is evident in the slasher's decision *not* to represent female bodies. However, such a conscious negation can also be read as resistance to public constructions of that body. As Penley writes in "Brownian Motion,"

The bodies from which they are indeed alienated are twentieth-century women's bodies: bodies that are a legal, moral and religious battleground, that are the site of contraceptive failure, that are publicly defined as *the* greatest potential danger to the fetuses they house, that are held to painfully greater standards of physical beauty than those of the other sex. (154)

Like the fans' much-debated resistance to professional standards of writing, the resistance to representing the female body enables the slashers to forge a potential alliance between the *Star Trek* fandom and gay men, whose bodies are similar battlegrounds. There is in the K/S world a "comprehension of the fact that *all* men (and women) must be able to recognize their own homosexual tendencies if they are to have any hope of fundamentally changing oppressive sexual roles" (156).

Constance Penley's ethnographic account of slash fandom upholds three important points about cyborg cultural politics made in Haraway's 1985 manifesto. First, new technologies offer new possibilities for resistance, especially when they intersect and overlap. (The slashers' hybrid genre of romantic pornography is the product of hybrid production techniques, including writing, sketching, VCR editing, and song-dubbing.) Second, this resistance is not articulated in the traditional languages of feminism and the Left, but may take ostensibly regressive or reactionary forms, as indicated by the slashers' resistance to representing the female body. Third, issues of sexuality and gender are paradoxically eroded and intensified within the networks producing such forms: homoerotic activities provide the topical ground for the articulation of heterosexual desires. Hence, while the absence of the female body from the slashers' work may appear complicitous with ongoing attempts to relegitimate masculine authority, that absence can also be seen as a telling pause, a hesitation that speaks volumes in the well-known line, "I'm not a feminist but . . ."

For as Penley writes, "the tension . . . between the feminist concerns of the fans and their unwillingness to be seen as feminists can teach those who work in the field of women and popular culture a great deal about how political issues get articulated in everyday life" (138). Slashing is not assimilable to a discourse that views pornography as inevitably demeaning to women, nor is it assimilable to an attempt to construct more wholesome erotic images of women's pleasures. What technocultural feminism might learn from the slashers is the libidinal power of resistance available among working women who ostensibly just want to "have fun." The size, range, and complexity of slash practices, together with the subversive loyalty of the slashers to the official *Star Trek* series, demonstrate a strong commitment to the Vulcan philosophy of Infinite Diversity in Infinite Combination — perhaps another way of articulating the cyborg manifesto's irreverently blasphemous message to socialist feminists in the 1980s.

In terms of method, Penley's work of ethnography in popular culture suggests that technocultural feminism is not only about women and technology, but also about ways of representing the subject from a nonuniversalizing perspective. It is also about respecting the differences between the terms "woman" and "feminist" for in these differences lie important lessons. As a *Star Trek* fan as well as an academic feminist, Penley respects these differences by juxtaposing her own interpretations with those of the slashers themselves. She protects the privacy of slash artists by *not* publishing their names, and she defends slashing against the reductive and unsympathetic label of "fag-hagging." Such a term "obscures the very real appreciation the fans have of gay men in their efforts to redefine masculinity" (156–157).

Of course, whether gay men appreciate such efforts is another issue open to debate. My limited reading of gay and lesbian slashing does indicate such an appreciation: the editors of a queer fanzine acknowledge K/S writing as a classic tradition that inspires their focus on the interactions of characters from *Star Trek: The Next Generation* and *Deep Space Nine*.[16] Penley also reports recently that "the fans are asking themselves if the AIDS crisis is having or should have an effect on what they are writing, for example whether Kirk and Spock should be shown practicing safer sex."[17] Here, I would suggest, is another version of those "dissident vernaculars" about AIDS that Peter Dickinson considers to be "vital counterdiscursive strategies" to the frequent apocalypticism of AIDS discourse.[18] The prospect of Kirk slipping a condom onto Spock's green corkscrew penis offers an occasion to laugh while we are reminded that safe sex is not just about survival; it's also about pleasure.

But when young Sarah Connor lays a handgun on her pregnant belly at the end of *The Terminator*, it is worth asking whose pleasure is being entertained here. What Kevin Pask calls the "pro-gun, 'pro-life' "[19] stance of our heroine offers disturbing support for Penley's description of late twentieth-century women's bodies as battlegrounds. As such, they are important sites for technocultural feminist intervention and critique. Rosalind Petchesky's "Foetal Images: The Power of Visual Culture in the Politics of Reproduction" is an important early example of such work.

Petchesky situates her discussion of visualizing technologies in reproductive medicine at "the overlapping boundaries between media spectacle and clinical experience when pregnancy becomes a moving picture."[20] Her focus is the antiabortion video *The Silent Scream* (1984), a text purporting to show the attempts of a twelve-week-old fetus to escape an abortion, as well as its distinctly "human" pain. Documenting the historical significance of photographs of the fetus since their first appearance in a 1962 issue of *Look* magazine, Petchesky argues that pro-choice rebuttals of this video on the basis of its technical fraudulence (camera tricks) or on the basis of alternative medical evidence (at twelve weeks a fetus cannot receive pain impulses) miss an important historical point. *The Silent Scream* works in spite of its fraudulence because a generation of viewers has been culturally conditioned to read the fetus as a human being.

An essential paradox of photography — namely its ability to represent reality "larger than life" by stripping objects of spatiotemporal contexts — partly enables this conditioning. The ubiquity of fetal images in

Western culture for the past forty years is another partial cause. Meta-phorically severing the fetus from the pregnant body, the ultrasound camera enables it to float free not only in the photographic image but also in the popular imagination. Hence, in the blockbuster film *2001: A Space Odyssey* (1968), the fetus acquires the symbolic import of a "Star Child" — figuring simultaneously "fertility and life" and "the technolo-gies of cosmic extermination."[21] The apocalyptic symbolism of the Star Child capitalizes on the absence of the pregnant body, retrospectively inscribing it as the site where such "cosmic extermination" is most likely to originate.

When reproduced in the interests of pro-life messages such as *The Silent Scream,* the apocalyptic fetus condenses issues of choice to a single, and singularly catastrophic one — the choice between human life and death. A woman's decision to abort a pregnancy takes on the symbolic dimen-sions of a global decision to terminate the hopes of the human race, while a decision not to abort (the obvious purpose of *The Silent Scream*) gains epic proportions similar to the model of guerrilla motherhood offered in *The Terminator.* Choice is in effect no choice at all when the future of humanity is at stake. Intersecting with religious, moral, and legal argu-ments for fetal rights, the superhuman "space-fetus" rhetorically disem-powers the liberal humanist argument for an individual woman's right to choose. Like the self-immolating cyborg in the last scenes of *Terminator 2,* it purports to "teach us about the value of human life."

How does the Star Child iconography of the 1960s play itself out in the popular films of the eighties? Here, I momentarily depart from Petchesky to consider the implications of fetal imagery for the pregnant body. From the Star Child perspective of *2001,* the pregnant body is by extension a spaceship — a machine. From the "human being" perspective of *The Si-lent Scream,* the pregnant body is largely a hostile environment. This cy-borgian melding of mechanical and environmental/organic views of the pregnant body is considered in Mary Ann Doane's analysis of science fiction/horror films,[22] which trouble the organically defined boundaries of the pregnant body. As such, they give popular voice to the increasing tendencies on the part of visualizing technologies in medicine to view the female body as a cybernetic machine.

Doane argues that the symbolic systems of films such as *Alien* (1979) address a contemporary revolution in reproductive technologies — rang-ing from birth control to surrogate mothering. They do so not only by directly representing maternal origins and the phenomenon of birth as horrifying and unnatural (the monster of *Alien;* the grotesque gestation of its offspring in men's bodies) but also by signifying maternity in the mise-en-scène. In *Alien,* the spaceship "seems to mimic in the con-struction of its internal spaces the interior of the maternal body," while in

Blade Runner (1982) the nonexistent but "desperately" invoked mothers of a cyborg community are symbolically represented in a photograph carried by Rachel the replicant.[23] The displacement of an abstracted concept of maternity into machines and artifacts enables a contemporary perception of the maternal body as similarly machine-like.

However, such a perception indicates more than the power of visualizing technologies to subject women to a masculinized and objectifying social gaze. According to Doane, it also indicates a link between the fascination with technology as embodied knowledge and the desire for a sense of history that imaging technologies constantly put under erasure. The photographic function of context-stripping enables a disembodied maternal concept in these films to fill in the space of an absent historical context, which in turn retrospectively inscribes the "mother-machine" with the social authority of organized, systematic, total knowledge.

A version of this social authority can be noticed in *Alien*, where the spaceship's computer system, called Mother, has a metanarrative power over the maternalized mise-en-scène. As indicated by the film's opening question to the computer ("What's the story, Mother?"), this is the power to tell a story from the mother-machine's point of view. Yet that story, as it unfolds in the plot of *Alien*, "is no longer one of transgression and conflict with the father but of the struggle with and against what seems to become an overwhelming extension of the category of the maternal, now assuming monstrous proportions."[24] Unlike the computer HAL in *2001*, whose power is clearly not in humans' best interests, the computer-mother of *Alien* assumes the power to warn humans about bad mothers. After all, wouldn't a computerized supermother know all about them?

It is hardly coincidental that *The Silent Scream* demonstrates a similar narrative alignment of the maternal body with the social authority of scientific knowledge. At the end of this video, we learn that both the woman who chose to abort the fetus ("a feminist") and the young doctor who performed the abortion have ultimately repented of their murderous act and vowed "never again."[25] By relegating doctor and feminist together to a narrative of sin and salvation, *The Silent Scream* situates the traditional authority of medicine in unholy alliance with feminist authority to speak about women's experience. Needless to say, a blasphemous text such as the cyborg manifesto, which deconstructs the totalizing effects of both kinds of authority, plays no part in this right-wing reduction of feminist plurality to a single position — pro-choice.

In the films discussed by Doane, anxieties about women meld with anxieties about machines to produce a particularly troubling obstacle to Haraway's utopian feminist cyborg. Despite the multiple, contradictory, and lively number of feminist viewpoints generated by the feminist critique of science in past decades, the view from outside its sphere of debate can be one of monolithic, maternalized control. In the right-wing imagination, which has made considerable inroads in the abortion debate in the past few years, "bad mothers" and "bad scientists" are one. The recent murders of doctors who perform abortions indicate the fluidity with which misogyny, antifeminism, and fear of scientific authority can meld.

Contemporary discussions of visualizing technologies in the abortion debate register the extent to which the use of these technologies alters perceptions not only of women, but also of the pro-choice position forged in the liberal humanist years of the women's movement. As Valerie Hartouni notes, even an ostensibly pro-choice video about abortion, *S'Aline Solution* (1991), is saturated with images that have already been appropriated for anti-choice purposes. The result is a contemporary discourse that speaks in only very limited ways of "the expanded sense of freedom and power that abortion has afforded many women in allowing them to take hold of their lives." As Hartouni writes, "freedom and power have an at best pejorative resonance and function" when they represent all women as one, for that one too often appears today as "the casual, capricious, career-minded woman who has abandoned hearth and home and kills without conscience."[26] Replaced by a discourse of loss, guilt, and suffering that younger viewers read as "evidence of a certain moral sensibility,"[27] freedom and power on the part of women now appear to be okay for a pro-choice woman, as long as she suffers in her choice.

While Hartouni's work illustrates a difference in perception between college-age women and older women viewing the pro-choice video, it also illustrates a similarity: neither group appears to have questioned the authenticity of the images presented. It therefore comes as a surprise to learn that "the sequence of images we are inclined to read as a saline abortion turn out to be ejaculation . . . the white fluid we construe as the saline solution is seminal fluid . . . [and] our expulsion from the body in the concluding frames of the video is not through a birth canal, but . . . through the urethra as ejaculate."[28] As in Petchesky's analysis of *The Silent Scream,* however, the fact that images of male ejaculation are used to represent an abortion is almost beside the point. What is more significant is the capitalization on viewers' technocultural illiteracy with a pro-choice discourse in which suffering for one's choice is the sign of moral sensibility.

At first glance, Doane's and Hartouni's essays might be taken as evidence against the cyborg manifesto's impulse to visualize women as cyborgs. Indeed, Mary Ann Doane has argued that the Harawayan cyborg is incapable of representing the varieties of contemporary power that elude visualization technologies, nor can it adequately represent feminist history in its constant orientation toward the future.[29] Yet what counts as history is very much part of ongoing debates in feminism, socialism, and postmodernism: the cyborg's purpose within the manifesto is primarily to embody the conditions of existence in which history might be written differently. Doane's and Hartouni's essays demonstrate Haraway's point that questions of who controls the interpretation of bodily boundaries become a major feminist issue in the visual politics of the late twentieth century.[30] They also demonstrate, with Petchesky, some ways in which the debate about reproductive rights has become a focal point for a variety of competing discourses.

Hence, Doane and Hartouni can also be said to support Petchesky's argument against the gendered axes of traditional feminist resistance to technology.[31] Such an argument is supported by the apprehension that something like a monolithic feminist mother-machine is being molded in contemporary visual culture. This mother-machine cannot be deconstructed with a speculum, but rather, as Carol Stabile suggests, "by engagement with technoscience and questions of postmodernity."[32] Petchesky's stance against a dominant understanding of visualization technologies as "male" mitigates the argument that reproductive technologies are imposed on all women as a class. Such an argument cannot explain why women of color and working-class women, who are likely candidates for ultrasound imaging because of their high rates of infertility and fetal impairment, are nevertheless the least likely to use ultrasound.[33] Neither can it explain the pleasures of ultrasound images for women without dismissing those pleasures as a form of false consciousness. While the propensity of much medical and scientific imaging has been shown to privilege masculine voyeurism and fetishism, Petchesky notes that women also construct fetishes for their viewing pleasure — as they do when they insert ultrasound images into the family photograph album.[34] An important difference here appears to be that neither these fetishes nor the pleasure in viewing them appears to hinge on an eroticized sense of domination.[35]

What's important in Petchesky's work, as with the cyborg manifesto, is the attempt to get beyond a binary opposition between pro- and anti-choice stances by compounding it with overlapping differences between public and private uses of the fetal image, as well as the institutionalized class and race differences that often control accessibility to ultrasound. Petchesky also points out the need for a feminist discourse on technology to distinguish between the power relations embedded in technologies and the technologies themselves: the objectifying tendencies of the camera and the photographic image are *not* inherently masculine. They are tools that feminist theory has inadequately addressed until recently. As Hartouni suggests, it is also important to consider differences in viewers' ages as they interpret these images. These multiple considerations help technocultural feminists to reimagine the maternal cyborg body not as a mother-machine, but as one in closer affinity with environmental activism.

Recontextualizing the fetal image is one step toward transforming the "hostile environment" image of contemporary maternity. Petchesky emphasizes that the fetus should be seen not only within a female body, but also within a body moving in social space. Such tactics help to represent the varieties of women who could or should be using ultrasound and also help medical authorities to assess the reasoning behind its uses. Picturing a pregnant woman "within her total framework of relationships, economic and health needs and desires"[36]—as subject and agent of technologically enhanced choice—is an alternative to the isolating, embattled image of pregnant women as spaceships, baby machines, or hostile environments. Images of pregnancy do not stop at the limits defined by an individual's body, but like the collective utopian cyborg image, extend to include multiple roles within the body politic.

Carol Stabile suggests another, more difficult task for technocultural feminism—distinguishing between pregnant bodies and maternal ones.[37] As pregnancy becomes independent of a heterosexual contract, as surrogate pregnancies enable us to see pregnancy as paid work, and as environmentalist concerns gain popular favor, it may be time, as Haraway suggests in a more recent context, to link maternity to the environment in resolutely non-nostalgic images and stories of "Mother Earth."[38]

In "A Manifesto for Cyborgs," the technocultural task of rewriting origin stories without nostalgia is largely dependent on the contributions of Third World women and women of color. In its status as part human, part machine, and part animal, the Harawayan cyborg is constructed partly by beast fables that have been instrumental in histories of colonial oppression.[39] In recent technocultural works by Rey Chow, such fables come to bear in startling ways on colonialist history and feminist postcolonial politics.

In "Violence in the Other Country: China as Crisis, Spectacle and Woman,"[40] Chow responds to the horror of Tiananmen Square by forging a relationship between historical trauma and gender politics:

[W]henever there is a political crisis, [Third World women] stop being women; when the crisis is over and the culture rebuilds itself, they resume their more traditional roles as wives and mothers as part of the concerted effort to restore order. (88)

Chow relates this experience of political crisis and gender suspension to the "futility of intellectual discourse at the moment of shock" when we learn of such crises (82). Canadian feminists hearing about the Montreal Massacre of 1989 experienced a similar sense of initial futility, which was compounded by strategies on the part of media and their representative experts aimed at erasing gender issues from ensuing commentary.[41]

Such moments of shock transform our conventional ways of thinking; indeed that moment of shock provides common ground here for my comparison of Tiananmen Square with the Montreal Massacre.[42] Nevertheless, an important difference between the two events is that women and feminists in the immediate aftermath of the Montreal crisis had the discursive mobility to speak as women and feminists, no matter how censored they were in doing so. In the case of Tiananmen Square, the suspension of gender at a moment of crisis enables us to understand gender not as an overarching category of explanation, but rather as a tool that must be adjusted to fit the task at hand.

In Chow's essay, the technocultural example of such a tool is the Goddess of Democracy statue, a facsimile of the American Statue of Liberty. Constructed by the students in Tiananmen Square, reconstructed in Hong Kong, Taiwan, and the United States, the statue became a frequent focal point for Western television cameras. As such, it reminds us of the cyborg image and the fetal image, with their powers to focus and mobilize a number of competing discourses. For Chow, this statue is one of the latest instances of the "King Kong syndrome" at work in the technologically mediated production of Western knowledge about China:

This is the cross-cultural syndrome in which the "Third World," as the site of the "raw" material that is "monstrosity," is produced for the surplus-value of spectacle, entertainment and spiritual enrichment for the "First World." (84)

Much like Fay Wray in *King Kong,* who "becomes the hinge of narrative progress, between enlightened instrumental reason and barbarism" (84), the Goddess of Democracy is endowed with the narrative authority to tell a tragic story of the Chinese dissidents' struggle, defeat, and annihilation. But the multiple, nongendered connotations of that statue for the dissidents who used it are categorically different from those imagined by Western spectators. What makes the statue so rhetorically powerful for Western cameras is its mobilization of a "white woman fetish" to bridge the gap between Western and Chinese versions of democracy while simultaneously assuming the authority of a benign neocolonial humanism.

I want to emphasize here that Chow does support the use of the Goddess of Democracy as an emblem of Chinese solidarity with the students' struggle. Its significance lies precisely in its ability to represent that struggle as a collective one and to mobilize communities in support. However, the surplus value of the statue — its feminized lack of modern "progress" — is linked in Chow's reading to the repressive function of veiling that images of women often perform. In this case, part of what is veiled is the Western media's role in engineering the crisis. Photographing Chinese people who expressly asked not to be photographed made it easier for the Chinese government to track them down, while the general framing of events in China as a spectacular crisis for Western consumption may well have encouraged protesters to act rashly (83). We are faced in Chow's essay with a powerful indictment of Western culture's appetite for apocalypse at a safe remove — in the "other country."

That indictment extends to a consideration of a film that helps Chow to encapsulate the risks entailed in consolidating Western gender values with technoscientific knowledge. In contrast with *King Kong*'s version of the white woman fetish, *Gorillas in the Mist* (1988) shows us the white female primatologist taking up the ape's habitat as a site for revolutionary resistance to Western civilizing ideals. Nevertheless, her benign insistence "that the 'wild' stay alive in their original, natural habitat" confronts Chow with the dilemma of a neocolonialism that fails to acknowledge the historical impossibility of "letting the other live" while simultaneously occupying its homeland (90). Like the Goddess of Democracy in Tiananmen Square, the primatologist in the wilds indicates that the "natural" habitat is always already denaturalized.

As a Westernized Chinese intellectual, Chow is firmly embedded within this dilemma. Confronted frequently with charges of complicity in her use of Western theory on Chinese literature and feminist theory on Chinese women, she finds that the Western desire to observe Chinese women in traditional surroundings can become a devastating attempt to reinstall them in traditional gender roles. In modern ethnographic case studies, they become victims of socialist patriarchy; in studies of classical Chinese history and literature, they become speechless inhabitants of an Edenic "culture garden." In both situations, the fact of Westernization "as an irreducible part of Asian modern self-consciousness" is under ongoing threat of erasure (94).

Chow's use of Western film to focus questions of historical memory, combined with her self-identification as a Westernized Chinese intellectual woman, illustrates the complication of race, class, and gender at work in global technoculture. As such, it supports Haraway's argument for political alliances based in consciously constructed identities rather than naturalized ones. In addition, Chow expands on the technocultural risks entailed in feminist nostalgia for organic myths of origin. The question is not how to let Third World women "live" by submitting to their traditions and histories, but rather how to make connections between subjects recently traumatized by consciousness of their hybrid, "impure" positions.

For Chow, the existence of the "non-Western, but Westernized, feminist subject" epitomizes the stakes involved in this self-conscious subject position:

Because it is "multiply organized," the space of the Westernized, non-Western feminist subject is an elusive one and as such always runs the risk of being elided. The China crisis shows us such an elision: at the moment of political shock, Chinese women become degendered, and join everyone else as "Chinese." In the long run, however, when the roots of violence can be probed more leisurely and analytically, the problems *embodied* by Chinese women . . . would serve as focal points through which the reverence for authority must be attacked. (95)

The Montreal Massacre — an event in which young women engineering students embodied feminism for their killer — might serve here as another focal point for attacking such reverence. Attempts to silence women and feminists in the aftermath of the massacre were purportedly based in a desire to perceive it as a tragedy for all (ungendered) Canadians. Yet, as Elspeth Probyn writes,

in the search to comprehend how such a thing could happen in Canada, one interpretation held quite amazing sway: the man (and sometimes the woman) on the street agreed with the expert on the screen that feminism made men scared; that in taking jobs away from men, feminists were responsible for this state of affairs.[43]

The problem embodied by women in the aftermath of the Montreal Massacre is a labor issue: working women are labelled feminists so as to serve as scapegoats for corporate and government cutbacks. The officially gender-blind reverence for dead "Canadians" demonstrates the complicity of humanist discourse in veiling the economic aspect of contemporary misogyny.

When gender is used in arguments against violence, as is appropriate and necessary in the comparatively privileged Canadian context, these arguments cannot be delivered from an uncontaminated position of historical or technocultural innocence. Chow's essay demonstrates the extent to which the category "woman" is, as Haraway argues in her vision of a feminist apocalypse, "non-innocent." In its status as a technocultural matrix of East and West, tradition and modernity, human rights and colonial privilege, the Goddess of Democracy statue demonstrates some of this non-innocence. For, as Chow notes, the use of sex and gender may be simply "pointless . . . if they refer only to the dominant sexual transaction of woman-versus-man" (87), but they become politically dangerous when used to represent Chinese dissidents to themselves. However, when considered as fluid technocultural commodities rather than transhistorical and global identities, sex and gender may also become tools for resisting the kinds of violence that install women in traditional roles. When Haraway writes that "cyborg gender is a local possibility taking a global vengeance,"[44] she is, I imagine, referring to such careful and politically astute uses of gender difference in a global struggle waged on many fronts.

In another context, Rey Chow offers a critique of "postmodern automatons" that contributes yet again to the surprising half-life of the "Manifesto for Cyborgs." She identifies the Harawayan cyborg as a social object animated by the critical look of the First World feminist. This animating look, at its idealistic limit, does not imitate the "God's-eye view" that Haraway, Petchesky, and other technocultural feminists locate in the power of photography, but rather "bears the history of her own dehumanization on her as she speaks for other women."[45] Beyond the postmodern privilege of self-reflexivity embodied in her critical look, the First World feminist cyborg might do well to consider Chow's point that

the task that faces Third World feminists is . . . not simply that of "animating" the oppressed women of their cultures, but of making the automatized and animated condition of their own voices the conscious point of departure in their intervention.[46]

"Violence in the Other Country," with its conscious adoption of a hybrid, technoculturally mediated subject position, as well as its understanding of gender as cultural commodity, illustrates some risks and rewards in speaking from this "automatized and animated" stance.

In this essay, I have argued that the cyborg manifesto's blasphemous vision of an apocalypse that has already happened charges its "surprising half-life" with issues of complicity and resistance for feminist technoculture. If the fragmentation of essentialized gender identity and the fractured feminisms of the 1980s make cyborgs and women "non-innocent," that non-innocence also allows for new constructions of feminist knowledge. And if popular cyborg narratives disperse gender hierarchies across the boundaries between human, animal, and machine, such dispersal is nevertheless recuperable on the battlegrounds of women's bodies today. At stake in technocultural feminism are continuing questions of who gets to do the recuperating, on whose terms.

Constance Penley's discussion of a hybrid practice of writing in combination with technologies of visualization notes resistance to the embattled construction of the female body in the slasher's choice not to represent it. In some ways analogous to Rey Chow's consideration of gender politics suspended at a moment of crisis, that erasure of the female body from representation nevertheless constitutes a privilege that is not universally available. Like the displaced and demonized figure of the pregnant woman in the work of Petchesky and others concerned with the effects of medical visualizing technologies on women's lives, the gendered body under threat of erasure delineates a multivocal site of struggle rather than a transcendent agent or victim of cosmic extermination. Like the written body of the feminist cyborg that has yet to find adequate visual representation, it reinforces the manifesto's concern to see both utopian and dystopian possibilities in the apocalyptic imagination of the late twentieth century.

Technocultural feminism demands more than new kinds of knowledge about the machines we encounter in our daily lives; it also demands a politics and an ethics that can deploy that knowledge in tactically subversive and (de) constructive ways. Haraway's definition of cyborg writing — a blasphemous writing which "must not be about the Fall, the imagination of a once-upon-a-time wholeness before language"[47] — helps in that task. Penley's ethnographic work, situated between the feminist academy and a community of nonfeminist women, redefines cyborg writing in the context of multiple techniques of representation. Meanwhile, the efforts of Petchesky and others to read the fetal image in the interlocking contexts of Hollywood entertainment and right-wing politics challenges a current tendency to conflate pregnancy with maternity, and maternity with scientific authority. Finally, Rey Chow's use of Western film and feminist theory to understand events in Tiananmen Square illuminates the technologically mediated contribution of the West to contemporary hybrid constructions of racial otherness.

These technocultural feminists demonstrate that the global task of reconstructing the social relations of science and technology begins locally and proceeds without hope of final resolution. They continue Haraway's anti-apocalyptic aims by considering the kinds of symbolic and material violence inscribed on women's bodies today, and by sympathetically responding to the languages in which that violence is resisted. Perhaps most importantly, they offer versions of pleasure, struggle, and feminist commitment that are also reasons to continue pursuing, again without hope of final resolution, the manifesto's claim that here and now, we are all cyborgs.

Notes

1. Donna Haraway, "A Manifesto for Cyborgs: Science, Technology, and Socialist Feminism in the 1980s," in *Coming to Terms: Feminism, Theory, Politics,* ed. Elizabeth Weed (New York: Routledge, 1989), 173. Further references in the text are to this edition.

2. See for example Joseph P. Rouse, "What are Cultural Studies of Scientific Knowledge?" in *Configurations* 1.1 (Winter 1993): 1–22; Istvan Csicseray-Ronay Jr., "The SF of Theory: Baudrillard and Haraway," in *Science Fiction Studies* 18 (1991): 387–403; Veronica P. Hollinger, "Cybernetic Deconstructions: Cyberpunk and Postmodernism," in *MOSAIC* 23.2 (Spring 1990): 29–44; and Michele Barrett, introduction, *Women's Oppression Today: The Marxist/Feminist Encounter,* rev. ed. (London: Verso, 1988), xxvi–xxvii.

3. See Jacques Derrida, "No Apocalypse, Not Now (Full Speed Ahead, Seven Missiles, Seven Missives)," in *Diacritics* (Summer 1984): 20–31.

4. Mary Carpenter, "Representing Apocalypse: Sexual Politics and the Violence of Revelation," this volume.

5. Haraway, after Chela Sandoval, "A Manifesto for Cyborgs," 180.

6. Derrida, "No Apocalypse, Not Now," 27–28, 26.

7. Haraway, "A Manifesto for Cyborgs," 174.

8. Constance Penley and Andrew Ross, introduction to *Technoculture*, ed. Constance Penley and Andrew Ross (Minneapolis: University of Minnesota Press, 1991), xiii.

9. Derrida, "No Apocalypse, Not Now," 31.

10. Haraway, "A Manifesto for Cyborgs," 204.

11. Kevin Pask, "Cyborg Economies: Desire and Labor in the *Terminator* Films," this volume.

12. For a discussion of the Montreal Massacre in the context of cultural studies and identity politics, see Elspeth Probyn, "Technologizing the Self: A Future Anterior for Cultural Studies," in *Cultural Studies*, ed. Larry Grossberg, Cary Nelson, and Paul A. Treichler (New York: Routledge, 1992), 295–337. For a variety of Quebecois feminist responses to the Montreal Massacre, see Louise Malette and Marie Chalouh, eds., *The Montreal Massacre*, trans. Marlene Wildman (Charlottetown, Prince Edward Island: gynergy books, 1991).

13. For a discussion of critical responses to the liquid cyborg in *Terminator 2*, see Scott Bukatman, *Terminal Identity: The Virtual Subject in Postmodern Science Fiction* (Durham, N.C.: Duke University Press, 1993), 304–307.

14. Constance Penley, "Brownian Motion: Women, Tactics, and Technology," in Penley and Ross, *Technoculture*, 137. Further references are given parenthetically in the text.

15. In an interview with Penley and Ross, Haraway describes the sensitive man as an androgynous, and therefore suspiciously totalizing figure. He adds "the privilege of gentleness" to his already considerable list of privileges. "If it's only added privilege, then it's a version of male feminism of which I am very suspicious." Donna Haraway, "Cyborgs at Large," in Penley and Ross, *Technoculture*, 19.

16. Sl'Tish Horr, K'Tel, and Gigi the Galaxy Girl, editorial, *Science Friction: The ST-TNG Magazine* 2 (May 1993): 5.

17. Constance Penley, "Feminism, Psychoanalysis and the Study of Popular Culture," in *Cultural Studies*, Larry Grossberg et al. (New York: Routledge, 1992), 479.

18. Peter Dickinson, "Go-Go Dancing on the Brink of the Apocalypse: Representing AIDS," this volume.

19. Kevin Pask, "Cyborg Economies," this volume.

20. Rosalind Petchesky, "Foetal Images: The Power of Visual Culture in the Politics of Reproduction," in *Reproductive Technologies: Gender, Motherhood and Medicine*, ed. Michelle Stanworth (Minneapolis: University of Minnesota Press, 1987), 59.

21. Petchesky, "Foetal Images," 63.

22. Mary Ann Doane, "Technophilia: Technology, Representation, and the Feminine," in *Body/Politics: Women and the Discourses of Science*, ed. Mary Jacobus et al. (New York: Routledge, 1990), 163–176.

23. Doane, "Technophilia," 169, 172.

24. Doane, "Technophilia," 169.

25. Petchesky, "Foetal Images," 60; emphasis in the original.

26. Valerie Hartouni, "Fetal Exposures: Abortion Politics and the Optics of Allusion," in *camera obscura* 29 (May 1992): 144.

27. Hartouni, "Fetal Exposures," 139.

28. Hartouni, "Fetal Exposures," 140.

29. Mary Ann Doane, "Commentary: Cyborgs, Origins and Subjectivity," in *Coming to Terms: Feminism, Theory, Politics,* ed. Elizabeth Weed (London: Routledge, 1989), 210.

30. Haraway, "A Manifesto for Cyborgs," 193.

31. Petchesky, "Foetal Images," 69.

32. Carol Stabile, "Shooting the Mother: Fetal Photography and the Politics of Disappearance," in *camera obscura* 28 (January 1992): 198. Stabile argues that "the promise of . . . [Haraway's] cyborg should not blind us to the cyborgs [i.e. fetal images] being forced upon us" (200).

33. Petchesky, "Foetal Images," 77.

34. Petchesky, "Foetal Images," 70.

35. My thanks go to colleague Avril Torrence for this observation.

36. Petchesky, "Foetal Images," 79.

37. Stabile, "Shooting the Mother," 199.

38. Donna Haraway, "The Promises of Monsters: A Regenerative Politics for Inappropriate/d Others," in *Cultural Studies,* ed. Lawrence Grossberg, Cary Nelson, and Paula A. Treichler (New York: Routledge, 1992), 318.

39. For a fuller discussion of the significance of animal stories in colonialist discourse, see Donna Haraway, *Primate Visions: Gender, Race and Nature in the World of Modern Science* (New York: Routledge, 1989).

40. Rey Chow, "Violence in the Other Country: China As Crisis, Spectacle, and Woman," in *Third World Women and the Politics of Feminism,* ed. Chandra Talpade Mohanty, Ann Russo, and Lourdes Torres (Bloomington: Indiana University Press, 1991). Further references are given parenthetically in the text.

41. See for example, Greta Hoffman Nemiroff, "Where Are the 49% When We Need Them?" in *The Montreal Massacre,* ed. Louise Malette and Marie Chalouh (Charlottetown: Gynergy Books, 1991), 145–149. See also "Violence Is Not a Women's Issue," *The [Toronto] Globe and Mail,* July 31, 1993, D6.

42. Elspeth Probyn writes of her experience of the Montreal Massacre,

> The awful recognition, that *shock* of recognition of where we are as women, the terrible feeling as the very space of the university, of the streets, is rearranged in fear, brought forward another tone. There was no way of not speaking as a woman and as a feminist. Nevertheless, this spontaneous move to speak of and to a collective of women was, in turn, represented as a speaking position founded upon the dead bodies of fourteen young women. ("Technologizing the Self" 502)

43. Probyn, "Technologizing the Self," 502.

44. Haraway, "A Manifesto for Cyborgs," 204.

45. Rey Chow, "Postmodern Automatons," in *Feminists Theorize the Political,* ed. Judith Butler and Joan W. Scott (New York: Routledge, 1992), 110.

46. Chow, "Postmodern Automatons," 112.

47. Haraway, "A Manifesto for Cyborgs," 198.

"Go-go Dancing on the Brink of the Apocalypse": Representing AIDS
An Essay in Seven Epigraphs

Peter Dickinson

in memoriam Mark B. and David P.

EPIGRAPH #1:

The past four decades have witnessed unprecedented success in controlling infectious diseases, an achievement that has created great confidence in medicine's ability to conquer sickness. Yet in only a few years,
the epidemic of human immunodeficiency virus (HIV) and acquired
immune deficiency syndrome (AIDS) has shaken this confidence and
revived fears at least as old as the medieval plagues.[1]

— American Institute of Medicine and the
National Academy of Sciences

With the AIDS pandemic well into its second decade, and with the millennium drawing to a close, the initial *dis*-ease surrounding the disease has
given way to a whole new industry of discursive inquiry. This has resulted
in the production and proliferation of a number of competing AIDS
discourses, many of which are characteristically apocalyptic in tone: from
the dire predictions of biomedicine to the sensational headlines in the
media; from the calls for mandatory testing and quarantine on the part
of Jesse Helms and other right-wing politicians to the holocaust imagery
and graphics employed by Larry Kramer and like-minded gay activists;
from the metacritical interventions of intellectuals like Susan Sontag to
the arresting visions created by artists like Tony Kushner.

However, the problem with abstract theorizing about AIDS is that it
frequently lacks a subject, a body, a corpus, a corpse. This would seem to
be even more the case when theorizing AIDS as apocalypse. As Jacques
Derrida states, with "[a]n apocalyptic superimprinting of texts: there is
no paradigmatic text. Only relationships of cryptic haunting from mark
to mark. No palimpsest. . . . No piece, no metonymy, no integral corpus."[2] In this sense, then, the discourses enumerated above potentially

threaten whole groups of marginalized peoples — specifically, persons living with AIDS and HIV — with erasure, if not complete annihilation.

And yet, AIDS is not only a condition, resulting from HIV, that attacks the cells of the immune system and impairs the body's ability to defend itself against viral, fungal, bacterial, protozoal, and parasitic infections, but also, in the words of Paula Treichler, "an epidemic of signification."[3] As Douglas Crimp states, "AIDS does not exist apart from the practices that conceptualize it, represent it, and respond to it."[4] Neither does apocalypse. To quote Derrida again: "What I write here is related to reading, writing, teaching as apocalypse, to apocalypse as revelation, to apocalypse in its eschatological and catastrophic sense."[5] Reading, writing, teaching as apocalypse. Reading, writing, teaching AIDS as apocalypse. Perhaps I would do well to locate myself, initially, in this particular apocalyptic moment.

Recently, during a trip to San Francisco, I came across an article by Gregg Taylor in the *San Francisco Bay Times*. In this article, from which I have appropriated the first part of my title, Taylor argues that it is the responsibility of young queers to practice "naughty, pro-active hooliganism" in the name of social advancement and change:

> Our predilection as the generation of the Apocalypse is to be contentious rather than content. Because our world has been informed by sound bites and infomercials, rather than history and analysis, our ingrained distrust of authority has geared us to base our futures in hope rather than expectations.[6]

Sound rhetorical advice, especially for the practice/praxis of queer activism. But how does this translate into the present context of academic theorizing? For it would seem that, in writing this essay, I am immediately confronted with an ethical dilemma. That is, given my own status as a seronegative gay man, how can I abstractly theorize a retrovirus (HIV) that inscribes and transcribes itself at the microcellular level of antibodies without effacing the very material *bodies* of the persons living with AIDS and HIV in which this virus resides? Can I legitimately equate the call for speaking out as a sign of resistance on the ACT UP frontlines (encapsulated in the slogan SILENCE = DEATH) with a deconstructivist framework inherent in cultural criticism that aims to demystify language and power and open up the traditionally desexualized spaces of the academy to a polyphony of marginalized voices and subversive practices?[7] In the representation of AIDS, where do cultural analysis and cultural activism collide/elide/align?

In his essay "The Plague of Discourse," Lee Edelman offers a somewhat cynical — and suitably apocalyptic — response to these questions: "[D]iscourse, alas, is the only defense with which we can counteract discourse, and there is no available discourse on AIDS that is not itself diseased."[8]

For his part, Stuart Marshall argues that competing apocalyptic discourses from the Right and Left tend to overshadow "an often unheard discourse of people living with AIDS that stresses hope, survival, healing, and personal triumph."[9] Why then should I heap yet another discourse onto this burgeoning pile, especially when so many other voices remain unheard?

But, as Michel Foucault reminds us, discourse is itself an *event,* an event, moreover, that involves not only the text or utterance but its position within a given social space, including the speaker, location, and hearers of discourse.[10] These last two elements are frequently overlooked, especially in academic theorizing focused almost exclusively on the "speaking" rather than the "listening" subject.[11] However, in my volunteer work with AIDS Vancouver this is precisely my role: to listen, to attempt actively, attentively, and sensitively to "hear" the needs of my Buddy. And then to respond to those needs accordingly. I am eager to apply this discursive model to my academic work as well (especially in this present context), to theorize listening as potentially as powerful an "act of resistance" as speaking.

For example, within a framework of "listening" it is possible to reconfigure Edelman's "zone of infection" into an examination, after Derrida, of the "tone of inflection" in a range of AIDS discourses. What is being said, how is it being said, by whom and for whom is it being said? In attempting to answer these questions, I hope to establish a taxonomy of the various modes of apocalypse at work in the discursive production of AIDS — from the marketing of apocalypse by biomedicine and the media to the ironizing of apocalypse by gay activists and artists — paying particular attention to the representation of identity and difference, safer sex, and persons living with AIDS and HIV.

*   *   *

In his essay "Of an Apocalyptic Tone Recently Adopted in Philosophy," Derrida comments as follows:

The overlordly tone acts on the authority of a *salto mortale* . . . , a leap from concepts to the unthinkable or the irrepresentable, an obscure anticipation of the mysterious secret come from beyond. This leap toward the imminence of a vision without concept, this impatience turned toward the most crypted secret sets free a poetico-metaphorical overabundance. To that extent this overabundance has indeed an apocalyptic affinity.[12]

Derrida claims that this overlordly or apocalyptic tone "is dominated by the oracular voice," which "speaks to you in a private code, and whispers secrets to you, while uncovering your ear, jumbling, covering, or parasitising the voice of reason that speaks equally in each and maintains the same language for all."[13]

Applying Derrida's discourse typology to contemporary representations of AIDS, it is at once possible to delineate an oracular voice at work in biomedical discourse, for example. Indeed, my first epigraph illustrates that the "rational" voice of science is itself embedded within the semantic conventions of language whereby past and future are revised in order to control present thinking about AIDS. Of course, our faith in modern science's and medicine's ability to triumph heroically over pestilence and disease perforce necessitates the adoption of an oracular voice by its practitioners. Or, to put it more cynically, apocalyptic thinking fuels epidemiological research. As early as 1985, Robert C. Gallo, one of the "co-discoverers" of HIV, in his introduction to Jacques Leibowitch's *A Strange Virus of Unknown Origin*, characterized AIDS as the crucible in which the field of immunology would have "its baptism by fire."[14] Likewise, Treichler cites another epidemiologist as stating that we face "an impending Armageddon of AIDS, and the salvation of the world through molecular genetics."[15] And, more recently, in a book with section headings like "A Calamity for Our Times," "The Oracles of Science," "A Look Back," and "Disaster: Its Extent and Causes," physician and scientific historian Mirko Grmek has called AIDS "the first of the postmodern plagues."[16]

The apocalyptic tone in biomedical discourse is perhaps nowhere more evident than in its propensity for quoting statistics and for naming.[17] Ironically, whereas the former activity stresses the global impact of the pandemic (as evidenced in the World Health Organization's [WHO] yearly projections of the numbers of people worldwide infected with HIV, either knowingly or unknowingly), the latter attempts to claim local ownership of the scientific knowledge needed to combat the disease (as evidenced in the debate over the naming of HIV or in the plethora of acronyms that have developed in connection with AIDS).[18] However, both strategies inadvertently highlight the racial, gendered, and sexual biases at work in the discourse.

In "AIDS, Homophobia, and Biomedical Discourse," Treichler points out that the American Centers for Disease Control's initial "4-H" list of high-risk categories included the following groups: homosexuals, hemophiliacs, heroin addicts, and Haitians. Not until 1986 was the center willing to revise its list to include a fifth H-category, namely heterosexuals, despite persistent evidence that heterosexual intercourse was the primary mode of transmission in Africa.[19] Moreover, listen to the American Institute of Medicine's comments on the "demographic impact of AIDS":

AIDS cases occur in higher proportions in black and Hispanic populations than in white populations, mainly as a result of higher HIV prevalence in black and Hispanic IV drug abusers and their sex partners and offspring. Recent data also suggest that the virus is spreading more rapidly among blacks and Hispanics at risk than among other population groups, especially in Northeastern cities, suggesting that the future composition of AIDS cases will consist primarily of poor, urban minorities.[20]

What the institute fails to mention, however, is that these same "poor, urban minorities" will not be included in clinical drug trials because of their inability to access, socially and economically, proper health care and their inability to fit, racially or sexually, into a homogenized group of white males between the ages of twenty-five and forty-five. To this end, Treichler has also demonstrated that biomedical discourse is constructed along explicitly gendered lines, resulting in women being consistently counseled against taking the HIV-antibody test by their (male) physicians.[21]

EPIGRAPH #2:

Of all the tragedies of this century, does AIDS stand alone as a robber of youth, creativity and potential? The last 20 years of the century will have been dominated by AIDS. There have been a great many scourges in this millennium. . . . you can't help thinking of the great tragedies. Six million Jews and 20 million Russians died in World War II. How many died at Nagasaki and Hiroshima? How do you quantify all this?[22]

— Bernard Gersten

In August 1986 the *Los Angeles Times Magazine* published an article by Neil Schram called "AIDS: 1991." Described as a "fictional scenario based on what is known about acquired immune deficiency syndrome," the article paints a decidedly apocalyptic picture of a United States where mandatory AIDS testing is required of every American citizen and where the president is given to pronouncements such as the following: "We have a crisis that requires drastic measures. Failure to follow these recommendations will undoubtedly lead to a need for even more drastic measures in the future."[23] Printed five years after the first reports on the "mysterious cancer" afflicting gay men started appearing in the *New York Times,* this article reflects a definite shift in tone in the media's coverage of AIDS. More specifically, Rock Hudson's death in 1985 (which was announced in the press with bold headlines declaring that "AIDS FINALLY HAS A FACE," and which succeeded merely in obliterating the existence of every other PWA, living or dead, from popular consciousness) sparked a flurry of panic in the media about the possibility of heterosexual transmission, altering the conception of AIDS as an epidemic affecting gay men to a pandemic affecting potentially all sexually active persons, regardless of their sexuality.[24] The "reality" of apocalypse was suddenly much closer. Indeed, in the prologue to his controversial book *And the Band Played On*, the late Randy Shilts, who reported for the *San Francisco Chronicle*, claimed that Hudson's death "became a demarcation that would separate the history of America before AIDS from the history that came after."[25]

For Simon Watney the apocalyptic tone in media discourse has manifested itself most noticeably in a reconfiguration of the traditional liberal distinction between "public" and "private" knowledges: "In all its variant forms the spectacle of AIDS is carefully and elaborately stage-managed as a sensational didactic pageant, furnishing 'us,' the 'general public,' with further dramatic evidence of what 'we' already 'know' concerning the enormity of the dangers that surround us on all sides and at all times."[26] Thus, instead of socializing a discourse on AIDS, the mainstream media have demonized it; instead of contextualizing the issues surrounding AIDS, they have compartmentalized them.

Most disturbing, however, is the fact that in sensationalizing AIDS, that is, in adopting an oracular voice and taking it to the nth degree, the media have ultimately rendered AIDS banal. To be sure, the death of a Rudolf Nureyev can still elicit reports such as the one from which my second epigraph is drawn, but what about the PWAs who die every day without so much as an obituary? In a recent issue of *Canadian AIDS News* devoted to the media's coverage of AIDS, Robert Burr, director of communications at the Canadian Public Health Association, identifies another tonal shift in AIDS reporting:

The Canadian public is already jaded by the failures of scientific credibility ranging from Three Mile Island [to] Chernobyl. . . . Now warning signs are appearing that the public — and the media — are disillusioned over the quality of AIDS information. Simply put, AIDS educators may not be able to count on the media sympathy they've enjoyed in the past.[27]

This would perhaps explain the impetus behind two articles that recently appeared in the *Vancouver Sun*. The first, titled "Apocalypse No," suggests that projections about the numbers of people infected with HIV have been greatly exaggerated.[28] The second, titled "Apocalypse Now," claims that the latest WHO estimate of 13 million people infected with the AIDS virus worldwide is, if anything, conservative.[29] Of course, the fact that the former article focuses on the impact of AIDS in the West and that the latter concentrates on AIDS in Africa may account for the discrepancy in tone. For, as Simon Watney points out, "[t]he discursive regularities of Western AIDS commentary are nowhere more apparent than in the construction of 'African AIDS.' "[30]

EPIGRAPH #3:

I may be the most radical person you've talked to about AIDS, but I think that somewhere along the line that we are going to have to quarantine, if we are really going to contain this disease.[31]

— U.S. Senator Jesse Helms

The preservation of "family values" has been the most persistent rallying cry of the neoconservative political right in its representations of AIDS. This has resulted in successful constitutional intervention in the policing of morality within several "Western liberal-democratic" countries. For example, the 1987 Helms Amendment in the United States and Section 28 of the 1988 Local Government Act in Britain have effectively legislated against representations of safer sex outside the confines of heterosexual monogamy, ostensibly in order to safeguard the micromoral polity of the family.[32]

Even more frightening, however, are the calls for the quarantine of persons living with AIDS and HIV that have repeatedly surfaced through-out the course of the pandemic (from Lyndon Larouche in the United States and Jean-Marie Le Pen in France, for example). While such oracles have, so far, been ignored, the spectre of mandatory testing has become much more of a reality. According to the Panos Institute, thirty-five of one hundred twenty-two countries surveyed specifically screen potential immigrants for HIV antibodies.[33] Canada and the United States are in-cluded among this thirty-five. In this sense, the AIDS pandemic serves to fuel First World political paranoia toward the Third World. This reaction-ary equating of contagion with social, cultural, racial, and sexual differ-ences is a contemporary configuration of apocalypse that is, in fact, a direct legacy of late nineteenth-century fin-de-siècle imperialism: fear of miscegenation, fear of not finding in the "Other" the inversed figure of the "Self."

EPIGRAPH #4:

It's not too early to see AIDS as the homosexuals' holocaust. I have come reluc-tantly to believe that genocide is occurring: that we are witnessing — or *not* witnessing — the systematic, planned annihilation of some by others with the avowed purpose of eradicating an undesirable portion of the population.[34]

— Larry Kramer

Ironically, the apocalyptic tone used by the political right seems to have contributed to the adoption of a similar tone by the activist left. Indeed, Kramer's holocaust allusions emerge as a direct consequence of the calls for quarantine outlined above.

Writer, activist, cofounder of the Gay Men's Health Crisis (GMHC) and founder of ACT UP in New York, Kramer has been a thorn in the side of both the American political system *and* the gay community since the early eighties. Witness the opening of his article "1,112 and Counting," first published in the *New York Native* in March 1983 and subsequently reprinted in Kramer's volume of essays, *Reports from the Holocaust:* "If this article doesn't scare the shit out of you, we're in real trouble. If this article doesn't rouse you to anger, fury, rage, and action, gay men may have no future on this earth. Our continued existence depends on just how angry you can get."[35] Always provocative, and frequently prophetic, Kramer has been accused of espousing a rhetoric that, at the very least, suffers from introversion, and, at the very worst, borders on paranoia. Nevertheless, Kramer's voice has been indispensible to AIDS activism and he remains steadfastly unapologetic in his comparison of holocausts, past and present: "Perhaps because I am both, I find it remarkable how many similarities I notice between homosexuals and Jews. . . . History recently made a pretty good attempt to destroy the Jewish people, and . . . I think history now has an opportunity to do . . . pretty much the same to homosexuals."[36]

As a result of such comparisons, the oracular voice of AIDS is perhaps nowhere more apparent than in the ACT UP slogan SILENCE = DEATH. First appearing in white type on posters, buttons, and T-shirts underneath a pink triangle on a black background, this simple graphic has, in a few short years, come to signify the forefront of AIDS activism to the gay community. Not without incurring its own share of controversy, however.

As Douglas Crimp states, the equation SILENCE = DEATH "does its work with a metaphorical subtlety that is unique, among political symbols and slogans, to AIDS activism":

Our emblem's significance depends on foreknowledge of the use of the pink triangle as the marker of gay men in Nazi concentration camps, its appropriation by the gay movement to remember a suppressed history of our oppression, and, now, an inversion of its positioning (men in the death camps wore triangles that pointed down; SILENCE = DEATH's points up). SILENCE = DEATH declares that silence about the oppression and annihilation of gay people, *then* and *now,* must be broken as a matter of our survival.[37]

Nevertheless, at a purely discursive level, the use of this graphic has just as much potential for violence as the rhetoric of the far right, particularly in its construction and mobilization of a "singular" AIDS community. Lost in the analogy between the current AIDS crisis and the internment of homosexuals in Nazi Germany, according to Marshall, "are all those aspects of difference and subjectivity that identity politics subordinates and suppresses precisely to ensure political solidarity and action. This has, on a subtle level, far-reaching and possibly reactionary consequences."[38]

As someone who has brandished this particular graphic in a variety of ways on a variety of different occasions, I find that I am suddenly on shaky ground in my examination of its apocalyptic tone. The academic in me says to deconstruct the equation; the activist in me says to wear it and feel empowered. In the end, however, I tend to side with Marshall when he states:

I am utterly convinced of the appropriateness of the legend SILENCE = DEATH, but I am unconvinced about anchoring the equation to the pink triangle. The powerful message contained in the slogan is the necessity of representation, but the use of the pink triangle immobilizes representation by locking it into an agenda of victimization and annihilation.[39]

EPIGRAPH #5:

It will have been said that with the appearance of AIDS something is reaching its end — provisionally or definitely.[40]

—Alexander García Düttmann

Of course, AIDS has also received much critical attention from the intellectual community (witness this very essay, for example), ostensibly as an "act of resistance" whereby the rational voice can intercede against the oracular. Susan Sontag's *AIDS and Its Metaphors* is one such example. Picking up where she left off in her earlier treatise, *Illness as Metaphor*, Sontag argues against the more punitive metaphorical representations of AIDS. Recognizing that "one cannot think without metaphors," she nevertheless asserts that "that does not mean there aren't some metaphors we might well abstain from or try to retire. As, of course, all thinking is interpretation. But that does not mean it isn't sometimes correct to be 'against' interpretation."[41]

And yet, for all her professed aversion to metaphorical thinking, Sontag cannot help falling into what Derrida calls a "poetico-metaphorical overabundance" of tone in her own representation of AIDS.[42] This is nowhere more evident than in her concluding discussion of apocalypse. Linking AIDS with industrial pollution, the stockpiling of nuclear weapons, the collapse of global financial markets, and "other unfolding disasters," Sontag unwittingly contributes to the imaging of apocalypse as "part of the ordinary horizon of expectation":

AIDS may be extending the propensity for becoming inured to vistas of global annihilation which the stocking and brandishing of nuclear arms has already promoted. With the inflation of apocalyptic rhetoric has come the increasing unreality of the apocalypse. A permanent modern scenario: apocalypse looms . . . and it doesn't occur. . . . AIDS is one of the dystopian harbingers of the global village, the future which is already here and always before us, which no one knows how to refuse.[43]

Given such pronouncements, Sontag inevitably "finds herself writing inside the outside of her own exclusion zone, re-articulating those futilities and fatalities she had hoped to oppose. . . . Plagued even within the confines of her own figural cordon sanitaire . . . , Sontag's high profile volubility amounts to a kind of silencing."[44]

EPIGRAPH #6:

History is about to crack wide open. Millennium approaches.[45]

— Tony Kushner

In turning to analyze the particular discourses at work in the artistic community, I want first to preface my remarks with the following declaration: I will be focusing exclusively on representations of AIDS produced by queer artists. I have made this admittedly arbitrary decision partly because of my own subject position as a gay man, but also because I believe, along with Richard Dellamora, in his reading of Edmund White's "An Oracle,"[46] and Ed Cohen, in his study of Oscar Wilde,[47] that apocalyptic utterance and fin-de-siècle theorizing have particular resonances within gay culture, signaling a double gesture of (dis)closure: an unveiling, after Foucault, of our "use of pleasure" in "the care of the self,"[48] as well as our dis-pleasure in the policing of same-sex desire as disease.[49]

Consider, for example, the recent multimedia exhibition *Fin-de-Siècle* by Toronto-based trio General Idea (consisting of A. A. Bronson, Felix Partz, and Jorge Zontal), which toured Germany and Spain and, most recently, appeared at Toronto's Power Plant Gallery.[50] Apart from the title piece, which features three white fake-fur seals lying on white polystyrene slabs arranged in the shape of an iceberg, the most arresting installation is "One Year of AZT and One Day of AZT." In it a daily ration of what Treichler correctly identifies as the only FDA-approved antiretroviral drug for "the treatment of the spectrum of AIDS problems"[51] covers the floor in the shape of five white and blue pills the size of coffins, while the walls of that room and three additional rooms are lined with a year's supply of 1,825 smaller pills. As John Bentley Mays suggests in his review of the exhibit, the tone here is indeed black, but ironically so, "in which the horror of death by AIDS and humourous, plucky charm exactly balance each other, with trademark GI finesse."[52]

Black humor also suffuses Gregg Araki's 1992 film *The Living End* and Tony Kushner's Pulitzer prize– and Tony award–winning play *Angels in America*. In the former, HIV-positive lovers, Jon and Luke, embark on an odyssey of sex and violence that evokes recollections of James Dillinger's apocalyptic gay novel *Adrenaline,* that makes Hollywood's *Longtime Com-*

panion look like an ultra-sanitized Tide commercial, and that gives new meaning to what Arthur and Marilouise Kroker have labeled "panic sex in America."[53] And in *Millennium Approaches,* the first part of Kushner's seven-hour "Gay Fantasia on National Themes," a valium-addicted Harper Pitt travels to Antarctica in order to confront for herself the hole in the ozone layer; the ghost of Ethel Rosenberg comes back to haunt her former prosecutor, Roy Cohn, now dying of AIDS; and Prior Walter greets the arrival of the Angel at his deathbed, amid "*a great blaze of triumphal music*" and "*a shower of unearthly white light,*" with the following awestruck words: "God almighty . . . *Very* Steven Spielberg."[54]

However, in *Perestroika,* the concluding portion of Kushner's epic theatrical event, the Angel turns out to be "a cosmic reactionary."[55] "YOU MUST STOP MOVING!" (52) she tells Prior in a resplendently apocalyptic voice punctuated by occasional hacking coughs, "On you in you in your blood we write have written: STASIS! The END" (54). Prior, having been given this glimpse of "the end of things," decides he wants no part of it and, as such, realizes that his "only resistance is to run" (56). When the Angel finally catches up with him, in Heaven no less, he explains that "[w]e can't just stop. We're not rocks. Progress, migration, motion is . . . modernity. It's *animate,* it's what living things do. We desire. Even if all we desire is stillness, it's still desire *for.* Even if we go faster than we should. We can't *wait*" (132).[56] Thus, standing before the "Seven Myriad Infinite Aggregate Angelic Entities," in the "Hall of Continental Principalities," in the midst of "Not-to-Be-Time," and "With Apocalypse Descending," Prior returns his prophetic implements (signified most prominently in the play by the "Tome of Immobility") and, moreover, manages to secure from the assembled company a promise of "more life": "We live past hope. Bless me anyway. I want more life" (135–136).

With respect to fiction, Sarah Schulman's *People in Trouble* offers an especially powerful depiction of AIDS as apocalypse. In this text a tale of doomed lesbian love unfolds against the backdrop of ACT UP (fictionalized in the text as "Justice") demonstrations in New York City. The result is a vision of the present, *not* the future, in which no one is safe, and from which no one is exempt: "It was the beginning of the end of the world but not everyone noticed right away. Some people were dying. Some people were busy. Some people were cleaning their houses while the war movie played on television."[57] Similarly, in *Dog Years* Canadian author Dennis Denisoff creates a portrait of twentysomething existence decidedly dissimilar to that popularized by compatriot Douglas Coupland, in which "Generation X-tasy" (that group of gay men who have never known sex without the association of death) is forced to contemplate not only its deferred future, but also, conceivably, the very end of history: "For Paul, history is recorded as before and after the Stonewall revolt; for me, history begins with AIDS and AIDS is still here. What I mean to say is, history ends with AIDS."[58]

*   *   *

But the end of history is also the beginning of histories. Or, as John J. Joughin suggests, "apocalyptic moments have always come and gone, and . . . this latest post-history would not be the first to claim to be the last."[59] I do not believe that Joughin is being deliberately flippant about the magnitude of the current AIDS pandemic here. Rather, he is pointing to a particular "configuration of a history of histories in crisis," whereby "critical moments, apocalyptic moments, occupy a necessary space in the oppressor's imaginary where there is never a lack without an attendant resolution."[60] And yet it is precisely in between this lack of and resolution of crisis, that is, within the critical moment itself, that we find the possibilities and contingencies of situational change. For apocalyptic thinking can open up spaces for the enunciation or utterance of hitherto silenced and marginalized voices.

As Derrida states, "[b]y its very tone, the mixing of voices, genres, and codes, apocalyptic discourse can also, in dislocating destinations, dismantle the dominant contract or concordat" ("Of an Apocalyptic Tone," 29–30). Moreover, he identifies an "apocalyptic *pli*," or message, that can induce a certain tonal change (28), "the possibility for the other tone, or the tone of another, to come at no matter what moment to interrupt a familiar music [tonality]" (24), a process of demystification that

imposes itself as the enigmatic desire for vigilance, for the lucid vigil, for elucidation, for critique and truth, but for a truth that at the same time keeps within itself some apocalyptic desire, this time as desire for clarity and revelation, in order to demystify or, if you prefer, to deconstruct apocalyptic discourse itself. (22)

In this context, the current AIDS crisis is no exception. In addition to the "official" discourses it has produced, it has also produced a number of "unofficial" counterdiscourses, or "vernaculars." I use this term not only as a deliberate juxtaposition to Derrida's use of the term "oracular," but also in order to signify one of the "post-histories" Joughin refers to in his essay, an apocalyptic moment that is frequently equated/conflated with the present AIDS pandemic, namely the bubonic plague that raged across Europe in the fourteenth century, or the first time the world (almost) ended.

In 1957 Norman Cohn published his groundbreaking study, *The Pursuit of the Millennium*.[61] In it he argues that the exterminating impulses of the twentieth century are a direct legacy of the fervent growth and equally fervent inquisition of heretical religious sects during the Middle Ages. More importantly, however, he claims that medieval millenarian thinking spawned revolutionary class and national struggles that spoke a local and popular language of religion (encapsulated in German, Flemish, or Italian vernaculars as opposed to papal Latinate) for the first (and the last) time. In a similar fashion, AIDS, like its medieval predecessor, the Black Death, has given rise to a number of "dissident vernaculars."[62] These vernaculars are presently operating within and across various communities, at once resisting the seductive rhetoric of endtime in dominant discourse, and wading through the morass of disinformation surrounding AIDS, to speak to marginalized subjects in a language they can potentially understand.

In her recent work, for example, Cindy Patton has begun to theorize "a 'pornographic vernacular' as a concept from which to produce better strategies for organizing communities or subcultures around safe sex." Recognizing the need to balance carefully cultural assumptions about sexuality and representation in assessing the potential for pornography to intervene positively in safer sex education, Patton nevertheless argues that "a theory of sexual vernacular makes no sharp distinction between 'sex' and 'text,' but views sexual performance, sexual identities, and sexual networks as constructed in and *as* language." As she puts it, "[s]exual vernaculars are the identifying characteristics of liminal sexualities — being 'in the life' historically precedes more visual markers of subcultural affinity."[63]

For his part, Samuel Delany identifies a double or twin process of rhetorical control and discursive regulation at work in the representation of AIDS. Distinguishing between "street talk" and "straight talk," he argues that whereas the former fashions a discourse of experience that leans toward life, hope, and sex, the latter produces a discourse of knowledge that leans toward death, fear, and antisex. Delany focuses, in particular, on the construction of "high risk" and "low risk" behaviors, claiming that such arbitrary designations "define a discursive substratum where *all* sexual behaviour becomes more or less dangerous, and all is subject to endless displacement and slippage along that discursive slope, now nearer to, now further from, death."[64]

Personally, I believe that in the areas of safer sex education and treatment activism these "dissident vernaculars" are important and vital counterdiscursive strategies. For example, there is a difference between the precision of the vernacular — "Don't get fucked up the ass without a condom"; "Use oral drugs like Pentamidine or Bactrium to treat PCP unless side effects occur, then use aerosol" — and the obfuscation of the oracular — "Penile-rectal intercourse without a condom brings with it a high risk of HIV transmission"; "Pentamidine intravenous infusion is a possible prophylactic mainstay for treatment of *pneumocystis carinii* pneumonia." Thus, the sexual, linguistic, and cultural vernaculars at work in the safer sex shorts produced by the GMHC in New York, or by Richard Fung and John Greyson in Canada, the "guerrilla theater" tactics of Puppets Against AIDS and other theater troupes from South Africa, the poster graphics of ACT UP, the native iconography of Heal Our Spirits in British Columbia, the peer counseling among female sex trade workers in Kenya, and cooperative newsletters such as *Project Inform Perspective, Treatment Issues,* and *The Body Positive* speak not to "target groups" about imminent risk and eventual demise, but to "constituent communities" about living with AIDS. Not necessarily displacing or even deferring AIDS as apocalypse; merely demystifying, or deconstructing the discourses surrounding it.

Still, speaking about/with AIDS is problematized only for some of the people some of the time. As Patton states, "[w]hat are ignored are the ways in which the vernacular terms are altered or are reinvested once they are linked to the dominant discourse through an enforced equivalency determined and policed by the culturally sensitive educator."[65] Or, as the late Michael Lynch has put it, "what to say is a problem for vigilants, not for the invigilated."[66] As Lynch suggests, the decision to say, in the vernacular, "with the upright personal pronoun, 'I have AIDS' " necessarily brings with it certain "Oracular Expectations":

When I withhold the avowal "I have AIDS," it's sometimes an attempt to escape the overdetermined readings of my body. When I say upfront "I have AIDS," it too is sometimes [an] attempt to resist overdetermination. Yet both the withholding and the giving may operate to further the overdetermination. Whether I say it, or I don't, Oracular Expectations escalate. Willy-nilly, my life becomes a sentimental, or antisentimental, deathbed.[67]

According to Alexander García Düttmann, however, speaking about/ with AIDS is potentially a way of avoiding, or at least resisting, apocalypse:

Ever since I decided to speak in the language of truth . . . , to speak of my AIDS and in its name — legitimated by this avowal — I rush headlong after the virus, I allow myself to be led by it, to follow it, to love and to hate it, as if I were one of the survivors of some imminent apocalypse. . . . The avowal, this precipitous testimony, which speaks of contamination, permits us in language to outlive ourselves: perverse punishment. In refusing to speak of AIDS without avowing my AIDS, in refusing to speak of myself without speaking of my AIDS, I am already my own survivor, the other in myself.[68]

What, then, "can be the limits of a demystification" of an apocalyptic tone?[69] For Derrida "this demystification must be led as far as possible, and the task is not modest. It is interminable, because no one can exhaust the overdeterminations and the indeterminations of the apocalyptic stratagems."[70] Moreover, just as Edelman argues that any discourse about AIDS is necessarily diseased, so Derrida claims that "all language on apocalypse is also apocalyptic and cannot be excluded from its object."[71] And so, as the end of this essay approaches, I find myself returning to the beginning. The question avoided then cannot be avoided now: that is, does any examination of the "tone of inflection" of AIDS discourses nec-essarily return us to the "zone of infection" from which they emerged? Apocalypse now instead of apocalypse not yet? Delany would seem to think so:

The range of discourses — and the rhetoric that falls out of them — must be lis-tened to, and listened to carefully, if only to suggest further operationalized studies. But to give conclusions drawn from unoperationalized rhetoric the same weight as such studies, while lacking their outcomes, is a discursive crime at one with murder. And the range of our society, from the highest to lowest, is guilty of that crime, on the grounds of what we say about AIDS.[72]

This returns us to the whole issue of discourse analysis and (inter)sub-jective agency. Recently, Derrida has argued that AIDS is an event "ab-solutely unique to our time," an event, moreover, that throws into ques-tion "the inalienable identity of anything like a subject," replacing the notion of subjectivity with that of "intersubjectivity," a tertiary trace, mark, caesura in time (located, presumably, within the *retro*virus itself) at once brand new and immemorial.[73] For García Düttmann, however, Der-rida's "gesture of recognition" here risks "being nothing more than a gesture of appropriation," in which "Derrida [is] able to say nothing about AIDS that he could not have and has not been able to say about deconstruction."[74]

Thus, in the representation of AIDS as apocalypse, who is speaking and who is listening? Or, perhaps more importantly, to whom are we speaking and to whom are we listening? In closing, I have chosen to give the penultimate word to Michel Foucault, whose theories have informed my notion of discourse throughout this essay, and who, since his own death from AIDS in 1984, has been the subject — I use the term loosely here — of much "discursive exhumation":[75]

Writing so as not to die . . . or perhaps even speaking so as not to die is a task undoubtedly as old as the word. The most fateful decisions are inevitably sus-pended during the course of a story. We know that discourse has the power to arrest the flight of an arrow in a recess of time, in the space proper to it. It is quite likely, as Homer has said, that the gods send disasters to men so that they can tell of them, and that in this possibility speech finds its infinite resourcefulness; it is quite likely that the approach of death — its sovereign gesture, its prominence within human memory — hollows out in the present and in existence the void toward which and from which we speak.[76]

EPIGRAPH #7:

SILENCE = DEATH

Notes

I wish to thank the following people for the helpful comments, criticisms, and suggestions that they made during the writing and revising of this paper: Richard Dellamora, Richard Cavell, Robert K. Martin, Alec Globe, Judy Segal, Marni Stanley, Lesley Ziegler, Julie Walchli, Danny O'Quinn, Jonathan Dollimore, and Felix Yaung.

1. Institute of Medicine and National Academy of Sciences, *Confronting AIDS: Update 1988* (Washington, D.C.: National Academy Press, 1988), 1.

2. Jacques Derrida, "Living On: *Border Lines,*" trans. James Hulbert, in *Deconstruction and Criticism* (New York: Continuum, 1986), 136–137.

3. Paula Treichler, "AIDS, Homophobia, and Biomedical Discourse: An Epidemic of Signification," in *AIDS: Cultural Analysis/Cultural Activism,* ed. Douglas Crimp (Cambridge, Mass.: MIT Press, 1989), 31.

4. Douglas Crimp, "AIDS: Cultural Analysis/Cultural Activism," in Crimp, *AIDS: Cultural Analysis/Cultural Activism,* 3.

5. Derrida, "Living On," 125.

6. Gregg Taylor, "Generation X-tasy," *San Francisco Bay Times* 13, no. 24, August 13, 1992, p. 36. For a somewhat more pessimistic, although no less personal, take on AIDS and the increasing rate of seroconversion among twentysomething gay men, see Stephen Beachy, "AIDS and the Apocalyptic Imagination," in *NEXT: Young American Writers on the New Generation,* ed. Eric Liu (New York: Norton, 1994), 17–37.

7. Cindy Patton elaborates on the link between deconstructivist theory and ACT UP praxis in the last chapter of her *Inventing AIDS* (New York: Routledge, 1990). I will be returning to the slogan SILENCE = DEATH and the critical debates surrounding it later in this essay.

8. Lee Edelman, "The Plague of Discourse: Politics, Literary Theory, and AIDS," *South Atlantic Quarterly* 88, no. 1 (Winter 1989): 316.

9. Stuart Marshall, "The Contemporary Political Use of Gay History: The Third Reich," in *How Do I Look?: Queer Film and Video,* ed. Bad Object-Choices (Seattle: Bay Press, 1991), 89.

10. See Michel Foucault, *The Archaeology of Knowledge and the Discourse on Language,* trans. A. M. Sheridan Smith (New York: Harper, 1972).

11. Notable exceptions include Linda Alcoff, "The Problem of Speaking for Others," *Cultural Critique* (Winter 1991/92): 5–32; Gayatri Chakravorty Spivak, "Can the Subaltern Speak?," in *Marxism and the Interpretation of Culture,* ed. Cary Nelson and Lawrence Grossberg (Urbana: University of Illinois Press, 1988), 271–313; and bell hooks, *Talking Back: Thinking Feminist, Thinking Black* (Toronto: Between the Lines, 1988). Hooks, herself an advocate of "speaking as an act of resistance," issues the following warning:

Appropriation of the marginal voice threatens the very core of self-determination and free self-expression for exploited and oppressed peoples. If the identified audience, those spoken to, is determined solely by ruling groups who control production and distribution, then it is easy for the marginal voice striving for hearing to allow what is said to be over-determined by the needs of that majority group who appears to be listening, to be tuned in. It becomes easy to speak about what that group wants to hear, to describe and define experience in a language compatible with existing images and ways of knowing, constructed within social frameworks that reinforce domination. (14)

12. Jacques Derrida, "Of an Apocalyptic Tone Recently Adopted in Philosophy," trans. John P. Leavey Jr., *Oxford Literary Review* 6, no. 2 (1984): 11–12. In many ways, Derrida's essay is a response to Immanuel Kant's 1796 treatise "On a Newly Arisen Superior Tone in Philosophy." Recently, Peter Fenves has collected these two essays, together with another essay by Kant, in a single volume: *Raising the Tone of Philosophy: Late Essays by Immanuel Kant, Transformative Critique by Jacques Derrida* (Baltimore: John Hopkins University Press, 1993). In his editorial introduction, "The Topicality of Tone," Fenves claims that Derrida's essay

> does not set out to reveal as yet unheard-of clauses or arcane articles in Kant's writing; rather it undertakes to examine their possibility as an enabling condition of universal communication and "enlightened discourse" in general. The possibility that an announcement hides certain unspoken clauses lies in its *tone;* tonality is, in turn, the preeminent vehicle of catastrophic revelations. . . . Showing how tone makes an *apocalyptic* event — the last event, the eventuality of every event — not only possible but also necessary and unfindable is the task undertaken in Derrida's address. (3, 36)

I am grateful to Danny O'Quinn for drawing my attention to this very important (con)text.

13. Derrida, "Of an Apocalyptic Tone," 11, 12.

14. Robert C. Gallo, introduction to Jacques Leibowitch, *A Strange Virus of Unknown Origin*, trans. Richard Howard (New York: Ballantine, 1985), xvii.

15. Treichler, "AIDS, Homophobia, and Biomedical Discourse," 62.

16. Mirko D. Grmek, *History of AIDS: Emergence and Origin of a Modern Pandemic*, trans. John Macquarie and Jacalyn Duffin (Princeton, N.J.: Princeton University Press, 1990), ix.

17. Derrida discusses the relationship between naming and apocalypse, or "the Apocalypse of the Name," in "No Apocalypse, Not Now (Full Speed Ahead, Seven Missiles, Seven Missives)," trans. Catherine Porter and Philip Lewis, *Diacritics* 14, no. 2 (1984): 30–31.

18. In 1984 Gallo, working out of the National Cancer Institute in the United States, reportedly isolated a virus that was believed to be the causative agent of AIDS, and that was subsequently designated HTLV-III. A year earlier Luc Montaigner, working out of the Pasteur Institute in France, had isolated a similar virus that he had called LAV. Bickering over the naming and ownership of the virus continued in various scientific journals for two years (with compromises like HTLV-III/LAV and LAV/HTLV-III being suggested by the United States and France, respectively), until the Human Retrovirus Subcommittee of the International Committee on the Taxonomy of Viruses proposed HIV as the official "in-

ternationalist" nomenclature in May 1986. For a comprehensive overview of the chronology and the permutations of the debate see Treichler, "AIDS, Homophobia, and Biomedical Discourse." On other naming strategies and acronyms associated with AIDS see Jan Zita Grover, "AIDS: Keywords," in Crimp, *AIDS: Cultural Analysis/Cultural Activism*, 17–30; and Grover, "Visible Lesions: Images of the PWA in America," in *Fluid Exchanges: Artists and Critics in the AIDS Crisis*, ed. James L. Miller (Toronto: University of Toronto Press, 1992), 23–51.

19. Treichler, "AIDS, Homophobia, and Biomedical Discourse," 44–45.

20. Institute of Medicine and National Academy of Sciences, *Confronting AIDS*, 52.

21. Treichler, "AIDS, Gender, and Biomedical Discourse," in *AIDS: The Burdens of History*, ed. Elizabeth Fee and Daniel M. Fox (Berkeley: University of California Press, 1988), 190–266.

22. Quoted in David Ansen, "I Will Show You Fear in a Handful of Dust," *Vancouver Sun*, January 23, 1993, C11.

23. Neil R. Schram, "AIDS: 1991," *Los Angeles Times Magazine* 11, no. 32, August 10, 1986. For an analysis of the background against which this article is set that is somewhat different from my own, see Simon Watney, *Policing Desire: Pornography, AIDS and the Media* (Minneapolis: University of Minnesota Press, 1989), 77–79.

24. Consider, for example, the August 12, 1985, cover of *Maclean's* magazine, which featured a photo of an emaciated Hudson. Under the headline "The New Terror of AIDS," a man identified only as Walter, "a Montreal AIDS victim," is quoted as saying: "Last week I had AIDS. This week I have Rock Hudson's disease." In a similar way, Magic Johnson's recent disclosure of his seropositive status has revived fears of heterosexual transmission of HIV. Ironically, whereas the media persistently avoided any mention of Hudson's sexuality in their initial construction of him as "heterosexual," the popular press has been scrambling to corroborate rumors that Johnson is gay or, at the very least, bisexual. See, for example, Thomas Bonk, "Suggestion That Johnson Had Gay Sex Gathers Momentum," *Vancouver Sun*, October 24, 1992, C4. On the pre- and post-AIDS representations of Hudson, see Richard Meyer, "Rock Hudson's Body," in *Inside/Out: Lesbian Theories, Gay Theories*, ed. Diana Fuss (New York: Routledge, 1991), 259–288.

25. Randy Shilts, *And the Band Played On: People and the AIDS Epidemic* (New York: St. Martin's Press, 1987), xxi. While Shilts deliberately constructs a discourse of apocalypse in his book, citing epigraphs from Camus and the Book of Revelation, and arguing that the first five years of AIDS in America "is a drama of national failure, played out against a backdrop of needless death" (xxii), he does so, paradoxically, at the same time as he constructs a Genesis story, his overwhelming emphasis on "Patient Zero" reflecting a quest for origins.

26. Watney, "The Spectacle of AIDS," in Crimp, *AIDS: Cultural Analysis/Cultural Activism*, 80.

27. Robert Burr, "Media Reflect Public Cynicism toward AIDS," *Canadian AIDS News* 6 (September/October 1992): 8.

28. Veronique de Turrene, "Apocalypse No," *Vancouver Sun*, January 16, 1993, C3.

29. Deborah Scroggins, "Apocalypse Now," *Vancouver Sun*, April 21, 1993, A15.

30. Simon Watney, "Missionary Positions: AIDS, 'Africa,' and Race," in *Out There: Marginalization and Contemporary Cultures*, ed. Russell Ferguson et al. (Cambridge, Mass.: MIT Press, 1990), 89. In addition, see Paula Treichler, "AIDS and HIV Infection in the Third World: A First World Chronicle," in *Remaking History*,

ed. Barbara Kruger and Phil Mariani (Seattle: Bay Press, 1989), 190–266; and Richard Chirimuuta and Rosalind Chirimuuta, *AIDS, Africa and Racism* (London: Free Association Books, 1989).

31. Quoted in Ronald Bayer, *Private Acts, Social Consequences: AIDS and the Politics of Public Health* (New York: Free Press, 1989), 169.

32. On the former, see Cindy Patton, "Safe Sex and the Pornographic Vernacular," in Bad Object-Choices, *How Do I Look?*, 31–63; on the latter, see Simon Watney, "School's Out," in Fuss, *Inside/Out*, 387–401.

33. The Panos Institute, *The 3rd Epidemic: Repercussions of the Fear of AIDS* (London: Panos Publications, 1990), 118.

34. Larry Kramer, *Reports from the Holocaust: The Making of an AIDS Activist* (New York: St. Martin's Press, 1989), 263.

35. Kramer, *Reports from the Holocaust,* 33.

36. Kramer, *Reports from the Holocaust,* 233.

37. Douglas Crimp, with Adam Rolston, *AIDS Demo Graphics* (Seattle: Bay Press, 1990), 14.

38. Marshall, "The Contemporary Political Use of Gay History," 86–87.

39. Marshall, "Contemporary Political Use of Gay History," 88.

40. Alexander García Düttmann, "What Will Have Been Said about AIDS: Some Remarks in Disorder," trans. Andrew Hewitt, *Public* 7 (1993): 96.

41. Susan Sontag, *AIDS and Its Metaphors* (New York: Farrar, Straus and Giroux, 1989), 5.

42. Derrida, "Of an Apocalyptic Tone," 12.

43. Sontag, *AIDS and Its Metaphors,* 44, 87, 93.

44. John J. Joughin, "Whose Crisis? AIDS/Plague and the Subject of History," in *Uses of History: Marxism, Postmodernism, and the Renaissance,* ed. Francis Barker et al. (New York: Manchester University Press, 1991), 148. For a critique more focused on Sontag's silencing of gay men, see D. A. Miller, "Sontag's Urbanity," *October* 49 (1989): 91–101.

45. Tony Kushner, *Angels in America: A Gay Fantasia on National Themes. Part One: Millennium Approaches* (New York: Theatre Communications Group, 1993), 112.

46. Richard Dellamora, "Apocalyptic Utterance in Edmund White's 'An Oracle,' " in *Writing AIDS: Gay Literature, Language, and Analysis,* ed. Timothy F. Murphy and Suzanne Poirier (New York: Columbia University Press, 1993), 98–116. In this article, reprinted in his recent book *Apocalyptic Overtures: Sexual Politics and the Sense of an Ending,* Dellamora applies the theories of Derrida and Foucault to White's short story about gay mourning in the age of AIDS. Dellamora claims that "[b]y siting the possibility of oracular utterance within the history of gay existence at a moment that is fraught with suffering, confusion, and anxiety, White supplements Derrida's reflections with others that open upon the possibilities of personal and social renewal" (101). Moreover, he concludes by claiming that "White's double glance, backward as well as forward, in the face of bereavement reminds gay men, in particular, of the need to continue this work [i.e., that begun by Foucault, namely aligning a politics of pleasure with an ethics of caring]" (114).

47. In *Talk on the Wilde Side: Toward a Genealogy of a Discourse on Male Sexualities* (New York: Routledge, 1993), Ed Cohen argues that Oscar Wilde's 1895 trial for engaging in "acts of gross indecency with another male person" became a turning point between late Victorian and modern bourgeois attitudes toward sexuality, helping to define the now commonplace distinction between "heterosexual" and "homosexual."

48. See Michel Foucault, *The History of Sexuality Vol. II: The Use of Pleasure,* trans. Robert Hurley (New York: Vintage, 1986); and *The History of Sexuality Vol. III: The Care of the Self,* trans. Robert Hurley (New York: Vintage, 1988).

49. See Watney, *Policing Desire.* I recognize that my principle of selection regarding the artistic representations of AIDS discussed in this section risks repeating the essentialist gesture interrogated under Epigraph #4 of creating a "singular" AIDS community, and that by invoking such criteria I, like Sontag, am effectively "writing inside the outside of [my] own exclusion zone." As such, let me hasten to point out that it is not my intention here to efface the multiple and material performances of mourning by nongay artists; rather, I am attempting to "que(e)ry" the ways in which (predominantly gay) artists articulate apocalyptic constructions of a (predominantly gay) subjectivity to a (predominantly gay) audience, focusing, in particular, on the complex interplay between ironized (dis)identification, camp performativity, self-determining agency, and political activism that these constructions frequently enact. See, in this regard, David Román, " 'It's My Party And I'll Die If I Want To!': Gay Men, AIDS, and the Circulation of Camp in U.S. Theater," in *Camp Grounds: Style and Homosexuality,* ed. David Bergman (Amherst: University of Massachusetts Press, 1993), 206–233. (My thanks to the anonymous reader from the University of Pennsylvania Press for suggesting further clarification of this point.) One exception to my "queer only" rule that I shall cite here is Yann Martel's short story, "The Facts behind the Helsinki Roccamatios," one of the most moving portraits of AIDS, gay or straight, that I have read in recent memory. In it Martel alternates the narrator's descriptions of his friend Paul's deteriorating illness with yearly "facts" gleaned from the past century in order to give the story-within-the-story (that of the Roccamatios) that they are composing together historical credence. The "story" ends with an oracle of its own: the narrator receives a note from Paul, after the latter's death, that propels the "story-within-the story" one year into the next millennium, thereby resisting apocalypse. See Martel, "The Facts behind the Helsinki Roccamatios," in *The Facts behind the Helsinki Roccamatios and Other Stories* (Toronto: Knopf, 1993), 1–75.

50. As it turned out, this was the last exhibit the group would mount together as a collective. Jorge Zontal died of AIDS-related complications on February 3, 1994. Four months later, on June 5, 1994, Felix Partz died, also of AIDS-related complications.

51. Paula Treichler, "How to Have Theory in an Epidemic: The Evolution of AIDS Treatment Activism," in *Technoculture,* ed. Constance Penley and Andrew Ross (Minneapolis: University of Minnesota Press, 1991), 80.

52. John Bentley Mays, "Illness as Metaphor," [Toronto] *Globe and Mail* March 20, 1993, C6.

53. Arthur Kroker and Marilouise Kroker, "Panic Sex in America," in *Body Invaders: Panic Sex in America,* ed. Arthur Kroker and Marilouise Kroker (Montreal: New World Perspectives, 1987), 10. More recently, Arthur Kroker has used the term "sacrificial sex" in connection with AIDS. See Kroker, "Sacrificial Sex," in Miller, *Fluid Exchanges,* 321–328. For a critique of the heterosexist assumptions implicit in *Longtime Companion,* see Bart Beaty, "The Syndrome Is the System: A Political Reading of *Longtime Companion,*" in Miller, *Fluid Exchanges,* 111–121.

54. Kushner, *Millennium Approaches,* 118.

55. Kushner, *Angels in America: A Gay Fantasia on National Themes. Part Two: Perestroika* (New York: Theatre Communications Group, 1994), 55. Further references to *Perestroika* are given parenthetically in the text.

56. Imbuing dialectical materialism with an apocalyptic spirituality in this manner, Kushner's play seems to echo the post-Marxist mysticism inherent in many of the writings of Walter Benjamin. Indeed, Benjamin's description of the "angel of history" not only underscores much of Kushner's personal theory of performance (and performance of theory) in *Angels in America*; it also serves as an appropriate model for the politicization of art "in the age of AIDS," at once allowing for the performance of mourning and the acceptance of loss as a precursor to change:

This is how one pictures the angel of history. His face is turned toward the past. Where we perceive a chain of events, he sees one single catastrophe which keeps piling wreckage upon wreckage and hurls it in front of his feet. The angel would like to stay, awaken the dead, and make whole what has been smashed. But a storm is blowing from Paradise; it has got caught in his wings with such violence that the angel can no longer close them. This storm irresistibly propels him into the future to which his back is turned, while the pile of debris before him grows skyward. This storm is what we call progress.

See Walter Benjamin, "Theses on the Philosophy of History," in *Illuminations: Essays and Reflections,* ed. Hannah Arendt (New York: Schocken, 1968), 257–258. Kushner discusses his debt to Benjamin in the afterword to *Perestroika*. See Kushner, "Afterword: With a Little Help from My Friends," in *Perestroika,* 154.

57. Sarah Schulman, *People in Trouble* (New York: Plume Books, 1991), 1. Schulman discusses the impetus behind her novel as well as the need for "developing a vocabulary of AIDS fiction" in an interview with Andrea Freud Lowenstein. See Schulman, "Troubled Times," in *In Versions: Writing by Dykes, Queers & Lesbians,* ed. Betsy Warland (Vancouver: Press Gang, 1991), 217–226.

58. Dennis Denisoff, *Dog Years* (Vancouver: Arsenal Pulp Press, 1991), 12. In "Jan. 01, 2000," the last chapter of Douglas Coupland's *Generation X,* Andy, the disaffected narrator, finally comes face to face with the spectre that has been haunting his diminished horizon of expectation since childhood, in this case a nuclear mushroom cloud as opposed to AIDS: "the cloud was on the horizon. It was not imaginary. It was the same cloud I'd been dreaming of steadily since I was five, shameless, exhausted, and gloating." See Coupland, *Generation X: Tales for an Accelerated Culture* (New York: St. Martin's Press, 1991), 176.

59. Joughin, "Whose Crisis?" 140.

60. Joughin, "Whose Crisis?" 140, 151.

61. Norman Cohn, *The Pursuit of the Millennium: Revolutionary Millenarians and Mystical Anarchists of the Middle Ages* (1957; London: Paladin, 1978). It has since become somewhat of a bible for contemporary anarchist movements. Greil Marcus uses Cohn's book, as well as a text by Cohn's son, Nik, called *Pop from the Beginning* (London: Paladin, 1972), to make a case for punk music being seen as a particular kind of anarchic vernacular in *Lipstick Traces: A Secret History of the Twentieth Century* (Cambridge, Mass.: Harvard University Press, 1990).

62. The term is Patton's. She argues that " '[d]issident vernaculars' also suggests that meanings created by and in communities are upsetting to the dominant culture precisely because speaking in one's own fashion is a means of resistance, a strengthening of the subculture that has created the new meaning. The idea of dissident vernaculars also places the health educator in a much different role, perhaps that of a technician rather than a translator." See *Inventing AIDS,* 148 n. 12.

63. Patton, "Safe Sex," 32, 44, 45.
64. Samuel Delany, "Street Talk/Straight Talk," *Differences: A Journal of Feminist Cultural Studies* 3, no. 2 (Summer 1991): 36–37.
65. Patton, "Safe Sex," 41.
66. Michael Lynch, "Last Onsets: Teaching with AIDS," *FUSE Magazine* 15, no. 5 (Summer 1992): 26 n. 5.
67. Lynch, "Last Onsets," 24.
68. García Düttmann, "What Will Have Been Said about AIDS," 97.
69. Derrida, "Of an Apocalyptic Tone," 29.
70. Derrida, "Of an Apocalyptic Tone," 29.
71. Derrida, "Of an Apocalyptic Tone," 30.
72. Delany, "Street Talk/Straight Talk," 35.
73. Jacques Derrida, "The Rhetoric of Drugs: An Interview," trans. Michael Israel, *Differences* 5, no. 1 (Spring 1993): 19–20. Derrida goes on to state that

[t]he [AIDS] virus (which belongs neither to life nor to death) may *always already* have broken into any "intersubjective" space. And considering its spatial and temporal dimensions, its structure of relays and delays, no human being is ever safe from AIDS. This possibility is thus installed at the heart of the social bond as intersubjectivity. . . . If I have spoken of an event and of indestructability, it is because already, at the dawn of this very new and ever so ancient thing, we know that, even should humanity some day come to control the virus (it will take at least a generation), still, even in the most unconscious symbolic zones, the traumatism has irreversibly affected our experience of desire and of what we cooly call intersubjectivity, the rapport to the alter ego, etc. (20)

See also Derrida's comments on AIDS in " 'Eating Well,' or the Calculation of the Subject: An Interview with Jacques Derrida," trans. Peter Connor and Avital Ronell, in *Who Comes After the Subject?*, ed. Eduardo Cadava et al. (New York: Routledge, 1991), 96–119.
74. García Düttmann, "What Will Have Been Said about AIDS," 111.
75. See, for example, Didier Eribon, *Michel Foucault*, trans. Betsy Wing (Cambridge, Mass.: Harvard University Press, 1991); James Miller, *The Passion of Michel Foucault* (New York: Simon and Schuster, 1993); and David Macey, *The Lives of Michel Foucault* (London: Hutchinson, 1993).
76. Michel Foucault, "Language to Infinity," in *Language, Counter-Memory, Practice: Selected Essays and Interviews*, ed. Donald F. Bouchard, trans. Bouchard and Sherry Simon (Ithaca, N.Y.: Cornell University Press, 1988), 53.

O.G. Style: Ice-T/Jacques Derrida

A Carousel CD recording (AAD) remixed by Darren Wershler-Henry for *Postmodern Apocalypse*

Darren Wershler-Henry

EVERY FUCKIN' THING I WRITE
IS GONNA BE ANALYZED BY SOMEONE WHITE.

— Ice-T, "Ice M.F. T"

Disc 5 Track 4: Home Invasion

There's a rap on the door. And I'm saying "yes" automatically, suddenly, perhaps irreversibly. Even if there *is* an interrogative inflection to my voice, I'm nevertheless rapt, answering a house-call,[1] a call that has much to do with the formation of my identity. The door bursts open, and I'm Being-thrown back into the room, guiltily[2] interpellated into the cover art of Ice-T's *Home Invasion* (Figure 7).

Front and center sits a white boy in a Fishbone T-shirt and Africa pendants, components of the standard uniform of a white rap fan. Being a white college boy myself, this is the position the album invites me to occupy: "THEY SAY I'M FUCKING UP THE MINDS OF LITTLE KIDS / BUT HALF MY FANS ARE IN COLLEGE."[3] Beside him/me sits a stack of gangster rap tapes by Public Enemy, Ice-T, and Ice Cube, and a pile of dog-eared books by Malcolm X, Iceberg Slim, and hard-boiled fiction writer Donald Goines. Rather than being specific works, these items are iconic of coldness, hardness, and blackness, the running subtexts of this scene. The other, unlabeled tapes might include albums by black gangster rappers Just Ice and Ice Cream T, for example, but it's a pretty safe bet that none of them are albums by Vanilla Ice or Snow, two white rappers with pretensions to street credibility. As for the books, the illustration provides no titles, but none are necessary. In typical postmodern fashion, Spike Lee has long since transformed Malcolm's "X" from a signifier for uncompromising black activism into a commodity fetish, marketing it as "culture" to black and white youth alike (the very white Jerry Steiner, wearing

Figure 7. Front cover, record jacket. Ice-T, *Home Invasion*. Photo: Patricia Seaman. Courtesy Rhyme Syndicate Records.

the omnipresent X baseball cap, says to the very white Parker Lewis: "Mr. Spike and I are big fans of Malcolm Ten, sir"). The other books in the pile also have resonances specific to the formation of a "cool," "black" identity; Ice-T is Iceberg Slim's namesake, while Goines's books bear titles like *Daddy Cool*. For reasons that will become evident shortly, it might also be appropriate to invoke Goines's *Street Players*, whose protagonist is "cool and sharp as an ice crystal."[4]

Around the white college boy and the commodities that describe his identity swirls a violent, phantasmatic Oedipal scene. The door hangs crazily on broken hinges; a shadowy figure with a handgun is entering. A balding, bespectacled white man in a suit lies bleeding under the rifle-butt of a masked commando. Another masked man, naked from the waist up, is in the process of raping a panic-stricken woman. Over it all hangs the disembodied face of Ice-T; swirling lines of power run from his right eye to the boy's headphones. Everything about this tableau suggests that it is the mise-en-scène of a particular desire. Through fantasy, it articulates symbolic positions for both the rapper and his rapt, white, college-educated fan. However, these positions are tentative and problematic; at times, they even blur into each other. So the question at hand is this: whose desires are being represented in this scene, or, to rephrase, what comes first, the (w)rapper or the rapt?

Disc 4 Track 10: O.G.

O.G.: Original Gangster . . . and *Of Grammatology*. These initials form a highly compressed metonym for the blurring between "Signifyin(g)," Henry Louis Gates Jr.'s "black trope of tropes"[5] (represented here by Ice-T's gangster rap), and "signification," in the sense that linguistic sign theory after deconstruction uses the term. This encounter is both postmodern and apocalyptic: "postmodern" because the discourses of the academy and the street, which traditionally occupy opposite ends of the sociocultural spectrum, are beginning to miscegenate; "apocalyptic" because of the often disturbing and surprising revelations that this encounter generates about both of these discourses, and about the types of subject positions that they strive to create. These positions are often complex and contradictory: a white college boy might turn out to be a Young Black Teenager, or, at least, infected with Anthrax's hip-hop/thrash virus.[6] Conversely, a streetwise rapper can be a Teacher (KRS-One), a Professor (Professor Griff), or a Doctor (Dr. Dre).

This blurring of borders occurs because neither white college boys nor rappers are always uncritical recipients of either rap or deconstruction. We and they are also always readers and interpreters of what we see and hear. Rappers and theorists are each in turn caught up in the folds of their others' aural canals — in Fredric Jameson's terms, they are *(w)rapped* by the process of listening/reading:

Wrapping can be seen as a reaction to the disintegration of that more traditional concept Hegel called "ground," which passed into humanistic thought in the form named "context," felt by its opponents to be basely "external" or "extrinsic," since it seemed to imply the double standard of two radically distinct sets of thoughts and procedures. . . . [Wrapping] retains the essential prerequisite of *priority*[7] — or even *hierarchy*— the functional subordination of one element to another (sometimes even called "causality") — but now makes that reversible. What is wrapped can also be used as the wrapper; the wrapper can also be wrapped in its turn.[8]

In a hip-hop scenario of continual citation and recitation, the status of an "Original" Gangster comes into question quickly. As Jonathan Culler points out, "There is such a thing as an original . . . style only if it can be cited, imitated, and parodied."[9] "Ice-T," for example, is a pseudonym, a supplementary (w)rapper formulated by a person born as Tracy Marrow,[10] but the latter is no longer (if it ever was) an original or core identity. The veneer of Ice — the (w)rapper of words and beats constructed around an absent center — is paradoxically what constitutes the "hard core": "I'M / A HARDCORE PLAYER FROM THE STREETS / RAPPIN BOUT HARDCORE TOPICS / OVER HARDCORE DRUM BEATS."[11] Whatever a rap recording claims it is re-presenting, it is never a fully present musician or musicians, as Simon Reynolds emphasizes: "In *The Recording Angel*, Evan Eisenberg argues that 'phonography' bears the same relation to live music that cinema bears to theatre. What a record documents is not an event, but a phantasm constructed out of different takes. It never 'happened.' Sampling takes the fictitious nature of recording even further, creating events that never could have happened. 'Deconstruction of the metaphysics of presence,' or what?!"[12]

In other words, a rapper — like any other subject position — is not the exemplar of an essence, but a site from which to practice a *G-Style*, or better yet, several *styles*, some of which might be capable of melting and re-fusing hard-core gangster rap's icy exterior armor. Furthermore, simplistic assumptions about who is producing the violent Oedipal fantasies associated with gangster rap might well be imploded by the tip of a deconstructed G-stylus, along with the capital "O" of "Original."

The apocalyptic postmodern implosion of the notion of origin implies that rap has the potential to reverse, parody, and Signify[13] in Gates's sense on contemporary theory as easily as the latter can parasitize the former. Fredric Jameson notes the tendency of contemporary readings to affirm their autonomy and unity by assimilating their "primary" texts into themselves, transcoding their elements, foregrounding echoes and analogies, even borrowing stylistic features in order to forge the neologisms that become their own theoretical terminology (of course, this essay is no exception; my hope is to set up a kind of oscillation so that neither discourse entirely overwhelms the other). However, Ice-T's raps affirm that this process is reversible.[14] On the track "First Impression," a cool, haughty feminine voice Signifies on the discourse of the academy:

UPON INITIAL CONTACT WITH ICE T'S MUSIC,
I HAD ENVISIONED HIM TO BE AN ILL-MANNERED AND
PSYCHOLOGICALLY UNSTABLE MAN WITH AN
EXTREMELY UNEDUCATED AND BARBARIC
FRAME OF MIND, WHOSE RAPS DISPLAYED NOTHING

BUT RIDICULOUS JARGON, SHOCKING SEXUAL
AUDACITY AND REPULSIVE IMAGES OF THE GHETTO.
HOWEVER, AFTER FURTHER ANALYSIS OF HIS MUSIC
I CAN DEDUCE THAT HE IS THE EPITOME OF
ANTIDISESTABLISHMENTARIANISM WHO EMBODIES
THE ENTIRE SPECTRUM OF THE URBAN EXPERIENCE
AND STRUGGLE, BUT TO MAKE THINGS MORE PLAIN
AND SIMPLE TO THE LAYMAN, I FIND ICE T TO BE THE
DOPEST, FLYIST, O.G PIMP HUSTLER GANGSTER
PLAYER HARDCORE MOTHERFUCKER LIVING TODAY.

TO BE HONEST I AM TOTALLY AND IRREVOCABLY
ON HIS DICK!!!!!!![15]

Disc 5 Tract 5: G-Style

With the Original under erasure, everything turns on the point of *style:*
"THE POINT OF THE ICE PICK,"[16] the tip of the Iceberg. *The Iceberg*— the
title of Ice-T's third album[17]— is a conflation of two of Derrida's examples of the spur / *éperon* of style: "the prow, for example, of a sailing vessel,
its *rostrum,* the projection of the ship which surges ahead to meet the sea's
attack and cleave its hostile surface. Or yet again, and still in nautical
terminology, the style might be compared to that rocky point, also called
an *éperon,* on which the waves break at the harbor's entrance."[18] The
Iceberg is a moving point, a point composed of the very matter it separates: temporarily crystallized, but capable of flow and reformation. And
there is always more to it than meets the eye.
     The stylus is also "the gangster tip," or "G-style":

> Style is almost beyond [language]: imagery, delivery, vocabulary spring from the
> body and the past of the writer and gradually become the very reflexes of his
> art. . . . Whatever its sophistication, style has always something crude about it: *it is
> a form with no clear destination, the product of a thrust, not an intention,* and, as it were,
> a vertical and lonely dimension of thought. Its frame of reference is biological or
> biographical, not historical: it is the writer's "thing," his glory and his prison, it is
> his solitude. . . . It is the private portion of the ritual, it rises up from the writer's
> myth-laden depths and unfolds beyond his area of control.[19]

Style is the battering rap on the door, the word from the (m)Other, the
outside wanting in . . . the boyz from the 'hood on a trip to the suburbs.
Nomadic and dromocratic, rap wanders aimless through the hallways of
culture, spray-painting its paraphs on subway walls, taking its subjects by
surprise, offering them the tools for their own reinscriptions. This is rap
style as stiletto or rapier, or, in a contemporary setting, something much

more violent: "GANG BANGERS / DON'T CARRY NO SWITCHBLADES / EVERY KID'S GOT A TEC 9 OR A HAND GRENADE."[20]

The violence of style displays itself in several forms. In its most mundane manifestation, violence appears in rap as metaphor. In its most interesting manifestations, though, rap eschews thematics to embody violence itself. As Jacques Attali points out in *Noise*, "*noise is violence:* it disturbs. To make noise is to interrupt a transmission, to disconnect, to kill. It is a simulacrum of murder."[21] "Bring the Noise,"[22] Public Enemy's 1988 rap classic, was one of the first signs of rap's imminent politicization, a call to use the violence of rap's noise against the complacency of the contemporary music scene. At the time of its release, it was one of the fastest and loudest raps ever written, an early example of producer Hank Shocklee's highly dense, cacophonous aesthetic. Ice-T's raps take up this legacy of speed and complexity, employing not only rapid-fire vocal delivery at a high bpm (beats per minute) number, but also samples from thrash and heavy metal. This music is not only about violence, it *is* violence.

In *Spurs*, Derrida hints at several possible productive uses for linguistic objects that present themselves in this fashion: "such objects might be used in a vicious attack against what philosophy appeals to in the name of matter or matrix, an attack whose thrust could not but leave its mark, could not but inscribe there some imprint or form. But they might also be used as protection against the threat of such an attack, in order to keep it at a distance, repel it."[23] One effect of rap's phonography, then, is the mounting of a simultaneous attack on and defense against white Western metaphysics in its role as enforcer of musical propriety. What makes this phonography possible, of course, is a *stylus*.

The stylus of the record player is not only a device that enables a passive listening, it is also a tool to effect a rewriting, as the hands of a rap DJ turn the tables backwards, against the grain of the voice, to produce rap's signatory "scratch." "ALL SONGS CUT THE *$@%& UP BY D.J. EVIL E THE GREAT!"[24] is a purely graphic paraph that co-signs with "Ice-T" on his albums, signifying the unavoidability of the spoken sign's passage through the written, and of the disorderly order that this passage produces: a graphic violence. Consequently, the sign in rap "can only be a mark at once written and spoken, vocalized as a grapheme and written as a phoneme, yes, in a word, *gramophoned*."[25] But if style is "a quill or a stylus,"[26] there is also a stylus in play *before* the voice *before* the technological mediation of the record player's needle. Ice-T's rap is always already a writing, and his albums are books.

GRAB THE PEN,
AND PLACE IT ON SOME LOOSE LEAF,

NOTHIN' SOFT, ALWAYS THE TOUGH MEAT.
THE WHITE PAPER AND BLUE LINES EXCITE MY MIND,
NOT ALLOW'N ME TO STOP THE RHYME,
UNTIL THE WHOLE MOTHERFUCKIN'
BOOK'S COMPLETE.
THEN I WRITE ON THE BACK OF THE SHEETS.[27]

This writing is not only prior to speech, but it is outside intention, spurring the rapper onward, past the point of completion into excess.

The excess of style is also what hypes the biological and biographical to the point of myth. Ice-T presents his subject matter as too large for pop rap: "WHEN I WROTE ABOUT PARTIES, / SOMEONE ALWAYS DIED. / WHEN I TRIED TO WRITE HAPPY, / YO I KNEW I LIED." He constructs from the raw material of his criminal past a style from which an identity emerges that is capable of presenting the rhymes:

WHO WOULD TELL HOW IT REALLY WAS?
WHO DARED?
A MOTHERFUCKER FROM THE WEST COAST, L.A.
SOUTH CENTRAL FOOL
WHERE THE CRIPS AND THE BLOODS PLAY. WHEN I
WROTE ABOUT PARTIES IT DIDN'T FIT,
SIX IN THE MORNIN,
THAT WAS THE REAL SHIT.[28]

Gangster rap operates as a new urban epic, presenting itself as a referential recounting of the feats of heroes and villains.[29] Ice-T frames himself as a black founding father: "This country was founded on the things I talk about . . . Paul Revere was running around saying, 'The redcoats are coming,' so he was basically saying, 'Here come the pigs, and a fuckup is going down.' . . . That was a revolutionary thought, and those were honorable thoughts in those days."[30] Like epic poetry, rap Signifies paradigmatically, but it pushes the digression from narrative further, piling on detail as its styles exfoliate, problematizing its own drive to communicate; "[w]hoever takes on the apocalyptic tone comes to signify [Signify?] to, if not to tell, you something."[31] Rap's message has been heard before, in a tone (or style — the tone arm is merely the extension of the stylus) that has been used before: "this is not the first time."[32]

Disc 5 Track 2: It's On

Jacques Attali claims that noise performs a prophetic or heraldic function; it anticipates the political organization of the era that is to follow it even as it disrupts the music of its own era (*Noise,* 19). Music is "noise given form according to a code . . . that is theoretically knowable by the listener" (25), and "noise" is the disruption of that code by another; thus, "noise" and "music" are solely relational terms (26). Each exists only in comparison to its other, and is entirely capable of becoming that other in a different context. This relationality raises particular problems for critics: "The simultaneity of multiple codes, the variable overlappings between periods, styles, and forms, prohibits any attempt at a genealogy of music, a hierarchical archeology, or a precise ideological pinpointing of particular musicians." However, Attali suggests that "it is possible to discern who among them are innovators and heralds of worlds in the making" (19).

The contemporary prophets of rage are hard-core and gangster rappers rhyming in apocalyptic G-styles: Public Enemy, on *Apocalypse 91 . . . The Enemy Strikes Black;* Ice-T and his Rhyme Syndicate, announcing "Rhyme Syndicate — we're in here! Peace! < ----- fuck that   WAR!"[33] Hard-core rappers know that "weapons and signs are the same thing," that "every combat is a semantic one, every meaning is warlike"; they might say, with (or against) Barthes, that "[w]e are at present engaged in a war, not of meaning (a war to abolish meanings) but of meanings: signifieds confront each other, furnished with all possible weapons (military, economic, ideological, even neurotic)."[34] G-style is Signifying by any means necessary.

Disc 5 Track 18: Message to the Soldier

Gangster rap's apocalyptic Signification is for particular ears only; you have to be "def" to hear "The Message."[35] The scenario unfolds like Kant's description of the mystagogues: rap communities constitute themselves around charismatic leaders, as "a sect ["I HOOKED UP WITH A NEW CREW / SOME BROTHERS WHO SEEMED LIKE THEY KNEW WHAT THE FUCK TO DO / YOU MIGHT CALL IT A GANG / WE CALLED IT A SE[C]T, AND IT WAS OUR OWN THANG"[36]] with a crypted language ["SPEAK IN CODE 'CAUSE YOU'RE NEVER ALONE / THAT'S WHY I USE THIS LOW TONE"],[37] a band, a clique or a small party with its ritualised practices."[38] *Home Invasion* stages itself as a harbinger of the coming apocalypse. "The injection of black rage into the American white youth is the 1st stage of preparation for the revolution. Prepare — It's goin' down."[39] It is the first Ice-T album not to include printed lyrics, for the following reason: "Lyrics to this LP have *not* been printed as a Syndicate security move to prevent reprint, analysis and explanations by squares, suckers, spies and traitors to the movement. Sorry but it's goin' down."[40]

In their essay on sampling, Simon Reynolds and David Stubbs ques-

tion the disruptive value of gestures such as this one, which identify
a privileged group within the music business: "As always, threat is directed outwards, seen in terms of shocks and blows to the record industry, 'the establishment,' the straights and squares. 'We,' of course, are
insiders, in the know, in control: it's never a question of disrupting our
value scheme, outstripping our ability to manage sounds, interfering
with the political structures inside our own heads."[41] During the Home
Invasion, however, "we" cannot be so sure that we have heard correctly:
are we down with the program, or suckers, spies, and traitors? *Rolling
Stone* says *Home Invasion* is "more squarely aimed at [Ice-T's] traditional
hard-core audience";[42] it takes the album's claim to be a "Message to the
Soldiers"[43] at face value. "THE BEATS ARE FAT AMMO DUMP TRACKS / THE
KIND THAT MAKE SPEAKERS CRACK / NOT MADE FOR SQUARES AND WEAK
PUNKS," raps "Ice Mother Fuckin' T," who adds "EVERYONE OF MY TRUE
FANS TOTALLY UNDERSTANDS / A NIGGA LIKE ME."[44] No doubt the first
track on the album, "Warning," attempts to ensure (perhaps even to
police . . . but this is a point that will be taken up later) the context of its
reception:

ATTENTION: AT THIS MOMENT YOU ARE NOW LISTENING TO AN ICE T LP. IF YOU ARE
OFFENDED BY WORDS LIKE SHIT, BITCH, FUCK, DICK, ASS, HO, CUM, DIRTY BITCH,
LOW MOTHERFUCKER, NIGGA, HOOKER, SLUT, TRAMP, DIRTY LOW SLUT TRAMP
BITCH HO, NIGGA FUCK SHIT, WHATEVER, TAKE THE TAPE OUT NOW. THIS IS NOT A
POP ALBUM. AND BY THE WAY: SUCK MY MOTHERFUCKIN' DICK![45]

. . . but it's always already too late; the damage is done, and the language
knows it. The context is hopelessly muddled: many copies of the album
are on compact disc, a format that the "Warning" neglects to mention.
With both LPs and CDs it is possible to bypass the "Warning" entirely by
selecting individual tracks. Even in the more linear tape format linearity
is a relative state because of fast-forwarding and the double-sided, even
duplicitous, nature of the medium: is it live or is it Memorex? And all
of this on top of the recorded voice (like any mark)'s guaranteed iterabil-
ity in the face of the total absence of every empirically determined addressee.[46] It's on: rap apocalypse, heavily mediated by the technological,
has no off switch.[47]

Disc 5 Track 8: Watch the Ice Break

"What holds for the addressee holds also, for the same reasons, for the
sender or the producer. To write is to produce a mark that will constitute
a kind of machine that is in turn productive, that my future disappearance in principle will not prevent from functioning."[48] "BUT WHEN I'M
GONE I'M GONNA NEED YOU TO CARRY ON / YOU GOTTA BE STRONG."[49] But

this is not only a future tense situation — Ice-T, like all speakers, is *not present* in general.[50] With his Gangster Origins under erasure, Ice-T is no more a unitary force than his audience; he is almost unthinkable without DJ Evil E, DJ Aladdin, SLJ, and Ammo Dump Productions. There are "[a]t least two spurs,"[51] then: *Home Invasion* features rap duets with Evil E, ragga-rapper Daddy Nitro, Brother Marquis of the 2 Live Crew, and Grip, Ice-T's teenage female protégé. G-style itself is a multiplicity; "if there is going to be style, there can only be more than one."[52] Chris Morris of *Musician* magazine writes that "Ice T's new rap album . . . plays less like an album than 3 different EPs crammed onto one 19-track package."[53]

Watch the Ice break. The coreless "hardcore," supposedly indivisible Iceberg is calving, heading off in all directions at once, *Speaking in Tongues*, like the Talking Heads. This is the apocalypse of all textuality:

No longer is one very sure who loans his voice and his tone to the other in the Apocalypse; no longer is one very sure who addresses what to whom. But by a catastrophic overturning here more necessary than ever, one can just as well think this: as soon as one no longer knows who speaks or who writes, the text becomes apocalyptic. And if the dispatches [*envois*] always refer to other dispatches without decidable destination, the destination remaining to come, then isn't this . . . also the structure of every scene of writing in general?[54]

Morris inscribes the countersignature of the listener-as-reader as the result of this polyglossia. "As Ice and his posse range all over the map, you'll find yourself heading for your CD player's programmable function locating for yourself the def beats (there are plenty of them) and the style that suits you best to pull together your own EP."[55]

As was suspected on the opening track, as much as the rapper in-forms the rapt listener (the white college boy), the rapt (listener) wraps the rapper, catching him up in the folds of his ear and his mind's eye.

[T]he signature becomes effective — performed and performing — not at the moment it apparently takes place, but only later, when ears will have managed to receive the message. In some way the signature will take place on the addressee's side, that is, on the side of him or hcr whose ear will be keen enough to hear my name, for example, or to understand my signature, that with which I sign.[56]

The listener who wants the "Power" proffered by Ice-T's music, like *Power*, the kid on "New Jack Hustler" who wants to be down ("I KNOW IT'S REAL, IT'S GOTTA BE REAL, / MAN YOU THE FLYEST BROTHER I SEEN IN MY LIFE! / YO MAN, I JUST WANNA ROLL WITH YOU MAN, / HOW CAN I BE DOWN?"[57]), anyone wishing to occupy the positions of the masked thugs on the cover of *Home Invasion* (only one of whom is even arguably identifiable as "black") is not listening with a very keen ear, or recognizing a lesson that Spiderman could teach to Superfly: "With great power comes great responsibility."

This is not simply the responsibility of separating the "true" or the "real" tracks from the "fictive" ones, as "Lethal Weapon" suggests. This is an argument that Ice-T has mobilized in interviews:

> Take somebody who never heard of Arnold Schwarzenegger, never saw the movie, and take that clip of him walking into a police station and killing everybody. If you showed that to somebody who didn't know Schwarzenegger or that it was a movie, they'd say, "Oh, my God, this is the most terrible person in the world." That's what America did: they took a clip of my life and said, "This is who this dude is." They just don't know what makes me tick.[58]

The problem, though, is that the difference between truth and fiction is ultimately an indeterminable distinction, as another version of Ice-T points out on "Pulse of the Rhyme": "IS THIS REAL OR FICTION? / YOU'LL NEVER KNOW / WHILE YOU'RE LOCKED TO THE / PULSE OF THE RHYME FLOW!"[59] The responsibility at the scene of reading or listening is more complicated because reception involves the active production of the entire text, a situation that makes any act of reading an explicitly political gesture.[60] The reader is responsible for the reading at least as much as the writer . . . and here, we are moving into the realm of *policing*, by both the self and the other.

Disc 6 Track 12: There Goes the Neighborhood

By the time anyone realized what was happening, both sides had already called in the border patrol.

Body Count is the name of a thrash metal band that features Ice-T on lead vocals. *Body Count* is the name of their first album — an album about which Ice-T has repeatedly said, "This is not a rap album — underline *rap* album. It's a rock album,"[61] and this is where the confusion begins. "Body Count," the title track of the album (maybe; the album also features tracks titled "Body Count's in the House" and "Body Count Anthem"), also appears in a slightly different version on Ice-T's *O.G. Original Gangster.* Both Ice-T (as rap group) and Body Count are part of Rhyme Syndicate Records, and feature some of the same personnel. It should come as no surprise that immediately after Ice-T makes the distinction between the Body Count project and his rap records, he states that a miscegenation is already in effect: "It's a rock album with a rap mentality."[62] Musical apartheid is always already an impossibility. As Ice-T explains in the staged interview that precedes "Body Count" on *O.G.,* "[A] lot of people don't realize that you know, rock and roll is truly black music; it was created by Chuck Berry, Little Richard, and black people like that."[63] What's at stake, then, is the regaining of lost territory.

"There Goes the Neighborhood": *Body Count* stages itself as a Home Invasion.

> Who gave them fuckin' niggas
> those rock guitars?
> Who let 'em in the club?
> Did you make 'em pay?
> Who let 'em on the stage?
> Whose lettin' 'em play?
>
> Don't they know rock's just for whites
> don't they know the rules?
> Those niggers are too hard core
> this shit ain't cool.[64]

In this scenario, the black musician (rapper) turns (Signifies) on his wrapper (the mainly white and often racist music industry), reversing the process of parasitization, deterritorializing the striated space of the suburbs in the process. "[I]t's an album that got into Texas and got inside suburbia a little deeper than a normal rap record would,"[65] says Ice-T. While this may not be *physically* true — *Body Count* sold approximately 300,000 copies in the United States, and 25,000 in Canada,[66] a drop in the bucket compared with the sales racked up by his rap albums, whose audience is 75 to 80 percent white[67] — the *psychic* and *economic* impact is still being felt in the form of censorship.

Disc 3 Track 12: Freedom of Speech

"We know that apocalyptic writings increased the moment State censorship was very strong in the Roman Empire, and precisely to catch the censorship unawares."[68] At present, apocalyptic discourses in and outside music are on the rise; this can be at least partially attributed to the repression engendered by the Nuclear Family. Nancy Reagan and Tipper Gore's regime of "Just Say No" crosses party lines, and is backed by the absolute censorship of their respective husbands' access to nuclear weaponry.[69] Rap had largely managed to avoid the attention of the censors — until the controversy over the last track on the *Body Count* album erupted.

Since July 28, 1992, when Ice-T decided to "voluntarily" remove "Cop Killer" from future pressings of the *Body Count* album (in the face of threats to himself and his label, Time Warner, in forms running the gamut from polite petitions from police unions to hate mail and bomb threats),[70] and his subsequent departure from the label for the independent Priority records, a number of rappers (including Whodini, DJ Pooh, Paris, Kool G. Rap, Boo-Yaa Tribe, FU2, Juvenile Committee, and Almighty RSO) have been directly affected by loss of contracts, removal of particular tracks from forthcoming albums, demands to change lyrics, police harassment, and other forms of covert and overt censorship.[71] On the surface, at least, this appears to contradict Derrida's musing that "we would perhaps think that the apocalyptic discourse can also get around censorship thanks to its genre and its cryptic ruses."[72] Certainly rap's mixing of voices, genres, and codes, its atonalities, and inadmissibilities have effected a dislocation in the dominant social contract, but in the process of the prophesied return of rap to independent labels,[73] will rap lose its audience and influence? This might be the "apocalypse *without* apocalypse,"[74] the end of the invasion, but then again, it might not.

The projected sales of Ice-T's new Home Invasion album and the Bodycount album combined wouldn't come close to offsetting the possibility of a multi-million dollar loss resulting from a police organization-led divestment in Time Warner stock. Warner Bros. simply let Ice-T shlep the Home Invasion album to the street savvy Priority label. Now Priority can take the heat, Ice-T can earn a much fatter royalty rate (rumoured to be as much as $4 per album) and Warner Bros. can quietly continue reaping the benefits of owning a sizable chunk of Home Invasion's song publishing.[75]

Fredric Jameson might well identify this situation as "one of those extraordinary postmodern mutations where the apocalyptic suddenly turns into the decorative."[76] To rephrase KRS-One's famous rhyme, it's about a salary, and *that's* the reality.

The Deleted Track: Cop Killer

The cover of *Rolling Stone* #637 features a photograph of Ice-T in the uniform of a police officer. Beside and beyond its ironic Signification, this image raises some interesting questions. No doubt, Ice-T's "grand airs" and "overlordly tones" (the phrases are Derrida's) have invoked the ire of the contemporary equivalents of Kant's philosophical police force,[77] but what kinds of policings are instigated by Ice-T himself?

Disc 5 Track 7: Question and Answer

QUESTION AND ANSWER: WHAT DOES A RAPPER DO WHEN HE STARTS OUT HARD CORE, BUT CAN'T SELL ENOUGH RECORDS TO REMAIN IN THE RECORD BUSINESS? ANSWER: HE GOES POP. THIS ANSWER IS NOT SET UP TO DIS ANYBODY WHO STARTS

OUT POP, OR FOR THE RAPPERS WHO STARTED OUT HARD CORE, AND NOW ARE MAK-
ING WEAK-ASS DANCE MUSIC, 'CAUSE THEY COULDN'T STAY DOWN WITH THE HARD
CORE. I JUST GOT A QUESTION FOR YOU: HOW DOES IT FEEL TO WAKE UP EVERY
MORNING AND LOOK IN THE MIRROR, AND REALIZE THAT YOU'RE A FUCKING HO?[78]

Ice-T's various policings follow this line very consistently: they are always
concerned with maintaining the integrity of hard-core rap and hard-core
rappers. It is not a stance unique to his persona either; it is a fairly
common one among other gangster rappers. The widespread nature of
this phenomenon has led critic Simon Reynolds to theorize rap as an
almost solely reactionary genre, promulgated by fascist subjectivities.

Hip hop is (to abuse Eldridge Cleaver's fine phrase) — SOUL ON ICE — a survivalist
retreat from engagement with the outside world or other people, back to the
frozen shell of a minimal self. There's a new kind of relation to the body, not the
slow suffusion of "getting in touch," but more domineering a regime, a priming
of the machine in readiness for self-defence.[79]

Reynolds extends this argument into a comparison between rappers and
the fascist soldier-males Klaus Theweleit describes in *Male Fantasies*. He is
swept up in the heat of his discourse on apocalyptic rap ("[Public En-
emy] dramatized themselves in a state of perpetual imminence, the eve of
apocalypse, with the huge clocks around their necks permanently fixed
at a minute to midnight"),[80] caught in the paradox to which such discourses always fall prey: "all language on apocalypse is also apocalyptic
and cannot be excluded from its object."[81] What's missing from his analysis is the recognition of a fluidity even in the frosty exteriors he describes: Ice floes/flows, and at his most crystalline moments there are still
detectable, self-recognized flaws (even at his most bombastic, Ice-T proclaims that "I AIN'T NO SUPER HERO / I AIN'T NO MARVEL COMIC").[82] As a
result, Reynolds mistakes a militant stance for a reactionary one, fixing
one facet of rap as its sole face. bell hooks has observed that "[w]hatever
its form, black militancy is always too extreme in the white supremacist
context, too out-of-order, too dangerous,"[83] or, as Public Enemy puts it,
"Too black / Too strong." In the name of a feminism-informed liberalism, Reynolds in fact produces a reading that is all too easily recuperated
by the discourse of neoconservative racism.

  Posing questions about the politics of pop culture phenomena like rap
music involves walking a delicate line. It involves the possibility of recognizing, along with Robert Christgau in *The Village Voice*, that Ice-T is one of
the only hard-core rappers to date to question homophobia in the rap
community.[84] Simultaneously, it involves dealing with the appalling misogyny of tracks like "99 Problems" (which, as Chris Morris indicates in
Musician, is definitely the low point of *Home Invasion*).[85] Still, as bell hooks

has warned, the ongoing analysis of rap's impact cannot be allowed to slip into a debate over "positive" and "negative" images. "Focus on good and bad images [of black subjectivity] may be more fundamentally connected to the western metaphysical dualism that is the philosophical underpinning of racist and sexist domination than with radical efforts to reconceptualize black cultural identities."[86] Fussing over representation is tantamount to continuing "in the best apocalyptic tradition to denounce false apocalypses."[87]

Disc 5 Track 19: Ain't a Damn Thing Changed

But what if hard-core gangster rap *itself* were the false herald of an anticlimactic apocalypse?

The advent of recorded music heralded the society of simulation, and the accompanying death of the spectacle; the ability to stockpile that music became an anticipatory enactment of the transformation of diverse cultures and subcultures into commodity fetishes.[88] In Attali's terms, culture moves from a basis of representation to one of repetition, but this shift does not signal an end to the forms of juridical power that hold sway under representation: "[M]odernity is not the major rupture in the systems for the channelization of violence, the imaginary, and subversion that so many anachronistic thinkers would like to see. Not a major rupture, but sadly, boringly, a simple rearrangement of power, a tactical fracture, the institution of a new and obscure technocratic justification of power in organizations" (83). When rebellion is packaged as a consumer product, the pseudoevent of the record's release replaces real movements for societal change. Nothing happens anymore . . . except that the corporations who own the record companies continue to make money, and thus continue to maintain their upper hand in power's ongoing agonistic struggle. From this perspective, as Attali puts it, mass-produced music "is a means of silencing, a concrete example of commodities speaking in place of people, of the monologue of the institutions. . . . [E]verywhere, it signifies the presence of a power that needs no flag or symbol: musical repetition confirms the presence of repetitive consumption, of the flow of noises as ersatz sociality" (111).

In this cultural milieu, musicians (rappers included), traditionally rebels, outsiders, criminals, and scapegoats, undergo a shift in function. They still continue to create a form of sociality by sublimating noise into music and affirming that society is possible. However, instead of inventing ways for different subject positions to connect, the "anticonformist" rappers become models for replication, regardless of "[w]hether they are manipulated, exploited by intermediaries who manufacture them, or are masters of their own game."[89] This is the very paradigm for a phallogocentric society, where identity is based on resemblance rather than difference. Rap, with its aesthetic of sampling, and priorization of the recording over the performance, is in many respects the music of repetition par excellence. Accordingly, Ice-T's lyrics may come back to haunt him.

Disc 4 Track 20: Escape from the Killing Fields

However, repetition too is having its crisis and will eventually be replaced. Attali envisions its replacement as a musical utopia beyond repetition, an order that he calls "composition." Composition is a space where the rapper and the rapt are in continuous oscillation: "beyond the realm of music, [it] calls into question the distinction between worker and consumer, between doing and destroying, a fundamental division of roles in all societies in which usage is defined by a code; to compose is to take pleasure in the instruments, the tools of communication, in use-time and exchange-time as lived and no longer as stockpiled" (*Noise* 135). This is not a return to an earlier mode of musical production, not a new ruse of power; it is something entirely other, a "*society without lack*" (147).

Once again, though, as Attali notes, "[c]omposition can only emerge from the destruction of the preceding codes" (136). The price that must be paid to achieve that utopia is an apocalypse that rap has never ceased to announce. If gangster rap is complicit with repetition, it also contains harbingers of the possibility of composition, perhaps even more so than other types of contemporary music. Attali mentions that composition is "incontestably aided by the existence of the records and representations it subverts, from which it draws its inspiration and innovations" (141); rap's DIY aesthetic, stronger than in any musical movement since punk, encourages the listener to insinuate him-/herself into the production by rapping along with the instrumental versions provided on many EPs, or to outright sample the rap records in the process of creating new ones. Composition will not happen in the studios of the record companies or their megacorporate owners; it will happen on street corners and in basements soundproofed with egg cartons stapled to the walls. Or, to paraphrase Public Enemy's "Countdown to Armageddon," perhaps this revolution will not be televised.[90]

Disc 2 Track 13: Outro

There are no answers to the question of apocalypse that are not also apocalyptic, but it may be possible to hint at the possibility of the scene of a different hearing, a space that Avital Ronell calls "a space of contact-taboo and wounding," where oppression aligns itself with the phantom other that comes rapping on the door.[91] Attali holds a similar opinion:

[Composition] plugs music into the noises of life and the body, whose movement it fuels. It is thus laden with risk, disquieting, an unstable challenging, an anarchic and ominous festival, like a Carnival with an unpredictable outcome. This new mode of production thus entertains a very different relation with violence: in composition, noise is still a metaphor for murder. To compose is simultaneously to commit a murder and to perform a sacrifice. It is to become both the sacrificer and the victim, to make an ever-possible suicide the only possible form of death and the production of life. To compose is to stay repetition and the death inherent in it, in other words, to locate liberation not in a faraway future, either sacred or material; but in the present, in production and in one's own enjoyment.[92]

You have to be def(t) to hear: the icicle-stylus punctures the eardrum, rends the veil, creating a wound or crack in the armor that admits alterity without colonizing it.

It rents it in such a way that it not only allows there the vision or production of the very (same) thing, but in fact undoes the sail's self-opposition, the opposition of veiled/unveiled (sailed/unsailed) which has folded over on itself. Truth in the guise of production, the unveiling/dissimulation of the present product, is dismantled. The veil no more raised than it is lowered.[93]

Perhaps, at the very same time as it rends the eardrum, the icicle-spur, both weapon and armor, melts, flows, trickling inside. If it ever were truly outside. "What is 'inside' and what is 'outside' a text, of *this* text, both inside and outside of these volumes [rap albums, perhaps] which we do not know whether they are open or closed?"[94]

Who's rapping on the door? Open it up and find out. Until they come in, the stereo's set on random play: chill and let the fat tracks flow.

Notes

1. Avital Ronell, *The Telephone Book: Technology, Schizophrenia, Electric Speech* (Lincoln: University of Nebraska Press, 1989), 2, 5. The "call" of rap music functions in a manner analogous with the telephone call as Ronell describes it.

2. Ronell, *Telephone Book*, 58.

3. Ice-T, "Home Invasion," *Home Invasion*, Rhyme Syndicate Records, P2 53858, 1993.

4. Quoted in *AMOK Fourth Dispatch: Sourcebook of the Extremes of Information in Print*, ed. Stuart Swezey and Brian King (Los Angeles: AMOK Press, 1990[?]), 209.

5. Henry Louis Gates Jr., *The Signifying Monkey: A Theory of African-American Literary Criticism* (New York: Oxford University Press, 1988), 51.

6. The Young Black Teenagers are a group of all-white rappers on the Def Jam label, created and managed by Hank Shocklee, producer of Public Enemy. Anthrax is an all-white speed-metal band who recorded *I'm the Man*, a rap pastiche

(Island Records ISM-1163, 1987), and then went on to do "Bring Tha Noize" (a version of Public Enemy's classic "Bring the Noise") with the members of PE themselves (Public Enemy, *Apocalypse 91 . . . The Enemy Strikes Black.* Def Jam / Columbia CK 47374, 1991). As the lyrics of both versions suggest, even thrash-metal bands like Anthrax can "rock bells."

7. Priority Records — the label that manufactured and distributed *Home Invasion* when Warner Brothers balked. This change in wrapper also effected what it wraps — the track "It's On" added after the recording of the rest of the album, despite the eponymous message of track 19: "Ain't a Damn Thing Changed."

8. Fredric Jameson, *Postmodernism, or The Cultural Logic of Late Capitalism* (Durham, N.C.: Duke University Press, 1991), 101–102.

9. Jonathan Culler, *On Deconstruction* (Ithaca, N.Y.: Cornell University Press, 1982), 120.

10. Alan Light, "Ice-T: The *Rolling Stone* Interview," *Rolling Stone* 637 (August 20, 1992): 28–32, 60, 30.

11. Ice-T, "O.G. Original Gangster," *O.G. Original Gangster,* Sire / Warner Bros., CD 26492, 1991. See also liner notes 10.

12. Simon Reynolds, "The End of Music," in *Blissed Out: The Raptures of Rock* (London: Serpent's Tail, 1990), 169.

13. This is Signifyin(g) as a Derridean paleonym — the retaining of an old name by one of the terms in a binary opposition in order to destroy the opposition to which it never really belonged in the first place (see Jacques Derrida, *Dissemination,* trans. Barbara Johnson [Chicago: University of Chicago Press, 1981], 4). In *The Signifying Monkey,* Henry Louis Gates Jr. strategically (re)defines the term as follows. Signifyin(g) — the final "g" bracketed as the trace of black *différance* (46), which disrupts the (white) conventional critical usage of the term, and hence constitutes a critique of the meaning of meaning itself (47) — is "the black trope of tropes, the figure for black rhetorical figures" (51). It chiefly involves the substitution and play of words along the paradigmatic axis; it outlines parallel universes of discourse, other possibilities through play, parody, and pastiche (49). What is crucial for my purposes here is that rap music was founded on the practices of Signifyin(g) in this sense; as such, "Signifyin(g), in Lacan's sense, is the Other of discourse, but it also constitutes the black Other's discourse as its rhetoric" (50).

14. Jameson, *Postmodernism,* 103.

15. Ice-T, "First Impression," *O.G. Original Gangster.* See also liner notes 4.

16. Ice-T, "Prepared to Die," *O.G. Original Gangster.*

17. *The Iceberg: Freedom of Speech . . . Just Watch What You Say,* Sire / Warner Bros., 92 60281, 1989.

18. Jacques Derrida, *Spurs: Nietzche's Styles,* trans. Barbara Harlow (Chicago: University of Chicago Press, 1978), 39.

19. Roland Barthes, *Writing Degree Zero and Elements of Semiology,* trans. Annette Lavers and Colin Smith (Boston: Beacon Press, 1967), 10–11. Emphasis mine.

20. Ice-T, "O.G. Original Gangster," *O.G. Original Gangster.*

21. Jacques Attali, *Noise: The Political Economy of Music,* trans. Brian Massumi, (Minneapolis: University of Minnesota Press, 1985), 26.

22. Public Enemy, "Bring the Noise," *It Takes a Nation of Millions to Hold Us Back,* Def Jam, BFCT-44303, 1988.

23. Derrida, *Spurs,* 37.

24. Ice-T, *O.G. Original Gangster,* liner notes. This paraph itself varies from album to album, a dissemanation within the very structure of the signature itself.

25. Jacques Derrida, "Ulysses Gramophone," in *Acts of Literature,* ed. Derek Attridge (New York: Routledge, 1992), 267.

26. Derrida, *Spurs,* 37.

27. Ice-T, "Mind Over Matter," *O.G. Original Gangster.*

28. Ice-T, "O.G. Original Gangster," *O.G. Original Gangster.* See also liner notes 9.

29. "On *Home Invasion,* Ice-T blows-up his cartoon-like image of the gun wielding outlaw to epic proportions." Tim Perlich, "T Chases Buck," *Now* 12: 32 (April 8–14, 1993): 43.

30. Light, "Ice-T: The *Rolling Stone* Interview," 32.

31. Jacques Derrida, "Of an Apocalyptic Tone Recently Adopted in Philosophy," trans. John P. Leavey, Jr., *Oxford Literary Review* 6, no. 2 (1984): 3–37, 24.

32. Derrida, "Of an Apocalyptic Tone," 8.

33. Ice-T, *Home Invasion,* liner notes.

34. Roland Barthes, "Digressions," in *The Grain of the Voice: Interviews 1962–1980,* trans. Linda Coverdale (New York: Hill and Wang, 1985), 127.

35. Grandmaster Flash and the Furious Five's "The Message," one of the first significant rap hits, was also a herald of the coming apocalypse: "Don't push me 'cause I'm close to the edge" ("The Message," Sugar Hill, 1007, 1982).

36. Ice-T, "That's How I'm Livin'," *Home Invasion.*

37. Ice-T, "Message to the Soldier," *Home Invasion.*

38. Derrida, "Of an Apocalyptic Tone," 9.

39. Ice-T, *Home Invasion,* liner notes.

40. Ice-T, *Home Invasion,* liner notes.

41. Simon Reynolds and David Stubbs, "The End of Music: Sampling," in *Blissed Out,* 167–171, 167.

42. Light, "Ice-T: The *Rolling Stone* Interview," 30.

43. Ice-T, "Message to the Soldier," *Home Invasion.*

44. Ice-T, "Ice M.F.T," *Home Invasion.*

45. Ice-T, "Warning," *Home Invasion.*

46. Jacques Derrida, "Signature Event Context," in *Margins of Philosophy,* trans. Alan Bass (Chicago: University of Chicago Press, 1982), 314–316.

47. Ronell, "A User's Manual," *The Telephone Book,* xv.

48. Derrida, "Signature," 316.

49. Ice-T, "Message to the Soldier," *Home Invasion.*

50. See Derrida, "Signature," 316.

51. Derrida, *Spurs,* 139.

52. Derrida, *Spurs,* 139.

53. Chris Morris, "Real Power Generation," *Musician* 175 (May 1993): 85–86, 85.

54. Derrida, "Of an Apocalyptic Tone," 27.

55. Morris, "Real Power Generation," 86.

56. Jacques Derrida, *The Ear of the Other: Otobiography, Transference, Translation,* ed. Christie McDonald, trans. Peggy Kamuf (Lincoln: University of Nebraska Press, 1985), 50.

57. Ice-T, "New Jack Hustler," *O.G. Original Gangster.* See also liner notes 6.

58. Alan Light, "Words from the 'Home' Front." *Rolling Stone* 657 (May 27, 1993): 20–21.

59. Ice-T, "Pulse of the Rhyme," *O.G. Original Gangster.* See also liner notes 16.

60. Derrida, *The Ear of the Other,* 51–52.

61. Light, "Ice T," 30.

62. Light, "Ice T," 30.

63. Ice-T, "Body Count," *O.G. Original Gangster.*

64. Body Count, "There Goes the Neighborhood," *Body Count,* Sire/Warner Bros., 9 26878-2, 1992. See also liner notes.

65. Light, "Ice T," 30.

66. Perlich, "T Chases Buck," 43.

67. Light, "Ice T," 60.

68. Derrida, "Of an Apocalyptic Tone," 29.

69.

> The worldwide organization of the human *socius* today hangs by the thread of nuclear rhetoric. This is immediately readable in the fact that we use the term "deterrence" or "strategy of dissuasion," as we say in French, for the overall logic of nuclear politics. Dissuasion, or deterrence, means "persuasion." Dissuasion is a negative mode or effect of persuasion. The art of persuasion is, as you know, one of the two axes of what has been called rhetoric since classical times. To dissuade is certainly a form of persuasion, but it involves not only persuading someone to think or believe this or that, but persuading someone that something *must not* be done. . . . The anticipation of nuclear war (dreaded as fantasy, or phantasm, of a remainderless destruction) installs humanity — and through all sorts of relays even defines the essence of modern humanity — in its rhetorical condition. (Jacques Derrida, "No Apocalypse, Not Now (Full Speed Ahead, Seven Missiles, Seven Missives)," trans. Catherine Porter and Philip Lewis, *Diacritics* 14:2 (Summer 1984): 21–31.)

70. Light, "Ice T," 31.

71. See "Editorial: Shooting Himself in the Mouth," *The Source* 45 (June 1993): 9; and Eddie Huffman, "Street Cred: Rap Returns to Its Indie Roots," *Option* 50 (May/June 1993): 51–56.

72. Derrida, "Of an Apocalyptic Tone," 29.

73. See Huffman, "Street Coed," and Light, "Words," 20.

74. Derrida, "Of an Apocalyptic Tone," 35.

75. Perlich, "T Chases Buck," 43.

76. Jameson, *Postmodernism,* xvii.

77. Derrida, "Of an Apocalyptic Tone," 10.

78. Ice-T, "Question and Answer," *Home Invasion.*

79. Reynolds, "Hip Hop," *Blissed Out,* 157.

80. Reynolds, "Hip Hop," 159–160. The power of the apocalyptic image has Reynolds seeing things: only one member of Public Enemy, Flavor Flav, wears a clock around his neck.

81. Derrida, "Of an Apocalyptic Tone," 30.

82. Ice-T, "O.G. Original Gangster," *O.G. Original Gangster.* See also liner notes 10.

83. bell hooks, "A Call For Militant Resistance," in *Yearning: Race, Gender, and Cultural Politics* (Toronto: Between the Lines, 1990), 186.

84. Robert Christgau, "Ice T Blinks," *The Village Voice,* August 11, 1992, 88.

85. Morris, "Real Power Generation," 86.

86. bell hooks, "The Politics of Radical Black Subjectivity," in *Yearning: Race, Gender and Cultural Politics* (Toronto: Between the Lines, 1990), 19.

87. Derrida, "Of an Apocalyptic Tone," 29.

88. Attali, *Noise,* 88.

89. Attali, *Noise*, 119.
90. Public Enemy, "Countdown to Armageddon," *It Takes a Nation.*
91. Ronell, *The Telephone Book*, 402.
92. Attali, *Noise*, 142–143.
93. Derrida, *Spurs*, 107.
94. Derrida, "Of an Apocalyptic Tone," 35.

An Absolute Acceleration: Apocalypticism and the War Machines of Waco

Christopher Keep

In March of 1993, Governor Ann Richards of Texas was asked by the Federal Bureau of Investigation and the Bureau of Alcohol, Tobacco, and Firearms (ATF) to authorize the use of Abrams tanks in their operation against approximately one hundred members of the Branch Davidian sect besieged in their compound near Waco. Though the use of armored vehicles against civilians is strictly controlled under U.S. law, Richards was persuaded to comply with the request under the Drug Interdiction Act. The Davidians, the ATF claimed, were concealing a "speed factory" — a facility for the production of methamphetamines — in the basement of their compound. Though it appears now that there was no such "factory," that its existence was a ruse used to coerce Richards into signing the release (the governor has since claimed that she was deceived by the federal officials), there seems nonetheless to be a grain of metaphorical truth to the charge. Ranch Apocalypse, as the Davidians called their home, was a speed factory: the events of the siege progressed with a subtle, but ever-increasing tempo that pushed inexorably toward the fiery consummation, the *absolute acceleration* of the apocalypse.

In the days before and after the immolation of the Davidians was broadcast live on CNN, media representations of the relationship between the sect members and the FBI agents sent to secure their surrender tended to emphasize the ideological distance between them. The two groups were regularly presented as occupying distinct, even diametrically opposed positions in the cultural field. It was precisely the foreignness, the perfect remoteness of the Davidians' apocalyptic beliefs from the secular common sense of the government agents that was most often invoked as an explanation for the debacle. "Even after 51 days of facing each other across the wind-swept plains of central Texas," ran one *Newsweek* article, "the FBI and the Branch Davidians were still aliens to each other — viewing reality through very different prisms."[1] The bureaucratic, authoritarian, but still rational state apparatus, in this scheme, was paired off against the criminal, irrational, but in some ways sympathetic religious cult, each of which was blind to the motivations of the other.

This emphasis on the absolute otherness of the Davidians was used by both those who wished to defend the government's actions and those who wished to attack them. On the one hand, there was President Clinton dismissing calls for Attorney General Janet Reno's resignation simply because "some religious fanatics murdered themselves."[2] On the other, there were those experts in millenarian religious sects who blamed the government for not understanding the Davidians' esoteric beliefs. "The FBI botched the whole situation," claimed Gilbert Greggs, an assistant professor of Religious Studies at the University of Missouri-Columbia. "If the FBI had bothered to read the *Book of Revelations,* they would have realized that it's filled with images of the world ending in fire. They didn't defuse the situation. They ignited it."[3] Ultimately, Clinton and Greggs differed only with regard to the extent to which the government negotiators should have striven to bridge that gap. The Davidians, all parties in the debate seemed to agree, were bound to an obscure worldview, one that divided them from the federal agents as surely as did the barbed wire fence the latter had erected around the perimeter of the compound.

But to present the events of April 19, 1993, as resulting from a case of "communications breakdown" is to obscure the real affinities that existed between the Davidians and the federal agents, affinities that were as much responsible for the outcome of the siege as were their differences. Far from being perfect strangers, the two groups were, in fact, blood relatives, bound by an eschatology of speed, by the desire for the end that comes quickly. And it is only through attending to the ways in which both were interpellated by the internal logic of the apocalypse that we will be able to understand the tragedy of Waco as something more than a "mistake" or a "miscalculation." The Davidians were not the only apocalyptic sect on the plains of Texas in April 1993: the militarism of the federal agencies was symptomatic of the doomsday mentality of the Reagan/ Bush administrations. With its fascination for the spectacle of instantaneity, American culture itself has become a speed factory. Driven by a thanatogenic urge toward closure, the actions of the FBI and the Branch Davidians reveal the extent to which the speed of the war machine has become the dominant characteristic of what Paul Virilio calls "dromocratic" society.[4]

*   *   *

For the followers of David Koresh, the end of the standoff could not come quick enough. Steeped in millennialist religious teaching, they believed the resolution of the confrontation would usher in the end of time itself, the descent of the New Jerusalem, and the marriage of the Lamb of God to the purified souls of the Elect. Their leader, Vernon Wayne Howell (better known as David Koresh), claimed to have received a revelation from God that he was the seventh angel of the Revelation of St. John the Divine, the heaven-sent messenger whose arrival would signal the beginning of the endtime. In his vision, Koresh foresaw that the Battle of Armageddon would be fought on the desert plains of Texas and would begin when the U.S. Army attacked him and his followers in the shadow of Mount Carmel. The one hundred heavily armed ATF agents who arrived at Ranch Apocalypse on February 28, 1993, to deliver a search warrant for suspected illegal weapons thus appeared to the Davidians as confirmation of their leader's vision. The four agents and six sect members that died in the firefight were but "the souls of them that were slain for the word of God" (Revelation 6:9). The Davidians had, in short, every reason to believe that the end was nigh.

While at least one of the FBI agents is reported to have thought that Koresh's seven seals referred to "seagoing creatures with whiskers," the same cannot be said for the presidents under which they served during the 1980s.[5] Both Reagan and Bush openly espoused an evangelical Christianity not dissimilar to that taught by David Koresh. Much impressed by Hal Lindsey's best-selling *Late Great Planet Earth* (1970), a sensationalist account of the ways in which the contemporary political scene fulfilled the endtime prophecies of the Bible, Reagan was particularly open about his apocalyptic beliefs. Speaking to an Israeli lobbyist in 1983, he confessed:

You know, I turn back to your ancient prophets in the Old Testament and the signs foretelling Armageddon, and I find myself wondering if we're the generation that's going to see that come about. I don't know if you've noted any of those prophecies lately, but believe me, they certainly describe the times we're going through.[6]

In the light of such statements, the steadily increasing arms expenditures of the eighties and the techno-utopian dreams of the Strategic Defense Initiative appear as preparations for an Armageddon that would never arrive.

The events at Waco, it is worth remembering, began while the Clinton administration was as yet nascent. On the day the ATF agents arrived at Ranch Apocalypse to deliver their ill-fated warrant, Janet Reno was still waiting to be sworn in as attorney general. The ATF's aggressive militarism was in keeping not only with the character of its previous operations, but with that of the administrations under which it had prospered. The ensuing siege was thus less an anomaly than the logical consequence of nearly a decade in which a particularly virulent form of apocalypticism functioned as an unofficial state policy. The assault against the Davidians was, in a sense, nothing less than the struggle of one apocalyptic sect jealously vying with another for the right to become the bride of Christ.

The FBI's Hostage Rescue Team (HRT), sent by Reno to replace the ATF agents after the bungled raid, also shared the Davidians' desire for the end. For fifty-one days they negotiated, coaxed, and cajoled the sect's leader through a series of surrender plans only to have him change his mind at the last moment. As the demand for a politically expeditious solution to the crisis mounted, Reno solicited assault plans from her advisers and from experts in chemical warfare. At a reported cost to the taxpayers of nearly a million dollars a day, the attorney general needed to accelerate events to a conclusion as quickly as possible, and she found ready support for her initiatives from the federal agents who had grown tired of the waiting game. In the end, Reno accepted a plan she had initially rejected — to fire canisters of O-chlorobenzalmalonnitrile, a form of tear gas banned for use in war by the Paris Chemical Weapons Convention (1989), into the Davidians' compound — in order to, in her words, "bring about a peaceful resolution."

This desire for an end united the Davidians and the federal agents under the apocalyptic sign par excellence, the sign of speed. The spectacularized towing of Koresh's black Camaro 427 by a specially equipped armored vehicle,[7] the "instant books" and made-for-TV movies (one of which went into production while the siege was still ongoing),[8] the pervasive sense of inevitability, of the expectation of another "Jonestown" — each of these were manifestations of the condition of urgency that seemed, paradoxically, to only increase as "real" events, "real developments" became fewer and fewer. The collective impatience that hung about Waco grew until, finally, it was a day on which nothing new had happened, a day, in fact, much like any other during the standoff, that everything happened.[9] It was perhaps only in this absence of an "event" that the apocalyptic desires of the Davidians and HRT could finally approach the terminal velocity they sought, the pure speed of the war machine unloosed. For Gilles Deleuze and Félix Guattari, speed — *celeritas* — is precisely the quality that defines the war machine and, in particular, its tendency toward opening out beyond the event horizon to the unstratified domain of "smooth space":

Laminar movement which striates space, which goes from one point to another, is weighty; but rapidity, celerity, only apply to movement which deviates to the minimum extent and thereafter assumes a vortical motion, occupying a smooth space, actually tracing smooth space itself.[10]

The war machine, in this problematization, is a multiple and variable form that has warfare as its immediate object only when it is appropriated by the State. In its pure or "nomadological" state it has as its object "not war, but the drawing of a creative line of flight, the composition of a smooth space and of the movement of people in that space" (422). It is in this way, then, that one might refer to both the apocalypticism of the Branch Davidians and the militarism of the HRT as war machines; each was caught up in its own desire for the unlimited speed of an inertialess surface.[11] Shifting the discussion of Waco from the domain of space to the domain of time reveals not two static objects paralyzed by the distance between them, but two similarly constituted vectors of violence, two bodies in motion along *the same line*. The question raised by Waco, then, is how this largely immobile array of bodies, technology, and weaponry somehow accelerated to escape velocity without anyone apparently noticing. How is it that the question of speed was obscured, when its figures were everywhere?

*   *   *

The imbrication of apocalypticism and the war machine is at least as old as the Revelation of St. John the Divine itself and, in part, suggested by its visions of the Battle of Armageddon and its depiction of Christ laying waste to the armies of the Beast with the sword "which proceeded from his mouth" (19:21). In his appeal to an imminent *eschaton*, Koresh, the high-school dropout and frustrated rock musician, was following in the steps of such dissident millenarian movements as the defenders of Masada, the fourteenth-century Hussites, and the Fifth Monarchy Men of the English Civil War. Like the blind Jan Žižka, who successfully led the Taborites against Emperor Sigismund in the 1420s,[12] Koresh used Revelation as the central tenet of his sect, finding in it a means by which not only to secure the fidelity of his followers to the very death, but to convince them of the necessity of taking up arms against the central government. According to the affidavits filed by the federal Bureau of Alcohol, Tobacco, and Firearms, the Davidians had the United Parcel Service deliver (C.O.D.) $199,715 worth of firearms and munitions, including 123 M-16 assault rifles, a grenade launcher, and the parts required for turning semiautomatic rifles into machine guns.[13] Koresh strove to maintain a military-style regimen at the compound, supplementing his six- to seven-hour sermons on the meaning of the seven seals with video screenings of Vietnam War movies such as *Platoon* and *Full Metal Jacket*— the only films he ever allowed to be shown.[14] When the ATF arrived to deliver its search warrant for illegal weapons, the Davidians were expecting them not only because they had been tipped off by a local TV news cameraperson, but because they had been preparing for, indeed, looking forward to, this event all along. "We're ready for war," Koresh told the FBI, "Let's get it on."[15]

The Davidians' AK-47 rifles and khaki combat jackets were, however, but the coruscations, the incendiary sparks thrown off by the war machine as it approached its own limit velocity, less important in and of themselves than for what they both alternately concealed and revealed. For if Koresh's guns remind us that the war machine is not the exclusive preserve of the State, they also obscure from us the speed that necessitated them. Speed is the condition of the war machine, both the horizon of its endeavors and its originating principle. "War is not," writes Paul Virilio, " 'a worksite of fire.' War has always been a worksite of movement, a speed factory."[16] The industrial revolution, or what Virilio calls the "dromocratic revolution," saw not only the invention of the means of mass production, but of the means for the fabrication of speed itself—the steam engine, the telephone line, the electric circuit. In this climate of perpetual acceleration, of faster engines and quicker microchips, the war machine has flourished; armored cars have given way to cruise missiles and cruise missiles to satellite-borne plasma weapons in an ever-increasing involution of space and time. "History as the extensiveness of time — of time that lasts, is portioned out, organized, developed — is disappearing in favour of the instant, as if the end of history were the end of duration in favour of instantaneousness, and of course, of ubiquity."[17] Directed toward "the end of duration," the war machine is also directed toward, as David Koresh knew, the nontime, the instantaneity, of the apocalypse.

*   *   *

When the first flames began to sweep through the main building of Ranch Apocalypse, Ruth Riddle leapt from a second story window and was dragged against her will to safety by HRT agents. In her pocket was a computer diskette containing the first pages of Koresh's exegesis of the seven seals of Revelation. The leader of the Davidians had promised the FBI that upon the completion of his manuscript he would surrender himself and his followers to the authorities. In a letter to his lawyer, Dick DeGuerin, he wrote, "I hope to finish this as soon as possible and to stand before man to answer any and all questions regarding my actions."[18] While the tanks were amassing outside the perimeter wire on the night of April 18, he was busy writing; survivors of the calamity claimed he worked the whole night, apparently caught up by the same sense of urgency that marks the text that was his subject. Christ's last words, indeed, the last words of the King James Version of the Bible, are an exhortation for *speed*.

"Surely I come quickly," the Savior promises, to which John of Patmos replies, "Even so, come, Lord Jesus" (22:20). Come, come quickly. The eschatological drive of Revelation, with its ardent expectation of the end of all things, evidently infected Koresh's commentary; its end, too, would mark not simply the end of a literary work, but a literal one as well, the end of the standoff. In the thirteen pages that survived on Ruth Riddell's diskette, Koresh, too, looks forward to the apocalypse in terms that implicitly relate it to the end of the siege. "Should we not eagerly ourselves be ready to accept this truth and come out of our closet and be revealed to the world as those who love Christ in truth and righteousness[?]"[19] The apocalypse for Koresh, as for John of Patmos, is the moment, the always arriving instant, at which the end of the text would be analogous with the end of the division between the literal and the literary, between the sign and the referent, the word and the Word.

In "No Apocalypse, Not Now (Full Speed Ahead, Seven Missiles, Seven Missives)," Jacques Derrida claims that the *eschaton* of the nuclear age is "fabulously textual," for the end of the world, if it can be thought at all, must necessarily remain in the realm of the imaginary, in the realm of signs and fiction.[20] Or perhaps not a realm at all, but a speed. Comparing the particular apprehensions of the end of the world aroused by the nuclear bomb with those of earlier periods, Derrida reminds us, "The most classical wars were also speed races, in their preparation and in the actual pursuit of the hostilities. Are we having, today, *another,* different experience of speed? Is our relation to time and to motion qualitatively different? Or must we speak prudently of an extraordinary . . . acceleration of the same experience?"[21] For Derrida, the apocalyptic genre is the dream of an "extraordinary acceleration," or what he will later call an "absolute acceleration," in which writing would finally master its own vagaries, in which the post will be received as sent, and meaning revealed in its perfect plenitude. It is, in short, the dream of the end of writing insofar as writing, as that which defers, which displaces, which prolongs, is also that which is produced by and produces time.

It is, thus, not surprising to find apocalypticism flourishing in the age of the war machine. The disappearance of duration in the age of the dromocratic revolution is the uncanny realization of the antihistoricism of the apocalypse and its desire to return the sign to the plenitude of the Word. But it is the paradoxical nature of apocalypticism that it necessarily forestalls the end in the very act of imagining it. As Jonathan Z. Smith has said, apocalypticism is primarily a "scribal phenomenon," a prophetic mode that consistently valorizes the written word over the spoken as a vehicle of divine revelation.[22] As such, Derrida has taken it as the very model of all writing. Referring to the confusion of sendings and receivings that mark the Apocalypse of John, he asks, "And if the dispatches

always refer to other dispatches without decidable destination, the destination remaining to come, then isn't this completely angelic structure,
that of the Johannine apocalypse, isn't it also the structure of every scene
of writing in general?"[23] For Derrida, it is the nonarrival of every sending
that is *apocalyptic* precisely in that it does not fix meaning in place, but *dis-*
places it, for what it causes to accelerate. If there was a speed factory at
Waco, I would suggest, it was Koresh's book on Revelation, for it was this
text that, in the very act of deferring the end, produced the conditions of
urgency that ensured its realization. As long as he claimed to be writing,
the federal agents allowed the siege to proceed, to slowly approach a
velocity that no amount of diplomatic brake-pushing could reverse. Hur-
rying toward the telos, Koresh's writing also opened up a moment of
duration (fifty-one days, to be precise) that both forestalled and ensured
the end. His exegesis was the necessary catalyst that, in the very act of
frustrating the State war machine, pushed it to the apocalyptic speed of
writing itself.

While Koresh labored away at his commentary the agents of the Hostage Rescue Team became increasingly dispirited by their failure to set
the tempo of events, to, in effect, *keep up* with the strange apocalyptic
speed that the Branch Davidians were manufacturing in their underground factory. The HRT was stymied by Koresh's ability to regulate time
at his own pace. "There were never any real negotiations," an FBI agent
told a *Time* reporter. "We stayed in touch to avoid provocation, but everything was done on his time — he was in strict control."[24] It was in order to
retrieve the temporal upper hand that the agents first formulated their
assault plans. "At some point," said Bob Ricks, the FBI's chief spokesper-
son, when explaining the rationale for the decision to move against the
Davidians on April 19, "we had to up the ante."[25] To this end, the bureau
tried to disrupt the flow of time at the compound, shining bright lights
into the compound at night, buzzing it with helicopters, and assaulting
the people inside with a sonic barrage of amplified Tibetan monk chants,
Nancy Sinatra songs, and the sound of rabbits being slaughtered.

These tactics, however, seemed to have taken a greater toll on the
federal agents than on the besieged Davidians. While Reno claimed (and
was then obliged to rescind)[26] concerns for the safety and security of the
sect's children as her topmost priority in ordering the assault, her initial
statements to the press reveal a different priority. After acknowledging
that her decision was not provoked by any change in the circumstances of
the six-week-old siege, or by any new ultimatums from Koresh, the attorney general conceded that the immediate reason for "increasing the
pressure" against the Davidians was that the HRT troops were exhausted.
"The experts," Reno told reporters, "advised me, that in those situations
where one had to be constantly on the alert that it was in the best interests

of everybody involved, to provide for really time off, and what I was told is that there were no back-ups."[27] It was, thus, as much out of concern for the well-being of the HRT agents as for any putative concerns for the children still in the compound that Reno ordered the attack when she did.

The point is worth dilating upon: the Branch Davidians, holed up in their ramshackle compound, with neither running water nor electricity, fed on scanty provisions from camp stoves, and deprived of sleep by a constant aural barrage, broke the back of the HRT troops manning the perimeter wire by simply standing still. The speed they discovered was not that of the machine in motion, but the vortical movement of the apocalypse, the speed released when the subject submits itself to the end that is always already coming. While the Branch Davidians traced out what Deleuze and Guattari call a "plane of consistency, a creative line of flight, a smooth space of displacement" (422–423), the HRT could only watch and grow increasingly furious at its own impotence, its own *flightlessness*. This inertia is the condition of the war machine when it is appropriated by the State: divorced from its nomadological impulse, it becomes bound to the bureaucratic need to occupy space, to regulate it through the imposition of quantified time and the carving out of distinct spheres of influence. Confronted with the Davidians' vortical motion, the war machine of the state could find no effective means of drawing close enough to engage them and, finally, exhausted itself in the effort. "Turning the war machine back against the nomads," as Janet Reno did with the Davidians, "may constitute for the State a danger as great as that presented by nomads directing the war machine against States" (419).

Frustrated with their inability to keep pace with the Davidians, the FBI concocted a plan that was meant to increase the pressure on Koresh, to narrow the space that the federal agency felt was key to its ability to control the pace of events. "Today was not meant to be D-Day," Reno explained. "This was just a step forward in trying to bring about a peaceful resolution by constantly exerting further pressure to shrink the perimeter."[28] But the plan miscarried precisely for its continuing attention to space ("shrinking the perimeter"). Reno and her advisers persistently failed to recognize that this, like all wars, was, as Derrida writes, "a speed race." But the point was not missing on other members of the State war machine. According to a *Newsweek* article, members of Delta Force, the military counterpart of the HRT, scorned the FBI plan, "since it violated a cardinal rule of counterterrorism: once an assault has begun, entry teams must quickly subdue the targets before they have time to regroup. 'Speed is of the essence,' said one former Delta officer. 'Once you have busted down walls, you've tipped your hand.' "[29] Apparently hoping that the mothers and their children would take the opportunity to flee the compound, the HRT sent their first Combat Engineering Vehicles in at 6 A.M. They pushed the noses of their specially mounted battering rams through the pink plasterboard walls of Ranch Apocalypse, fired off their tear gas canisters, and withdrew. When the Davidians showed no sign of surrendering, they simply repeated the process and waited for the people inside to come out. It was this hesitation that was to prove fatal, for in the gap, the strange aporia between 6 A.M. and noon, the Davidians and their unwitting accomplices, the Hostage Rescue Team, suddenly accelerated to a speed at which the very ground on which they were standing caught fire.

It is significant, in this regard, that we may never know exactly how or by whom the fires that destroyed Ranch Apocalypse were started. According to the FBI, the Davidians, under Koresh's orders, ignited ammunition stores stockpiled for just such an eventuality and killed themselves. Survivors of the debacle claim nothing could be further from the truth. According to some, the tanks punctured a propane tank that was barricading the door. The highly flammable gas ignited and the flames quickly spread, feeding on the bales of hay and the canisters of lantern fuel stocked nearby, to the rest of the compound. According to others, a videotape shows that the conflagration was started by a tank armed with a flamethrower that fired into the main building. While the government has staunchly denied such allegations, the recent Treasury investigation into the ATF's handling of "Operation Trojan Horse" and the Justice Department's report on the subsequent siege and its outcome have revealed the extent to which the federal agents regularly mismanaged critical situations and then knowingly misinformed their superiors and the public.

*   *   *

Responsibility for the debacle of April 19, 1993, must ultimately lie, as Reno has acknowledged, with the federal government. But to excuse or vilify either Koresh or Reno is to overlook the ways in which the flames that engulfed Ranch Apocalypse were kindled by neither party, but by their mutually constituted desire for the telos. Driven by the war machine's desire for speed, the Davidians and the HRT fulfilled one another's deepest desires and played them out before the hungry eyes of millions live on television. The events of Waco, then, foreground the sovereignty of speed in what Fredric Jameson calls the "cultural logic of late capitalism."[30] In an age in which telecommunications and high speed transportation — both by-products of the war machine — have effectively collapsed space to that increasingly short interval required to cross it, the apocalypse is revived as the spectacle of our own longing for the instant, for the satisfactions of closure that, like Jesus, comes quickly. And the eighty-five Branch Davidians (including seventeen children) who perished on April 19, together with the ten people killed in the shoot-out of February 28, serve to remind us of the profound cost of such speed.

Notes

1. Barbara Kantrowitz et al., "Day of Judgment," *Newsweek*, May 3, 1993, 22.

2. Remarks by the president in a question-and-answer session with the press, April 20, 1993 (televised [CNN]; also available on-line from the White House).

3. Elizabeth Ommachen and L. E. Ohman, "Waco's Lessons Linger," *Columbia Missourian* April 25, 1993, A1.

4. Virilio argues that Western "democracies" are more accurately described as "dromocracies," *dromo* meaning "running" or "racing." The emphasis on the relationship of wealth to power has obscured what is for Virilio a more primary relation, that of speed to power. "The one who goes the fastest possesses the ability to collect taxes, the ability to conquer, and through that to inherit the right of exploiting society" (Paul Virilio and Sylvère Lotvinger, *Pure War*, trans. Mark Polizzotti [New York: Semiotext(e), 1983], 44). Dromocratic society is thus characterized by the reduction of space to time: "The violence of speed has become both the location and the law, the world's destiny and its destination" (Paul Virilio, *Speed and Politics: An Essay on Dromology*, trans. Mark Polizzotti [New York: Semiotext(e), 1986], 151).

5. Melinda Beck et al., "The Book of Koresh," *Newsweek*, October 11, 1993; 27.

6. Quoted in Paul Boyer, *When Time Shall Be No More* (Cambridge, Mass.: Harvard University Press, 1992), 142.

7. Koresh's prized black Camaro became the subject of intense scrutiny in the last week before the April 19 assault. Frustrated by their failure to coax, intimidate, and, finally, force Koresh into further negations, the HRT had an armored vehicle tow the car away. The tactic succeeded; Koresh was visibly upset by the incident, while news commentators tried to make the most of this gesture of symbolic castration. But if the car was a symbol of the phallus, and thus of Koresh's maddening power over the State, its removal must also be seen as the contestation of speed itself, what Virilio would call a dromological conflict in which competing vectors vie for supremacy.

8. Courtenay Thompson, "Apocalypse Now: Waco and the Lure of Instant Books," *Columbia Journalism Review* (July/August 1993): 10–11.

9. Stephen Labaton, "Reno Calls Assault on Texas Cult 'Obviously Wrong' in Hindsight," *New York Times*, April 20, 1993, A21.

10. Gilles Deleuze and Félix Guattari, *A Thousand Plateaus: Capitalism and Schizophrenia*, trans. Brian Massumi (Minneapolis: University of Minnesota Press, 1987), 371. All subsequent citations of this work appear in parentheses.

11. Deleuze and Guattari themselves extend the term "war machine" to objects not normally associated with the military: "an 'ideological,' scientific, or artistic movement can be a potential war machine, to the precise extent to which it draws, in relation to a *phylum*, a plane of consistency, a creative line of flight, a smooth space of displacement" (422–423).

12. On Žižka and the Taborites, see Howard Kiminsky, *A History of the Hussite*

Revolution (Berkeley: University of California Press, 1967), and Bernard McGinn, *Visions of the End: Apocalyptic Traditions in the Middle Ages* (New York: Columbia University Press, 1979), 259–269.

13. Jill Smolowe, "February 28: Sent into a Deathtrap?" *Time* (Canada) May 3, 1993, 21.

14. Marc Breault and Martin King, *Inside the Cult* (New York: Signet, 1993), 184.

15. Andrew Phillips et al., "One Lived, One Died," *Maclean's* May 3, 1993, 19.

16. Paul Virilio, *Speed and Politics,* 140.

17. Virilio and Lotringer, *Pure War,* 46.

18. Nancy Gibbs, " 'Oh, My God, They're Killing Themselves,' " *Time* (Canada), May 3, 1993, 28.

19. Beck et al., "The Book of Koresh," 27.

20. Jacques Derrida, "No Apocalypse, Not Now (Full Speed Ahead, Seven Missiles, Seven Missives)," *Diacritics* 14 (1984): 23.

21. Derrida, "No Apocalypse," 20.

22. Jonathan Z. Smith, "Wisdom and Apocalyptic," in *Religious Syncretism in Antiquity,* ed. Birger A. Pearson (Missoula, Mont.: Scholars Press, 1975), 154. On the "scribal" nature of apocalypticism, see also Bernard McGinn, "Early Apocalypticism: The Ongoing Debate," in *The Apocalypse in English Renaissance Thought and Literature,* ed. C. A. Patrides and Joseph Wittreich (Ithaca, N.Y.: Cornell University Press, 1984), 5.

23. Jacques Derrida, "Of an Apocalyptic Tone Recently Adopted in Philosophy," *Oxford Literary Review* 6, no. 2 (1984): 27.

24. Gibbs, "They're Killing Themselves," 22.

25. Murray Campbell, "Koresh Predicted Apocalyptic Ending," *Globe and Mail,* April 20, 1993, A2.

26. In the Justice Department's investigation into the government's handling of the events at Waco, Reno admitted to having "misunderstood the bureau's data about the children (authorities had no evidence they were molested during the siege)." See "The Waco Whitewash," *New York Times,* October 12, 1993, A22.

27. Labaton, "Reno Calls Assault," A21. Similarly, in his question-and-answer session of April 20, President Clinton claimed his "number one" reason for moving on that particularly inauspicious Monday morning was that "there was a limit to how long the federal authorities could maintain with their limited resources the quality and intensity of coverage by experts there. They might be needed in other parts of the country."

28. Sam Howe Verhovek, "Cult Siege Comes to Fiery End," *Globe and Mail,* April 20, 1993, A2.

29. Melinda Beck et al., "The Questions Live On," *Newsweek* May 3, 1993, 28.

30. Fredric Jameson, *Postmodernism, or, The Cultural Logic of Late Capitalism* (Durham, N.C.: Duke University Press, 1991).

Part IV
Coda

Agrippa, or, The Apocalyptic Book

Peter Schwenger

> All techniques meant to unleash forces are techniques of disappearance.[1]
>
> — Paul Virilio

Black box recovered from some unspecified disaster, the massive case opens to reveal the textures of decay and age. Yellowed newspaper, rusty honeycombing, fog-colored cerement enveloping a pale book. On the book's cover, a burned-in title: *Agrippa (A Book of the Dead)*. Within it, page after page printed with cryptic letters.[2]

    TGTGG
    CCATA
    AATAT
    TACGA
    GTTTG

These are the combinatory possibilities of genetic codes, as recoded by scientists. The pages are singed at their edges; more fragments of old newspaper are interspersed. And at intervals, engravings by New York artist Dennis Ashbaugh reproduce the commercial subjects of a previous generation, subjects that later acquire a fuller meaning: a telephone ad ("Tell Daddy we miss him"), a diagram for the assembly of a pistol, an advertised magnesium gun "for nighttime photography." Black patches like burns smudge these images. With exposure to light the images gradually fade; the black patches reveal themselves to be the rhythmic chains of the DNA molecule as captured in microphotography. Embedded in the last pages of the book is a computer disk containing a text by cyberpunk novelist William Gibson. When activated, it runs once; then a built-in computer virus destroys the text, leaving a blank disk.

No matter, for now, what the evanescent content of that disk may be. Its specific content is less important than the fact of its disappearance. In a gibe at the art world's commercialism, publisher Kevin Begos Jr. suggested to Ashbaugh that "what we should do is put out an art book on computer that vanishes" (personal communication). Ashbaugh took him seriously, took him further; Gibson was enlisted shortly after. For all its complex resonances as an object, then, *Agrippa* is based on this one idea: a book disappears.

The idea has precedents. Maurice Blanchot's essay on "The Absence of the Book" argues from writerly experience that a work always becomes something other than what it is intended to be — what it is intended to be being, of course, a book. But the book (icon of law, presence, and textual-cultural wholeness) is always betrayed by what Blanchot calls "the disaster." This disaster has to do with the necessary falling short of a work's concept at the same time that an unexpected otherness beyond the work is evoked. A book never realizes its desired full presence; its realization occurs only and paradoxically through absence — "the prior deterioration of the book, the game of dissidence it plays with reference to the space in which it is inscribed; the preliminary dying of the book."[3] In the end the original concept, and even the very idea of "concept" must be exploded, Blanchot argues, citing Mallarmé's curious statement that "there is no explosion but a book."[4]

Yet Mallarmé also felt that the world existed in order to be put into a book. And he made this book — Le Livre — the ongoing preoccupation and project of his last twenty years, a project that came to nothing. Le Livre never appeared; its absence may have been the very point of it. The book's nonappearance is linked to the disappearance of the world, a crucial component of Mallarmé's art — so Sartre argues.

Meaning is a second silence deep within silence; it is the negation of the world's status as a thing. This ever unspoken meaning, which would disappear if one ever attempted to speak it . . . is quite simply the *absence* of certain objects. What is involved here is not the mere absence of a particular being but a "resonant disappearance."[5]

Sartre is here quoting Mallarmé's "disparition vibratoire," which was for him the condition of any possible meaning or truth. Speaking of his own writing, Mallarmé said that "whatever truth emerged in the process only did so with the loss of an impression which, after flaring up for a brief instant, burned itself out."[6]

Kevin Begos has acknowledged the influence of both Mallarmé's book and Blanchot's "Absence of the Book." One more book was needed to catalyze *Agrippa*, however — an old photograph album discovered by Gibson on a trip back to his home town of Wytheville, Virginia. His computerized text reproduces its commercial title page:

ALBUMS
C.A. AGRIPPA
Order extra leaves by letter and name

The print is dim, scrawled over with something indecipherable. The opening words of Gibson's text describe the opening of the album:

> I hesitated
> before untying the bow
> that bound the book together
> a Kodak album of time-harmed
> black construction paper

These words describing a hesitation themselves hesitate before they begin scrolling past. Then, one by one, the old photographs are rendered in words, each with its caption — though these captions are sometimes indecipherable, their obscurity described along with the rest of the book's "time-harmed" textures. This electronic book, book of the future, evokes through its words the ghost of antiquated pages.

That this ghostly book is a photo album means that it is already a book of the dead. In the photographs a whole world of people and objects is depicted in intense specificity: shadows cast on the brims of straw hats, grass that needs cutting, electric wires strung over street intersections. Yet all these things fall into a Mallarméan absence. Viewing a photograph, Roland Barthes says, "I shudder . . . *over a catastrophe which has already occurred.* Whether or not the subject is already dead, every subject is this catastrophe."[7] The black box of the camera is a temporal mechanism; Gibson speaks of the fall of the shutter as dividing time.

The description of the album's discovery is followed by the recollection of an earlier discovery by Gibson: As a boy he opened a drawer to find another mechanism of disappearance, his father's pistol. He took it out of the drawer and it unexpectedly discharged; when he dropped it, it went off again. Beyond the biographical fact, there may be a link here to another pair of explosions half a world away: Gibson's father worked on the Manhattan Project. Another possible disappearance of the world is adumbrated, not literary but literal; the singed, disastrous look of the black box's contents takes on a new significance. This "relic from the future," as Begos has called it (personal communication), replicates a typical pattern of nuclear-war fiction. Relic of a past event which is yet to take place in the future, the nuclear narrative is transmitted backward to us in the present, which is that future's past. The paradoxes shuttle and blur into "time no more," as announced by the angel of the apocalypse; and that "no more" is echoed in the last resonances of a disappearing world.

The men who moved the world closer to disappearance have, most of them, themselves disappeared; Gibson's father died when his son was six. To the degree that *Agrippa* is a memoir of Gibson's father, its irreversible passing is like his life, or any life. We can reread a human life only in memory. We can, of course, *write* of a human life, write "in memory of." When we do, we inhabit a paradoxical space, according to Jacques Derrida:

[D]oes the expression "in memory of" mean that the name is "in" our memory — supposedly a living capacity to recall images or signs from the past, etc.? Or that the name is in itself, out there somewhere, like a sign or symbol, a monument, epitaph, stele or tomb, a memorandum, aide-mémoire, a memento, an exterior auxiliary set up "in memory of"? Both, no doubt; and here lies the ambiguity of memory, the contamination which troubles us, troubles memory and the meaning of "memory."[8]

Following a distinction in Hegel, Derrida suggests that there are two kinds of memory: mechanical memorization (*Gedächtnis*), associated with writing, and interiorized recollection (*Erinnerung*), associated with mourning. For Derrida, these are at odds with each other: "[T]he inscription of memory [is] an effacement of interiorizing recollection, of the 'living remembrancing.' "[9] Or, as Paul de Man puts it, art "*materially* inscribes, and thus forever forgets, its ideal content."[10] But the process can be reversed: writing that disappears can make another kind of writing appear. This is an unforgetting, in Heidegger's terms — the return from Lethe — *aletheia* or truth, a version akin to Mallarmé's truth. To lose the text commemorating a loss is not, then, to redouble loss; it is to move away from the loss that is always inherent in memory's textual mechanism. It is once again to take into one's keeping the memory that is interiorized recollection.

What I have just said may give the impression that Gibson's text is exclusively past-bound, father-oriented, in one way or another an act of mourning. This is not so. At a certain point in the album, and in his own book, the photographed small-town streets that are his father's memories fuse with Gibson's own memories. He then detaches himself from those past streets, remembers the process of forgetting them. By way of the draft board office on the town's main street, Gibson recalls his one-way trip to the Canadian border; when he crosses that border, time is divided as if by a shutter. He describes the unfamiliar feel, the texture, of his first days in Toronto. Finally, a leap into an even stranger future, so remote from these that it might be a scene from one of Gibson's own novels. In a Far Eastern city, a typhoon drives "horizontal rain" at the speaker's face. Yet this destructive future elicits neither mourning nor fear. In the last words to scroll by, the speaker is "laughing in the mechanism."

What mechanism? The word "mechanism" is repeated at intervals in *Agrippa,* and the idea is implicit throughout it.

• The camera is a mechanism for dividing time.

• The gun, when it discharges, enforces in the silence that follows an "awareness of the mechanism."

• Behind the gun, the bomb—and a mechanism extending beyond the bomb casing to the Manhattan Project and the forces that produced it.

• On a still night in Wytheville, the boy can hear the clicking as traffic lights change a block away, and this too is described as an awareness of the mechanism. How far away does the mechanism extend?

• The photograph album is referred to as a mechanism; any book is a mechanism.

• Language is a mechanism; for Jacques Lacan, it is the mechanism we are born into, the set of the structuring principles of our lives.

• An affinity between chains of signifiers and chromosomal chains. If we are born into the mechanism of language, we are born out of a genetic mechanism—out of which we cannot move, for it composes us.

• The mechanisms of our genes and our nervous systems, insofar as they are mechanisms, are linked to those of the computer in a cybernetic field.

When the disk has run its course, everything in the text—book, camera, gun, explosion, father, town, time, memory—is encrypted into a mechanized code much like that on Ashbaugh's pages, before it contorts and vanishes. Always, and in all its versions, the mechanism is involved with absence and its ultimate end is disappearance.

That disappearance is apocalyptic: I am using the word not only in its sense of overwhelming destruction, but also in its original Greek sense of revelation. The last book of the Bible has forever linked destruction with revelation—as Blanchot does, as Mallarmé does. Moreover, it does so repeatedly through a *book.* The Book of the Apocalypse describes the opening of a book; that opening, seal by seal, unleashes a series of terrible endings. The Last Judgment is initiated when the Book of the Dead is opened. And finally the sky disappears "as a scroll when it is rolled together." Microcosmic apocalypse, *Agrippa* too is destroyed by being opened, its images fading, its text scrolling past us into irreversible emptiness. But if there can be no rereading, the reading we have finished may not be finished with us. After the final destruction of heaven and earth in the Bible a new heaven and earth come to pass; and something like this comes to pass in reading, even if what is read can never be read again. Blanchot has said that writing is "the opaque, empty opening into that which is when there is no more world, when there is no world yet."[11] He hovers here between "no more" and "not yet," between loss and potential: the emptiness is apocalyptic, in both its senses. Through the necessary destruction of the text (all texts), something comes to pass. Though the question of what comes to pass is ultimately beyond us, the question of *how* it comes to pass is not.

A book, says Blanchot, is "a ruse by which writing goes towards *the absence of the book*."[12] The ruse in *Agrippa,* as in other books, has to do with framing. The final disappearance of *Agrippa* takes place within multiple frames, some literal, some literary: the black box, the corroded coffin in which the shrouded book is laid; the book's cover and title; the time-bound pages of newspaper, commercial images, genetic codes; the embedded disk of magnetic code; the code of language; rhythm and recurrence — all that I have articulated of what this work articulates, and more. All of these are mechanisms that, rightly combined, explode into revelation, the immanence of something *beyond*. But in the revelation of what lies between or beyond these framing elements, they are annihilated. For what is apprehended is exactly what is other than these separate elements, a sum that exceeds these parts. We move toward the famous conclusion of Wittgenstein's *Tractatus* — a tautology that is saved from the "intense inane" by being itself framed, the product of a certain process in time. At the end of the process that is *Agrippa* we are left not merely with emptiness, but with our awareness of that process both in and beyond the mechanism. Knowing that there *has been* a process in time, the blank page (as in Isak Dinesen's tale) may be the most eloquent text. "The most beautiful and perfect book in the world," says Ulises Carrión, "is a book with only blank pages, in the same way that the most complete language is that which lies beyond all that the words of man can say."[13] In the very act of disappearing, then, *Agrippa* makes something appear.

Notes

This work was supported by the Social Sciences and Humanities Research Council of Canada. Special thanks to Veronica Hollinger and Sasha Sergejewski.

1. Paul Virilio, *The Aesthetics of Disappearance,* trans. Philip Beitchman (New York: Semiotext(e), 1991), 23.

2. William Gibson and Dennis Ashbaugh, *Agrippa (A Book of the Dead)* (New York: Kevin Begos Publishing, 1992).

3. Maurice Blanchot, "The Absence of the Book," in *The Gaze of Orpheus and Other Literary Essays,* ed. P. Adams Sitney, trans. Lydia Davis (Barrytown, N.Y.: Station Hill, 1981), 151.

4. Maurice Blanchot, *The Writing of the Disaster*, trans. Ann Smock (Lincoln: University of Nebraska Press, 1986), 134.

5. Jean-Paul Sartre, *Mallarmé, or the Poet of Nothingness*, trans. Ernest Sturm (University Park, Pa.: Pennsylvania State University Press, 1988), 140.

6. Letter from Mallarmé to Eugène Lefébvre, May 17, 1867, in *Stéphane Mallarmé: Correspondance, 1862–1871*, ed. Henri Mondor (Paris: Gallimard, 1959), 245–246.

7. Roland Barthes, *Camera Lucida: Reflections on Photography*, trans. Richard Howard (New York: Hill and Wang, 1981), 96.

8. Jacques Derrida, *Mémoires: For Paul de Man*, trans. Cecile Lindsay, Jonathan Culler, and Eduardo Cadava (New York: Columbia University Press, 1986), 50.

9. Derrida, *Mémoires*, 56.

10. Paul de Man, "Sign and Symbol in Hegel's *Aesthetics*," *Critical Inquiry* 8 (1982): 773; cited in Derrida, *Mémoires*, 67.

11. Maurice Blanchot, *The Space of Literature*, trans. Ann Smock (Lincoln, Neb.: University of Nebraska Press, 1982), 33.

12. Blanchot, "Absence of the Book," 147.

13. Ulises Carrión, quoted in *Artists' Books: A Critical Anthology and Sourcebook*, ed. Joan Lyons and Gibbs M. Smith (Rochester, N.Y.: Visual Studies Workshop Press, 1985), 38.

Contributors

EDITOR: *Richard Dellamora*, who recently completed a year as Visiting Fellow in the department of English at Princeton University, lives in Toronto and is a professor of English and cultural studies at Trent University. Dellamora is the author of *Apocalyptic Overtures: Sexual Politics and the Sense of an Ending* (Rutgers University Press, 1994) and *Masculine Desire: The Sexual Politics of Victorian Aestheticism* (University of North Carolina Press, 1990).

Jonathan Boyarin is the editor of *The Ethnography of Reading* (University of California Press, 1993); the author of *Storm from Paradise: The Politics of Jewish Memory* (University of Minnesota Press, 1992) and *Polish Jews in Paris: The Ethnography of Memory* (University of Indiana Press, 1991); and coeditor of *From a Ruined Garden: The Memorial Books of Polish Jewry* (New York: Schocken Books, 1983). An anthropologist, he has done field work in Paris, Jerusalem, and New York City. Boyarin teaches at the New School for Social Research in New York City and held a Guggenheim Fellowship in 1994–1995.

Mary Wilson Carpenter, an associate professor of English at Queen's University, is the author of *George Eliot and the Landscape of Time* (University of North Carolina Press, 1986). She has published essays in *Victorian Poetry, Diacritics,* and *Genders,* and is currently completing a book on the representation of sexuality and the body in commodified biblical interpretation in nineteenth-century Britain.

Ken Cooper completed his doctoral work at Vanderbilt University and is an assistant professor of English at SUNY Geneseo. He was a Visiting Fellow at the Banting Institute at Radcliffe College in the summer of 1994. His essay, " 'Zero Pays the House': The Las Vegas Novel and Atomic Roulette," appeared in the Fall 1992 issue of *Contemporary Literature.*

Peter Dickinson is currently writing a doctoral thesis on nationality and sexuality in contemporary Canadian literature at the University of British Columbia. In addition to essays published in *Studies in Canadian Literature* and other journals, his prose and poetry have appeared in *Samplings, S.I.R.,* and in *Queeries: An Anthology of Gay Male Prose,* ed. Dennis Denisoff (Vancouver: Arsenal Pulp Press, 1993).

Teresa Heffernan is completing her doctoral dissertation at the University of Toronto. She has published articles in *Canadian Literature, The Popular Culture Review,* and *Virginia Woolf Miscellanies.*

Andrew Hewitt, an associate professor of comparative literature at SUNY Buffalo, is the author of *Fascist Modernism: Aesthetics, Politics, and the Avant-Garde* (Stanford University Press, 1993) and the forthcoming *Political Inversions: Homosexuality, Fascism and the Modernist Imaginary* (Stanford). He has published essays in *ELH* and *New German Critique.*

Linda Howell teaches in the department of English at Mount Royal College in Calgary and recently completed her Ph.D. candidacy examinations at the University of Rochester. She is writing a thesis on women and technology in twentieth-century literature and film.

Christopher Keep teaches in the department of English at Queen's University and recently completed his doctoral work there. His articles have appeared in *Sulfur, Mosaic, Cinémas,* and the *Frontenac Review.* Keep is currently completing a book on nineteenth-century apocalypticism and the crisis of masculinity.

Kevin Pask lives in Montréal, Québec. He is the author of a forthcoming book, *The Emergence of the English Author: Pre-Scripting the Life of the Poet in Early Modern England* (Cambridge University Press).

David Robson teaches in the department of English at the University of Western Ontario and completed his doctoral degree there in June 1994.

Peter Schwenger, professor of English at Mount St. Vincent University in Halifax, is the author of *Phallic Critiques* (Routledge, 1984). He has published essays on nuclear criticism in special issues of *PMLA* and *PLL.* His most recent book is *Letter Bomb: Nuclear Holocaust and the Exploding Word* (Johns Hopkins University Press, 1993).

Darren Wershler-Henry is a doctoral student at York University, where he is completing a dissertation on the history and ideology of the typewriter as a cyborg assemblage. His first book of concrete poetry, *Nicholodeon: A Book of Lowerglyphs,* is forthcoming (Toronto: Coach House Press).

Index

University of Pennsylvania Press
New Cultural Studies
Joan DeJean, Carroll Smith-Rosenberg,
and Peter Stallybrass, Editors

Jonathan Arac and Harriet Ritvo, editors. *Macropolitics of Nineteenth-Century Literature: Nationalism, Exoticism, Imperialism.* 1991

John Barrell. *The Birth of Pandora and the Division of Knowledge.* 1992

Anne E. Becker. *Body, Self, and Society: The View from Fiji.* 1995

Bruce Thomas Boehrer. *Monarchy and Incest in Renaissance England: Literature, Culture, Kinship, and Kingship.* 1992

Carol Breckenridge and Peter van der Veer, editors. *Orientalism and the Postcolonial Predicament: Perspectives on South Asia.* 1993

E. Jane Burns. *Bodytalk: When Women Speak in Old French Literature.* 1993

Roger Chartier. *Forms and Meanings: Texts, Performances, and Audiences from Codex to Computer.* 1995

Joseph W. Childers. *Novel Possibilities: Fiction and the Formation of Early Victorian Culture.* 1995

Richard Dellamora, editor. *Postmodern Apocalypse: Theory and Cultural Practice at the End.* 1995

Jones DeRitter. *The Embodiment of Characters: The Representation of Physical Experience on Stage and in Print, 1728–1749.* 1994

Julia V. Douthwaite. *Exotic Women: Literary Heroines and Cultural Strategies in Ancien Régime France.* 1992

Barbara J. Eckstein. *The Language of Fiction in a World of Pain: Reading Politics as Paradox.* 1990

Jean Marie Goulemot. (James Simpson, trans.) *Forbidden Texts: Erotic Literature and Its Readers in Eighteenth-Century France.* 1995

Katherine Gravdal. *Ravishing Maidens: Writing Rape in Medieval French Literature and Law.* 1991

Jayne Ann Krentz, editor. *Dangerous Men and Adventurous Women: Romance Writers on the Appeal of the Romance.* 1992

Carole Levin. *The Heart and Stomach of a King: Elizabeth I and the Politics of Sex and Power.* 1994

Karma Lochrie. *Margery Kempe and Translations of the Flesh.* 1991

Linda Lomperis and Sarah Stanbury, editors. *Feminist Approaches to the Body in Medieval Literature.* 1993

Alex Owen. *The Darkened Room: Women, Power and Spiritualism in Late Victorian England.* 1990

Jacqueline Rose. *The Case of Peter Pan or The Impossibility of Children's Fiction.* 1992

Alan Sinfield. *Cultural Politics — Queer Reading.* 1994